Foreign Policy in a Transformed World

Foreign Policy in a Transformed World

MARK WEBBER AND MICHAEL SMITH

WITH

David Allen, Alan Collins,
Denny Morgan
and Anoushiravan Ehteshami

An imprint of **Pearson Education**

Harlow, England · London · New York · Reading, Massachusetts · San Francisco · Toronto · Don Mills, Ontario · Sydney
Tokyo · Singapore · Hong Kong · Seoul · Taipei · Cape Town · Madrid · Mexico City · Amsterdam · Munich · Paris · Milan

Pearson Education Limited
Edinburgh Gate
Harlow
Essex CM20 2JE
United Kingdom

and Associated Companies throughout the world

Visit us on the World Wide Web at:
www.pearsoned.co.uk

First published 2002

ISBN 978-0-13-908757-8

British Library Cataloguing-in-Publication Data
A catalogue record for this book is available from the British Library

Library of Congress Cataloging-in-Publication Data
A catalog record is available from the Library of Congress

8   7
08

Typeset in 10/13pt Sabon by 35
Printed in Malaysia   PJB

Contents

10. | East Asia and the Pacific Rim: Japan and China   287

Alan Collins

Part 3   Conclusion   323

11. | The Challenge of Foreign Policy   325

Mark Webber

Contributors

David Allen is Senior Lecturer in Politics and Jean Monnet Senior Lecturer in European Politics in the Department of European Studies, Loughborough University. He is the author of numerous articles and book chapters on European foreign policy and other aspects of European Union policy making, including contributions to all four editions of Helen Wallace and William Wallace (eds), *Policy-Making in the European Union* (4th edition, Oxford University Press, 2000). He is also joint author (with Mike Smith) of the 'External Relations' section of the *Journal of Common Market Studies* Annual Review.

Alan Collins is Lecturer in the Department of Politics at the University of Wales, Swansea. Prior to this appointment he was a British Academy Post-Doctoral Fellow in the Department of International Politics at the University of Wales, Aberystwyth. He is the author of *The Security Dilemma and the End of the Cold War* (Keele University Press, 1997) and *The Security Dilemmas of Southeast Asia* (Palgrave, 2000).

Denny Morgan is Post-Doctoral Research Fellow in International Relations and member of the African Studies Centre at Coventry University. Her research interests include institutionalisation, focusing on the impact of organisational behaviour on the politics of agenda setting in Europe and West Africa.

Anoushiravan Ehteshami is Director of the Institute for Middle Eastern and Islamic Studies and Professor of International Relations at the University of Durham. His most recent publications include: (as editor) *From the Gulf to Central Asia: Players in the New Great Game* (University of Exeter Press, 1995), (as author) *After Khomeini: the Iranian Second Republic* (Routledge, 1995), (as co-editor), *Islamic Fundamentalism* (Westview Press, 1996), (as co-author) *Syria and Iran: Middle*

Powers in a Penetrated Regional System (Routledge, 1997), and (as author) *The Changing Balance of Power in Asia* (1998). His current research is focused on four projects: the Asian balance of power in the post-Cold War era, the international politics of the Red Sea sub-region, foreign policies of Middle Eastern states since the end of the Cold War, and the impact of globalisation on the Middle East.

Michael Smith   is Jean Monnet Professor of European Politics in the Department of European Studies, Loughborough University. He is author, co-author and editor of many books and articles on EU external policies and European integration, including *Europe's Experimental Union* (Routledge, 2000), *Negotiation and Policymaking in the European Union* (Special Issue of the *Journal of European Public Policy*, 7(5), 2000) and *Beyond Foreign Economic Policy: the United States, the Single European Market and the Changing World Economy* (Pinter, 1997). He is also joint author (with Brian Hocking) of *World Politics. An Introduction to International Relations* (2nd edition, Prentice Hall, 1995) and joint editor (with Brian White and Richard Little) of *Issues in World Politics* (2nd edition, Palgrave, 2001).

Mark Webber   is Senior Lecturer in the Department of European Studies, Loughborough University. He is the author of *The International Politics of Russia and the Successor States* (Manchester University Press, 1996), *CIS Integration Trends: Russia and the Former Soviet South* (Royal Institute of International Affairs, 1997), co-author of *The Enlargement of Europe* (Manchester University Press, 1999) and editor of *Russia and Europe: Conflict or Cooperation?* (Macmillan, 2000). His current research focuses on NATO–Russian relations and the issue of exclusion in European security.

Preface

This is a volume which has given its principal authors sleepless nights. The normal business of writing and editing has contributed to this, but its primary cause has been the intellectual challenges which the book has presented. Conceived initially in the mid-1990s, *Foreign Policy in a Transformed World* was intended as a primer on foreign policy analysis (FPA) for use by undergraduate and postgraduate students alike. There are several books – some of them very good – on FPA, but very few have attempted to place the analysis of foreign policy within an analytical and thematic framework sustained by the far-reaching alterations in world politics that have been felt over the last two to three decades (and, in particular, following the end of the Cold War).

In this light, the central purposes of the book are to elaborate frameworks for the analysis of foreign policy while at the same time linking these to the study of change and transformation in world politics more generally (Part One). These frameworks then guide a series of case studies of contemporary foreign policies drawn from five separate geographic regions (Part Two). The purpose of the frameworks is to encourage a consistency across the case studies while not losing sight of the distinctive features and trends in each of them. It is our firm hope that students who read this book will learn something not just about a range of foreign policies and their regional settings, but also something about the nature of transformation in world politics. This is a view that has been informed by our own experience of teaching. Students, we believe, prosper best in the acquisition and application of knowledge when it is contextualised rather than narrowly focused, when it is analytically and theoretically informed, and when it is presented in a stimulating and open fashion. This book strives towards these ends.

We would like to extend our thanks to the various contributing authors, all of whom, despite the very different natures of their expertise, gladly wrote their case studies with the central themes of the book uppermost in their mind. Thanks are also due to the editorial staff at Pearson Education who have regarded this book with continuing interest and patience.

Mark Webber and Michael Smith, Loughborough University

Abbreviations

ABM	Anti-Ballistic Missile (Treaty)
ACRI	African Crisis Response Initiative
AEC	African Economic Community
ANC	African National Congress (South Africa)
ANIE	Asian newly industrialised economies
APEC	Asia-Pacific Economic Cooperation
APPA	African Petroleum Producers' Association
ARF	ASEAN Regional Forum
ASEAN	Association of South East Asian Nations
ASEAN-PMC	Association of South East Asian Nations-Post Ministerial Conference
BSF	Black Sea Fleet
CCP	Chinese Communist Party
CEFTA	Central European Free Trade Area
CESDP	Common European Security and Defence Policy
CFE	Conventional Forces in Europe (Treaty)
CFSP	Common Foreign and Security Policy
CIA	Central Intelligence Agency
CIS	Commonwealth of Independent States
CMC	Central Military Commission (China)
CMEA	Council for Mutual Economic Assistance
CPU	Communist Party of Ukraine
CSCE	Conference on Security and Cooperation in Europe
CTBT	Comprehensive Test Ban Treaty
DFA	Department of Foreign Affairs (South Africa)
DJD	Democratic Party of Japan
DPP	Democratic Progressive Party (China)
DRC	Democratic Republic of Congo

EAEC	East Asia Economic Group
EC	European Community
ECE	East-Central Europe
ECO	Economic Cooperation Organisation
ECOMOG	(Economic Community of West African States) Military Monitoring Group
ECOWAS	Economic Community of West African States
EEC	European Economic Community
EFTA	European Free Trade Area
EPC	European Political Cooperation
ESDI	European Security and Defence Identity
ESDP	European Security and Defence Policy
EU	European Union
FALSG	Foreign Affairs Leading Small Group (China)
FDI	foreign direct investment
FPA	foreign policy analysis
FPI	foreign policy implementation
FPM	foreign policy making
FRG	Federal Republic of Germany
FSU	former Soviet Union
FTAA	Free Trade Area of the Americas
G7	Group of Seven
G8	Group of Eight
GATT	General Agreement on Tariffs and Trade
GCC	Gulf Cooperation Council
GDP	gross domestic product
GDR	German Democratic Republic
GNP	gross national product
GNU	Government of National Unity (South Africa)
GUUAM (group)	Georgia, Ukraine, Uzbekistan, Azerbaijan, Moldova
IFIs	international financial institutions
IMF	International Monetary Fund
JETRO	Japan External Trade Organisation
JSDF	Japanese Security Defence Force
KEDO	Korean Peninsula Energy Development Organisation
LDP	Liberal Democratic Party (Japan)
LP	Liberal Party (Japan)
MFA	Ministry of Foreign Affairs (China)
MITI	Ministry of International Trade and Industry (Japan)
MOE	Ministry of Education (Japan)

MOF	Ministry of Finance (Japan)
MOT	Ministry of Transportation (Japan)
MPT	Ministry of Posts and Telecommunications (Japan)
NAFTA	North American Free Trade Association
NATO	North Atlantic Treaty Organisation
NGO	Non-Governmental Organisation
NMD	National Missile Defence
NPT	(Nuclear) Non-Proliferation Treaty
OAU	Organisation of African Unity
OECD	Organisation of Economic Cooperation and Development
OPEC	Organisation of Petroleum Exporting Countries
OSCE	Organisation for Security and Cooperation in Europe
PAS	Parti Islam Se-Malaysia
PECC	Pacific Economic Cooperation Council
PJC	(NATO–Russia) Permanent Joint Council
PLA	People's Liberation Army (China)
PLO	Palestinian Liberation Organisation
PRC	People's Republic of China
PUWP	Polish United Workers' Party
SACU	Southern African Customs Union
SADC	Southern African Development Community
SSA	sub-Saharan Africa
START	Strategic Arms Reduction Treaty
TMD	Theatre Missile Defence
UMNO	United Malays' National Organisation
UN	United Nations
UNSC	United Nations Security Council
US	United States
WEU	Western European Union
WTO	World Trade Organisation

Map 1: The Americas

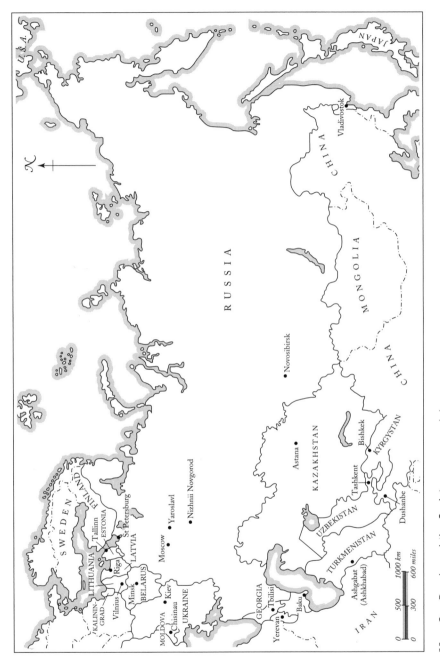

Map 2: Russia and the Soviet successor states

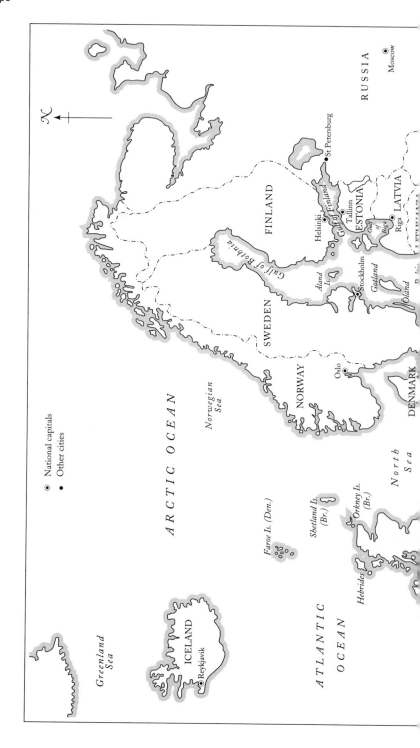

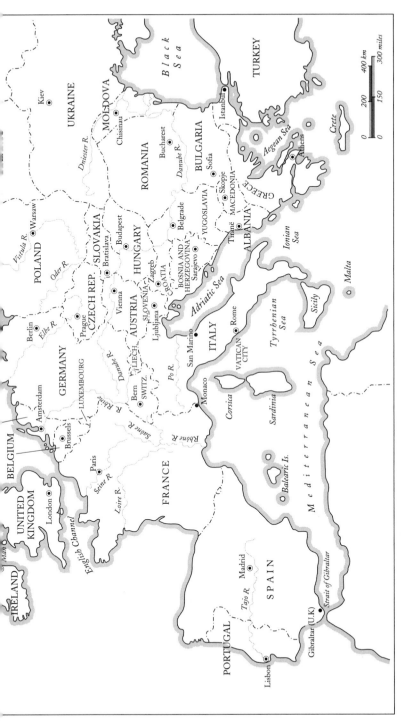

Map 3: Europe

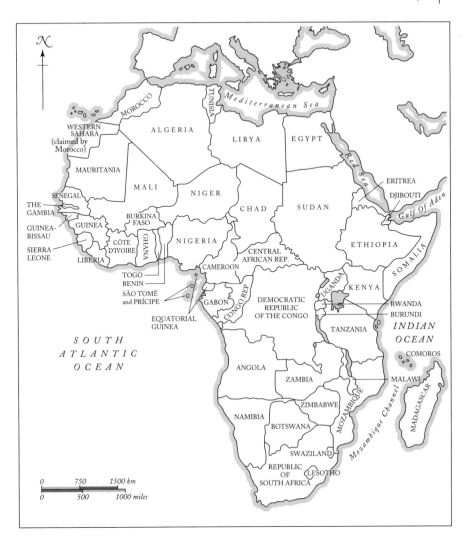

Map 4: Outline political map of contemporary Africa

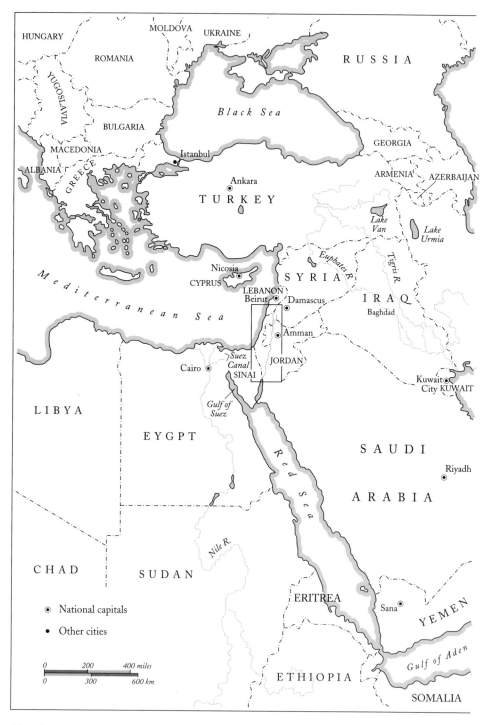

Map 5: The Middle East

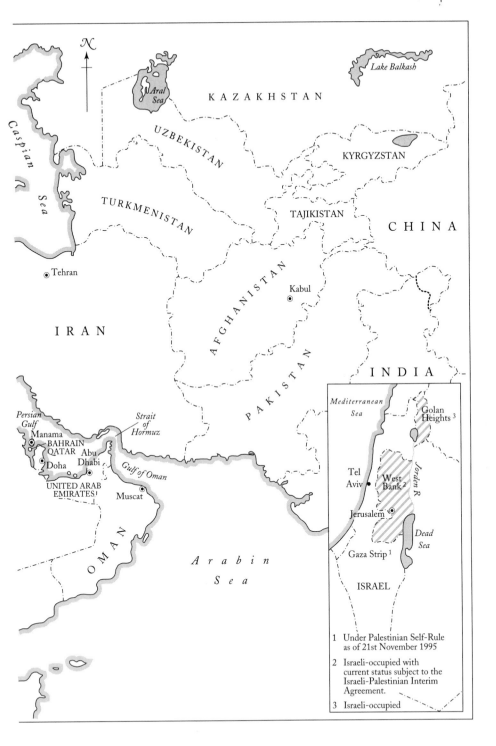

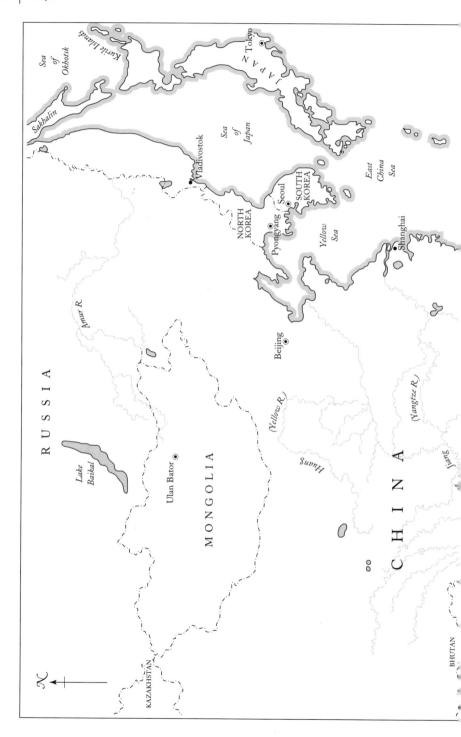

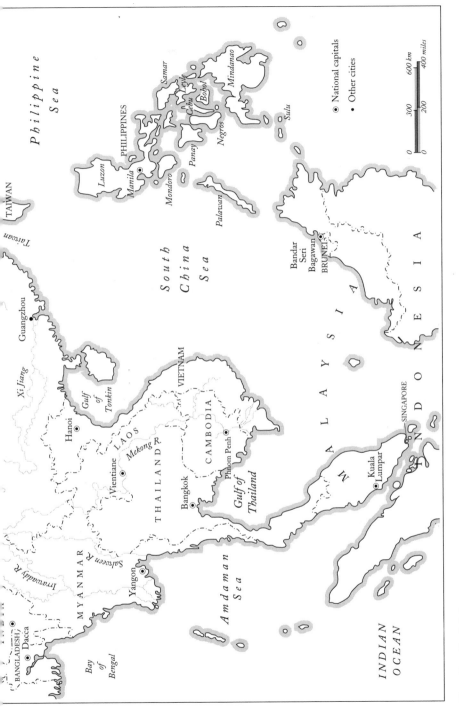

Map 6: East Asia

Publisher's Acknowledgments

We are grateful to the following for permission to reproduce copyright material:

Guardian Newspapers Limited for an extract from 'Short slams "vile and dishonest" officials' by Patrick Wintour, published in *The Observer* 30th August 1997, © *The Observer*, August 1997; the North Atlantic Treaty Organisation for an extract adapted from *NATO Handbook, Edition 2001*, © NATO Office of Information and Press; Central Intelligence Agency for Tables 5.1, 6.1, 7.1, 8.2, 9.1 and 10.1 from *The World Fact Book, 2000*.

In some instances we have been unable to trace the owners of copyright material, and we would appreciate any information that would enable us to do so, in particular Figure 2.1. The concentric circles of power in foreign policy decision-making from *How American Foreign Policy is Made* by John Spanier and Eric M. Uslaner, which was published in 1974 by Praeger Publishers, New York and Washington.

Introduction

Mark Webber and Michael Smith

Since at least the end of the 1980s, the student of world politics and of foreign policy has been confronted by a demanding intellectual challenge: the need to make sense of a world undergoing a profound transformation. In the first place, with the end of the Cold War, followed in short order by the collapse of the Soviet Union and Yugoslavia, there has been a proliferation of new states and the emergence of new patterns of cooperation and conflict both among these new states themselves and within the system of states more broadly. In parallel, a second trend of somewhat longer pedigree has gained ground, albeit one which has accelerated in recent years. In short-hand usually referred to as 'globalisation', this has involved the development of trends in international trade, communication, migratory movements and so on, which, according to some observers, have fundamentally challenged the competence of national governments. Alongside this process, the growth of regional economic and political integration and the emergence of major transnational policy issues, such as those of the environment or international crime, have posed further challenges to the traditionally tidy distinction between the nation state and its international context. Another change frequently noted, and linked to those already mentioned, has been the shifting balance between 'warfare and welfare' in both national societies and international settings; foreign policy makers for a long time have had to confront the complex balance between economic, political and military objectives, and this has been given greater force by the developing world political economy.

This book explores the persistent search for national identity and foreign policy effectiveness in this transformed world. It does not make the claim that hitherto the conduct and analysis of foreign policy has been trouble-free. Indeed, in the early 1960s, for example, decolonisation and the multiplication of new states in the so-called 'Third World', coupled with a growth of regional and global institutions, formed a superficially similar set of circumstances. What makes the period after the late 1980s (the watershed provided by the end of the Cold War) so much different, however, is the pace, pervasiveness and profundity of change, something that has meant a questioning of the very relevance of concepts of statehood and foreign policy. That said, the state (and its principal agent, national government) still retains a primacy in international life. It is the main subject of international law, the principal member of international organisations and the organising entity of political, military, diplomatic and, to some extent, economic power. In this light, our perspective on the nature of foreign policy can be expressed initially in the following definition:

> Foreign policy is composed of the goals sought, values set, decisions made and actions taken by states, and national governments acting on their behalf, in the context of the external relations of national societies. It constitutes an attempt to design, manage and control the foreign relations of national societies.

Contemporary foreign policy is focused sharply – as is this book – on the ways in which, and the extent to which, national governments have succeeded in dealing with the challenges of a substantially transformed world. Conceiving foreign policy in these terms may smack of an overly traditional approach, one which focuses on states to the detriment of other actors. However, the approach is cognizant of these other actors, be they non-governmental organisations (NGOs), large transnational corporations, stateless nations such as Kosovo, Chechnya and Kurdistan or international organisations such as the European Union (EU), the United Nations (UN) and so on. Indeed, we do not deny that these actors are important or even that they may pursue activities which resemble foreign policy. For our purposes, these 'foreign policies' are regarded as a part – often a very major part – of the context in which national government has become enmeshed. It may even be the case that the foreign policy pursued by a national government is, in some senses, synonymous with these other 'foreign policies'. This is apparent to some degree in the 'Common Foreign and Security Policy' of the EU and the actions pursued by NATO, in that in both cases EU and NATO policies often conform closely with, and are the consequences of, the foreign policies and preferences of their member states.

Our focus then is the ways in which national government has come to terms with and attempted to manage the changing world around it. This central *problématique* enables us to achieve unity of focus without neglecting the ways in which actors other than national governments and societies have developed new patterns of international activity. It also forms an essential starting point for a comparison and an evaluation of the effectiveness with which the challenges to national policies have been met. The central teaching aim of the text is thus to stimulate discussion on the extent to which foreign policy formed and conducted by national governments has come to terms with the transformed world.

Elaborating upon these themes, the foundations of our approach to foreign policy are informed by the following:

- First, foreign policy is intimately linked to the notions of statehood and government, but these notions are not taken to be unchanging and uniform. Rather, they are sources of important questions about the ways in which national societies adapt to changing circumstances.

- Second, foreign policy implies a capacity to distinguish between the domestic politics and the external relations of national societies, and to form policies directed towards external 'targets'. This statement instantly raises vital questions about how the 'foreign' is defined or pursued in an increasingly interconnected world.

- Third, foreign policy cannot be detached from notions of strategy and action which embody goals, values and decisions. These notions are not seen as inflexible and unvarying. There is no rigid definition of what goals, values and decisions count as 'foreign policy' and which do not: although there is a substantial body of conventional wisdom as to what should be included and excluded, this wisdom is there to be questioned and evaluated.

- Fourth, foreign policy involves tasks of design, management and control. In an ideal world these would be easily achievable by national government. However, in practice, they give rise to numerous problems and thus impede the attainment of the goals, values and decisions noted above.

These foundations are, in turn, informed by two central issues which link foreign policy analysis (FPA) to the broader academic discipline of International Relations. The first is that of theory development. Foreign policy analysis (FPA) has not been left untouched by theoretical developments in its mother discipline and so this text highlights and utilises theoretically-informed models where appropriate. Furthermore, our approach is informed both by the literature of International Relations and by that of Comparative Politics and other branches of policy analysis. This arises from the fact that in studying foreign policy, inevitably one has to confront the relationship between 'national politics' and 'international politics', between public policy at the national level and the ways in which this is projected beyond.

A second analytical issue is that of 'theory and practice'. More than in many other areas of analysis, in FPA the student is constantly confronted by the 'real world'. There is thus a constant need to apply the frameworks of theory and comparison to the diversity of actual foreign policies themselves. For this reason it is difficult to propose a 'general theory of foreign policy' except at a very high level of abstraction. More relevant and useful is a range of 'middle range theories' which can encompass the variety of national experiences and foreign policy actions while still remaining informed by general theoretical insights. Linked to this is the matter of the relationship between policy analysis and the 'policy community'. Theories of foreign policy are inevitably subject to the 'so what?' question posed by those directly engaged in the policy process. This, in essence, boils down to a tension between those who seek to explain and understand foreign policy in general terms, and those who advocate analytical approaches which have a direct relevance to actual foreign policy conduct. While by definition the student of foreign policy in an academic sense cannot expect to penetrate the day-to-day untidiness and complexity of foreign policy action, it is nonetheless possible to ask well-directed questions and to see the 'theory/practice divide' as a source of insight rather than a source of frustration.

In a sense, all foreign policies are the same, as implied by the definition deployed above: all national governments are faced with the challenge of responding to the demands of their regional and more broadly international setting. But equally, each foreign policy is unique, given the range of demands and possible responses shaped by the global and regional setting, by national forces, by the process of policy making itself and not least by what happens when foreign policy is implemented. There is thus a constant need not only to compare one foreign policy with another, but also to compare foreign policy with other areas of public policy, with which it may intersect or by which it may be constrained.

This approach is reflected in the structure of the text. Essentially, the book falls into two interconnected parts:

Part One aims to set out the key elements of the analytical framework. Chapter 1 explores in some detail the analytical issues raised by the study of foreign policy, while Chapter 2 provides an introduction to the notion of the 'foreign policy arena' and to those who participate in it. Chapters 3 and 4 take this further by exploring the foreign policy process – the making and implementation of foreign policy. The overall purpose of Part One is twofold: to provide a range of analytical tools with which to approach FPA and to delineate a picture of a transformed world where these tools are to be applied.

Part Two applies this framework to a series of case studies. These are organised on a broadly regional basis, reflecting the argument that foreign policy is shaped by a combination of global, regional and national forces. Each case-study chapter incorporates a review of the foreign policy arena (focusing specifically on the regional arena but also considering how the region has been affected by wider global trends) and relates this to the range of foreign policies to be found within that region. This review is followed in each chapter by two national case studies, selected on the basis of the countries' importance to the region or to the broader global arena. These are not intended to be exhaustive studies of the foreign policies concerned; rather, they are designed to show the distinctive ways in which the relevant country has received and responded to the challenges of transformation.

Each of the chapters contains both an introductory summary of the main themes and questions addressed, and a concluding summary. At the end of each chapter, there is a full set of references and in most cases a short review of additional reading, designed to support further study of the concepts or cases dealt with. Where they are deemed useful, we have also included a number of relevant web site page addresses. The chapters also contain a number of boxes and tables. These are intended to provide schematic illustration of concepts or comparisons and (in the case study chapters) to furnish basic data of the relevant regions and the states which occupy them.

Our assumption is that the users of the text will have some prior knowledge of International Relations, world politics or Comparative Politics, but that this text will constitute their first major and sustained engagement with the area of FPA itself. We have thus tried throughout to ensure accessibility and clarity for those approaching the study of foreign policy from a variety of backgrounds.

Part One
Frameworks

Mark Webber and Michael Smith

1 | Problems and Issues in Foreign Policy Analysis

In the Introduction, it was argued that in analysing foreign policy, the key element was the focus on national governments and their responses to changing global conditions. In this chapter, we aim to identify a number of key issues in foreign policy analysis, and to 'problematise' them, that is, explore their analytical implications for the assessment and comparison of foreign policies.

This chapter falls into five main sections. First, we identify a number of the 'puzzles' which have long preoccupied students of foreign policy. Second, we consider some conventional assumptions about foreign policy. Third, we look at the ways in which global transformation has questioned the continuing relevance of such assumptions. Fourth, we offer an overview of the main schools of thought in foreign policy analysis. Finally, we summarise the main elements of the framework of analysis developed in this chapter. This will then be carried forward in Chapters 2–4 (which explore specific areas of foreign policy itself: the policy arena, the policy-making process and the implementation of policy) and will also be used as the basis for case studies in Part Two.

Foreign policy puzzles

In common with other areas of policy analysis, foreign policy analysis (FPA) starts with a number of central questions about the nature of what is to be studied. Perhaps the most fundamental question is the broadest: what is foreign policy? In the Introduction, we set out a definition, and it is useful to repeat it here as the basis for moving on to a more detailed enquiry:

> Foreign policy is composed of the goals sought, values set, decisions made and actions taken by states, and national governments acting on their

behalf, in the context of the external relations of national societies. It constitutes an attempt to design, manage and control the foreign relations of national societies.

Just how useful is this definition? Consider the following example. During late 1997, there was a severe financial crisis affecting a number of the countries of East Asia. The impact of fluctuating currencies, of financial speculation and of instabilities within the governments of the region caused wild shifts in confidence and undermined the ability of national governments to maintain stable economic conditions. The Prime Minister of Malaysia, Mahathir Mohammed, made a number of sharp public attacks not on the other countries in the region, but rather on the activities of international financiers, who were accused of deliberate economic destabilisation for the sake of private financial gain. Major commitments were made by leading countries such as the United States (US) and Japan, and by international financial institutions, to the re-establishment of economic stability and to containing the crisis. The latter was a particular concern given fears (in part, subsequently realised) that the 'infection' could spread to the countries of Latin America, Eastern Europe, and even into the US and Western Europe.

Do the responses to this crisis constitute 'foreign policy'? In many respects, the answer would have to be 'yes' in that actions taken clearly conform to the definition of foreign policy set out above. Efforts were made by national governments aimed at identifying goals, setting values and taking action – all in the light of their external financial position and the needs of their national societies. There was also a clear effort to 'design, manage and control' the foreign relations of those societies, specifically their external economic relations. But even the brief outline of the case stated gives rise to some key puzzles:

- First, were the goals of foreign policy always clear, and were the values set equally acceptable to all members of the national society? Although the aim of economic growth and stability is very widely shared in national societies everywhere, there will always be those who see their interests as lying in speculation, profit and individual gain. In other words, a tension exists between the general good and a sectional or specific good.

- Second, is it always national governments who take decisions or action? Foreign policy implies essentially that the government acts on behalf of the country, but it seems that on occasion at least, there can be doubts about the unity or stability of the government itself. During the crisis outlined above, not only did one government in the region (that of Thailand) change, but the country concerned was also in the process of adopting a new constitution which would lead to major political changes. So national governments need not be regarded as monolithic.

■ Third, are national governments the only actors on the international stage? As the above example makes plain, a number of governments were assailed by the activities of international speculators. In other circumstances, they have been challenged by international criminal cartels, terrorist organisations and migratory flows of population.

■ Fourth and related to the points above, how much power to 'design, manage and control' do national governments really have? It seems clear that in many international economic transactions, national governments are only a part of the story, and the flows of international finance, together with the activities of firms or individual speculators, can have important effects in constraining or undermining the authority or 'management capacity' of the governments in question.

Each of the elements in our initial definition is thus subject to questioning. That said, as an analytical convenience some definition has to be offered. That presented above provides us with a check-list of the characteristics to look out for in any national foreign policy. But teasing out some of the implications of the definition alerts us to the fact that in seeking to pin down the meaning of foreign policy, some uneasy questions arise. However, for any foreign policy, the simple questions 'what's going on here?' and 'who is doing what to whom?' are an essential starting point. We now move on to consider the ways in which analysts have attempted to deal with these types of question in the past, and the ways in which they might need reformulating.

Foreign policy: traditional assumptions

Traditionally, foreign policy has been seen as inextricably linked to the 'world of states', in which the primary actors are nation states and their governments, and in which a series of policy problems emerge to reflect the competitive and insecure nature of international politics. This has given foreign policy a very powerful image in the study of International Relations. To put it very simply, foreign policy is often seen as 'special' or 'privileged' by virtue of the answers given to the types of question raised above: What are the aims and values of foreign policy? Who makes foreign policy? How is it made? How is action taken?

In this light, let us first look at the links between foreign policy, statehood and the world of states. The study of International Relations for many years was conducted within the context of what has been termed 'state-centric realism'. Central to this perspective was the assumption that states were the primary actors in world politics (if not the only actors), that foreign policy was pursued by governments on behalf of the state and that a sharp distinction existed between domestic policy making and foreign policy making. The aims of foreign policy by this view were related to the pursuit of sovereignty and independence. The key value espoused was that of the 'national interest', defined in terms of independence and security. But the fact that the national interest was pursued in a world where all states were pursuing the same aim had a number of important consequences. Specifically, it meant that international politics was characterised by competition and insecurity and the chief task of foreign policy makers was to guard against threats and the actions of competitors. This state of affairs was exacerbated further by what some realists viewed as a central driving force of human motivation, namely a quest for power (Aron, 1962: 21–93; Morgenthau, 1960: 3–15).

Given these basic assumptions about the world of states and the place of foreign policy within it, there was in principle little difficulty in establishing the main characteristics of foreign policy. During the Cold War era, there was a strong tendency in many countries to identify foreign policy very closely with 'national security policy', and to see the military security of the society as the principal if not the only aim of policy making. This had direct and important implications for the question 'who makes foreign policy?' The answer simply was that foreign policy was made by a specialised elite defined by education, training and experience. This elite had the role – indeed, the duty – of establishing and pursuing the national interest and of speaking on behalf of the national society. When it came to the formulation of decisions and actions, this elitist context had further effects. Decision making was necessarily confined to a small circle, and was characterised even in democratic societies by a pervasive secrecy.

From this it might reasonably be inferred that foreign policy was not only specialised but also dangerous. The stakes were high, ultimately expressed in terms of national independence or national survival. Competition from other states might generally be muted and peaceful, but in principle it could always turn nasty and lead to conflict if not war. Whereas national societies could be described as 'security communities', the wider world was an 'insecurity community', in which there were no universally accepted rules and in which there were constant risks of damage. But this was not a 'war of all against all'. What saved the system from constant system-wide conflict was the institution of statehood itself, through which responsible authorities could practise diplomacy, adjust their differences and cooperate either tacitly or openly to avoid the worst risks and costs of international competition (Hobson, 2000: 50–5; Morgenthau, 1960: 167–223).

Foreign policy in the traditional view, therefore, was conducted not only within a world of states, but also within a society of states, in which there was a number of powerful unwritten rules about the ways in which national governments should behave (Bull, 1977: 13–16, 23–52). The essence of 'responsible statehood' was in the conduct of responsible foreign policies – not shirking international competition or the defence of the national interest, but using the practice of diplomacy to conduct the business of the nation. Only in extreme circumstances could the use of force or a declaration of war be justified. Governments which flouted this rule could easily find that large numbers of others would group up to retaliate or to contain them, as in the case of Napoleonic France, Nazi Germany or (during the Cold War) the Soviet Union. But to state this 'rule' is to raise further questions. National governments would be faced in such a context with constant delicate choices, and the consequences of those choices were by definition uncertain. Foreign policy, therefore, hinged ultimately on the judgement and decisions of a small number of specialists whose knowledge of the consequences of their actions was imperfect; if things went badly wrong, it could mean national loss or national extinction.

According to this view, foreign policy action is one of the most demanding of political acts. The attempt to influence behaviour across national boundaries where there are none of the supports provided by national law, culture or habits of obedience, where knowledge is restricted and where the consequences of actions are very difficult to estimate, gives a fundamental element of delicacy and risk which is absent from any other areas of policy making. Even between the closest of national allies, there is the potential for confusion, recrimination, escalation and ultimately war. While the practices of 'responsible statehood' can contain many of these uncertainties and risks, they cannot eliminate them. In addition to being elitist, secretive and linked with national security, foreign policy is consequently also risky.

Thus far, we have established that the essence of foreign policy, as traditionally viewed, is the same for all states. The problem, however, as you may have suspected, is that foreign policies are characterised by considerable variety. Traditional views of foreign policy do not entirely neglect this variety. Central to much traditional thinking is the notion of power. Often described in terms of military power, this can be seen as an essential way of discriminating between foreign policies, not only in terms of their key characteristics but also in terms of their prospects for success. Thus descriptions of countries as 'Great Powers', 'Middle Powers' or 'Small States' are intended to give an indication of the scope and responsibilities of foreign policy; they also give a broad description of the potential for action and of success in any given venture (Berridge, 1992: 9–25). During the Cold War period, the description of the US and the Soviet Union as 'superpowers' was intended to convey the impression that they were unlike any previous global powers, and thus, by extension, that their foreign policies were shaped by a distinctive if not unique set of influences. The 1960s and 1970s saw not only the consolidation of this superpower status for the two states concerned, but also the emergence in the Third World of a large number of new, often small and poor states, which greatly increased variety within the world of states.

Another element in the variety of foreign policies accounted for by traditional views concerned the policy makers themselves. Policy, arguably, is not formed until the commitment to pursue a goal is brought into balance with the capabilities necessary for its implementation. Not all policy makers or governments are going to be equally competent at performing this balancing act, and much of the effort of traditional FPA has been devoted to understanding the ways in which performance can fall below expectations or potential. One of the key distinctions between foreign policies is thus the efficiency and effectiveness of the 'foreign policy machine', and one of the key problems is that the 'machine' is really a collection of rather imperfect human beings.

Size, status, resources and human factors are thus key elements in the traditional study of foreign policies. Another is what might be described as 'circumstances': both the long-term geopolitical situation of a country and the short-term challenges it faces. For a very long time, foreign policies have been described in terms of location – the 'island state', the 'buffer state' – and in terms of the general political context within which governments operate – democracy, dictatorship, stability and instability (Wallace, 1971). Such factors are clearly important in shaping the choices available to foreign policy makers, and in influencing the ways in which actions are taken. As much as anything else, they affect expectations and perceptions, both on the part of foreign policy makers in one country and on the part of their counterparts in other countries. But these long-term factors can also be supplemented if not supplanted by short-term factors, such as those contained in threatening or crisis situations.

We hope it is clear from this discussion that what we have described as 'traditional' views of foreign policy based on state-centric realism do not eliminate complexity or variety from the study of the policy-making process. It is also clear, however, that such views seem most appropriate to the conditions of the Cold War and do not happily encompass the processes of change and development which were already apparent in the Cold War period itself but which have become much more prominent with its demise. We now discuss a number of these processes, and then look at the ways in which these have generated new approaches to the study of foreign policy.

A transformed world

One of the most common descriptive labels of world politics in recent years has been that of transformation (Held et al., 1999). In this section, we discuss a number of the far-reaching processes of change that have been identified in global affairs and link them to the ideas about foreign policy outlined earlier.

An important point must be made at the outset. Although the period from the late 1980s on has frequently been presented as constituting a watershed in many senses, it is necessary to retain a historical perspective. Change in world politics does not occur overnight. Many of the apparently sudden and radical shifts that have taken place at key points in history reflect longer, sometimes hidden trends of development. For instance, the emergence after the Second World War of the two superpowers was the consummation of processes which had been going on for the previous fifty years – not just the rise of the two new world powers, but the decline of others, such as Britain and France. Similarly, while the years 1989–91 seemed to witness a sudden revision of the political map of the world (with the collapse of the Soviet Union and Yugoslavia most notably), it should be remembered that this process had gestated for a considerable period of time owing to the long-term structural problems of communist political systems.

Moreover, fixing on these events as somehow characteristic of wider global developments is also misleading since it tends to play down autonomous but still important processes of change taking place in areas outside Europe and the North Atlantic region, in Asia and Latin America for example. Such cautionary notes are not simply for the benefit of students; policy makers themselves are in many ways less well-adjusted if they ignore the longer term and the historical or operate on the basis of cultural 'blinkers'.

These qualifications aside, there is nonetheless a commonly held view that since the 1980s we have witnessed radical, widespread and in many senses irreversible changes in world politics and the world economy, and that these must be taken into account when studying foreign policy (Light, 1994).

Beyond the 'world of states'

We have already seen that traditional views of foreign policy depend heavily on assumptions about the 'world of states'. This is not seen as an unchanging or undifferentiated world: there has always been a place for discussion of the variety of states and statehood.

More recent changes, however, seem to have gone well beyond the assumptions of the traditional view. Two developments are particularly important in this context: first, the sudden increase during the 1990s in the number of states, many of which are fragile and the source of instability. And second, the accelerated development of political and economic networks which seem to demand more than mere statehood for their operation and regulation.

Taking the first of these – the expansion of the 'world of states' – it should be noted that this is not an unprecedented process. During the early 1960s, the dismantling of the British and French colonial empires led to a major influx of new participants on to the international scene, and many of these new states brought with them new problems of political and economic development as well as significant international or domestic conflicts (Jackson, 1990). They also brought with them new problems for FPA, in the sense that it had now to encompass not only well-developed (and, therefore, predictable) 'western' or 'northern' states, but also fragile, less-developed (and, therefore, unpredictable) 'southern' ones as well (Calvert, 1986). This upsurge of state creation was, however, balanced by the stabilising factor of the Cold War which, through the creation of spheres of influence between the superpowers (and, to a limited extent, by China also), harnessed (but did not eliminate) many of the system instabilities brought about by this influx. The Cold War also brought a certain analytical tidiness, allowing as it did an analysis of foreign policy in terms of where a state stood in the bipolar competition between the two superpowers.

The collapse of Yugoslavia and the Soviet Union has upset this picture of stability. Fifteen states have arisen from the ruins of the Soviet Union and a further five have so far emerged within what was once the Socialist Federative Republic of Yugoslavia. These have brought with them economic, political, ethnic and other tensions, resulting in the Balkans and the Transcaucasus regions in vicious local wars and external intervention. Even where states are not 'new', in the sense that they had previously had an independent existence (as in the case of most of states of Eastern Europe once subject to Soviet power) these same states have frequently been assailed by a variety of political and economic instabilities. Such developments are clearly a significant challenge to the rather cosy idea of a 'society of states' based on 'responsible statehood'. Quite simply, there is less prospect of a functioning 'society' where there are extensive and fundamental conflicts over territory, assets and ideas; and there is less prospect of 'responsible statehood' where states are new, fragile and subject to conflicting pressures of global change. It is important to remember, nonetheless, that these types of problem are not entirely new. The twentieth century was characterised by Balkan conflicts in both its second and final decades.

The earlier spasms of the 'society of states' took place in a world where there were no really substantial challenges to state dominance. The 'ideology' of sovereign statehood has been the most potent symbol of the twentieth century, responsible for many of its most dire conflicts as well as many of its economic and political gains. During the 1970s and 1980s, there was a growing recognition that this image of state dominance, while not disappearing, was contested by the development of new forces, the second of the two developments alluded to above (Keohane and Nye, 1977; Mansbach et al., 1976). One product of the appearance of new and fragile states has been the increased incidence of sub-national challenges to the state, either through threats of secession and resultant civil war (as in the nominally Russian republic of Chechnya) or through more peaceful movements to regionalism or federalism (as in the case of the European Union (EU)). At the same time, the development of the world economy has led to a new focus on transnational forces, such as those embodied in powerful corporations such as Microsoft and Nestlé and in a variety of political movements such as those which have mobilised against perceived injustices in world trade and global financial arrangements. It has been argued that such forces represent a powerful movement towards globalisation, in which social, economic and political activities everywhere are connected with such activities everywhere else. Opinions differ greatly as to whether such forces are harbingers of new wealth and global prosperity, or of new inequalities and forms of exploitation (Hutton and Giddens, 2000).

Related to the development of non-state forces has been the emergence of new forms of international organisation. One of the key claims made by states to dominate international affairs has been that they are better organised on the whole to achieve the requirements of citizens for order, prosperity and development. The extent to which this claim was borne out in many cases can be challenged. As indicated above, the 'society of states' is a diverse one. During the past twenty or thirty years, however, there has been an immense proliferation (or consolidation) of forms of organisation whose operation have detracted from the competencies of states. These range from global bodies such as the United Nations (UN) or the World Trade Organisation (WTO) to regional or sub-regional institutions such as the Council of Europe and the North American Free Trade Association (Keohane and Martin, 1995).

The net effect of these processes is a substantial but incomplete transformation not only of the 'world of states' but also of the world in which states exist. This is not to say that states are on the way out – many of them are more vigorous, wealthy and powerful than ever before. But it is to argue that national governments have to deal with a new and more complex reality, the product of many years of evolution, which appears in important respects to be irreversible. We will discuss the implications of these changes more fully in Chapter 2.

New issues

The traditional image of foreign policy depends heavily on a certain view of the foreign policy 'agenda'. As noted above, the competing claims of states in international affairs created insecurity and, as a result, the pursuit of national security was indisputably at the head of national priorities. Although this has economic and social aspects, the ultimate expression of national security was the ability to ensure military security for the territory and its citizens. From this sprang many of the claims of states to design, manage and control not only their foreign relations but also the activities of their citizens both at home and abroad. Even the apparently mundane details of national passports and customs controls are in this sense a powerful symbol of the claim to state dominance.

How has this traditional agenda been affected by changes in the contemporary era? Again, it is important to have some historical perspective. Even during the Cold War, the ability of most states to provide for their own national security was often challenged: either states were inherently weak, as were many in the Third World, or they had to depend upon powerful patrons, particularly the superpowers with their nuclear arsenals. This is a state of affairs that has changed little. Very few states, even after the demise of the Cold War, have asserted a self-sufficiency in national security affairs; and those that have – North Korea, Iraq, Libya, Cuba and, to some degree, China – tend to be regarded as unusual. The continuing pattern is, in fact, collaboration, a condition to which even the most powerful of states – the US (through the North Atlantic Treaty Organisation [NATO]) or Russia (through arrangements with partners in the Commonwealth of Independent States [CIS]) – still resort. National security has then remained a key aim of foreign policy – indeed, the fact that certain of the transformations of world politics have been so disruptive makes this a seeming necessity.

The provision and meaning of national security has, however, altered in recent years. The emphasis which the Cold War placed on the military instruments of security (and, by extension, foreign policy) has been downgraded both by governments and by foreign policy analysts. For many states, the Cold War imposed a considerable opportunity cost in the form of expenditures foregone on economic and social development. With the disappearance of the Soviet threat this has led in the West to the exploitation of a 'peace dividend' – the diversion of resources away from the military (apparent in a fall in defence expenditure as a proportion of gross domestic product) towards civilian needs. This pattern is not, however, a uniform one. Many states elsewhere feel no such luxury in their security situation. Indeed, in large swathes of Africa, the Middle East and the Asian sub-continent military instruments and threats continue to fixate national leaderships. Even here, however, the meaning of security is no longer seen as fixed. The 'military sector' of security may be the most pressing for some, but it is buttressed by threats to states, national populations and individuals that derive from other economic, environmental, political and societal 'sectors' (Buzan et al., 1998). This is also the case in the more settled states of Europe and North America. Here, the threats to the human environment, the burdens of migration and refugees or the task of promoting economic prosperity have come to many governments to appear far more immediate and challenging items on the foreign policy agenda. It is not that economic and social priorities have never been given a place; rather, it is that historically they have always been 'trumped' by the primacy of national security. Since the 1980s, it has not been so easy to play the national security card in its traditional form. New issues have become more immediate and, importantly, many of these issues are inherently transnational or global in their implications.

How much of a transformation?

The picture we have painted so far is necessarily an outline, one that will be developed more fully in the following chapters. It is important, though, to be aware of this general context for the study of contemporary foreign policy. We have identified a number of key areas in which the pressures of change have been felt. But how much of a transformation do these represent? Although the context of foreign policy has clearly been subject to major shifts, does this mean that our initial definition of foreign policy, with its emphasis on states and their national governments, is in any way less appropriate? We would argue that the definition is, in fact, still a relevant one. It is still the case that national governments seek to 'design, manage and control' the foreign relations of national societies, that the institution of statehood remains central to the ordering of international life, and thus that the foreign policies of states enjoy an influence that privileges them above non-state actors. Of course, there is variety. It would be manifestly obtuse to suggest that the foreign policies of all states enjoy this degree of importance (the foreign policy of the US is clearly more significant in a global sense than that of say Sri Lanka or Nepal) or that all states, in practice, are more influential than other actors in international life (the US may be more important than the United Nations in many instances, but the UN is more important in many other instances than Sri Lanka or Nepal). Furthermore, as we have made clear throughout this chapter, foreign policy is made and conducted in a context characterised by a number of changing features. In short, these constitute the following:

- Changes in the numbers, resources and status of both states and non-state actors, including the rise of 'non-state foreign policies'.

- Changes in the nature of national security and other national objectives and values.

- Changes in policy-making processes, including the new salience of cross-departmental and cross-national processes.

- Changes in the nature of power and influence, and in the effectiveness of particular methods of policy implementation.

This does not mean that foreign policy is marginalised or uninteresting. We would maintain that it is not only central to national and international life, but also interesting in new and challenging ways.

Changing perspectives on foreign policy

In view of what we have said so far, it is not surprising that one of the central features of the study of foreign policy has been a competition between different perspectives. The study of International Relations in general has been distinguished by tensions between a variety of approaches, and FPA has shared in this process of development. We have already pointed out the central features of a 'Realist', state-centric view of foreign policy, or what we have also described as the 'traditional' view. This is a compelling image of foreign policy, which sets the national government as the representative of a society against the world and casts success or failure in Mancihean terms of triumph or disaster. As with all such images, it is not representative of all day-to-day events or processes in foreign policy, although it is clear from what we have said that there is still some mileage in such a perspective. Indeed, the proliferation of new states, each with their own national identity and role to develop, and confronted by an often uncertain and sometimes hostile international environment, could be said to have given it new life (Goldgeier and McFaul, 1992).

A related approach is that of 'Neo-Realism'. While still giving a central role to the state, this approach attributes state behaviour less to qualities which inhere within the state itself (such as the quality of leadership or the quest of leaders for power and glory) and more to the conditioning effects of the international system's anarchical structure (or, in other words, the absence of world government). Anarchy creates conditions of suspicion and competition among states and consequently imposes one compelling motivation upon them, that of self-preservation. This need not mean that states are engaged in a constant round of wars and conquest. Indeed, Neo-Realism suggests that states are constrained in their behaviour by 'the distribution of capabilities' within the international system. The most obvious manifestations of this include nuclear weapons-based deterrence and also more traditional forms of balance of power. Kenneth Waltz, the best known Neo-Realist, was clear in his writings that this perspective did not constitute a theory of foreign policy; however, certain important inferences can be drawn. Foreign policy, according to this view, can be seen as guided ultimately by national survival, the related objective of exploiting opportunities that enhance state capabilities and a general predisposition against anything but expedient forms of cooperation with other states (Waltz, 1979).

While there are those who might present foreign policy as essentially about competition, insecurity and threat, the reality is that much of foreign policy is about cooperation between states. Working on this assumption, perhaps the most sustained challenge to Realist and Neo-Realist conceptions of foreign policy has come from what is often termed the Pluralist perspective (Viotti and Kauppi, 1993b: 7–8). In many ways, this approach is a direct response to the perceived inadequacies of the traditional approach, especially in the light of changes to domestic and world politics. Pluralist approaches takes these changes as central influences on foreign policy and thereby demand new concepts and methods of analysis. Pluralists have identified a number of pervasive global trends which have had the effect of reducing the 'insulation' of national governments and national societies. One influential approach in this vein is Keohane and Nye's (1989) notion of 'complex interdependence'. According to this view, world politics has, since at least the 1970s, become increasingly characterised by an agenda of 'multiple issues' and thus foreign policy has moved away from its traditional concern with military and security matters towards economic, social, environmental and other concerns. As a consequence, links between governments have multiplied as new issues and areas of cooperation have emerged, and many of these have given rise to new forms of international organisation. In many ways, although there is still no world government, world politics and the world economy are increasingly 'governed' by intricate sets of rules and institutions. Thus, the 'cast of characters' on the world stage has expanded, and it is not always clear that individual national governments hold the whip hand in dealing with political or economic issues.

Another key characteristic of this new context is that international issues affect much wider parts of domestic populations, and thus that a range of 'private' or non-governmental organisations can become interested in foreign policy making. Pressure groups, organised interests and other domestic forces can gain a role in the shaping of foreign policy, particularly on economic and social issues. In the implementation of policy, equally, a wide range of organisations can become involved, through systems of cross-departmental and cross-national policy activity. Notions of power and of coercion become less prominent than notions of influence, access and communication. A logical development of this line of argument is to see foreign policy as in many ways the 'international dimension' of domestic policies and, indeed, to deploy many of the analytical tools of Comparative Politics or Policy Analysis more generally to explore the foreign policy process (Evans et al., 1993; Risse-Kappen, 1995).

A further strand in the study of foreign policy has been what can be termed the Dependency perspective. This bears particular relation to the emergence noted above of many new states in the Third World. Although these states could lay claim to the classical properties of statehood –

sovereignty, recognition, control of territory – it was apparent from the outset that many of them were incapable of exercising their independence. By this view the world was (and still is) one of profound inequalities between states and within societies, which means that the small, the poor and the unstable are effectively subordinate to the large, the rich and the stable. For FPA, this perception leads to the conclusion that less developed countries have few realistic policy choices – they succumb to a form of economic servitude upon rich states and international financial institutions and, in regional terms, become preoccupied with immediate threats to their national security that arise from arbitrary borders (a legacy of the colonial period) and unresolved territorial claims (Thomas, 1987). Their policy-making processes, meanwhile, are often characterised by a lack of stable structures, a severe lack of resources both human and administrative and by a close linkage between domestic political contests and foreign policy actions. For such states, the making and implementation of foreign policy is often a matter of reflexes, in the sense that the actions are demanded if not compelled directly by pressing national need and dependence on others. Lest it be thought that these features are somehow in the past, it should be remembered not only that there are still large numbers of less developed countries of the 'classical' type, but also that the 1990s saw (as already noted) the emergence of large numbers of 'new' states often with these same features of dependency and vulnerability.

Since the 1990s, (Neo) Realism, Pluralism and Dependency approaches have been joined by what can be termed the Globalist approach. In International Relations, the 'globalisation' process has been noted most dramatically in the area of political economy, with the growth of transnational processes of production, exchange and communication. Some would argue that this is itself a very long-standing phenomenon, starting with the growth of maritime trade in the Middle Ages and proceeding through the growth of the great nineteenth-century empires. Equally, in the area of global security, the twentieth century has seen a consistent attention to the process whereby the security and integrity of different countries or regions have become linked. What is said to be distinctive about more contemporary globalisation processes is their rootlessness: in other words, they are less constrained by territorial or national divisions, or by the authority of national governments, than previously (Sasken, 1996). This is clearly a distinctive basis on which to approach foreign policy, since it effectively challenges the credentials of national governments at the most fundamental level, and threatens to undermine some of the most cherished elements of national security and national action. Globalisation might in principle mean that 'foreign policy' is often powerless in the face of a multiplicity of external influences. Whereas the Realist, Pluralist and Dependency approaches all rely on strong assumptions about power, influence and the rules to which they give rise, a Globalist view assumes no such structures. For foreign policy decision making and action, this produces a very indeterminate world; indeed, some have defined such a world as essentially 'postmodern', one in which there are no settled structures of authority and in which individuals or groups hold no settled positions (Devetak, 1996).

This review shows that the concept of 'foreign policy' itself has been subject to considerable debate, and that this debate has intersected with broader developments of a global character. It is not possible to draw simple lines of cause and effect between the 'real world' and the analysis of foreign policy, but it is clear that the relative certainty and predictability of the 'world of states' which might be said to have characterised the 1950s and 1960s has disappeared. It is also apparent that theories of foreign policy are not simply mechanical descriptions of processes and events but embody value-laden assumptions about what is or is not significant. Thus, for example, Realist and Neo-Realist approaches may be described as essentially 'conservative', Pluralist approaches as 'reformist', and Dependency and Globalist theories as 'radical', in the sense that each takes a position on the acceptability of the status quo that implies actions to maintain, amend or transform the structures of world politics.

Another distinction which has been made, and which is particularly relevant to the study of foreign policy, is that between 'problem-solving theories' and 'critical theories'. The former takes the existing order as given and seeks to make it work more effectively, while the latter sees the existing order as a reflection of power relations and ideologies which represent particular dominant groupings in international affairs. In this context, both Realism and Pluralism might be seen as 'problem-solving' approaches, while Dependency and Globalist approaches would contain strong elements of critical theory (as, for example, would approaches to foreign policy and world politics more generally, such as feminism and environmentalism). For easy reference, the approaches we have identified are summarised in Table 1.1 below.

Summary and conclusion

To conclude this chapter, and to form a basis for the more detailed treatment in Chapters 2–4, we put forward here a summary of our framework

Table 1.1 Perspectives on foreign policy

	Nature of the international system	Foreign policy issue	Value-laden assumptions
Realism	Competitive. Prone to war. Influence of high-level diplomacy, balances of power. Society of states.	Acquisition of power. State survival. Glory and prestige. The 'national interest'.	Conservative
Neo-Realism	Anarchic. Competitive. Balances of power.	State survival. Preoccupation with national security.	Conservative
Pluralism	'Complex interdependence'. Increased likelihood of cooperation.	Multiple issues with no hierarchy. Economic issues as important as military ones.	Reformist
Dependency	Unequal. Economically weak states unjustly dependent on richer states.	For the weak states survival and manoeuvre in constrained circumstances. For the richer states entrenchment of beneficial exploitation.	Radical
Globalist	Acceleration of transnational processes of production, exchange and communication. Security of different countries or regions increasingly linked.	Multiple. States overwhelmed by this multiplicity.	Radical

for analysis of foreign policy. As indicated at several points in the chapter, we base our framework on a combination of the initial definition of foreign policy and specific elements in the foreign policy process. The key elements are three:

- First, the foreign policy arena. In this chapter we have intimated at a notion of an arena in which foreign policy is conditioned and takes place, but we must take this further and analyse the nature of this arena and the ways in which particular national governments are affected by and form a view of this arena. We must also assess in more detail the ways in which changes in the foreign policy arena are 'registered' by national governments, and the ways in which this relates to the groups, organisations and interests which 'populate' the foreign policy arena. This is undertaken in Chapter 2.

- Second, foreign policy decision making. We have dealt in a very general way with ideas about how governments make policy, and how policy making has responded to processes of transformation . We now need to take this analysis further, and to explore the ways in which different models of foreign policy making can be used to assess specific cases. This is the focus of Chapter 3.

- Third, the implementation of foreign policy. This chapter has talked in general terms about issues affecting the implementation of policy, including the changing nature of power and influence and some of the instruments of policy. Chapter 4 will focus in more detail on the implementation process, and will assess the ways in which implementation has responded to the transformation of world politics.

Further reading

Foreign policy analysis (FPA) is an important sub-field of the academic discipline of International Relations. Two useful surveys of the FPA literature are Hill and Light (1985) and Light (1994). Texts dedicated to the analytical and comparative study of foreign policy include Clarke and White (eds) (1989), Macridis (ed.) (1992), and Neack, Hey and Haney (eds) (1995). Useful surveys of different perspectives in International Relations (and by extension in FPA) can be found in Brown (1997), Viotti and Kauppi (eds) (1993a) and Walt (1998). On the recent transformation of world politics there is now quite a sizeable literature. See, for instance, Halliday (2001) and Hocking and Smith (1995). Work on transformation and foreign policy is much less in evidence (hence this volume). However, see Rosati, Hagan and Sampson (eds) (1997) for recent foreign policy responses to change, and Boyd and Hopple (eds) (1987) and Smith (1981) for more general approaches on foreign policy adaptation.

References

Aron, R. (1962) *Peace and War. A Theory of International Relations*. London: Weidenfeld and Nicolson.

Berridge, G.R. (1992) *International Politics. States, Power and Conflict since 1945* (2nd edition). Hemel Hempstead: Harvester Wheatsheaf.

Boyd, G. and Hopple, G.W. (eds) (1987) *Political Change and Foreign Policies*. London: Pinter.

Brown, C. (1997) *Understanding International Relations*. Basingstoke: Macmillan.

Bull, H. (1977) *The Anarchical Society. A Study of Order in World Politics*. Basingstoke: Macmillan.

Buzan, B., Wæver, O. and de Wilde, J. (1998) *Security. A New Framework for Analysis*. Boulder, CO, and London: Lynne Rienner.

Calvert, P. (1986) *The Foreign Policy of New States*. New York: St Martin's Press.

Clark, M. and White, B. (eds) (1989) *Understanding Foreign Policy. The Foreign Policy Systems Approach*. Aldershot: Edward Elgar.

Devetak, R. (1996) 'Postmodernism', in Burchill, S. and Linklater, A. (eds), *Theories of International Relations*. Basingstoke: Macmillan, 179–209.

Evans, P.B., Jacobson, H.K. and Putnam, R.D. (eds) (1993) *Double-Edged Diplomacy. International Bargaining and Domestic Politics*. Berkeley: University of California Press.

Goldgeier, J.M. and McFaul, M. (1992) 'A Tale of Two Worlds: Core and Periphery in the Post-Cold War Era', *International Organisation*, **46**(2), 467–91.

Halliday, F. (2001) *The World at 2000*. Basingstoke: Palgrave.

Held, D., McGrew, A., Goldblatt, D. and Perraton, J. (1999) *Global Transformations: Politics, Economics, and Culture*. Oxford: Polity Press.

Hill, C. and Light, M. (1985) 'Foreign Policy Analysis', in Light, M. and Groom, A.J.R. (eds), *International Relations. A Handbook of Current Theory*. London: Pinter.

Hobson, J.M. (2000) *The State and International Relations*. Cambridge: Cambridge University Press.

Hocking, B. and Smith, M. (1995) *World Politics. An Introduction to International Relations* (2nd edition). Hemel Hempstead: Harvester Wheatsheaf/Prentice Hall.

Hutton, W. and Giddens, A. (eds) (2000) *On the Edge. Living with Global Capitalism*. London: Jonathan Cape.

Jackson, R.H. (1990) *Quasi-States: Sovereignty, International Relations and the Third World*. Cambridge: Cambridge University Press.

Keohane, R.O. and Martin, L. (1995) 'The Promise of Institutionalist Theory', *International Security*, **20**(1), 39–51.

Keohane, R.O. and Nye, J.S. (1977) *Power and Interdependence. World Politics in Transition*. Boston and Toronto: Little Brown.

Keohane, R.O. and Nye, J.S. (1989) *Power and Interdependence. World Politics in Transition* (2nd edition). Boston: Little Brown.

Light, M. (1994) 'Foreign Policy Analysis', in Groom, A.J.R. and Light, M. (eds), *Contemporary International Relations. A Guide to Theory*. London: Pinter, 93–108.

Macridis, R.C. (ed.) (1992) *Foreign Policy in World Politics. States and Regions* (8th edition). London: Prentice Hall International.

Mansbach, R.W., Ferguson, Y.H. and Lampert, D.E. (1976) *The Web of World Politics*. Englewood Cliffs, NJ: Prentice-Hall.

Morgenthau, H. (1960) *Politics among Nations. The Struggle for Power and Peace* (3rd edition). New York: Alfred A. Knopf.

Neack, L., Hey, J.A.K. and Haney, P.J. (eds) (1995) *Foreign Policy Analysis. Continuity and Change in Its Second Generation*. Englewood Cliffs, NJ: Prentice-Hall.

Risse-Kappen, T. (ed.) (1995) *Bringing Transnational Relations Back In: Non-State Actors, Domestic Structures and International Relations*. Cambridge: Cambridge University Press.

Rosati, J.A., Hagan, J.D. and Sampson, M.W. (eds) (1997) *Foreign Policy Restructuring: How Governments Respond to Global Change*. Colombia: University of South Carolina Press.

Sasken, S. (1996) *Losing Control? Sovereignty in an Age of Globalization*. NewYork: Columbia University Press.

Smith, S.M. (1981) *Foreign Policy Adaptation*. Aldershot: Gower.

Thomas, C. (1987) *In Search of Security. The Third World in International Relations*. Brighton: Harvester Wheatsheaf.

Viotti, P.R. and Kauppi, M.V. (eds) (1993a) *International Relations Theory. Realism, Pluralism, Globalism* (2nd edition). New York and Toronto: Macmillan.

Viotti, P.R. and Kauppi, M.V. (1993b) 'Theory, Images and International Relations: An Introduction', in Viotti, P.R. and Kauppi, M.V. (eds), *International Relations Theory. Realism, Pluralism, Globalism* (2nd edition). New York and Toronto: Macmillan, 4–22.

Wallace, W. (1971) *Foreign Policy and the Political Process*. London and Basingstoke: Macmillan.

Walt, S.M. (1998) 'International Relations: One World, Many Theories', *Foreign Policy*, **110**, 29–46.

Waltz, K. (1979) *Theory of International Politics*. Reading, MA: Addison-Wesley.

2 | The Foreign Policy Arena

This chapter explores the foreign policy arena: that is to say, the terrain on which foreign policy is conducted, and the ways in which that terrain is 'populated' by forces which shape foreign policy making and implementation. The chapter looks at the arena in terms of the contexts within which policy emerges: the international context, the governmental context and the domestic context. It then moves on to examine three factors that structure the foreign policy arena: actors, issues and interests. The overall argument of the chapter is that the traditional insulation and 'specialness' of foreign policy has come under pressure from a number of forces which emphasise linkages and complexity, and that this has important implications for governmental decisions and actions.

Introduction

Chapter 1 dealt in general terms with a number of the ways in which foreign policy analysis (FPA) has had to cope with the impact of change. One of the most important dimensions of change, and thus of pressure on policy makers and analysts, is change in the foreign policy arena. In this chapter, the central aim is to identify the major features of this arena. By doing this, the chapter will lay the basis for a more detailed exploration of policy making and implementation in Chapters 3 and 4.

What is the foreign policy arena? In broad terms, it can be described as the terrain on which foreign policy decisions are made and actions taken. This terrain has a certain topography – in other words, it has 'landmarks' which will differ according to the foreign policy under examination. But the arena is not simply a collection of physical features; it also represents a set of potential resources for the policy maker. Some of these resources are physical, some are human, and many are political or economic in their nature. One of the key tests of an effective foreign policy is, therefore, the ways in which a government can access the resources available in the arena, and the efficiency with which it can put them to use for policy purposes. Inevitably, the other side of the resources coin is that of constraints: no government faces a foreign policy arena in which there is no competition for access to resources, or in which all resources are equally available.

One reason why access is not assured lies in the second aspect of the arena. It is a terrain, to be sure, but this terrain is populated in various ways and by various forces, each of which is likely to have an impact on the government in the formulation of its foreign policy. The foreign policy arena is, in other words, occupied by a range of significant actors, issues and interests, all of which give it a dynamism and life. One of the key tests of an effective foreign policy is thus the ways in which the foreign policy makers can appraise the shifting array of forces in the arena, respond to those forces and use the opportunities they create. More negatively, it might be said that withstanding the challenges and insecurities of the arena is the minimum requirement of an effective foreign policy.

This chapter sets out to assess the ways in which the foreign policy arena may have changed during the contemporary era. It deals first with the arena in terms of *contexts*: the interrelated settings within which foreign policy emerges, and which are central to the 'terrain' outlined above. It then moves on to deal with those forces (actors, issues and interests) which give life and dynamism to the foreign policy arena.

Contexts

Analysis of foreign policy has invariably pointed to a special feature: the fact that policy makers simultaneously need to take account of developments both at home and abroad (Morse, 1970). At its simplest, the image is of the foreign policy maker either as a 'barrier' against the incursion of alien forces, or as a 'bridge' linking the domestic scene with the outside world. This image is fundamental to the argument that foreign policy is distinctive, and that it thus requires special processes of policy making and implementation. It is clear, however, that as the nature of the international system and domestic politics changes, there are likely to be major shifts in how these two realms relate to one another and consequently in the policy responses to which this shifting relationship gives rise. This state of affairs is best understood by examining three 'contexts' of the foreign policy arena: the international context, the governmental context and the domestic context.

The international context

Traditionally, there has been an overriding tendency in the study of foreign policy to present the international context as the predominant concern of policy-makers (Zakaria, 1992: 179). It is in the international domain that the challenges and opportunities for foreign policy largely arise, and as a result it is here that the stakes, the uncertainties and the risks are at their most demanding. Such a view of foreign policy, as you will recognise, arises directly from the image of International Relations as a competitive system of relations among states. Here, the foreign policy-maker is seen as responsible for maximising the gains and minimising the losses that arise from such competition – particularly in the area of national security. A series of military, economic, political and geographic factors feed into the international context, something which, in turn, gives rise to hierarchies of power and influence. This hierarchy is in some senses fixed, certainly at the top and bottom ends, as the states which either possess or lack resources tend to be the same over the short to medium term (the sudden demise of Soviet power is a rare exception). That said, considerable fluctuation exists in the middle of the hierarchy as states find that the possession or non-possession of certain resources (a particular commodity such as oil) or geographic position provides them with temporary advantages or places them in a situation of disadvantage. Furthermore, the hierarchy is also affected by fluctuations in the currency placed upon resources and other factors.

What this tells us is that for any government, status will be a key concern in confronting the international context. During the Cold War, for instance, both the United States (US) and the Soviet Union tended to view the international context in terms of each others' relative power positions (for a time, the Soviet Union was also preoccupied with the position of China). For those lower down the hierarchy of states it was also the case that the international context was viewed as structured by the apparent availability of resources, for example through membership of the key alliances of the North Atlantic Treaty Organisation (NATO) or the Warsaw Pact. After the Cold War (and to some extent, even during it) the balance of advantage between military and economic resources has shifted towards the latter. This has not fundamentally affected the US, owing to both its military and economic prowess, but it has had a profoundly negative impact on a state such as Russia. Similarly, geographic considerations have altered. States such as Cuba, Ethiopia and Afghanistan, which assumed a heightened importance during the years of Soviet–American competition, are now of marginal consequence. Others, such as Azerbaijan, Kazakhstan and Turkey, have, however, acquired a new importance that reflects changing geopolitical and geoeconomic concerns (in this case a proximity to newly-discovered energy resources and transportation routes).

Broadly speaking, how can we evaluate the impact of the international context and assess the ways in which it has altered? In response, it might be helpful to highlight three broad dimensions of change.

A first dimension is related to shifts in the *location* of activity – away from the Cold War concentration on Europe as the centre of international concern and towards other locations which reflect more pressingly the importance of new foreign policy issues. This, for some, has meant an attention to new 'arcs of crisis', in the Transcaucasus, Central Asia and the Great Lakes region of Africa; for others, a renewed emphasis on sites of poverty, famine and displacement such as the Horn of Africa; and for others still, demands for international action on environmental degradation in the Amazon Basin or equatorial Africa (White et al., 2001).

A second dimension of change concerns the *focus* of activity. This relates to the rise to prominence of new issues, already noted in the previous chapter. In simple terms this has meant an increased attention both by analysts and policy makers to matters of economic regulation, and social and environmental concern. It is worth repeating that these issues are not entirely 'new'. However, more so than in the Cold War period, they have given rise to debates of wider relevance that relate to the global distribution of wealth, patterns of inclusion and exclusion in international life and the need for new forms of international or global governance (Falk, 1995; Linklater, 1998). These debates have not simply been confined to academic circles. Bodies affiliated to the United Nations (UN) have advanced proposals for 'the management of global affairs [in a manner that] is responsive to the interests of all people in a sustainable future' (Commission on Global Governance, 1995: xvii) and powerful national governments have been compelled to act (albeit sometimes begrudgingly) in a more concerted manner on issues of debt and famine relief, and conflict resolution.

A third dimension, finally, is that of the *instruments* of activity. We have already noted that the traditional axes of international competition have altered and with them the instruments used to effect policy. The

Cold War stress on military instruments was never absolute. Indeed, both the US and the Soviet Union engaged in a form of ideological warfare, backed by a range of political, cultural and economic instruments. However, these instruments of 'soft power' are now even more important (Nye, 1990). Certainly among the established democracies this has long been the case; indeed, their interactions are characterised by an almost total absence of recourse to hard military measures. Even where relations are more competitive, the military component is less prominent. Consider, for instance, the conduct of relations between the US and Russia (or, for that matter, between the US and China) where trade, diplomacy and economic assistance are at least as important as the Cold War legacies of nuclear weapons and competitive military alliance systems. Of course, this is not a uniform pattern. As noted in Chapter 1, states residing in less stable parts of the world have continued to frame foreign policy with an eye to traditional threats to their security and thus still place an emphasis on military instruments.

The governmental context

In Chapter 1 it was noted that traditionally FPA assumed that all governments were in principle the same, although each had a different version of the foreign policy problem. Governments were seen as representing national states, whose claims to sovereignty and security were the key issues in foreign policy. National policy makers, in effect, had to assume that all other governments were out for the same things as they were: maximisation of their freedom of action and security in a competitive international system.

The implications of this view of government in foreign policy have been and still are powerful and far-reaching. Essentially, it leads to a view of government which is elitist and specialised (see Chapter 1). At the same time, government is also seen as insulated, because foreign policy should not be subject to the hurly-burly of 'normal politics'. Thus, in many governments, the Foreign Ministry, and alongside it the Defence Ministry, have historically been shielded from the scrutiny of legislatures and the broader political scene.

The assumptions encapsulated in this view of foreign policy are not simply matters of philosophy or of abstract argument. They have had powerful and direct effects on the entire structure of governments the world over, often through constitutional provisions which give a special place to foreign policy. The American constitution grants special powers to the President as Commander-in-Chief; the constitutions of the French Fifth Republic and the Russian Federation, similarly, contain provisions for centralisation of foreign policy with the chief executive (the President). In more autocratic systems both constitutional provision and political practice ensure a tight oversight of foreign policy by the executive. Indeed, in places such as Iraq, Turkmenistan, Syria and Libya foreign policy is, in effect, a special preserve of personal rule. Yet no matter how powerful the role of the executive, states almost without exception rely on specialised foreign ministries to implement and, in many case, to formulate, foreign policy. The existence of these ministries expresses in tangible form the primacy of the international context and the need to respond to it. Some would also argue that there is a powerful cultural factor at work in foreign ministries, buttressing their image as special arms of governmental policy making and providing them with a special status in society more generally (Frankel, 1963: 28–33). This does not, however, rule out frictions between the claims of foreign offices to special status and the demands of other government departments. Even the most traditional approaches to FPA allow for the fact that foreign ministries do not exist in a vacuum, and that intra-governmental politics can lead to challenges, for example where foreign policy is at odds with national prosperity or where there is broader instability in government itself. These frictions exist most transparently in established democracies but even in less democratic societies departmental competition occurs, albeit in a form that is often mysterious and not clearly observable to the outsider.

In recent years it has become ever more apparent that government structures for foreign policy making are open to challenge and change. One element of this has been organisational restructuring to reflect changes in the international context. For instance, most foreign offices had departments dealing with the affairs of East Germany, a state which in 1990 ceased to exist. During the early 1990s, the proliferation of new and newly-liberated states in the former Soviet bloc placed a great strain on the capacities of many foreign offices, both in the quantitative sense ('do we have enough people to staff new embassies or departments?') and in the qualitative sense ('is there anyone here who knows about Azerbaijan?') The governmental context for foreign policy making was in many countries thrown into a mild form of turmoil – not least in those new and newly-liberated countries which had to establish foreign policy making almost from scratch. This was not unprecedented: during the 1960s, with the ending of the British and French empires, dozens of new and often poor states had to establish foreign policy machines. In their cases as well, the international context was often challenging and turbulent.

Another type of challenge within the governmental context of foreign policy making has been the growth and diffusion of 'government' itself. The traditional approach to FPA assumed that government is unified, and that the leading role is taken by the Foreign Ministry (with the Defence Ministry often closely allied). In a way, this is not only a statement of perceived fact but also a statement of the way things ought to be in a well-regulated governmental machine. Since the 1980s it has become apparent that the idea of unified government is under pressure. One source of this pressure is simply the growth of government itself. Certainly in Western societies, the scope and scale of the governmental machine have increased, often as a response to the demands of international life. Thus, foreign offices that used to be staffed by a relatively small number of dedicated diplomats have become large and complicated bureaucracies. While this was true even before the 1980s, it can be argued that the increasing impacts of globalisation and regionalisation, and the proliferation of new states and organisations, have made for new pressures to expand. As expansion takes place, there is inevitably a problem of fragmentation, as bureaucrats develop their own distinct interests and organisational capacities. As will be seen in Chapter 3, this can lead to outbreaks of 'bureaucratic politics' and competition between government agencies.

These trends suggest that there are limits to the extent to which foreign policy is insulated from the broader process of government. When foreign policy could be defined largely in terms of diplomacy and defence, there were many reasons for the insulation of the foreign policy machine. When 'international policy' comes to include aspects of virtually every department of government, then there are clearly new incentives and challenges. In terms of incentives, many departments of government might feel that there are good reasons for international activity: contacts with their opposite numbers in other countries or in international agencies, the sheer necessity of international policy coordination, and the satisfaction to be gained from trips abroad. These incentives in turn hold the seeds of new challenges: of policy coordination across expanding areas of activity, of collective policy implementation, and so on. They also generate the involvement of a wider range of government departments, and of agencies or groupings outside government – in other words, an expanding 'foreign policy community' (Hocking, 1998: 2–3).

The notion of policy communities implies the growth of stable 'extended families' of those with an interest in international activities. Less stable or permanent are 'policy networks' – often *ad hoc* coalitions of those with foreign policy interests, which may be less easily penetrated or controlled by government. Both policy communities and policy networks are not necessarily in opposition to traditional models of government organisation in foreign policy, but do reflect modifications to the ways in which policy is shaped or conducted (Atkinson and Coleman, 1992).

The net effect of such developments in the governmental context is that the long-established image of foreign policy as the preserve of a skilled diplomatic (and sometimes military) elite is at least modified. In some lesser-resourced societies, it may be modified by the limitations of governmental capacity and structure. In others, it may be modified by the sheer extent of the structure, and may become less of a diplomatic problem than a management problem, where coordination of overlapping structures and institutions, and the intersection of various policy communities or networks, create major problems of collective action. We shall explore many of these issues more extensively in Chapters 3 and 4, and they will resurface in the case studies conducted in Part Two of the book.

The domestic context

Implicit in much of what we have said so far are important arguments about the role played in foreign policy making by the domestic context. Traditional images of foreign policy give a largely peripheral role to the domestic political or economic setting. The presumed delicacy of the foreign policy undertaking, and the need to insulate it even within the government structure, has led to a view of domestic pressures which relegates them to the margins. It must also be noted that this elitism and insulation have been in part accepted and often supported by informed domestic opinion. It is often considered right and proper that foreign policy is kept away from the domestic hurly-burly, in order to promote consistency and stability in policy making.

The domestic political context of foreign policy has thus historically been seen as permissive, allowing the policy makers considerable freedom of action. Domestic views of foreign policy, except in times of major national crisis, have often been described in terms of a restricted 'attentive public' and a great mass of those who are uninformed and uninterested. Foreign policy making is thus seen as profoundly and necessarily undemocratic, focused not on short-term political or economic advantage but on longer-term necessities. This is not to say that the domestic context can never influence foreign policy. For example, national political crisis or economic collapse can clearly make for severe constraints on the foreign policy makers. But even in such conditions, there is a strong tendency to argue, even in democratic political systems, that foreign policy should be insulated and untainted.

It is not surprising that such restricted views of the domestic influences on foreign policy have come under pressure, but the results of the pressures are not all in the same direction. In fact, there is a profound conflict of influences to be found (Gourevitch, 1978; Kapstein, 1995). On the one side, there has been a growth of new patterns of communication and new information sources (especially electronic media). This means that there is potentially far wider access to information about events that might have seemed impossibly 'distant' even in the recent past. There is also the potential for contacts between citizens in new and uncontrollable settings, such as the Internet. At the national level, therefore, the context is in principle less permissive than in the past, and this is so even in societies where there has traditionally been restricted access to international information, such as China and particularly states of the former Soviet bloc. Alongside the newly-informed citizen go newly-energised institutions of domestic opinion and politics. Pressure groups are more capable of informing themselves and of communicating their messages, legislatures at national and regional or local level are better able to form views on the foreign policy process and foreign policy actions.

But there is another side to this coin. While in principle there is a strong basis for a more 'information rich' domestic context which might constrain the foreign policy makers, there are trends which work to preserve or even to enhance their insulation from the domestic scene. For example, the growth of international mechanisms of governance means that the newly-informed citizen may find that decisions are taken elsewhere than at the national level, or that the increasingly complex process of coordination within the governmental machine may make it more difficult to exert pressure or make opinions felt. Thus, at the same time as the domestic context becomes richer in information and opinions, so the insulation of the foreign policy makers may increase. It is possible for the domestic forces we have described to counter this, for example by forming transnational alliances with those of similar views, but it is by no means a simple process.

Somewhat more elusive to grasp than the political features of the domestic context are characteristics which have been broadly defined as constituting national identity or culture. These are, of course, rather slippery concepts and thus difficult to define. However, taking just the former, it might be assumed that it constitutes a sense of similarity among the inhabitants of a state born from a national history, common experience and exposure to the same myths and symbols of nationhood. National identity consequently generates a sense of the state's place in the world, its national interests and its aspirations, and thus points to the appropriateness of certain courses of foreign policy action (Hyde-Price, 1999: 57–65). Not all national identities are perfectly formed. New states often lack a clear sense of identity (a fact plain to see among some of the post-Soviet states) and it may take decades before even a rudimentary national identity emerges (hence, forty years after independence, many states in Africa are still riven by deep-seated disputes because of the weakness of any over-arching sense of commonality among their populations). However, national identities are sufficiently developed among a wide range of states, thus allowing the concept to be employed as a useful means of understanding and comparing foreign policies. Adrian Hyde-Price (1999: 62–5), for instance, on the basis of a scheme outlined by Ilya Prizel (1998: 21–33), has forwarded six 'categories of relationships between national identity and the conduct of foreign policy'. These include the institutionally or constitutionally based identities of the US and the United Kingdom (UK) which result in foreign policies with a strong legalistic streak; the cultural pretensions of French identity which generates a foreign policy premised on asserting France's self-proclaimed position of *grandeur*; and the reconstructed identities of post-war Germany and Japan which, in the German case, has given rise to a strong foreign policy commitment to European integration and involvement in multilateral institutions.

Evaluating the contexts of foreign policy

The chapter so far has presented a view of three interrelated contexts for the framing and conduct of foreign policy: the international, the governmental and the domestic. Traditionally, the linkages between these contexts have been seen as restricted: policy by necessity was composed by the designated policy makers operating with an eye primarily to the international context, and at an arm's length relationship with domestic forces. It has been suggested here, however, that trends in these three contexts have fundamentally altered this traditional picture. As a result, it could be argued that the key problem in contemporary foreign policies – notwithstanding variations between governments and their capacities – is that of extracting resources from a set of inter-linked contexts, where many policy problems are both cross-departmental within government and cross-national between societies. How can governments in such circumstances position themselves and produce consistent policy both in the procedural sense (how they do it) and in the substantive sense (what they do)? In the second part of the chapter, we explore three features of the foreign policy arena which provide part of the answer to these questions: actors, issues and interests.

Actors, issues and interests

As pointed out earlier in the chapter, it is difficult to separate the contexts of foreign policy making from the actors, issues and interests which give dynamism and life to those contexts. We have already found ourselves talking in terms of groups, individuals and organisations, of their views and of the pressures they can exert. In this part of the chapter, we address these features of the foreign policy arena explicitly.

Actors

Who makes foreign policy? In the traditional analysis of foreign policy, the answer is obvious: the designated political and bureaucratic elites, who have a continuous responsibility for pursuing foreign policy object-ives, and who are specially qualified for the task (see Chapter 1). Foreign ministers and diplomatic officials are in many countries subject to training and experience which set them apart from the main streams of develop-ment within government. They form a restricted 'community' which has a great deal in common with foreign policy elites in other countries, and often it seems less in common with their colleagues elsewhere in govern-ment. Foreign offices are staffed according to this assumption of special-ness and specialisation, with the emphasis on close contact with the affairs of the 'target' countries or regions. The foreign policy 'machine' is set up and attuned in accordance with the geopolitical and other priorities of the country concerned, and adapts only slowly to the emergence of new challenges and opportunities.

This elitist view of foreign policy does not mean, however, that the foreign policy machine is completely sealed off. Rather, there is a key distinction to be made between those who participate continuously and effectively – the policy makers – and those who shape or influence policies from time to time. Access to the policy-making process is restricted, but it is not completely impossible to achieve. The notion is one of hierarchy, with inner and outer circles of influence. An example of the ways in which this might be expressed is in Figure 2.1, which shows 'concentric circles'

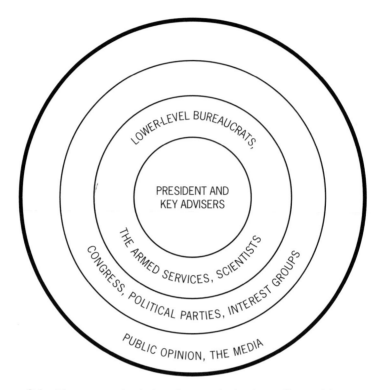

Figure 2.1 The concentric circles of power in foreign policy making

of policy making and influence in the case of the US. Although a general pattern can be discerned in which certain groups or individuals are close to the centre, it is clearly possible for movement to take place between the circles over time or in specific circumstances. Thus in wartime, for example, the military is likely to move closer to the centre of policy making (and it has often been argued that during the Cold War, foreign policy participation was 'militarised' on a long-term basis).

In looking for the actors in foreign policy making, even traditional analyses can cope with short- and long-term shifts in the level, intensity and effectiveness of participation. The traditional perspective is not unaware of problems of access and influence, or for that matter of the distinction – vital to all policy analysis – between formal structure and informal processes of participation. What traditional analyses find more difficult to cope with, however, are the problems created by changes in the context of foreign policy that create much wider participation by a broader array of actors from the international, the governmental and the domestic contexts. Participation in such a system is diffused, but remains within the boundaries of government; this is complicated, though, by the fact that 'government' has become a more elastic concept. Thus, national policy making may be heavily influenced by international agencies (for example, the European Union), international financial institutions (as in the case of International Monetary Fund officials advising governments in parts of Africa and Latin America) and foreign militaries (as in the role of NATO officers in Albania and Macedonia, for instance).

Beyond government, we must also register the fact that influence upon foreign policy has diffused much more broadly through societies. Clearly this has much to do with the changing subject matter of foreign policy itself (see below), and it also reflects the widening awareness of international issues noted earlier in the chapter. But it must be noted that the impact of this diffusion of participation will vary enormously depending on the specific characteristics of a country and its foreign policy process. Perhaps the most obvious contrast is between countries where there is a long-standing tradition of 'managed pluralism' (such as in the US and in Western Europe) and those where the political circumstances and the political culture are much less stable and secure. It has been argued, for example, that in many of the new states emerging from the former Soviet Union, organised criminal elements can play an important role in foreign policy making. Such arguments have also been made in the past about new states in the Third World.

The relationship between the foreign policy machine and the broader society is thus important to an understanding of patterns of participation, both formal and informal. So too is an appreciation of the types of policy which are at issue.

Issues

Just as participation in foreign policy making has traditionally been seen as hierarchical and relatively restricted, so have the issues on the foreign policy agenda reflected a powerful set of priorities. As noted in Chapter 1, there has historically been a very strong and intimate linkage between foreign policy and national security. Some analysts have pointed to the growth during the Cold War years of the 'national security state', in which the pre-eminence of national security as an issue was reflected in the close relationships between foreign policy, defence policy and industrial organisation (Hogan, 1998). Both the US and the Soviet Union reflected these pressures and processes, but they were also present in different ways in a large variety of other countries. For example, newly independent states in the Third World placed a high priority on the military not only as defenders of national independence but also as agents of modernisation within society. Governments as a result were often heavily militarised, and foreign policy along with them. In such cases, issues of national security had a high priority for the allocation of national resources, and in the competition between 'welfare and warfare' the latter tended to predominate (Clapham, 1985: 113–59).

This strongly hierarchical view of the issues on the foreign policy agenda has come under powerful attack from two directions during the past couple of decades. First, the nature of 'national security' itself has come under pressure. Partly, this arises from the fact that predominantly military indices of national security have been increasingly overtaken – hence the importance of 'soft power' noted above. Developments in military technology have also been important. First nuclear weapons and latterly 'smart' weaponry and the 'revolution in military affairs' more generally has meant that a truly modern and effective national defence can only be obtained by a handful of relatively wealthy states (the US, for instance) or attempted by those willing to sacrifice civilian needs for military expenditure (India, Pakistan and Iraq). In parallel, the leakage of military capabilities to non-state groupings such as terrorist organisations, organised criminal cartels and other interests has led again to the erosion of the military 'trump card' in foreign policy.

Second, a broadening of the national security agenda to new areas of activity has occurred and security has come to be defined in terms that range across economic, environmental and 'societal' concerns (see Chapter 1). To take just the first of these, for many countries (and for some time past) economic security has been at least as important as military security. However, only relatively recently has it become apparent that economic security might be at least as fundamental as the 'harder' military variant. For many citizens, the agenda is not dominated by fear of attack or subjection by military means; rather, it is dominated by issues of employment, welfare and prosperity (Cable, 1995). Allied to this, the agenda of foreign policy has become increasingly congested as processes of regionalisation, transnationalism and globalisation have accelerated. The traditional preoccupation with security (however broadly defined) has now to compete with a multiplicity of other, more everyday issues relating to economic management, environmental degradation, trans-border communication and cultural interaction (White et al., 2001).

These are issues at one and the same time of international (and foreign policy) concern and of local, regional or national sensitivity. They raise important questions of national or collective management, since they often demand long-term commitments of considerable resources. Once again, we are back to the central significance of resources in foreign policy, this time related to issues. Does a government have the capacity to extract resources from the context in which it has to operate, and what are the political, economic and social constraints on this extraction and the allocation of the resources themselves? The new issues of the foreign policy agenda came, during the 1970s, to be termed 'intermestic', since they engaged the domestic and the foreign policy processes of societies, and created new types of political and organisational challenge (Manning, 1977). Thus, the intersection of a changing context with changing issues is vital to the analysis of foreign policy. It affects participation, it affects institutions, and it affects interests. It is to interests that we now turn.

Interests

Historically, it has in principle been easy to describe the interests around which foreign policy centres. Because of the close link between foreign policy and national security, the idea of 'national interest' is fundamental to traditional notions of foreign policy (see Chapter 1). This does not mean that the national interest is always easy to identify and describe or is beyond active manipulation (the national interest may merely equate to whatever the policy makers say it is at any given time). But the notion of irreducible national aims, even if these are expressed in terms of no more than survival, is persistent and pervasive in the study of foreign policy. The notion has a kind of transcendental, mystical quality, but it can also serve as an important instrument of policy itself, rationalising and justifying the actions of policy makers to both domestic and international audiences. There is, however, an inherent tension built into the concept: the national interest will inevitably compete with the interests of other states, and also with any notion of an 'international interest' expressing the common standards or goals of the world community. In principle, such tensions are easy to resolve for a state: the national interest, like national security as an issue on the foreign policy agenda, trumps all others.

The notion of a monolithic national interest expressed by the foreign policy makers is clearly difficult to relate to the untidiness of actual foreign policy making. Traditional FPA thus spends a good deal of time and energy making distinctions between fundamental national interests and the goals of foreign policy. Such goals are assumed to be directed towards ultimate defence of this national interest, but they may involve apparent contradictions. For example, it may be necessary to give up territory to ensure national survival, or to enter an 'entangling alliance' to ensure independence. Many analysts have thus distinguished between short- and medium-term goals of foreign policy and the long-term goals expressed in the national interest. Arnold Wolfers (1962: 73–80, 91) has made an important distinction between 'possession goals' (defence of what one is or has) and 'milieu goals' (maintenance of broader international order or standards). He has also distinguished between goals of 'self-extension', goals of 'self-preservation' and goals of 'self-abnegation', each of which may in its own way contribute to fundamental national interests. The point is that even in traditional analysis, the definition of national interests is not an easy or simple matter.

Things become even more complicated when we consider the impact of the contextual and other changes dealt with earlier in this chapter. International and domestic constraints mean that no government can ever set national goals in a vacuum. Some would argue that this means that foreign policy has become essentially 'domesticated' in the sense that it is part of a seamless web of governmental policies and societal interests (Moravcsik, 1997). Others have proposed that the opposite, but nonetheless complementary, process has occurred: that the growing transnationalisation of interests has 'domesticated' the previously unruly setting of world politics (Hanrieder, 1978). The implications of both processes are the same, since they suggest that there is a growing emphasis in foreign policy on the satisfaction of sectional interests at the same time as there is an increasing incentive to respond to international interests and governance structures.

Arriving at a definition of the national interest has never been easy, and has always involved actual or potential conflicts between goals, but in the contemporary era it appears that foreign policy interests have been both diffused through society and politicised to an unprecedented degree. Much as foreign policy makers might long for the days when one could talk about the notion of national interest with some conviction, the ability of government to clearly define and pursue this interest has changed fundamentally.

Evaluating actors, issues and interests in foreign policy

Part of the conclusion from this review of actors, issues and interests in foreign policy must be that there are intimate links between the three: actors focus on issues and espouse interests, while changes in issues can shape the emergence of new patterns of participation and interests. We have argued that:

- Traditional assumptions about 'who makes foreign policy' have been challenged and modified by the diffusion of participation and by new processes of access and influence in foreign policy, which reflect, at least in part, the changes taking place in the context of policy making.

- The foreign policy agenda, traditionally centred on, if not dominated by, national security issues, has broadened to encompass new dimensions of security as well as new issues of welfare and humanitarian concerns.

- The interests shaping foreign policy can no longer be expressed in terms of a monolithic national interest, and the challenge of foreign policy is that of managing and negotiating different interests as well as allocating scarce resources between them.

What does this means for the nature of policy itself? One way of bringing these elements together and 'mapping' the foreign policy arena is to relate the changing nature of issues to the changing nature of interests and participation. In doing this, we can start by identifying three types of foreign policy issue: 'high politics', 'low politics' and 'sectoral politics'. The first of these is concerned with the traditional issues of national security and independence, the second with the vast mass of technical and administrative issues confronting foreign policy makers and the last with issues such as the environment, transnational migration and crime, and external economic relations that cut across the high/low politics divide. Importantly, each of these types of issue generates a characteristic pattern of participation: 'high politics' conforms to the restricted and elitist model outlined earlier, 'low politics' to the more administrative and organisational patterns we have also noted, and 'sectoral politics' to a more pluralist and negotiated type of participation.

Summary and conclusion

This chapter has dealt with two main topics. First, it has analysed the foreign policy arena in terms of contexts – international, governmental and domestic – within which foreign policy emerges. In doing so, it has established that a number of important changes have come to fruition, affecting the ways in which foreign policy makers can recognise and respond to contextual pressures. Central to these changes is a number of factors: the focus and composition of international activity, the resources available to and allocated by governments and the growth in awareness of international issues. The second topic on which the chapter has centred is that of the dynamics set up by actors, issues and interests in the foreign policy arena. The chapter has identified important trends in patterns of participation, in the priorities given to issues on the foreign policy agenda and in the range of interests shaping foreign policy.

At the beginning of the chapter, we noted that the foreign policy arena expressed both relatively static and relatively dynamic elements. It is firstly a terrain on which foreign policy takes place, and secondly a 'populated area' in which there is a continuous interplay of actors, issues and interests. Having explored these two interrelated aspects, we can now proceed to look at the heart of foreign policy: its formulation and its implementation.

Further reading

The notion of 'arenas' is not well developed in FPA. However, see Hocking and Smith (1995) Part 1 for its elaboration as a tool of International Relations. For the various 'contexts' of foreign policy (the international, the governmental and the domestic) the reader can turn to a number of works for conceptual assistance. A good place to start is Onuf (1995) and Singer (1961) which explore the complementary notion of 'level of analysis' in International Relations. The work of Rosenau (1980) on the 'external environment' of foreign policy and 'linkage politics' (the linkage that is between the national and international contexts of foreign policy) is also instructive, if a little difficult. For works which offer a more applied view of the various contextual influences on foreign policy, see Allen (1989) and Holsti (1992). For more on the actors of foreign policy, see Chapters 3 and 4 of this volume. On the issues relevant to foreign policy, see White, Little and Smith (eds) (2001). On foreign policy interests, see Jones (1979: 35–43) for a fairly traditional view, and Hyde-Price (1999: 32–9) for a more conceptually informed discussion.

References

Allen, D. (1989) 'The Context of Foreign Policy Systems: The Contemporary International Environment', in Clarke, M. and White, B. (eds), *Understanding Foreign Policy. The Foreign Policy Systems Approach*. Aldershot: Edward Elgar.

Atkinson, M. and Coleman, W. (1992) 'Policy Networks, Policy Communities and the Problems of Governance', *Governance*, 5(2), 154–80.

Cable, V. (1995) 'What is International Economic Security?', *International Affairs*, 71(2), 305–25.

Clapham, C. (1985) *Third World Politics. An Introduction*. London: Croom Helm.

Commission on Global Governance (1995) *Our Global Neighbourhood*. Oxford: Oxford University Press.

Falk, R. (1995) *On Human Governance: Toward a New Global Politics*. Cambridge: Polity Press.

Frankel, J. (1963) *The Making of Foreign Policy. An Analysis of Decision Making*. London: Oxford University Press.

Gourevitch, P. (1978) 'The Second Image Reversed: the International Sources of Domestic Politics', *International Organisation*, 32(4), 881–912.

Hanrieder, W.F. (1978) 'Dissolving International Politics: Reflections on the Nation-State', *American Political Science Review*, 72(4), 1276–87.

Hocking, B. (1998) 'Introduction. Foreign Ministries: Redefining the Gatekeeper Role', in Hocking, B. (ed.), *Foreign Ministries. Change and Adaptation*. Basingstoke: Macmillan, 1–15.

Hocking, B. and Smith, M. (1995) *World Politics. An Introduction to International Relations* (2nd edition). Hemel Hempstead: Prentice Hall/Harvester Wheatsheaf.

Hogan, M. (1998) *A Cross of Iron. Harry S. Truman and the Origins of the National Security State, 1945–1954*. Cambridge: Cambridge University Press.

Holsti, K. (1992) *International Politics. A Framework for Analysis* (6th edition). Englewood Cliffs, NJ: Prentice-Hall.

Hyde-Price, A. (1999) 'Interests, Institutions and Identity: Towards a New Model of Foreign Policy Analysis', Economic and Social Research Council/Institute of German Studies (Birmingham University), Discussion Paper Series, No.99/8.

Jones, R.E. (1979) *Principles of Foreign Policy. The Civil State in Its Modern Setting*. Oxford: Martin Robertson.

Kapstein, E.B. (1995) 'Is Realism Dead? The Domestic Sources of International Politics', *International Organisation*, 49(4), 751–74.

Linklater, A. (1998) *The Transformation of Political Community*. Cambridge: Polity Press.

Manning, B. (1977) 'The Congress, the Executive, and Intermestic Affairs', *Foreign Affairs*, 55(2), 306–24.

Moravcsik, A. (1997) 'Taking Preferences Seriously: a Liberal Theory of International Relations', *International Organisation*, 51(4), 513–53.

Morse, E.L. (1970) 'The Transformation of Foreign Policies. Modernization, Interdependence, and Externalization', *World Politics*, 22(3), 371–92.

Nye, J.S. (1990) 'The Changing Nature of World Power', *Political Science Quarterly*, 105(2), 177–92.

Onuf, N. (1995) 'Levels', *European Journal of International Relations*, 1(1), 35–58.

Prizel, I. (1998) *National Identity and Foreign Policy. Nationalism and Leadership in Poland, Russia and Ukraine*. Cambridge: Cambridge University Press.

Rosenau, J.N. (1980) *The Scientific Study of Foreign Policy* (revised edition). London: Pinter.

Singer, J.D. (1961) 'The Level-of-Analysis Problem in International Relations', *World Politics*, **14**(1), 77–92.

White, B., Little. R. and Smith, M. (eds) (2001) *Issues in World Politics* (2nd edition). Basingstoke: Palgrave.

Wolfers, A. (1962) *Discord and Collaboration. Essays on International Politics.* Baltimore, MD: Johns Hopkins Press.

Zakaria, F. (1992) 'Realism and Domestic Politics', *International Security*, **17**(1), 177–98.

3 | The Making of Foreign Policy

In this chapter our aim is to consider, quite simply, how foreign policy is made. In order to do this we will outline three different 'images' of foreign policy making. These allow us to make generalisations about policy making, although each approaches the subject with quite different analytical assumptions. We then consider the manner of foreign policy making in the context of a transformed world, focusing on how this process has been affected by a more fluid and complex agenda and an increased diversity of international actors. The chapter, finally, looks at ways in which foreign policy making can be compared and examines in particular the distinction between routine and crisis policy making and differences that derive from the type of political system (be this democratic, authoritarian or transitional) in which policy is constructed. Our assumption throughout the chapter is that foreign policy making is a far from straightforward process. The demands upon policy makers are many and often onerous, something that reflects the complexity of foreign policy itself.

Introduction

The formulation of policy is a central concern of many fields of study. Psychologists, economists and political scientists have all in different ways invested considerable intellectual effort in the study of how and why certain policies are made. This focus of study is not simply important but can also be exciting. It takes one to the very heart of a subject. Policy making involves decisions, sometimes routine and unnoticed, but occasionally, bold, innovative and conditioned by risk. Nowhere is this more evident than in the formulation of foreign policy. Here the dreary practicalities of diplomatic protocol coexist with issues that can help determine national welfare and even national survival. The making of policy, moreover, is a dynamic process. It suggests action, choice and an assumption of a desired state of affairs. It is never static, involving as it does continuous adaptation and refinement in light of experience, altered domestic and international circumstances or simply the folly of individual policy makers.

Given its importance, not surprisingly, the study of foreign policy making (FPM) is far from straightforward. It confronts the student with several analytical issues. The first of these is a 'level of analysis' problem. Where analysis is pitched, be this at the level of the international system, at the national or state level or at the level of the individual policy maker, not only predisposes the selection of variables to be considered in the study of policy formulation, but confronts the analyst with fundamental questions. To what extent is foreign policy formulation predetermined by the constraints of the international system? What scope is there for choice and free will among policy makers?

A second set of issues is concerned with the nature of decisions. These constitute a core component of policy making, the point at which a policy is initiated, options having been considered, and either discarded or retained. Yet to focus only on decisions can obscure as much as it reveals. Much foreign policy activity does not involve decisions as such (for instance, an ambassador reporting a piece of information to his or her home ministry). Moreover, the act of deciding is arguably much less important than the content of the policy itself. To concentrate on the former can lead one into the error of what Stanley Hoffman (cited in White, 1978: 159) once dubbed 'proceduralism' – a fixation with the 'how' rather than the 'what' of policy.

These sorts of problem can be partly answered with the assertion that much foreign policy *is* decisional and that the analysis of policy making is informed by an awareness of policy content (something this volume hopefully illustrates). Yet a third set of issues remain, those that relate to the practicalities of investigation. Reliable analysis of foreign policy requires the acquisition of information to test hypotheses and reach conclusions. In closed societies such information is scant or may have been screened to conform to a government-approved view. In such cases, the analyst is forced to view information with a trained scepticism and to infer from limited sources the decision processes by which policy is formulated. This was long the approach to the study of Soviet foreign policy and still determines how one views established authoritarian states such as North Korea, Iraq and China (see Chapter 10). In states with more open political systems, by contrast, information problems are usually of a different order. In general, data is much more accessible and plentiful; yet this too causes problems. Too much information may be as unhelpful as too little, supporting as it may all manner of mutually inconsistent arguments on how the policy-making process functions or how particular decisions are reached. Two examples of this include the decision processes that led to the initiation of the First World War and the decisions surrounding the 1962 Cuban missile crisis. In both cases a plethora of official documentation and frank memoirs of key participants has not promoted scholarly consensus but has rather prolonged and deepened disputes on the key issues. This type of problem is compounded by the nature of the information itself. A common source, the memoir, may be less than frank and somewhat self-serving in its choice and description of events. Less tainted primary source information (minutes, and, in some cases, verbatim transcripts) is often to hand in democratic states and this may prove invaluable in reconstructing decision behaviour. Yet even this may provide only a fragmentary account in that many foreign policy decisions simply go unrecorded and hence remain impervious to scrutiny.

Images of foreign policy making

Some of the analytical problems outlined in the previous section suggest, in part, unavoidable limitations of knowledge. The non-participating observer (and as we shall see below, even many of the participants) cannot obtain a complete picture of how or why particular policies have been chosen. Moreover, the intrinsically complex environment in which policies are made means that even if one was fortunate enough to possess perfect information, this need not result in perfect understanding.

One response to this problem is to consider policy making on the basis of case histories, utilising the methods of the diplomatic historian to explain the formulation of particular policies within a limited time frame. This may have its merits in explaining a single event, but the conclusions drawn from the analysis may not prove useful in studying other cases. Such an approach will tend, almost by definition, to focus on what is unique about the specific instance under investigation. If generalisations are to be obtained, a more transportable method of analysis needs to be employed. One way of doing this is to approach policy making with the assistance of particular analytical models or 'images' of how the process operates. Rather than attempting the near impossible task of identifying all the influences that shape policy, an image of this sort isolates particular factors in order to arrive at propositions that have a general application. In what follows we will look at three types of image:

- 'Rational actor' images.

- Images of 'political' foreign policy making.

- 'Psychological' images.

'Rational actor' images

The baldest image of this type is based on what may be termed 'procedural' rationality. This assumes the government of the state as the basic unit of analysis and suggests that united, purposive individuals acting on its behalf engage in goal-directed behaviour. In selecting an appropriate course of action, policy makers undertake a lengthy process of 'means-ends analysis'. This involves the identification of a foreign policy problem or situation; goal selection – that is, defining what is to be accomplished; the consideration of all possible alternatives that might achieve the goal; and, finally, selecting the one alternative that best 'maximises the goal' (Verba, 1969: 225). This approach is highly exacting and in practice policy making rarely, perhaps never, proceeds in such a logical, comprehensive and purposive manner. As we shall see below, limitations of time, information and intelligence confront the policy makers, such that they seek to satisfy minimum not maximal objectives (a process known as 'satisficing') or to pursue policy through incremental adjustment rather than a striving towards an ideal future goal.

Given these qualifications, in what sense is it still helpful to employ notions of rationality in analysing FPM? To answer this question, in what follows we will outline some other approaches that retain an assumption of rationality. These, as we shall discover, ascribe somewhat different meanings to the term but all share the opinion that it is a fruitful guide to understanding.

The first is the conventional 'Realist' view. This may not be expressly concerned with FPM as such, but does make propositions which have a bearing on how we understand this process. Its central claim is that a human preoccupation with power results in a competitive international system. This creates an imperative for survival which becomes the guiding national interest and thus the central purpose of foreign policy (see Chapter 1). Rationality equates with the identification and pursuit of this single goal. But who or what pursues it? At first glance, Realist scholars seem to place great emphasis on the actions of individual leaders. Henry Kissinger (1973: 312–31), for instance, in his study of the nineteenth-century Concert of Europe, elevates to centre stage the 'individual rationality' of just two figures – the Austrian and British Foreign Ministers, Prince von Metternich and Viscount Castlereagh – in explaining the durability of this great power arrangement. Similarly, Hans Morgenthau (1960: 5) argued that in order to 'give meaning to the factual raw material of foreign policy, we must approach political reality with a kind of rational outline', placing ourselves in 'the position of a statesman who must meet a certain problem of foreign policy' and asking ourselves 'what the rational alternatives are from which a statesman may choose'. Crucially, however, the calculations and actions of these individuals are seen to equate with the purposes of the state. Foreign policy is the preserve of a governing elite, an elite that acts authoritatively on behalf of the state and which is united in its outlook. The state is, in other words, a 'unitary actor', untroubled in its foreign policy by internal division and facing the outside world as an integrated unit.

Neo-Realism holds to the unitary state assumption but departs from the more conventional Realism in certain respects. As noted in Chapter 1, the Neo-Realist perspective places an emphasis on the structural features of the international system (and thus avoids the stress of conventional realism on the human striving for power), in particular its anarchic nature. The absence of a world authority, it is argued, means that states are preoccupied with survival. In such circumstances international politics reflects a condition of 'self-help', in which those acting on behalf of states are required, logically, to act in certain prescribed ways: assessing the changing distribution of power among states; weighing up how these changes influence their prospects for survival; and making a foreign policy that minimises any vulnerabilities and maximises opportunities. Rationality is, in other words, 'behaviourally engineered'. Those states which do not respond rationally to the cues of the system risk either servitude, or even worse, elimination (Buzan, 1996: 55). Neo-Realism's focus on the determining impact of the structure of the international system, then, allows policy makers very little discretion. The only sensible role for foreign policy practitioners is to read the signals of the system and act accordingly. Rationality seemingly rules out any selection from alternatives.

Such determinism is ironic in view of the fact that Neo-Realism is based partly on a way of thinking known as 'rational choice'. This is an approach whose influence extends well beyond Neo-Realism, so it will be regarded here as a distinct rational actor image. The form of rationality employed by rational choice is far less demanding than the procedural version noted earlier. It accepts that policy makers operate under constraints of time, knowledge and place. They remain rational, however, in an 'instrumental' sense in that they are capable of recognising and acting upon their perceived interests. Rationality is simply 'the efficient pursuit of consistent goals', the goal being seen in general terms as the maximisation of expected utility or welfare. When confronted with alternatives, policy makers will choose that option which they believe most effectively secures their goals (Nicholson, 1996: 150–7). Significantly, while the assumption of rationality is pitched at analyses of individual policy makers, for the approach to have any use in explaining the behaviour of organisations such as states, the preferences of these individuals have to be regarded as synonymous with the organisation as a whole – the state remains, in other words, a unitary actor. Proceeding from these assumptions, rational choice explanations have been employed in several different guises. They have been used to account for the decisions of national leaders to go to war, the decision calculations that underpin the operation of deterrence and, via the use of game theory, the reasons states choose (or fail to choose) to cooperate.

The considerations of rationality that are central to the different accounts above are, in turn, supported by three arguments. To begin with, policy makers themselves often claim to be acting in a rational manner, and when responding to the foreign policies of others make a similar assumption of policy makers elsewhere. Rationality, in other words, is implicit in the everyday language of foreign policy.

A second argument considers the distinctive nature of foreign policy. According to Sidney Verba (1969: 224, 229), foreign policy is set apart from domestic politics in that the overall goals of policy are more immediately apparent and at the same time much less controversial (for instance, the bipartisan nature of foreign policy in the United States [US]). What is more, those involved in foreign policy formulation make up a cohesive and distinctive group, a politically competent elite more likely to possess the knowledge and skills that limit the impact of non-rational, 'personality-oriented' behaviour.

A third and final argument relates to the seeming simplicity and analytical elegance of the idea of rationality itself. Confronted with the complex and relatively closed world of FPM, rationality can act as a useful working hypothesis. As Graham Allison (1971: 254–5) once put it: '[rationality] permit[s] a quick, imaginative sorting out of a problem of explanation or analysis. It serves as a productive shorthand, requiring a minimum of information. It can yield an informative summary of tendencies, for example, by identifying the weight of strategic costs and benefits.' Moreover, even when information is plentiful, the rationality assumption remains productive in that it can bring an overarching meaning to disparate and perhaps incoherent data.

Yet for all its seeming persuasiveness, the rationality assumption has not been without its detractors. Certain problems – those associated with the concept of procedural rationality – have already been noted. Two further, more general points are worth making. The first is terminological. What exactly is meant by 'rationality'? What is it to be 'rational'? At the hands of Morgenthau or Neo-Realists such as Kenneth Waltz (1979) the answer appears obvious: maximising power or ensuring survival. Yet both authors make clear that states can behave in ways other than rationality dictates. Morgenthau (1960: 7) is particularly frank in this regard, suggesting that '[t]he contingent elements of personality, prejudice, and subjective preference, and all . . . the weaknesses of intellect and will which flesh is heir to, are bound to deflect foreign policies from their rational course'. As for rational choice explanations, here the meaning of rationality is also problematic. Simply put, it seems to equate more with the *act* of choosing, than with the nature of the chosen course of action itself. What is specified with regard to the latter is that the choice will conform to the principle of maximising utility. As an explanation, however, this is incomplete and leaves important questions unanswered. How do policy makers act when confronted with two options, both of which yield comparable expected benefits? And what of the substance of the goal itself? How rational, in other words, is a policy-making process that yields choices that are seemingly mistaken?

A second general point relates to the nature of the policy-making unit. Approaches that utilise the rationality assumption, as we have seen, regard the state in traditional terms, as a unitary actor. This can be justified up to a point if one assumes that foreign policy is an elite activity, that the preferences of the individuals who make up any given elite are uniform, and that these preferences are untroubled, either by partisan political intervention or by alterations in the personnel of leadership (Hug, 1997: 2, 6; Nicholson, 1997: 3). All three assumptions are, however, open to question. To understand why we need to turn to a second set of images of FPM.

Images of 'political' foreign policy making

This type of analysis shares an assumption that policy making is the outcome of political activity broadly defined (involving elements of power, influence and interests). As distinct from the image of the rational actor, FPM, it is assumed, does not usually amount to some objective process of calculation among a collection of united policy makers. Rather, policy is seen as the outcome of bargaining processes among those groups and individuals which make up or influence government. Bargaining occurs because, crucially, these bodies often have interests which are in conflict and may hold differing views of any given issue or problem requiring a decision (McGrew and Wilson, 1982: 227).

The best-known and among the most influential approaches of this type is the 'governmental' or 'bureaucratic' politics model associated with Graham Allison. The views foreign policy makers strive to promote are, according to Allison, largely determined by their bureaucratic positions. This amounts, in an oft-quoted aphorism, to saying that 'where you stand depends on where you sit' (Allison, 1971: 144, 176). Consider, in this light, the example outlined in Box 3.1. Here the United Kingdom (UK) Minister for International Development is reported to be furious at an alleged by-passing of her department by the Foreign Office and the Prime Minister's Office in responding to a crisis spurred by volcanic eruptions in

Box 3.1: 'Short slams "vile and dishonest" officials' by Patrick Wintour

Clare Short, the Secretary of State for International Development, was at the centre of a new storm last night after she launched an attack on 'vile and dishonest' government spin doctors and claimed that a reactionary wing of the Foreign Office was trying to destroy her fledgling Whitehall department.

Ms Short's intervention came after newspaper reports last week [claimed] that she and her department had been sidelined in dealings with the volcanic island of Montserrat. . . .

[Ms Short] attacked the staff of the Foreign Office, which has overall responsibility for Montserrat, claiming that they and Downing Street had sought to give the impression that a new committee had been set up in the Foreign Office to coordinate the government's response. In fact, the committee had long been in existence . . .

Ms Short said there had been a briefing last week 'out of the reactionary end of the Foreign Office . . .'

She claimed that she was 'the whipping girl for people who cannot bear the idea of an independent department with an aid budget which is committed to development and not to Britain's short-term interest. They are out to destroy the department.'

Ms Short added that there were 'voices that look backward at Britain's role in the world and rather yearn for empire. They want the aid budget to be spent on short-term political and financial relationships.'

Source: *The Observer*, 30 August 1997, p. 1

the British Overseas Territory of Montserrat. This she claims is a conflict both of bureaucratic prerogative and of competing policy views. As this example makes clear, a variety of interests feeds into FPM. Each will bring to bear political resources to promote its particular preference, the upshot, typically, being a compromise of some sort and, therefore, an outcome somewhat different both from the choice that would have been made by a unitary actor or that which any of the bureaucratic actors would have chosen if acting alone.

The merits of the bureaucratic politics model can be seen to lie in its conscious attempts, first, to plug some of the explanatory gaps left by rational actor images (specifically, the weakness of the unitary actor assumption), and second, to explain FPM through an explicit focus on government, rather, that is, than simply assuming that the state's external circumstances determine its policy choices. The model does, however, paint only a partial picture of the politics of policy making. Bureaucratic position alone may, in fact, be a poor predictor of policy preference. Policy-making actors can sometimes act out of line with expectations (military officials, for instance, may adopt 'dovish' stances). It is also important to bear in mind that the process of bargaining differs according to circumstances. On some occasions, it can be a rather straightforward process. Insofar as a President or Prime Minister is capable of intervening to get his or her own way and given also that in many cases there will be policies over which there is little disagreement, then it would be fair to argue that policy making may be subject to very little 'pulling and hauling' among competing groups. By contrast, there will also be occasions of far greater complexity; when, for instance, domestic political considerations are brought to foreign policy. Policy makers are often involved in what Robert Putnam (1988) has dubbed a 'two-level game', attempting to cope with the demands of their own political systems while simultaneously dealing with international developments. These two levels often interact. In some circumstances the attempt to satisfy domestic pressures may constrain the policy maker (in the US, public opinion and Congressional opposition has, since the Vietnam War, ruled out large-scale American troop deployments in war situations), while in others it may embolden him or her, as the attempt to impress domestic support groups results in a forceful foreign policy based on a determined and unequivocal approach to decisions.

Whatever the merits and distinctiveness of political images of FPM, it is worth noting that these images do not dispense entirely with assumptions of rationality. Indeed, such assumptions can be said to survive in at least two senses. First, through the ability of the actors engaged in bargaining to make complex calculations designed to maximise their influence, and second, through the assumption that individual policy makers continue to act instrumentally, choosing the course of action calculated to yield a preferred result. As we have already seen, however, rationality of this type is analytically problematic. What is more, both the rational and political images tell one little about the nature of the values and beliefs held by policy makers or about how they perceive their environment. For these reasons, it is instructive to turn to a third type of image.

'Psychological' images

Intuitively, we expect important decisions to be made by important people. Because of this we assume also that the personal characteristics of political leaders will have a determining impact on the nature of policy. Political skills, emotions such as fear, anxiety and empathy, the character traits that predispose individuals towards certain courses of action, and the physiological effects of ill-health, age and medical dependency have all been considered germane in this regard (Crawford, 2000; Holsti, 1992: 299–302; Vertzberger, 1990: 172–89). Take as two examples, the former US President Ronald Reagan and his one-time opposite number, Leonid Brezhnev, leader of the Soviet Union. Both men were for long periods at the helm of the foreign policies of a superpower. Both possessed consummate skills of political manoeuvring yet neither could be considered an intellectual. Both were also relatively advanced in age. In Brezhnev's case, these traits had a harmful impact; the decision to send Soviet troops into Afghanistan in 1979 was taken by a small group of Soviet leaders, among whom an ill and medically dependent Brezhnev was the crucial mover. Reagan, by contrast, remained largely unaffected by ill-health during his two terms in office (despite an assassination attempt). His influence lay rather in his imposition upon American foreign policy of an assertive anti-communism. Reagan was also noted for his personal charm and good humoured nature, something that enabled him to strike up a productive personal relationship with one of Brezhnev's successors, Mikhail Gorbachev, in spite of the immense ideological differences between the two men.

A focus on leaders, however, can only tell us so much. Studies of this type tend to focus on the exceptional rather than the ordinary. Biographically based, they may tell us a good deal about one individual, but little about the nature of leadership in general. Of more general use are approaches which concentrate on the sorts of behaviour which are common to foreign policy makers as a whole. One influential approach of this type considers FPM in terms of concepts borrowed from psychology. Its central assumption is that what matters in the framing of policy is the perceptions held by the policy makers. Equally, it is also assumed that these perceptions form a realm that is distinct from reality. As spelt out in an influential formulation put forward by Harold and Margaret Sprout (as cited in Vogler, 1989: 136) in the 1950s: '[w]hat matters in the process of policy-making is not conditions and events as they actually are but what the policy-maker imagines them to be'. Thus, two environments exist, the 'operational' and the 'psychological'. Crucially, the two are often at odds; there is, to put it another way, a discrepancy between the 'objective' world that exists 'out there' and the 'subjective' world that exists in the minds of policy makers.

To this distortion is added bias that arises from the peculiar stresses and demands of foreign policy. High levels of uncertainty and complexity, the gravity of the issues at hand, and the practical problems of dealing with a huge array of different actors, large amounts of information, and of communicating across linguistic and cultural boundaries means policy makers are particularly prone to error. This may involve what has been termed cognitive bias, a perceptual distortion which arises out of the mental processes of dealing with huge amounts of information. In attempting to make sense of a complex world, individuals fall back on core beliefs. These, however, are often contradicted by our perceptual knowledge of the world. 'Cognitive dissonance' results, and in such situations, rather than adjust beliefs, individuals will more usually attempt to maintain cognitive consistency through mechanisms of reconciling new or discrepant information, the upshot often being a belief system that, while modified in a limited sense, is still inappropriate to the circumstances the policy maker faces.

The search for cognitive consistency, however, is not the only manner in which policy makers handle information. Other mental aids may also be employed to cope with policy-making problems: 'satisficing', 'cybernetic' mechanisms or programmed responses (Steinbruner, 1974) and the use of 'scripts' or 'schema' drawn from past experience. Such devices can be beneficial, particularly in dealing with simple problems. They are, however, ultimately imperfect – a deliberate simplification of a complex reality that is likely to lead to a deficient policy resolution.

Studies of motivational bias are equally downbeat. Here the effects of cognitive processes are acknowledged but greater emphasis is placed on the emotions that policy makers feel and, in particular, how they cope with the personal conflicts that arise when decisions have to be made.

Irving Janis and Leon Mann (1977), in a wide study, acknowledged that while some decisions may give rise to little conflict, others occasion stress and anxiety, either because the decision has to be taken under extreme time pressure or because the policy maker feels it is not possible to find a satisfactory solution to the issue at hand. In such circumstances, coping strategies are employed all of which depart from the more thorough and optimally desirable procedures of 'vigilant' policy making.

As portrayed so far the cognitive and motivational processes at work have been applied to individuals. Yet policy is usually made in a group setting, hence collective modes of thinking or 'group psychology' are important too. On the one hand, such dynamics may have a beneficial effect, cancelling out or moderating the biases of any individual by allowing the airing of alternatives and critical judgements. On the other hand, however, they introduce problems of their own. This may be because groups and organisations more broadly are, like individuals, constrained in their ability to process information or because these groups encourage their own peculiar forms of misperception and error. Irving Janis (1972), for example, has shown in the American case how the phenomenon known as 'groupthink' has resulted in adverse policy making and consequently in several ill-fated foreign policy adventures.

Studies such as these tend to focus on *why* individuals or groups view the world in the way they do rather than on *how* they see the world. Actual beliefs themselves (whether in the guise of an ideological outlook, an 'operational code' or a set of ideas) are, in other words, not at issue. The cognitive and motivational processes at work are treated in a manner that separates them out from any specific set of beliefs that may be held. Yet these approaches are nonetheless premised on the assumption that the beliefs themselves are psychologically valid, serving as a kind of mental filter ordering information imparted to the individual from the outside world. Beliefs, in turn, influence policy making. According to Judith Goldstein and Robert Keohane (1993: 3–30), these serve as 'road maps' that clarify goals, and as 'focal points' defining the choice of options. To take just one example, various Western states have periodically stressed the importance of human rights as a standard for conducting foreign policy, a position which reflects liberal beliefs in the sanctity of the individual. When these standards are influential (they can be overruled at times by material interests), they may act as a short-cut in policy making, ruling out, for example, close relations with certain governments (as we shall see in Chapter 8, South Africa during the 1970 and 1980s fell foul of such calculations). What is more, the impact of beliefs can go beyond specific decision instances. If incorporated into institutions, they can have a lasting effect, defining the parameters of policy choice and the limits of the possible. Again, human rights is a case in point, standards in this field being used as a benchmark for inter-state relations in a multiplicity of intergovernmental organisations.

Having given an overview of psychologically-based approaches, how might one assess their strengths and weaknesses? Part of their importance lies in the fact that they highlight factors missing from other approaches. They depart from rational images of policy making by highlighting processes which suggest, at best, a flawed or 'bounded' rationality and, at worse, the outright unintelligible. Thus, they may help us to understand why so many foreign policy decisions are misconceived and wrong-headed. They depart also from political approaches, stressing as they do individual and group psychology rather than the influence of position or political exigency.

Yet psychological approaches also labour under certain difficulties. Their proper application, for instance, requires us to undertake several arduous analytical tasks. These may include: (1) selecting the beliefs one wishes to study and extrapolating those relevant to foreign policy from more general beliefs held by policy makers; (2) wading through huge amounts of information to construct a picture of a belief system; and (3) arriving at a judgement as to whether the observed beliefs are in fact the 'real' beliefs held by an individual. And even when we have completed these steps are we in any position to correctly judge what drives the policy maker? To claim that we are rests on the dubious assumption that the outsider is better suited to 'determining "reality" in reference to the motives of actors in foreign policy and is insulated from his or her own forms of misperception' (Hermann, 1984: 28). Given these problems, those who employ psychological approaches are usually careful to point out that theirs is an incomplete explanation of FPM.

The three types of image outlined in this chapter offer quite different ways of approaching the analysis of FPM. Yet there need be no assumption that any one is necessarily better than another. As we have seen, all three have something to commend them yet, equally, all have their shortcomings. It is rare to encounter any one approach commended without qualification and even rarer to meet the argument that a particular approach is a complete explanation of all types of FPM. Indeed, the very complexity and variety of the phenomenon may well lead us to conclude that all three images of FPM have their uses. They ought not to be regarded as competing alternatives but rather as transferable parts, individually offering a partial account and together aspiring to comprehensive explanation.

In light of this injunction two methods are possible in examining FPM. The first involves moving between different images, depending on the circumstances of FPM under scrutiny. Rational actor assumptions may be best in examining decisions of high national security that involve a small elite; political approaches more beneficial in situations where FPM involves multiple organisations and groups and the presentation of numerous options (for instance, in cases of external economic policy); and psychological approaches of merit in situations of stress and uncertainty. Yet this method may still be less than satisfactory, for policies are often made when many and, in some cases, all of these conditions are combined. Hence, a second method can be followed. This involves employing simultaneously elements of more than one type of image of FPM. The perceptions or beliefs of policy makers, for instance, may act, as Robert Jervis (1976: 28–9) has suggested, as a 'proximate cause' of behaviour, with influences at other levels of analysis (Jervis labels these the international, domestic and bureaucratic) also being important. To return to an earlier example, the anti-communism of Ronald Reagan may have shaped American foreign policy through much of the 1980s, but it was influenced also by the domestic constituencies which helped put Reagan in power, the bureaucratic groups (notably, the Pentagon) who found him receptive to their blandishments and the global predicaments the US found itself in upon Reagan's assumption of the Presidency (a relative decline in economic power and a loss of political influence in Third World areas).

Foreign policy making in a transformed world

In Chapters 1 and 2 we described in detail the processes of change which characterise contemporary world politics. Changes of this order and magnitude pose problems both for the student of foreign policy, who aims to make sense of an ever-moving subject, and for policy makers themselves, who have to be responsive to a fluid, more complex agenda and an increasing diversity of actors upon the world stage. To consider how we might approach the analysis of FPM in this environment we shall return in this section to the three images outlined above, noting their applicability as a route to describing and understanding FPM in a transformed world.

Our first set of images, those based on notions of rationality, retain a currency of sorts. Rational choice may still be held up as a good description of the process of choosing, even if, as we saw above, it fails to say much about the intrinsic properties of the choice itself. Similarly, even the rather static assumptions of rational state calculation that lie behind Realism can be retained if, as Neo-Realists argue, the presumption of change is itself open to dispute. The significance of what others regard as fundamental alterations to the international system – the growth of inter-dependence and the end of the Cold War – is discounted by analysts such as Waltz (1993) because its central property, the anarchic structure, remains. Consequently, the policy-making calculus of foreign policy is unaltered, its rational imperative continues to be state survival, its auxili-ary objectives the promotion of gain and the minimising of loss.

This sort of argument, moreover, is not just abstract reasoning. Using the notion of the state as rational and preoccupied with self-help strat-egies, Neo-Realists have pointed to what they consider the shaky progress of European integration, the dim prospects for political and military stability in Europe and the emergence of new forms of competition between the great powers after the Cold War (Grieco, 1995; Meirsheimer, 1990; Waltz, 1993). Some working outside the Neo-Realist perspective have also con-tinued to see the analytical tidiness of the rational actor model as a useful means of imputing foreign policy designs to certain authoritarian states (Smith, 2000).

Yet while rational-actor images have something to commend them in identifying what are claimed to be enduring influences upon foreign policy decisions, their price, arguably, is oversimplification, understating as they do the shifting hierarchy of issues in world politics and the growing com-plexity of FPM. In this light, an alternative approach is to highlight not what endures in the international system, but rather what has changed.

This type of approach underlies the more politically-based images of FPM. These make a link between the changing nature of foreign policy and political processes on three separate grounds. The first is that the increased complexity of international events has necessitated an almost continuous process of adaptation on the part of traditional foreign policy institutions. This may involve the reassignment and retraining of diplomatic personnel, the creation or abolition of new departments and, more fundamentally, the launch of policy reviews. The extent of adapta-tion, however, varies. Organisational characteristics (for instance, the use of standard operating procedures) and the vested interests of bureaucra-cies in their commitment to established policies may well mean change is grudging and incremental. Second, complexity has increased the domestic political significance of foreign policy. We have already encountered this phenomenon in Robert Putnam's (1988) notion of the 'two-level game' – a state of affairs that is the natural consequence of the growing importance of economic issues to foreign policy and the consequent inter-twining of domestic politics and international relations. A domesticated foreign policy agenda can also have other effects. Keohane and Nye's (1989) typology of world politics as 'complex interdependence' assumes a growing agenda of 'multiple issues' (see also Chapter 1) and thus several 'domestic' government departments (for instance, those related to energy, telecommunications, food and environmental concerns) being involved in foreign policy formulation. This, in turn, presents organisational diffi-culties in coordinating the work of different branches of government. It also generates political problems as a proliferation of newly created policy coalitions seek to influence foreign policy.

And it is not just at the domestic level that this process arises. A third link between foreign policy and political process suggests that the formula-tion of foreign policy, while still the preserve of the home state, is none-theless influenced by actors from outside domestic political structures. Several distinct forms of influence can be seen to exist in this regard, what Keohane and Nye (1989: 33–4) have termed 'multiple channels of contact among societies'. These may not have emerged newly formed in recent decades but their scope and impact have assumed greater proportions.

The first channel of this sort is *intergovernmental* organisation. Here, the state retains its formal autonomy but is constrained in its policy-making options by virtue of commitments to multilateral bodies. Exam-ples include joint NATO defence planning and (albeit at a lesser level of development) the EU's Common Foreign and Security Policy and, more common outside Europe, the requirements laid down by international financial institutions such as the International Monetary Fund. Although the conditions that this organisation attaches to loans are largely of con-sequence for national economic policy, they can also have foreign policy effects. Among less developed countries and, more recently, the former communist states, such conditionality makes express provisions relating to external economic policy (currency valuation, import and export con-trols) and even to levels of defence expenditure.

A second channel is *transgovernmental* relations, something that in-volves direct contacts between governments usually below the level of the executive policy makers. Relations of this type may be born of functional necessity, as in the case of comparable government ministries engaged in joint decision making on technical projects (Franco-British collaboration in the early 1970s on the Concorde project or, more recently, Russian-American space cooperation). They may also be the outcome of more expressly political pressures. Ministries in separate countries may form coalitions against rival ministries within their own domestic governments

– the American State Department and the British Foreign Ministry working in unison against their respective Defence Ministries, for example. When applied to multilateral settings – for instance negotiations on debt relief and the law of the sea – such contacts can assume a considerable complexity. Here, transgovernmental coalitions operate not simply to influence the formulation of government policy, but also to affect any subsequent coordination of policy into a joint intergovernmental position. In such circumstances state and coalition actors are numerous and the bargaining calculations of these actors ever more intricate.

FPM, finally, can also be affected by *transnational* relations, occasions where interactions involve non-state actors as well as governments. The influence of these actors on FPM, however, is by no means assured. It depends on how skilful they are in infiltrating national policy-making processes and on how receptive the targeted government is to external pressures. Although, as Risse-Kappen (1995) has pointed out, it is not easy to draw a neat distinction between democratic and authoritarian states in this regard (see the next section), it does seem sensible to suppose that democratic polities do afford transnational non-state actors greater access, and that such opportunity is often translated into limited policy-making influence. This may involve lobbying by internationally-organised pressure groups, transnational 'epistemic communities' of economists and scientists relaying ideas and information to policy makers on issues of trade, monetary and environmental concern, and non-governmental central bankers (for instance, in Germany) seeking to shape the foreign policies of EU states regarding Economic and Monetary Union.

Political images of FPM, then, are useful in highlighting the rise to prominence of new issues and channels of influence. These images, however, tell one little about how change is received in the minds of the policy makers themselves. To appreciate this process we need to return to the psychological images of FPM outlined earlier.

These may well lead us to expect that change is a discomforting experience. Situations of uncertainty and flux not only exacerbate the already difficult problems of information processing, but can also result in cognitive inconsistency, as unfolding events seemingly contradict individual belief systems. The various methods by which these inconsistencies are dealt with were noted above. These tended to suggest either resistance to change or an inadequate adjustment to new circumstances. The upshot in all cases is the survival of a set of perceptions perhaps more suited to the past than to new realities. Three examples can be used to illustrate this.

The first is the influence exerted upon policy makers by historical analogies. These may sometimes be employed constructively but just as often they lead to poor quality policy making as the analogy chosen turns out to be a faulty guide to current action. British Prime Minister Anthony Eden's reliance on the 'Munich analogy' adversely affected his handling of the 1956 Suez crisis. Similarly, the Korean War analogy proved mistaken in America's approach to Vietnam, while the 'lessons' of Vietnam, in turn, were arguably a poor guide to the American response to the wars in the former Yugoslavia. Enemy images can exert a similar effect. These may linger long after the original circumstances that gave rise to them have passed. America's post-Cold War hostility to Cuba may be seen in this light. And third, policy makers may retain an outdated view of their country's role based on a previous, now lost position. Thus the British elite's quest for post-imperial great power status, the view held by some in France that Paris should play an interventionist role in Africa and the belief held among some Russians that their country ought to maintain the military capacity essential for foreign policy influence even in the face of a catastrophic economic collapse.

These examples suggest that responses to change are often ill-conceived. However, this need not always be the case. Policy makers are at times capable of flexible adaptation. This may be because change occurs in a manner that is incremental, such that it can be dealt with in a piecemeal fashion, or because it is anticipated, thus allowing its gradual absorption into pre-existing beliefs. Far more taxing circumstances can also arise but these too can be accommodated. Consider the following two examples.

First, situations in which long-term trends undermine central beliefs. Such, for instance was the type of situation which confronted the leaders of the Soviet Union (and, to some degree, China) by the early 1980s. At this point two externally generated problems for Marxist-Leninist ideology had become clearly apparent: the continuing economic vitality of the capitalist world system and the socialist system's inability to confront capitalism in a revolutionary struggle owing to the danger of nuclear annihilation. When combined also with failures in domestic performance, these developments served to undermine a central ideological assumption, namely that socialism was a superior form of social organisation which would eventually triumph over its capitalist rival. In cognitive terms, such information was so powerfully at odds with the core beliefs that cognitive consistency could not be satisfactorily achieved. As studies of Mikhail Gorbachev and his associates have shown, this did not lead to a paralysis in FPM; in fact, quite the opposite. The adaptation and even the abandonment of core beliefs, apparent in what became known as the 'new political thinking', had a profound effect, fundamentally altering the bases of Soviet foreign policy (Kull, 1992).

A second type of situation concerns change that is sudden, dramatic and occasioned by far-reaching uncertainty. This approximates the environment that confronted policy makers in the immediate post-Second World War years and which faces their successors in the wake of the more recent end of the Cold War. At first sight, this appears to be precisely the sort of environment that policy makers find the most perplexing. However, such 'big bang' events need not always leave policy makers confounded. Well-developed belief systems may, in some senses, be confirmed by these events, as was the case with the triumph of political and economic liberalism over Nazism in 1945 and, more recently, over communism. When this occurs, policy makers are able to impose some understanding upon their changed surroundings. The specifics of FPM may appear as difficult as ever, but at least the policy makers can approach strategic themes with a confidence of having seemingly being proven right on the big issues. Hence, in the post-Cold War period, the Western insistence on the durability of NATO as the basis of European security and on market-led reforms as a panacea for the transitional economies of Russia and Eastern Europe.

Foreign policy making in a comparative context

The application of the various 'images' of FPM presented above could suggest quite easily that a common logic applies to policy makers. Yet just how compelling this logic is depends on the nature of the environment that policy makers face. The manner of FPM, in other words, differs according to the situational circumstances in which it is made. One interesting way of illustrating this point is to consider the nature and spread of change that has occurred in the international system. While all states may in some way have been touched by the consequences of the growth of post-war interdependence and by the end of the Cold War, the extent and benefits of change have varied. Grouping states along these lines leads us to view international politics as consisting of 'two worlds' (Goldgeier and McFaul, 1992), each with quite different hierarchies of policy issues. The first, the core, comprises the states of Western Europe, North America and the 'tiger' economies of East Asia. Here, military issues are of low significance, economic interdependence profound and mutually beneficial, and institutional linkages well-established. In such circumstances the effects of anarchy are mitigated and the survival motive relegated to a 'perfunctory national objective'; wealth rather than power frames FPM. In the periphery, by contrast, military threats persist, economic relations are characterised by underdevelopment and subordination, and institutional cooperation is notable by its absence. FPM in this setting is conditioned by the power and influence calculations beloved of realists.

Crisis versus routine policy making

As well as a hierarchy of issues, the situational context of FPM can also be seen in terms of how urgent are the issues that face foreign policy makers. Here a clear distinction can be drawn between policies that are framed in a routine manner and those which are occasioned by crisis (see Table 3.1).

Routine policy making, although perhaps the least noticed, constitutes, in fact, the bulk of FPM. Much foreign policy activity occurs through regular channels, on the basis of coordinated, planned preparation. The exchange of delegations, participation in the activities of international organisations, and a wide range of diplomatic and protocol functions fall into this category. It is a type of work that is in itself demanding and often time-consuming. It is, however, also frequent and predictable, more likely to engender boredom and fatigue among foreign ministers than panic and adrenaline.

Crisis policy making is of a quite different order. In such situations the policy maker is tested to the limit and, moreover, engages in the making of decisions which carry huge consequences, both for the state on whose behalf he or she acts and sometimes for international politics on a regional or even global scale. The stakes in these situations are certainly higher, and so too are the pressures. This necessitates a suspension of many of the methods of routine FPM and the devolving of policy making to a small number of key officials. Crises also increase the likelihood of

Table 3.1 Styles of foreign policy making

Routine policy making	Crisis policy making
Policy initiation based on incremental adjustment.	Policy making as a response to a surprise.
Low/moderate stress levels.	High levels of stress.
Wide number of policy makers.	Small number of policy makers.
Broad range of options.	Narrow range of options.
Long lead time in policy formation.	Limited time to respond.
Blurred criteria for judging success; low cost of policy 'failure'.	High costs of policy failure.
No likelihood of force.	Likelihood of force.

error as stress accumulates and the pressures of time allow only a few (but not necessarily the best) options to be considered.

Crisis FPM is also generally regarded as involving an actual or latent use of force. Consequently, much attention has been given either to policy making in the lead-up to military intervention and war or how key policy makers take decisions that help avert conflict (Vertzberger, 1998). To take just the American case (perhaps the most studied example), the Cuban missile crisis, the onset of the Vietnam War and the Gulf War all fall into this category. Yet force alone need not be a defining characteristic. Crises can also occur owing to the unexpected nature of international events and the intensity and rapidity of the changes they usher in, regardless of whether force is used. They may also arise because foreign policy makers are constrained by unforeseen domestic problems. An embattled Foreign Minister, for instance, may regard his or her international activities as a test of popularity and competence, and consequently approach foreign policy matters acutely aware that upon their outcome rests his or her political survival. As the following extract (Box 3.2) from the memoirs of the former Soviet Foreign Minister, Eduard Shevardnadze, makes clear, such international and domestic circumstances, are certainly regarded as crisis ridden and the consequent stress, feeling of unpreparedness and necessity for quick response may be little different from those confronting policy makers in wartime. Indeed, in Shevardnadze's case they were enough to prompt his resignation.

Types of political system

As well as situational circumstances, state type is also important in building up a picture of FPM. States differ perhaps most obviously in terms of their political systems, and whether they are democratic, authoritarian or transitional will affect how foreign policy is made.

To take *democracies* first. Here, the political system is organised in a manner which encourages participation, diversity of opinion and the accountability of government. The consequent separation of powers among the institutions of government and the toleration of mechanisms of political opposition mean that policy making is often influenced by the preferences of a multiplicity of actors. Of these, the most important is the political executive – the office of a President or Prime Minister (see also Chapter 2). Its predominance stems both from the efficiency that is gained from centralisation and the constitutional and organisational advantages that the office enjoys. In addition, the very high stakes of foreign policy

Box 3.2: Eduard Shevardnadze on crisis foreign policy making

Only those close to me knew that I wasn't clinging to any post, except for the sake of our political future. . . . My colleagues and I outwardly defended the cause, but really we were losing hope. The threats to unseat the Foreign Minister were heard not somewhere out on the streets, but in the corridors of power. Worse, they were not challenged by those whose business it was to respond. . . . Some highly placed representatives watched impassively as the facts were distorted and the Foreign Ministry was cast in a false light. Top officials in other ministries also remained silent, although they shared equal responsibility with the Foreign Ministry for some of the foreign policy decisions and had given their consent. While conducting negotiations abroad, I kept stumbling on discrepancies in positions I thought had been agreed upon at the highest level.

It was very hard to work normally in such an atmosphere, but we managed. . . . We prepared and signed agreements with Germany and other major European powers. . . . We called for a European summit to lay the groundwork for new continental security structures, now that the division of Europe and the Cold War were over. We continued the traditional agenda with our American partners. . . .

The year 1990 was equivalent to several decades. We lived through it without pausing for breath, preoccupied with numerous external worries and constant internal pressure.

Source: Shevardnadze (1991: xiv–xv)

decisions – involving matters of national security and the promotion of national interests – has meant, historically, that the executive has retained a superior influence in the control of policy. This has not diminished with time. The blurring of international and domestic issues and the increased visibility of international affairs has increased both the motivation for, and political dividends to be reaped from, close executive involvement. As a consequence, Presidents and Prime Ministers are involved in person in the framing of important foreign policy decisions and, if not, set the overall policy context in which lower-level policy making is carried out.

Yet in a democracy executive direction is far from total. Three very important sources of countervailing influence are significant. First, the office of executive is an elective one, its incumbent is often restrained in the choice of policy by the rigours of re-election and the desire to remain in tune with public opinion. To what extent these pressures matter does vary. For a directly elected President (as in the US) or a prime minister with a clear parliamentary majority (the norm in the UK) these constraints tend to be more urgent with the approach of an election. They are also generally less pressing than in cases of coalition (commonplace in Western Europe) where government drawn from more than one party is the norm and policies have to be framed with a close eye towards the preferences of more than one party.

Second, constitutional arrangements can constrain executive policy-making to some degree. Legislatures in democratic states can play a limited but nonetheless important role through their oversight of the budgetary and treaty-making processes, their input into policy debates through standing committees and their share of responsibility in war and peace decisions. Again there are variations. The American Congress enjoys an influence over the executive not apparent among other legislatures. The British parliament, by contrast, has far fewer powers (it lacks, for instance, legal powers of treaty ratification) and is, in any case, closely tied to the executive through the majority party. A further but less commented upon constitutional arrangement is the referendum. With this device decisions of the executive are determined through the direct intervention of the voting public. This is a fairly common practice in Switzerland. It is used far less on matters of foreign policy in other democracies but when instituted can be of defining influence – in certain instances confirming executive preferences (British entry into the European Economic Community and Spanish entry into NATO), while in others countermanding them (as, for instance, in the cases of the 1992 Danish referendum that opposed ratification of the Maastricht Treaty and the 1994 referendum in Norway that rejected proposed membership of the European Union [EU]).

Third, the executive is subject to the influence of other agencies of the state. The impact of bargaining within government has already been noted above with reference to 'political' models of FPM. In addition, the bureaucracy (understood here as permanent administrative officials such as the civil service) may be considered to have a procedural impact on policy making. It acts as a gatekeeper of information, something that influences which issues rise to the level of executive or how other issues are interpreted. In situations of complex policy making, such a state of affairs is both necessary and indeed inescapable. It is, however, often, perceived as detrimental to good policy, its detractors claiming that bureaucracy encourages inflexibility and inertia. Moreover, permanent officials may perceive foreign policy issues in a manner different from the elected political masters, leading to conflicts in policy making. These problems have often led democratically-elected leaders to rely on a separate politically appointed staff of foreign policy advisers, a practice institutionalised in the US with the office of the National Security Council and in many European democracies with specialists attached to the office of the Prime Minister.

In democracies FPM is not simply a function of the elective, constitutional and bureaucratic structures outlined above. Also at work are less formal processes of influence. Democracies are open to all manner of sectional interests. In the case of the US, the impact of the so-called 'military-industrial complex' (an amalgam of government agencies, industrial concerns and research bodies) has long been detailed with regard to issues of military expenditure and arms procurement. The US and, indeed, democracies more generally also permit the operation of specialist interest groups that seek to influence FPM. Their impact, however, tends to be limited either because they have no established authoritative position in the policy-making process or, as is often the case, their priorities markedly diverge from those of government – the campaigns for nuclear disarmament in the UK, France and the US is a clear example. That said, interest groups may contribute to shifts in public opinion and at critical junctures be one influence among many pushing a government towards decisions that initiate policy change. Such, for example, was the influence of the anti-apartheid lobby in the US during the 1980s.

FPM in *authoritarian* states differs from democracies in several respects. In authoritarian regimes – even those with a pretence to forms of collegiate rule (military and communist states) – power is often concentrated in the hands of a single individual and foreign policy decisions tend to be closely shaped by the personal attributes of one person. This state of affairs is exaggerated further where such a 'predominant leader' is insensitive to advice and holds strong beliefs on foreign policy issues. This often has ruinous consequences, a fact plain to see in the Iraqi invasions of Iran (1980) and Kuwait (1990).

A concentration of power, however, is rarely absolute. While in stable authoritarian states leaders do not usually compete with autonomous centres of power such as interest groups, political parties or an independent legislature, they are often constrained by the existence of political factionalism from within the ruling regime itself. In the case of the Soviet Union, for instance, decisions on matters of arms control, military intervention and the end of the Cold War were all shaped by personal rivalries within the ruling Politburo and bureaucratic struggles involving the Communist Party, the Ministry of Defence, the KGB and so on. Similar dynamics are often also at work within military regimes; in these cases they are the product both of leadership and inter-service rivalries, and divisions between the military junta and its civilian administrators.

Political conflict, then, is not absent within authoritarian states. While it might be true that some of these states have displayed a remarkable durability and have successfully eliminated or neutered political opposition (such is still the case in China and Cuba and among dynastic states such as Saudi Arabia), many others have succumbed to democratic pressures or have experienced a sorry history of civil war and recurrent coups. Military and socialist regimes in Africa seem to have been particularly prone to these 'praetorian' tendencies. In cases such as Rwanda, Liberia, Sierre Leone and Somalia, the consequent disruptions of governance and, in some cases, even the termination of government itself, have rendered all forms of official policy making not just unsettled but at times simply inoperative (see also Chapter 8).

Since the mid-1970s authoritarianism as a form of rule has been on the wane. The removal of corporatist or military rule in southern Europe (Greece, Portugal, Spain and Turkey) was followed by a retreat of the military from Latin America and parts of Africa and latterly the collapse of communist rule in the Soviet Union and Eastern Europe. Only in southern Europe, however, have these transitions resulted in the consolidation of stable democracies. Elsewhere, the deeper structural problems of transition and the insufficient passage of time means one cannot yet safely judge the durability of these nascent regimes. They thus remain transitional in nature, exhibiting democratic features but influenced strongly by their recent authoritarian past.

Such *transitional* political systems are characterised by a number of peculiarities that affect FPM. First, the survival of personnel and practices from the old regime. It is a lengthy and costly business to replace administrative staff among foreign and defence ministries. Even at the higher ambassadorial and ministerial echelons where the political imperative for change is stronger many continuities of personnel exist. This is particularly striking in the Russian and Polish cases where parts of the former communist ruling elite have been assimilated into the post-authoritarian order. Certain political practices may also linger: an exaggerated secretiveness, a distrust of public involvement and a tendency towards insulating executive policy making from constitutional constraint.

Alongside these elements of continuity there is often considerable political disruption. As in South Africa and many post-communist states, this affects foreign ministries (for instance, in the reorganisation or relocation of departments and personnel) and, perhaps more pertinent for FPM centrally, it also involves the re-ordering of institutions. The break with an authoritarian past and the removal of a coordinating locus of power (a ruling party or a military junta) often requires the establishment of some form of constitutional settlement. Two patterns are evident here. When the process has been well prepared, has enjoyed popular support and has been executed by a strong ruling party the reconfiguration of the balance of power among institutions within the new constitution has been relatively clear-cut (Spain and South Africa). By contrast, in a large number of post-communist states initial democratic consolidation has been accompanied by political fragmentation and/or fierce political competition. Constitutional reform has consequently tended to be *ad hoc* or the result of political confrontation. This has resulted in an initial uncertainty concerning the location of authority for foreign policy making and a competition to carve out prerogatives that has pitted the executive against both legislatures, ministers and the armed forces. Almost without exception, however, these battles have been won by Presidents or Prime Ministers, foreign policy consequently becoming an almost unchallenged executive preserve.

Contrasts in FPM practices clearly exist across different types of political system. Two important qualifications, however, need to be made. First, there are also important similarities. In all cases the most important domestic actor is the political executive. It is also commonplace for FPM to be subject to internal processes of bargaining and competition. These processes may vary in intensity and effect but the executive does operate within constraints imposed by other important political actors. Second, political system differences may often seem less stark when considered in the light of other criteria of comparison. Whether a state is large or small, economically developed or underdeveloped, helps to determine the complexity of the foreign policy agenda and the resources a state can bring to bear in formulating its policies. Looked at in this way the similarities between say American and Chinese FPM may be just as important as the politically-derived differences. Similarly, Hagan (1995: 120) has suggested that 'it is difficult to generalise about any type of political system . . . political effects vary across different issues, situations and leaders'. Put another way, who is involved, what is at stake and how quickly decisions are reached depends less on the political context but more on the urgency of the issue and the personal priorities of the person holding executive office.

Summary and conclusion

This chapter has focused on FPM largely through an analysis of different 'images' of the policy-making process. These are summarised in Table 3.2.

Table 3.2 Images of foreign policy making

	Core assumptions	Supporting arguments	A transformed world
'Rational actor' images	Unitary state; means-end analysis (procedural rationality); determining impact of structure and survival motive (neo-realism); consistent and utility-maximising goals (instrumental rationality).	Policy makers aspire to rationality; distinctive nature of foreign policy; quick route to understanding.	Enduring influences on foreign policy making.
Images of 'political' foreign policy making	State is not a unitary actor; policy is the outcome of political bargaining; interaction between the international and the domestic.	Policy makers often complain of political influences on policy making; reflects the complexities of the policy-making process.	Points to new issues and channels of influence upon foreign policy making.
'Psychological' images	Perceptions of policy makers (as individuals and in groups) diverge from reality; this introduces distortion or bias into the perceptions of foreign policy makers.	Foreign policy gives rise to peculiar stresses and demands; this also gives rise to misperception; coping strategies are adopted.	Change increases stress upon policy makers and leads to problems in adapting perceptions and beliefs.

It seems clear that a 'traditional' approach – that most closely associated with rational actor images – is insufficient for understanding FPM in a changing world. Its reliance on the concept of the unitary state, the rationality of state action and the simplicity of the foreign policy agenda is at odds with the complex domestic and international environments against which foreign policy is formulated and inferences that can be drawn about the psychological characteristics of policy makers themselves. For these reasons it is fruitful to consider other images of FPM which stress the essentially political nature of policy making, the range of actors and influences that are brought to bear upon decisions and the manner in which policy makers respond to change in the international system. Yet while rational actor models do not suffice, we have also suggested that neither of the two other approaches, alone, is completely satisfactory. It is best to be eclectic in how one analyses FPM. Alternative images simply explain the same thing in different ways. In this chapter we have also drawn out some of the comparative differences of FPM, considering some of the situational and political differences that affect policy, but highlighting also certain commonalities.

Having demonstrated just how multifaceted and complex FPM is, it is worth returning to the starting point of this chapter. There we suggested that policy making involves a direct link between choice and action. This link is, however, not straightforward. To understand why we turn in the next chapter to a consideration of foreign policy implementation.

Further reading

Foreign policy making (or decision making) is well covered in the foreign policy analysis literature. The classic text is Allison (1971) which has recently been revised and re-issued – see Allison and Zelikow (1999). This work covers rational actor and what, in this chapter, we have called political models of decision making. For the various approaches which we have grouped under the psychological image, the reader should first consult Kinder and Weiss (1978), Rosati (1995) and Vogler (1989). These provide good introductions to what is a disparate literature. For crisis decision making, see Vertzberger (1998), and for a useful introduction to the impact of political system type on policy making, see Hagan (1995). Good general overviews of foreign policy making, meanwhile, include Goldstein (1994), chapter 3, Kegley and Wittkopf (1999), chapter 3 and Ray (1995), chapter 4.

References

Allison, G.T. (1971) *Essence of Decision. Explaining the Cuban Missile Crisis.* Boston, MA: Little, Brown and Company.

Allison, G.T. and Zelikow, P. (1999) *Essence of Decision. Explaining the Cuban Missile Crisis* (2nd edition). New York: Longman.

Buzan, B. (1996) 'The Timeless Wisdom of Realism?', in Smith, S., Booth, K. and Zalewski, M. (eds), *International Theory. Positivism and Beyond*. Oxford: Clarendon Press, 47–65.

Crawford, N.C. (2000) 'The Passion of World Politics. Propositions on Emotion and Emotional Relationships', *International Security*, 24(4), 116–56.

Goldgeier, J.M. and McFaul, M. (1992) 'A Tale of Two Worlds: Core and Periphery in the Post-Cold War Era', *International Organisation*, 46(2), 467–91.

Goldstein, J.S. (1994) *International Relations*. New York: HarperCollins.

Goldstein, J. and Keohane, R.O. (1993) 'Ideas and Foreign Policy: an Analytical Framework', in Goldstein, J. and Keohane, R.O. (eds), *Ideas and Foreign Policy. Beliefs, Institutions and Political Change*. Ithaca, NY, and London: Cornell University Press, 3–30.

Grieco, J.M. (1995) 'The Maastricht Treaty, Economic and Monetary Union and the Neo-Realist Research Programme', *Review of International Studies*, 21(1), 21–40.

Hagan, J.D. (1995) 'Domestic Political Explanations in the Analysis of Foreign Policy', in Neack, L., Hey, J.A.K. and Haney, P.J. (eds), *Foreign Policy Analysis. Continuity and Change in Its Second Generation*. Englewood Cliffs, NJ: Prentice-Hall, 117–44.

Hermann, M.G. (1984) 'Personality and Foreign Policy Decision Making: a Study of 53 Heads of Government', in Sylvan, S.A. and Chan, S. (eds), *Foreign Policy Decision Making. Perceptions, Cognition and Artificial Intelligence*. New York: Praeger, 25–52.

Holsti, K.J. (1992) *International Politics. A Framework for Analysis* (6th edition). Englewood Cliffs, NJ: Prentice-Hall.

Hug, S. (1997) 'Non-Unitary Actors in Spatial Models. How Far is Far in Foreign Policy?', paper prepared for the European Consortium for Political Research Workshops, Bern.

Janis, I.J. (1972) *Victims of Groupthink*. Boston, MA: Houghton Mifflin.

Janis, I.J. and Mann, L. (1977) *Decision-Making: a Psychological Analysis of Conflict, Choice and Commitment*. New York: Free Press.

Jervis, R. (1976) *Perception and Misperception in International Politics*. Princeton, NJ: Princeton University Press.

Kegley, Jr., C.W. and Wittkopf, E.R. (1999) *World Politics. Trend and Transformation* (7th edition). Basingstoke: Macmillan.

Keohane, R.O. and Nye, J.S. (1989) *Power and Interdependence. World Politics in Transition* (2nd edition). Boston, MA: Little Brown.

Kinder, D.R. and Weiss, J.A. (1978) 'In Lieu of Rationality. Psychological Perspectives on Foreign Policy Decision Making', *Journal of Conflict Resolution*, 22(4), 707–35.

Kissinger, H.A. (1973) *A World Restored: Castlereagh, Metternich and the Problem of Peace, 1812–22*. London: Victor Gollancz.

Kull, S. (1992) *Burying Lenin. The Revolution in Soviet Ideology and Foreign Policy*. Boulder, CO: Westview Press.

McGrew, A.G. and Wilson, M.J. (1982) 'The Politics of Decision Making', in McGrew, A.G. and Wilson, M.J. (eds), *Decision Making. Approaches and Analysis*. Manchester: Manchester University Press/Open University, 227–30.

Meirsheimer, J.J. (1990) 'Back to the Future. Instability in Europe after the Cold War', *International Security*, 15(1), 5–56.

Morgenthau, H. (1960) *Politics among Nations. The Struggle for Power and Peace* (3rd edition). New York: Alfred A. Knopf.

Nicholson, M. (1996) *Causes and Consequences in International Relations. A Conceptual Study*. London and New York: Pinter.

Nicholson, M. (1997) 'Rational and Irrational Actors and the Stability of Preferences', paper prepared for the European Consortium for Political Research Workshops, Bern.

Putnam, R.D. (1988) 'Diplomacy and Domestic Politics: the Logic of Two-Level Games', *International Organisation*, 42(3), 427–60.

Ray, J.L. (1995) *Global Politics* (6th edition). Boston, MA: Houghton Mifflin.

Risse-Kappen, T. (1995) 'Bringing Transnational Relations Back In: Introduction', in Risse-Kappen, T. (ed.), *Bringing Transnational Relations Back In. Non-State Actors, Domestic Structures and International Institutions*. Cambridge: Cambridge University Press, 3–36.

Rosati, J.A. (1995) 'A Cognitive Approach to the Study of Foreign Policy', in Neack, L., Hey, J.A.K. and Haney, P.J. (eds), *Foreign Policy Analysis. Continuity and Change in Its Second Generation*. Englewood Cliffs, NJ: Prentice-Hall, 49–70.

Shevardnadze, E. (1991) *The Future Belongs to Freedom* (trans. Fitzpatrick, C.A.). London: Sinclair-Stevenson.

Smith, H. (2000) 'Bad, Mad, Sad or Rational Actor? Why the "Securitization" Paradigm Makes for Poor Policy Analysis of North Korea', *International Affairs*, 76(3), 593–617.

Steinbruner, J.D. (1974) *The Cybernetic Theory of Decision*. Princeton, NJ: Princeton University Press.

Verba, S. (1969) 'Assumptions of Rationality and Non-Rationality in Models of the International System', in Rosenau, J.N. (ed.), *International Politics and Foreign Policy. A Reader in Research and Theory*. New York: Free Press, 217–38.

Vertzberger, Y.Y.I. (1990) *The World in Their Minds. Information Processing, Cognition, and Perception in Foreign Policy Decisionmaking*. Stanford, CA: Stanford University Press.

Vertzberger, Y.Y.I. (1998) *Risk Taking and Decisionmaking*. Stanford, CA: Stanford University Press.

Vogler, J. (1989) 'Perspectives on the Foreign Policy System: Psychological Approaches', in Clarke, M. and White, B. (eds), *Understanding Foreign Policy. The Foreign Policy Systems Approach*. Aldershot: Edward Elgar, 135–62.

Waltz, K. (1979) *Theory of International Politics*. Reading, MA: Addison-Wesley.

Waltz, K. (1993) 'The Emerging Structure of International Politics', *International Security*, 18(2), 44–79.

White, B.P. (1978) 'Decision-making Analysis', in Taylor, T. (ed.), *Approaches and Theory in International Relations*. London and New York: Longman, 142–63.

4 | The Implementation of Foreign Policy

This chapter shifts the focus from the making of foreign policy to its implementation: the mechanisms through which and the instruments with which decisions are translated into action and outcomes. The chapter starts by making some essential distinctions between decision making and action, and between the capacity to act and the capacity to get results. It then moves on to consider four components of foreign policy implementation: first, assumptions about the nature of the implementation process (rational, political and psychological); second, assumptions about the actors in foreign policy implementation; third, the nature of instruments in foreign policy implementation; and finally, the evaluation of outcomes from foreign policy implementation. The final part of the chapter considers the ways in which these aspects of implementation are affected by the transformed world in which implementation has to take place.

Introduction

What does it mean in analytical terms to move from the study of foreign policy making (FPM) to the study of its implementation? As we have seen in Chapter 3, the study of FPM implies a focus on the nature of decision making and the nature of decision makers, within a context of transformation. Many studies of foreign policy have tended to assume that once decisions are made, they are almost automatically translated into action, and that the results of those actions are easy to discern (Clarke and Smith, 1989: 182). But it is apparent even from a cursory study of foreign policy mistakes, failures and disasters that decisions about the broad aims or the general direction of foreign policy do not lead inevitably to effective implementation. More than this, even where implementation of a policy takes place as planned, it may well not lead to the predicted or anticipated results. One major study of American foreign policy in the Vietnam War concluded that while military means were efficiently implemented, these tools were put in service of a misguided set of foreign policy objectives. Military intervention could not, in other words, compensate for the political mistake of executing a prolonged military campaign in a region of marginal American interest, or overcome the seemingly unbreakable resolve of the Vietcong. The military instrument was efficiently applied in the sense of the numbers of service personnel mobilised and of military material committed, but ineffective in that the ultimate objective of military victory could not be achieved (Gelb and Betts, 1979)

To focus on implementation, then, is not to focus on a purely mechanical or automatic seeing through of agreed foreign policy objectives. Rather, it is to focus on actions and behaviours and the obstacles which face them. It is these actions and behaviours, and the reactions to them, which constitute the 'flow' and the substance of policy itself. Implementation also forms an obvious and important link with decisions. Just how important can be seen if we consider a counter-factual example. If a set of policy makers agreed to invade their neighbour's territory but then took no subsequent action, it is in some ways as if the original decision had never been made at all. Clearly the decision has to be implemented (i.e., an invasion has to take place) before we can talk of foreign policy being 'live'. Implementation is thus crucial to an understanding of the direction, the efficiency and the effectiveness of policy. The actions encapsulated in the process of implementation have to be chosen, they often have to be combined and coordinated in uncertain circumstances, and they require monitoring and evaluation by the policy makers as the basis for subsequent decisions and actions. This means that the implementation of foreign policy, like the making of policy, demands decisions and choices and the matching of commitments to capabilities. As such, implementation is clearly not just the residue after the policy has been made; it is subject to many of the same pressures and problems that were identified in Chapter 3, and thus to at least some of the same analytical investigations.

A central relationship in the implementation of foreign policy is that between the capacity to act and the capacity to get results. The capacity to act is a function of the 'raw material' available to policy makers in the form of resources or capabilities (see Chapter 2), but it also entails the ability to translate and combine those resources in pursuit of specific foreign policy goals. Because of this, it is clear that different countries will have distinct capacities to act. Moreover, as we have already suggested, the capacity to do something does not automatically carry with it the capacity to achieve a given result. In the first place, policy makers, while possessing adequate material resources, may still initiate misguided actions that stem from calculations of political expediency or human frailties of miscalculation and misperception. Second, and just as important, the taking of a particular action may produce unintended and undesired results owing to intervening circumstances. This is true in all areas of policy making and implementation, but arguably there are special reasons why in foreign policy implementation there should be a greater danger of adverse results: the uncertainty of the policy arena, the high stakes, and the lack of control over the actions of other national governments or internationally acting bodies.

In this chapter, we will explore these broad issues of foreign policy implementation (FPI), by focusing on four specific questions:

- First, how can we assess different images of implementation? This question links back to the treatment of images of foreign policy making in Chapter 3.

- Second, who implements foreign policy?

- Third, how is foreign policy implemented? What instruments are used, and how are they combined?

- Finally, what are the outcomes of FPI?

The chapter falls into two parts. The first part deals with the questions in general and comparative terms, while the second looks at the questions specifically in relation to the 'transformed world' of the late twentieth and early twenty-first centuries.

Implementation in perspective

Images of implementation

In Chapter 3, we distinguished between three broad 'images' of FPM: the rational, the political and the psychological. While these could be separated for the purposes of analysis, it was clear that any full explanation of FPM required elements of all three. Each of the images carried with it particular questions about the FPM process, and also implied distinct forms of evidence and explanation. In many ways, the same holds true in the study of FPI: depending on the starting point of analysis, the investigator can come up with competing and apparently contradictory 'stories' about the process and its results.

In the first place, it is possible to conceive of FPI as a rational process, a 'scientific' matching of agreed means and instruments with agreed objectives. In this, image implementation is essentially 'top down' and policy is deemed to be effective when the conditions of rationality are met (Lane, 1995: 101). This is not an easy process, and even the most rigorously rational analysis will leave some space for the uncertain or the unknown.

This image of FPI links directly with theories of rational decision making; indeed, it is a direct descendant of those theories, defining the problem of implementation again as one of information, calculation and coordination by rational policy makers. A particular development of this image is what might be termed a form of 'cost–benefit analysis' in foreign policy: the implementation of a given policy is best if it uses resources most efficiently and achieves the objective with the least expenditure of human or non-human capabilities. This means that the choice of instruments is a very delicate operation, because in foreign policy the inventory of instruments can include the large-scale use of force or economic coercion. Here, the cost–benefit calculation is particularly acute both because the instrument is often politically controversial and because it can invoke unpredictable responses by the state upon whom it is targeted.

The problem is, of course, that, as with FPM in general, it is not possible to fulfil the requirements of rationality on a consistent basis. Information about resources, about the possible reactions of adversaries or partners, about the likely costs of a particular course of action, or about the ways in which certain combinations of instruments might work, is not comprehensive. Indeed, where the 'target' of particular actions is hostile and secretive, information may be very difficult to come by. Where conditions are especially uncertain, as for example in a crisis, the dilemma is particularly acute, since the premium on rationality is high but the likelihood of achieving it is low. This means that much of FPI should be seen as political in nature. Far from being the mechanical application of principles of rationality and a form of cost–benefit analysis, implementation is untidy, contested and unpredictable.

One source of this untidiness and uncertainty is the nature of the implementors themselves. As pointed out in Chapter 3, foreign policy makers are guided not necessarily by principles of rationality but more often by considerations of political advantage. Such advantage can be seen in terms of party politics, of politics within the government itself or of politics within broader domestic or international contexts. In terms of implementation, political factors can mean that choices of actions or instruments are guided by political criteria rather than by a calculation of means and ends. When deciding to punish or reward the target of a particular policy, this can lead, on the one hand, to awkward compromises or half-measures (as in the case of the rather lukewarm sanctions applied against Russia or China by Western states over human rights infractions in Chechnya and Tiananmen Square). On the other hand, it can lead to the 'sledgehammer and nut' syndrome, where excessive means are used to achieve a relatively limited objective (as in the American military invasion of the small Caribbean island of Grenada in 1983). In either case, the political symbolism of the use of certain measures is important, not only in the domestic politics of the government doing the implementation, but also in the broader international context. This desire to impress, to reward or to be seen to take a hard line on a given issue is far from the calculated balancing of means and ends implied by the rational image and, as such, almost inevitably FPI will be 'inefficient'.

The political interactions surrounding FPI can also produce apparently perverse or self-defeating results. According to the influence of particular actors in the process, or the political stakes attached to a specific course of action or instruments, there will be a greater or smaller 'gap' between the rational standard and the political reality. This does not mean that rationality disappears completely; rather it means that it is modified and constrained by political considerations, whether these concern the political future of governmental leaders, the bureaucratic interests of certain participants or the natural caution of policy makers confronted with adverse domestic or international reactions.

In turn, this means that psychological aspects are important to the implementation of foreign policy. One way of viewing implementation is as a process of communication, whereby the intentions of the policy makers are converted into actions, which are then targeted on other governments or non-state actors (Lewis and Wallace, 1984). Because it is a process of communication, it is subject to the possibility of misunderstandings, inaccuracies or communications failures. In the first place, the conversion of intentions and decisions into actions will imply a complex process of communication within the governmental machine, and between the central foreign policy makers and their 'agents' (who may literally be on the other side of the globe). Second, the process of communication between one government (or its agents) and others is subject to cultural differences, to corruption by time and distance, and by the fact that actions taken by one government are themselves 'digested' by a complex policy machine in the 'target' country or organisation. We must never forget, as pointed out in Chapter 3, that policy makers are individually or collectively human, and thus that they suffer from the potential limitations of understanding to which all humans are prey.

This set of possible complicating factors means that at the heart of FPI are questions of communication, perception and credibility. Just as a decision is not automatically implemented, so implementation is not automatically understood in a uniform way by the wide range of individuals or groups to which it might apply. Thus, intentions may be misread, actions may be misinterpreted, expectations may be thwarted. Matters are complicated further by the fact that policy making and implementation are not one-off or discrete events. They are part of a flow, in which the effects of actions feed back into the perceptions and actions of foreign policy makers. If a process of implementation seems to be successful, then the commitment to it of the policy makers may be strengthened (a process of positive feedback). On the other hand, if implementation fails or is seen to be inefficient, then there may be a search for other methods (a process of negative feedback). Because of these feedback processes, which are themselves subject to possible failures or misperceptions, it is possible to see FPI as a process of continuous learning by the policy makers. It is in implementation that their commitment to aims and objectives may be strengthened or challenged, and it is through implementation that policy can be adjusted in the light of events.

It can be seen that, as in the case of FPM, the process of implementation can be judged by a variety of different standards. On the one hand, it would be wrong to ignore the search for rationality and the matching of means to ends. But it would equally be inappropriate to neglect the ways in which political or psychological factors can enter into the process, creating the possibility of misguided, inappropriate or unexpectedly successful (or failed) policy initiatives. Implicit in this discussion is the importance of the implementors of policy, and it is to this that we now turn.

Who implements?

The traditional view of implementation in foreign policy would see the question 'who implements?' as almost redundant. Governments make foreign policy decisions, and governments implement, moving in a coordinated way towards agreed objectives (Taylor, 1978: 127). Such a monolithic view of state action, though, is not likely to represent reality. The actors or agents through whom implementation takes place can be diverse, located in a variety of institutional and political settings and thus often difficult to coordinate. Furthermore, even when foreign policy implementation is seen to take place through the actions of political leaders, this may be in a context that is intergovernmental or transgovernmental in nature.

The lines of FPI, in other words, become blurred within a setting that is wider than simply the national context. To give an example, when meetings occur of the heads of state of the 'Group of Eight' and more so of the European Union (EU) and NATO (in the guise of the European Council and the North Atlantic Council, respectively) it may seem that the political executives of the countries in question are the key actors. But this relatively simple picture is deceptive. In the periods that intervene between these meetings a wide range of officials (at ministerial, ambassadorial and lower diplomatic levels) is continuously engaged both in implementing the agreements from one high-level meeting and also in framing the agenda for the next. These officials may also meet on an *ad hoc* basis to consult on issues of mutual concern involving countries or organisations outside the group. What is more, the foreign policy preferences of the national governments involved are subjected to bargaining, policies are adapted and implementation occurs through intergovernmental bodies as well as national ones (see Box 4.1.)

Implementation of policy, even at the highest political level, is built on a broad set of foundations. These foundations may centre on foreign offices and their diplomatic personnel, but they are also likely to include other administrative arms of government (for example, finance, trade and defence ministries). For any given foreign policy initiative, there will be a variety of agents: political leaders, government departments and diplomats. Some of these will be located in the 'home' country (in the Foreign Ministry), but others will be located in a wide variety of places abroad (embassies, consulates and, as Box 4.1. suggests, the headquarters or administrative offices of international organisations) depending upon the issue at hand.

The analysis of public policy and its implementation has often focused on what can be described as 'implementation chains' – the range of linked agents who must be coordinated if effective implementation is to take place. It is apparent that in foreign policy, implementation chains are distinctive because they extend internationally and may involve agents distant from the home country. During the nineteenth century, it might often appear that diplomatic agents could make independent decisions about the ways in which government policies might be carried out. This situation was changed by the development of telecommunications, first through the telegraph and later the telephone and associated technologies. But well into the twentieth century, examples can be found of relatively independent action by diplomatic and sometimes military agents, for instance in wartime conditions. As the twentieth century went on, the development of international organisations and such private organisations as major corporations or charitable actors meant that implementation

Box 4.1: Foreign policy making and implementation in NATO

The North Atlantic Council (NAC) has effective political authority and power of decision. . . . Many committees and planning groups have . . . been created to support the work of the Council or to assume responsibility in specific fields such as defence planning, nuclear planning and military matters. . . . Each government is represented on the Council by a Permanent Representative with ambassadorial rank. Each Permanent Representative is supported by a political and military staff or delegation to NATO, varying in size. When the Council meets in this format, it is often referred to as the 'Permanent Council'. Twice each year, and sometimes more frequently, the Council meets at Ministerial level, when each nation is represented by its Minister of Foreign Affairs. Meetings of the Council also take place in Defence Ministers' Sessions. Summit meetings, attended by Heads of State or Government, are held whenever particular important issues have to be addressed or at seminal moments in the evolution of Allied security policy. . . .

Items discussed and decisions taken at meetings of the Council cover all aspects of the Organisation's activities and are frequently based on reports and recommendations prepared by subordinate committees at the Council's request. . . . Permanent Representatives act on instructions from their capitals. . . . Conversely, they report back to their national authorities on the views expressed and positions taken by other governments. . . .

The work of the Council is prepared by subordinate Committees with responsibility for specific areas of policy. . . . The Senior Political Committee . . . meets in advance of Ministerial meetings to draft . . . texts for Council approval. Other aspects of political work may be handled by the regular Political Committee, which consists of Political Counsellors or Advisers from national delegations.

When the Council meets at the level of Defence Ministers, or is dealing with defence matters and questions relating to defence strategy, other senior committees, such as the Executive Working Group, may be involved as the principal advisory body. If financial matters are on the Council's agenda, the Senior Resource Board, or the Civil or Military Budget Committees, or the Infrastructure Committee, depending on which body is appropriate, will be responsible to the Council for preparing its work. . . .

The Secretariat of the Council is provided by the relevant Divisions and Offices of the International Staff, and in particular by the Executive Secretariat, which has a coordinating role in ensuring that Council mandates are executed and its decisions recorded and disseminated.

Source: Office of Information and Press, NATO (2001: 149–51)

chains could come to include a variety of intergovernmental or non-governmental bodies. Again, the range of actors and the length of the chain can be seen as a potential issue in the implementation of policies.

The picture is complicated further by the fact that implementation need not occur solely within an international context. In Chapter 2, we noted that the idea of foreign policy as directed solely towards foreigners has always been questionable. When it comes to the implementation of policy, there is scope for involvement by a variety of 'domestic' groups. Politically, there may be a need to 'sell' foreign policy in domestic politics, especially if major foreign policy issues coincide with electoral processes (see also Chapter 3). This is most pertinent in established democracies and although here foreign policy is often not a prime consideration of voters, politicians cannot ignore groundswells of opinion when they occur. Thus, United States' (US) President Lyndon Johnson was forced from office in 1968 because of his continued execution of the unpopular Vietnam War. Even in less democratic states, public opinion can still be a factor in implementation; the Soviet execution of the war in Afghanistan, having been initiated with no consideration of the public mood, finally proved unsustainable owing, in part, to an absence of popular feeling in favour of the Soviet occupation.

In short, the 'who implements?' question presents us with an issue of agency. An issue which pertains to the identification of roles in the process of implementation, the coordination of the actions of a range of participants and the control of individuals or groups responsible for implementing policy decisions. Where these tasks are less than clear-cut, or where there is disagreement over them, then the scope for a gap between policy making and policy implementation is apparent. In terms of the discussion earlier in this chapter, this is where the political, the bureaucratic and the organisational inefficiencies can often be at their sharpest. Commentators on FPI have pointed out that such factors can shift the process of implementation from that of activating a 'chain of command' towards that of 'coalition building' where politics is central (Smith and Clarke, 1985: 6–7). Others might add that the problems inherent in implementation give rise to a less than perfect process of execution in which the implementors are happy simply to 'muddle through' (Lindblom, 1959).

What instruments?

In a sense, we have already touched on the issue of instruments of FPI, since the actors or agents discussed above will typically operate with a specific range of instruments or – perhaps literally – weapons. As we saw in Chapter 2, foreign policy has often been conceptualised in terms of power. Attention to the instruments of its implementation brings us face to face with the translation of power into action. At one end of the 'power spectrum' may be said to lie the instruments of communication and persuasion: the diplomacy and administrative interaction around which much of day-to-day policy implementation centres. Policy in this sense is implemented through the sending, receiving and interpreting of messages, either in written or spoken form, with the aim of expressing the government's intentions and the intensity of feeling about specific issues. This is the stuff of classical diplomacy, through which the relatively dispassionate interaction of professional agents can stabilise, routinise and 'civilise' international interactions. Foreign policy implementation in this perspective is a form of continuous negotiation, in which views are exchanged and agreements, open or tacit, are reached (Berridge, 1995).

Diplomacy, however, has always had to coexist with other, harder-edged instruments. At the other end of the spectrum from persuasion is military intervention: the attempt not to reach agreement but to compel compliance through the destruction of human or non-human assets. This may seem a rather arid way of expressing what can be a tragic and at least a disturbing process, but it is one of the implications of a power-based assessment of foreign policy instruments. It can be argued that the use of a certain degree of force may be a good 'investment' if it contributes towards longer-term stability and the promotion of the national welfare. Thus, for example, pre-emptive attacks such as that by Israel on Egypt in the 1967 Middle East War can be seen as forcible and costly attempts to avert national destruction. These are high-risk and high-cost instruments to use, but clearly the imperatives of national survival may require them. Other, more recent examples of the use of force have tended also to be justified, in part at least, on humanitarian grounds. This was the case with Operation Desert Storm deployed against Iraq in 1991 and of Operation Allied Force directed against Yugoslavia (Serbia/Montenegro) in 1999. These humanitarian concerns may have camouflaged more instrumental concerns (Western access to oil supplies in the Persian Gulf and the containment of sources of instability in southeastern Europe) but from the point of view of implementation the end result looked the same, whatever the justification: the mobilisation and deployment of a massive use of military force.

Between the two ends of the spectrum – persuasive diplomacy and naked force – lie many nuances, and arguably the most demanding implementation choices. Where it is not clear what might be the implications of using different instruments or different combinations of instruments, the policy makers are faced with heightened risks and uncertainty. Use of diplomatic means where the adversary will not respond can make it necessary later to use force. On the other hand, use of force where the adversary or target might respond to diplomacy can create not only practical issues of cost and the risk of escalation, but also ethical issues (to which we will return later). For these reasons, there has been considerable attention to the interaction between diplomacy and military means, and also to the use of coercive but non-military means such as economic sanctions. Where a target is not open to persuasion, but force is unavailable or undesirable, then 'coercive diplomacy' or the use of threats can become a major element in the implementation of policy.

Two examples serve to illustrate this. First, the acquisition of nuclear weapons, either by the original nuclear powers or by newcomers such as India and Pakistan, can be seen as part of a deterrent posture, in which the simple knowledge of their possession by others can affect behaviour. Second, the use of economic measures such as embargoes or blockades (for instance, those imposed upon Iraq by the US and its allies after the Gulf War) can provide a means of punishing or rewarding which does not carry the immediate risk of military escalation (or in the Iraq case, serves partially to replace the use of force once an initial military objective has been achieved). The problem is, of course, that the deployment of a particular instrument may not bring about the reactions or outcomes predicted by the policy makers. Indian and Pakistani leaders have found that instead of stabilising their positions they have contributed to heightened tensions in the region and the risk of escalation. In a clear-cut case of the 'security dilemma', India and Pakistan, by deploying military instruments to strengthen their security, may have actually undermined it. Similarly, the US, having resorted to economic measures and the policing of 'no-fly zones' against Iraq, has found that they have been singularly ineffective in destabilising the regime of Saddam Hussein (the same may also be true of the economic blockade mounted for nearly forty years against Fidel Castro's regime in Cuba).

The deployment of foreign policy instruments – the use of force particularly – often highlights the fact that no one government can act alone in foreign policy. The twentieth century has seen a massive growth in collective implementation of foreign policies, either through such military/political alliances as NATO (see Box 4.1 above) or through economic organisations such as the World Trade Organisation, the International Monetary Fund and the World Bank. These bodies express a fundamental tension in the implementation of foreign policy. While it is often the case that no one country can unilaterally achieve a desired outcome, and thus there is an incentive to cooperate, this does not eliminate either competition among those who are cooperating, or the pursuit of particular national interests even while collective action is being undertaken. Thus, in dealing with the conflict in former Yugoslavia during the 1990s, there were large numbers of collective decisions by such bodies as the EU or NATO, but there were also enduring conflicts of national positions. In Bosnia in the mid-1990s, the US was often at loggerheads with the French and the British over the wisdom of air strikes, while in Kosovo in 1999, the US, British and French found themselves on the same side in carrying out air strikes that on this occasion were less than welcomed by some of NATO's southern members – Greece, Spain and Portugal. This is, in fact, a long-standing problem, expressed for example in the tensions between allies during the Second World War, or between the members of NATO when confronted with the Vietnam War in the 1960s and 1970s. In its economic/political form, it was encountered with considerable force among NATO members during the 1980s when the US held to a much harder position than their European allies on the wisdom of applying economic and political sanctions against the Soviet Union and certain other communist regimes in East-Central Europe (ECE).

The implementation of foreign policy thus requires a delicate balance: the ability at the national level to match instruments to purposes and to combine instruments effectively, along with the capacity to engage in collective measures where appropriate or necessary.

What results?

Assuming that foreign policy can be implemented efficiently, and the issues of coordination and control are resolved at the national level, the discussion above points to another set of problems. Even the best-framed and best-executed foreign policy can produce unintended outcomes, and the judgement of success and failure is far from easy. The examples of American policy in Vietnam and of nuclear weapons acquisition on the Asian sub-continent have already been alluded to above in this connection.

From this, it should be clear that the issue of success or failure in FPI is difficult to assess. One possible measure of the effectiveness of policy might be that of control: how far does the implementation of policy demonstrate not only the policy makers' control of their own policy and its implementation, but also their capacity to control the behaviour of others?

We have already seen that this entails the ability to know what is being done by a potentially wide variety of agents, to combine instruments and calibrate them to the aims of the policy, and to apply the instruments in such a way that they hit their target without causing damage to others. Given the fluid nature of foreign policy-making situations, this is a taxing set of requirements.

Another possible measure of success in policy implementation is the extent to which actions serve specific goals. Given the standard of a 'national interest', it may be possible in principle to establish whether given sets of actions contribute to or detract from the achievement of such an interest. We have already seen, however, that this is a rather amorphous concept (see Chapter 2). In reality also, the long-range nature of any national interest has to be related to the huge variety of medium-term and short-term goals that may be affected by multiple, sometimes conflicting lines of foreign policy, not to mention the sectional interests represented by powerful groups within society, whose interests in many foreign policy issues may be diametrically opposed. Further, as already noted, the national good often has to be balanced against powerful collective goods which may be institutionalised in such bodies as the United Nations (UN), NATO or the EU. Such institutions may have the benefits of making governments think in the long term and about the collective costs or benefits of particular policies, but they may equally appear inconvenient and intrusive when it comes to the implementation of specific measures.

How then do we know whether or when a foreign policy has succeeded, or when it has failed? At its most extreme, where a foreign policy leads to the break-up, invasion or extinction of a given country, then maybe it is easy to spot failure. The case of the Soviet Union is instructive here. It now seems in retrospect that the foreign policy goals of maintaining military parity with the US, of preserving control over Eastern Europe and maintaining clients in the Third World were misdirected. They proved a costly economic and political burden upon the Soviet Union itself and although efforts to address this state of affairs were made by Mikhail Gorbachev from the late 1980s, the accumulated costs were already considerable enough to have contributed to a major weakening of the Soviet state (Halliday, 1994: 191–215).

However, such absolute criteria can be misleading. State collapse is often the result of a multiplicity of domestic and external circumstances and disentangling these to the point where failures of foreign policy are evident is an analytically difficult, not to say dubious, task. Once discussion moves beyond the bald issues of national survival or extinction, into more nuanced economic, cultural or social issues, then judgement becomes even more uncertain. One way out of this impasse is to focus on specific policy lines, or on policies towards specific targets, where the aims may be set explicitly and thus the immediate issue of success, delay or failure becomes sharper. Examples abound here, but even so judgements can still be ambiguous. Take just one example, the foreign policy objective of a number of former communist states to join the EU and NATO. In 1999, three such states – the Czech Republic, Hungary and Poland – did, indeed, enter NATO and thus implementation could be regarded as a clear success. These states, however, have found it much more difficult to join the EU, despite having fixed target dates for doing so. At face value, this may be regarded as a failure of foreign policy. However, one must take into account the severity of obstacles to membership that these three states face within the EU, something that, in part, explains and arguably excuses the 'failure' of implementation in the aspirant country itself.

In general terms, it is clear that foreign policy makers themselves often talk in terms of success or failure, of threat or challenges and of response. What we need to be aware of are the limitations surrounding such statements, and the ways in which the process and context of implementation can change the standards by which any foreign policy may be judged. In the remainder of this chapter, we move to develop these arguments in the specific context of a transformed world.

Implementing foreign policy in a transformed world

Thus far, this chapter has focused on the problems and processes of FPI in a broad sense. We have noted that the images of FPI give us several different 'stories' about how implementation takes place. Is it a rational balancing of ends and means, costs and benefits, or is it rather a political process in which competition among groups and organisations shapes the choices of instruments and the assessment of success or failure? Is it even, more accurately, seen as a process subject to problems of misperception, of incomplete information and especially of imperfect understanding of the consequences of a given set of actions? Who are the implementors of foreign policy, and how do they choose the technique or combination of techniques with which to pursue particular objectives? In order to put these questions in the context of a substantially transformed world, we need to explore the impact of change on FPI.

Reassessing images of implementation

When we consider the impact of radical change on the ways in which implementation may be analysed, one of the most prominent implications is the twofold impact of diffusion and variety in world politics. Statehood, as noted in Chapter 1, has become diffused and contested in ways not unprecedented but certainly more pervasive than ever before. At the same time, statehood and governmental characteristics have become subject to greater variety as political change – for instance, the fall of communism – have reverberated around the globe.

What does this mean for the rational image of FPI? It has always been the case that owing to political and cultural differences between states, the rather conventional Western model of rationality is difficult to apply in many cases. As change accelerates, this is even more the case. Varieties of nationalism, of religious orientation and of ethical consideration can make for radically different judgements – each of them in its own way rational – about the use of foreign policy instruments. This is particularly true of the use of force, an area in which different cultures are subject to significant differences of justification or notions of costs and benefits, and in which the imposition of a dominant Western morality or rationality may appear provocative to others. For those in the EU who have built much of their post-1945 prosperity on the idea that force between them has been renounced, it may come as a surprise that political leaderships elsewhere may find force an altogether more rational instrument of policy (we are reminded here again of the Iraqi invasion of Kuwait in 1990).

In similar fashion, the analysis of constraints on foreign policy makers has to take into account the new international politics of transformation. A rational model is not blind to constraints on implementation but tends to view these as predictable and manageable. Hence, the notion of constraints in a mature democratic system may focus on political parties, interest groups and the like. This has always been much less relevant when applied to military-authoritarian systems and is equally problematic when considering the large number of new, formerly communist transitional states. Such a state of affairs means that we need to take a much broader view of the politics of FPI. In established democracies we may be able to concentrate on well-oiled constitutional and legislative processes and predictable lines of government authority. Elsewhere, however, the leading role of the military or of religious leaders may be the focus of attention, or (as in several post-communist states) we may need to take account of a certain fuzziness in implementation owing to underdeveloped government, contested lines of authority and personalised politics. Likewise, the notion of bureaucracy or of organisational influences on FPI needs to be considered broadly. Where there is little foreign policy bureaucracy (as is the case, for instance, in many poor African states or some of the new post-Soviet states of Central Asia) and where the most highly organised elements in society are not to be found in the governmental machine (but rather in say the private economy or, as in parts of west Africa and the former Soviet Union, in private militias and organised criminal networks), FPI is likely to be very different from what happens where there are many layers of administrative process. The result may be important differences in the style of implementation and in the choice of specific combinations of policy instruments.

In turn, these elements of variety and difference mean that the psychological aspects of FPI are inevitably affected. Where implementation is conceived as a process of communication – both within and between governments and other actors – it matters greatly how reliable and comprehensive the process of communication is. There are really two ends of a spectrum here. First, in highly-developed governmental machines, the processes of institutionalisation and bureaucracy can mean that there is almost too much information. This may mean that too many competing methods for implementation can be canvassed, but it may also mean that the growth of routines and 'standard operating procedures' can create rigidities and inefficiencies. One response to this situation on the part of political leaders is to set up their own 'private' foreign policy machines, relying on personal advisers and a small, close-knit team (see also Chapter 3). But this in its turn creates its own dangers, that of insulation for instance, with foreign policy made in a closed unit and thus insufficient consideration given to alternative forms of implementation.

At the other end of the spectrum, the problem is that of insufficient information, either about the resources available for implementation or about the possible consequences of certain lines of action. Many foreign ministries created in former Soviet states during the early 1990s relied literally upon a handful of personnel, and initially found it difficult to develop a foreign policy strategy independent of post-Soviet Russia. This was not an unprecedented problem given the similar difficulties experienced by ex-colonies in the 1950s and 1960s. But arguably the pace of change and the scale of sophistication needed in the twenty-first century is far greater than that ever confronted by those states at their birth. The dangers of misperception, of either over-caution induced by uncertainty or over-exuberance produced by the personalisation of implementation, is clear.

When it comes to feedback, the potential range and variety of such feedback, from the foreign ministries of the world but also from the media of mass communication or from transnational pressure groups, is likely to be far greater than before. For example, when the French government decided in 1995 to resume nuclear testing in the face of opposition from most other governments and from world opinion, it had to contend not only with diplomatic feedback of a negative kind, but also with popular demonstrations, with economic boycotts, and with the activities of a range of transnational groupings such as Greenpeace. In many theatres of conflict, foreign policy makers and their agents in the military have also had to come to terms with the ways in which the 'CNN factor' can influence feedback, either because they come to rely on news broadcasters for reliable information or because the rapid diffusion of news results in popular pressures to adjust policy. For example, American foreign policy makers have frequently evinced fear of the ways in which the sight of 'body bags' returning from conflicts may influence public opinion against the use of military means. It was considerations such as these that helped push the US into military action over Kosovo in 1999 but then ensured that such action would be limited to high-altitude air strikes in order to avoid American casualties (Freedman, 2000).

It is not necessarily the case that these problems are entirely new. However, the fact that they are occurring in a world with far greater speed of communication, with new 'technologies' of implementation and with unprecedented complexities of institutionalisation in areas such as the world economy means that the notion of choice has been transformed. Insofar as they are possessed of the necessary material resources, skills and knowledge, some sets of policy makers may see themselves as possessing far greater areas of choice than their predecessors, in economic, military or diplomatic domains. But at the same time they are likely to be significantly more tightly constrained by the development of new institutional and other networks (hence, the increase of obligations to international organisations, for instance) and by the emergence of new patterns of international communication (which may create an international public opinion against the pursuit of certain courses of action).

The net effect of these processes is that the tensions between rational, political and psychological aspects of implementation are heightened. Implementation has to take place through an increasing multiplicity of channels, and has to take into account an increasing range both of targets and of audiences. Does this mean that a 'new image' of implementation is necessary? Perhaps the most obvious area in which the established models may need supplementing is that of institutions, since it is apparent that we have to contend with a multilayered implementation setting, with substantial institutionalisation both at the level of international organisations and at the level of more informal networks. Implementation will often take place through such institutions, and at a variety of levels; at the same time, it will be shaped by them and have to take account of their demands, alongside those of the more familiar 'audiences' for FPI. We must now explore what this might mean in terms of who carries out the implementation of policy.

Who implements?

As we have seen, long-standing assumptions about the actors or agents of foreign policy indicate that top political leaders, diplomats and sometimes the military are the prime implementors of foreign policy. Depending on the circumstances, the balance between the three elements may be more or less even and more or less taxing, but this is the central 'triangle of forces' around which foreign policy action revolves. In the changed conditions of the twenty-first century, though, it is clear that each of the components is open to challenge, and also that new agents have become prominent in the implementation process. The diffusion of statehood, and the new variety of international relations in the broadest sense, means that there has been a diffusion of agency in the implementation of foreign policy.

Perhaps the most important effects of this diffusion can be seen in the notion of 'the diplomat'. Traditionally seen as specialists in the practice of international communication and negotiation, the occupants of this position have been regarded as a different breed from domestic officials. No other government servants can rely on spending regular periods abroad, or as having special responsibility for the coordination of the external actions of the state, both at home and in the field. This rather cosy image has, however, to be qualified. As noted in Chapter 2, there has, in fact, always been limited participation in diplomacy by other officials, from ministries of defence, and increasingly in the post-Second World War period by government personnel located in departments concerned with economic and social affairs (see also Hopkins, 1976). But it has only been from the 1980s that the full extent of the transformation of diplomacy has become apparent. Alongside the traditional diplomat, it is now commonplace for overseas missions to contain members of 'domestic' departments, while at the same time there has been a rapid growth in international dealings, such as on agriculture and the environment, which engage specialists from outside foreign ministries. It is not accurate to conclude that foreign ministries have now been supplanted, but particularly among countries of the EU and North America, it can be argued that conventional diplomacy is now only a small part of what goes on through the implementation of foreign policies.

Clearly, such a trend reflects the changing substance of foreign policies themselves. The move from 'high politics' towards 'low politics' and 'sectoral politics' has been noted in previous chapters, and it inevitably brings with it a change in the diplomatic setting and of diplomatic agents. Sometimes, it can lead to 'diplomatic' initiatives from agents beyond central government. For example, the overseas missions of American states such as California or Georgia have been increasingly active in trade and investment promotion; equally, regions or cities from within Russia have conducted forms of diplomacy as a way of advancing their economic regeneration. It can also lead to an increasing involvement of individuals or groups from outside government altogether as has been seen in the context of trade, environmental or human rights negotiations, and conflict resolution efforts (witness here the crisis diplomacy efforts of ex-US President Jimmy Carter in North Korea and Haiti). These bodies increase the range of interlocutors that government agents have to deal with and thus complicate further the process of FPI (Barston, 1997).

This does not mean, though, that 'foreign policy by diplomats' has ended. In some ways it has been extended. For example, in the EU, the growth of cooperation between foreign ministries and diplomats has led to new forms of diplomatic interaction which have certainly extended the roles of diplomats in both small and large member states. The same can be said of the traditional links between diplomats and the defence community. With the end of the Cold War, there were expectations in many countries that the role of the military in the implementation of foreign policy would diminish or even be eliminated. This has certainly not been the case, but the eruption of new forms of conflict, alongside the growth of activities such as peacekeeping or humanitarian intervention, has led to a re-direction of military concerns in a wide range of countries (member states of NATO in particular). In others, of course, the perceived threats to newly-established independence, or problems of internal order, have underlined the central importance of the military to national well-being. In this sense, while not formally military regimes, states such as Georgia and Azerbaijan in the former Soviet Transcaucasus, for instance, are nonetheless heavily militarised.

What has been experienced in the 1990s and beyond has been a process of diffusion and differentiation in the agents of FPI. In turn, this has demanded a readjustment on the part of political leaders, who have increasingly found themselves involved in forms of multilateral decision making and governance at the international level. The growth of international organisations generally has created a new demand for diplomatic skills in order to service new forms of cooperation and coordination. Many of these forms are economic or social in their focus, but not all. The growth of regional cooperation, most intensely in the EU but also in many other parts of the world, has meant in some ways an 'extra-nationalisation' of the established forms and concerns of government, widening the range of political leaders involved as well as that of officials. Many policies agreed at the regional or broader levels pose specific challenges of implementation: they have to be implemented across national boundaries, and 'sold' to a variety of domestic audiences in the countries concerned. Thus, for example, in the North American Free Trade Association (NAFTA) there is a proliferation of mechanisms for implementation in the member states (Canada, Mexico and the US), but there has also been considerable resistance on the part of domestic groups to free trade in particular sectors (for example, agriculture). These cross-national problems of implementation create new networks of contacts between agents in different countries, fostering either transnational or transgovernmental coalitions much more intense and active than those which had been the object of study during the 1970s (see Chapter 3). And this is a process not simply confined to the industrialised West. In the Asia-Pacific region, for example, a wide and growing range of such contacts (institutionalised within the Association of South East Asian Nations [ASEAN]) between both rich and newly-industrialising or less developed countries can be observed.

Alongside relatively traditional diplomatic, political or military agents for FPI, we can thus observe a growing range of new participants and 'quasi-diplomats'. Implementation, traditionally seen as taking place at national level with other national authorities as the targets, increasingly takes place within densely-institutionalised contexts, with multilateral contacts or networks as the central focus. This clearly places considerable pressure on the conventional mechanisms of communication, control and coordination discussed earlier in this chapter. This leads us directly to the issue of instruments.

New instruments?

Earlier in the chapter, we noted the existence of a spectrum ranging between persuasive and coercive instruments, with some of the most challenging situations for policy makers occurring where persuasion and coercion were in a subtle and shifting balance. It is logical to suppose that the changing nature of agency in FPI will be accompanied by, and affected by, new forms of instrument, and that there will be new challenges of control and coordination.

The first instrument to be affected is diplomacy. As noted above, the notion of the diplomat is under challenge from a variety of sources, and this reflects the changing nature of diplomatic activity itself. Early in the twentieth century there began a marked shift away from purely bilateral or secret diplomacy towards multilateral, conference and often public diplomacy. This trend continued unabated after the Second World War with the establishment of the UN and associated intergovernmental organisations. It is only from the 1980s, however, that there has been a full blooming of a number of trends in diplomatic practice. One of these might be termed the practice of collective diplomacy, in which there is a continuous and often institutionalised set of contacts between a group of countries, for example in the EU or NATO (see Box 4.1 above). More than ever before, the processes of communication, negotiation and persuasion in such contexts are continuous, with the aim of coordinating policy not only over specific sectors or cases, but also over the whole range of diplomatic concerns. In such contexts, the processes of persuasion exist at a number of interconnected levels: within the countries concerned, between them and within the common institutions to which they are committed, between the collective position and other contexts such as the UN or third-country capitals. A process of continuous, often unconscious mutual adjustment is thus characteristic of diplomatic persuasion in the twenty-first century.

What does this imply for the other end of the spectrum, that of coercion and force? We have already seen that despite the hopes of some that these instruments could be sidelined or eliminated, they have proved remarkably persistent. The persistence and diffusion of military capacity is not, however, the only way in which coercion remains central to FPI. One logical response to the perceived unacceptability of force is the resort to new forms of coercion – economic punishment, diplomatic isolation, and others – which are seen as being both less risky and more humane. The problem is that such methods are often slow to act, they are subject to evasion, and they often depend upon broad multilateral implementation with a variety of public and private agents. Thus, the attempts to impose sanctions on Yugoslavia, on Iraq and on Cuba, for example, have involved the proponents of sanctions in management of often fractious coalitions, and have been subject to 'leakage' either because certain countries do not support them or because private individuals or groupings persist in seeking commercial advantage. There is still a good deal of coercion around in international life, but in a global political economy it is not easy to apply it efficiently or effectively.

Attempts to coerce or to use force in the contemporary practice of foreign policy are also arguably more subject than before to two sets of additional constraints: the legal and the ethical. The post-war growth of international institutions, coupled with an increased emphasis on international law, means that governments in general are now subject to very high levels of legal constraint and as a result have reduced their freedom of action (albeit usually in return for perceived economic or political advantage). At the extreme, some governments may have signed away certain instruments of implementation altogether – for example, as in the EU, by giving responsibility for trade policy to the European Community subject to agreement between the member states. More typically, the legal constraints on the use of force are not absolute, but they are backed up by a strong presumption of adherence to a collective position expressed through regional (NATO) or more general groupings (the UN). Equally, there can be powerful constraints on the use of diplomatic or economic contacts, for example in respect of Iraq, Libya or Yugoslavia where the UN has imposed collective restraint on its members from dealing with these so-called 'pariah states'.

Such legal and political constraints often intersect with important ethical considerations, promoted either by international humanitarian organisations or by non-governmental groupings. Ethical constraints on the use of foreign policy instruments are not new. Since the 1990s, however, international awareness of the implications and increased ability to exert pressure on most governments has given a new power to the humanitarian dimension. Governments are under greater pressure than before to assert the ethical dimension of their foreign policies, although as the British government found when it proclaimed an ethical foreign policy in 1997, this dimension is often difficult to pursue when commercial, political and other pressures run counter to it (Wheeler and Dunne, 1998).

If implementation is seen as a process of communication, then it is clear that in the twenty-first century, most governments have a wider range of possible instruments than ever before, ranging from weapons of mass destruction to the ability to 'sell' policy on the Internet. But it is equally clear that these instruments are subject to unprecedented awareness and institutional constraints. Put simply, it may be more difficult than ever before for governments to get away with anything. Not only this, but the unprecedented range of instruments demands new levels of coordination and continual evaluation. When foreign policy intentions can be conveyed at the press of a computer key or an aside to the global media 'circus', the onus on the policy makers to maintain control is heightened at the same time as the control becomes more difficult to achieve.

What results?

Our focus on the new and contemporary developments need not suggest that older, more enduring problems of FPI have disappeared. Rather, what has happened is a transformation of the context in which these arise. What does this mean when we evaluate FPI outcomes?

One immediate conclusion is that the persistent tension between the national and the collective in assessing foreign policy has taken on new forms. We noted earlier that this tension lies at the heart of notions of success or failure, efficiency and effectiveness in foreign policy. What is beneficial to the national interest of national welfare will often be at the expense of the more general good – a tension sometimes expressed as a conflict between communitarian and cosmopolitan perspectives (Linklater, 1998: 49–50). Traditional conceptions of FPI see no insuperable difficulty here, in the sense that foreign policy makers' priorities will always be determined by the national rather than the collective good. But the discussion above indicates that for many governments, the balance has shifted quite radically. Nowadays, it appears, there is often great difficulty in distinguishing between the national and the collective. Not only this, but the increasing power of international institutions and the decreasing self-sufficiency of many national societies means that often there is no choice for foreign policy makers but to implement policy through collective channels, judging its quality by the standards of collective effect and collective benefit. This is not to say that the tension has disappeared, but the balance for many countries and in many situations has shifted substantially. If the purpose of FPI is to safeguard national independence and autonomy, then it appears that the very mechanisms of implementation themselves are sometimes at odds with this aim.

A linked conclusion is that implementation of foreign policy often requires that it be 'sold' to a variety of audiences in a variety of institutional contexts – to such an extent that the effectiveness of the 'selling' is almost more important than the substance of the policy actions taken. Foreign policy in many countries has become more subject than ever before to the attention of the public and the mass media, and this has had an impact on the ways in which efficiency and effectiveness can be defined and pursued. To return to a point made early in this chapter, FPI has moved a long way from the idea of the 'chain of command' impervious to external pressures, and has become very much centred on coalition-building along several dimensions. Support has to be mobilised within government itself, a taxing task when implementation has to span many departments and agencies. Support has to be mobilised among the variety of domestic audiences who have views on the ways in which policy should be carried out. Finally, support must be ensured among the international audiences (often linked to governmental or domestic political groupings in the home country) whose approval and resources are significant to the achievement of policy outcomes.

If we accept this version of implementation, then it becomes very difficult to conceive of 'success' in foreign policy as the positive achievement of agreed objectives. Rather, FPI in many cases resembles a continuous act of negotiation on several fronts, with no final resolution of the central issues. Here, process is everything, and the balancing of commitments and capabilities referred to earlier in the chapter is an unending story, rather than a formula with a single solution. This is a rather indefinite form of conclusion, but it is important to an understanding of foreign policy in the twenty-first century. For most countries and their governments, at most times, there is no way in which, with one mighty bound, they can free themselves of international constraints or domestic limitations. Even governments that acquire substantial new assets, such as those which have developed nuclear weapons, find that they are in some respects less free than they were before, given the degree of international suspicion and institutional restraint to which they become subject.

It must not, however, be assumed that all governments are affected equally or in the same ways by these changes. After all, one of the main messages of this part of the book is that variety among states and the challenges that they face have increased. Chapters 1, 2 and 3 pointed out that while all states have been touched by transformation, the manner of change and the responses to it are, nonetheless, subject to variation, depending on the state or group of states under consideration. This applies no less to the implementation of policy. What was said in Chapter 3 about the 'core' and the 'periphery' in world politics and FPM is also relevant to FPI. In the core, implementation is likely to reflect the decline of military issues, the intensity of economic interdependence, and the density of institutional frameworks, while in the periphery, implementation is on balance more likely to reflect the persistence of military threats and the salience of military means, by perceived inequalities and dependency, and by the relative 'thinness' of institutional networks. It follows that at least in general terms, the two regions will demonstrate distinctive patterns not only of FPM but also of FPI. Sometimes, however, the pattern will be upset, as has happened in the former Yugoslavia, where conflict – and militarised foreign policy responses – have literally become implanted in the heart of Europe.

We conclude by noting a paradox at the centre of foreign policy outcomes. Although much of FPI in the twenty-first century is concerned with demands of international coordination (the building of institutions, networks and new kinds of governance), alongside this more particularist demands exist, of state-building, of national independence and of national security. Countries in the core tend to be preoccupied with the first of these tasks, while those in the periphery find the latter more of a burden.

Summary and conclusion

This chapter has dealt with four issues concerning the nature of FPI. First, it has linked images of implementation with those of policy making developed in Chapter 3, and shown how their assumptions condition the ways in which we assess implementation. Second, it has dealt with the question 'who implements?' and in so doing has stressed the importance of agency in the implementation of foreign policy. Third, it has illustrated the importance of instruments to the analysis of foreign policy, by evaluating the ways in which instruments are chosen, combined and deployed. Finally, it has examined the question of foreign policy outcomes, using criteria of efficiency and effectiveness, success and failure. Throughout, the chapter has emphasised the ways in which difference and variety are central to foreign policies in the twenty-first century, and has also noted the ways in which constraints on foreign policy actions are experienced in different ways by different sets of foreign policy makers.

This completes our setting out of the framework for analysis of foreign policies, which has been the purpose of the first part of the book. We now move on to explore a number of regional and national case studies, with the aim of testing the framework and demonstrating the difference and variety which are central to our study.

Further reading

The literature on foreign policy implementation is fairly slight and somewhat dated. Among the few treatments readers are advised to consult Clarke and Smith (1989), Lewis and Wallace (eds) (1984) and Smith and Clarke (eds) (1985). Given this dearth of material it is worthwhile also considering more general works on policy implementation, for instance Ham and Hill (1993), chapter 6 and Lane (1995), chapter 4.

References

Barston, R.P. (1997) *Modern Diplomacy* (2nd edition). London and New York: Longman.

Berridge, G. (1995) *Diplomacy. Theory and Practice*. London: Prentice Hall.

Clarke, M. and Smith, S. (1989) 'Perspectives on the Foreign Policy System: Implementation Approaches', in Clarke, M. and White, B. (eds), *Understanding Foreign Policy. The Foreign Policy Systems Approach*. Aldershot: Edward Elgar, 163–84.

Freedman, L. (2000) 'Victims and Victors: Reflections on the Kosovo War', *Review of International Studies*, **26**(3), 335–58.

Gelb, L.H. and Betts, R.K. (1979) *The Irony of Vietnam: The System Worked*. Washington, DC: The Brookings Institution.

Ham, C. and Hill, M. (1993) *The Policy Process in the Modern Capitalist State*. New York: Harvester Wheatsheaf.

Halliday, F. (1994) *Rethinking International Relations*. Basingstoke: Macmillan.

Hopkins, R.F. (1976) 'The International Role of "Domestic" Bureaucracy', *International Organisation*, **30**(3), 405–32.

Lane, J.-E. (1995) *The Public Sector. Concepts, Models and Approaches* (2nd edition). London: Sage.

Lewis, D. and Wallace, H. (eds) (1984) *Policies into Practice. National and International Case Studies in Implementation*. London and Exeter, NH: Heinemann.

Lindblom, C. (1959) 'The Science of Muddling Through', *Public Administration Review*, **19**(8), 79–88.

Linklater, A. (1998) *The Transformation of Political Community*. Cambridge: Polity Press.

Office of Information and Press, NATO (2001) *The NATO Handbook*. Brussels.

Smith, S. and Clarke, M. (1985) 'Foreign Policy Implementation and Foreign Policy Behaviour', in Smith, S. and Clarke, M. (eds), *Foreign Policy Implementation*. Hemel Hempstead: George Allen and Unwin, 1–10.

Smith, S. and Clarke, M. (eds) (1985) *Foreign Policy Implementation*. Hemel Hempstead: George Allen and Unwin.

Taylor, T. (1978) 'Power Politics', in Taylor, T. (ed.), *Approaches and Theory in International Relations*. London and New York: Longman, 122–40.

Wheeler, N.J. and Dunne, T. (1998) 'Good International Citizenship: a Third Way for British Foreign Policy', *International Affairs*, **74**(4), 847–70.

Part Two

Case Studies

5 | The Americas: the United States and Brazil

Michael Smith

The United States (US) and Brazil both occupy the American continent, although plainly the northern location of the former and the southern location of the latter marks a real distinction and brings with it important policy consequences. Moreover, the US is not only a regional actor in the Americas but also arguably the world's 'only superpower'. The emphasis in this chapter, therefore, is on what might be termed the 'politics of predominance' in US foreign policy and the ways in which this has changed during the post-Cold War period. As for Brazil, it is a large and potentially influential country, but one which has a rather different experience of change and challenge. Its domestic economic and political circumstances have been much more turbulent than its northerly neighbour and (also unlike the US) it cannot be regarded as a significant global actor. The foreign policy of Brazil is perforce one in which the regional dimension is the dominant trend.

Introduction

The Americas constitute, in terms of International Relations, one of the longer-established state systems in the world. Most (but not all) states in what is often termed the 'western hemisphere' came to independence during the eighteenth and nineteenth centuries, as the result of various processes of decolonisation involving the British, Spanish and Portuguese empires. The states that emerged were often the subject of military or other forms of authoritarian rule. A key feature of the Americas as a historical state system was, therefore, the unevenness of democratic rule and the variety of forms of government (Calvert, 1994: chapter 2). As the nineteenth century passed, a second key feature became apparent: the growing predominance of the US, both in economic and military terms.

For many states in the Americas, ranging from Canada in the north to Argentina and Chile in the south, the key foreign policy concern was dealing with the US. In fact, the Americas in some respects can be treated as a *domaine reservée* for the US, one in which Washington can call the shots and shape the terms of engagement with the wider world. The most explicit expression of this feature was the 'Monroe Doctrine' of the early nineteenth century, by which the US effectively declared South America 'off limits' to European powers. In the early twentieth century this was succeeded by the 'good neighbour' policy in which the US continued to exercise sway over the foreign policies and alignments of the lesser American states (Iriye, 1993; LaFeber, 1993).

At the same time, however, other processes of change and realignment were occurring. From early in the twentieth century, the development of 'inter-American' institutions took place, with a central place occupied by the Organisation of American States and various other legal and political agreements. This, of course, was in potential conflict with the reality of US power – a conflict between unilateralism and multilateralism which is still evident in the Americas today (see below). As the century proceeded, changes were also apparent in the political economy of the region. Most countries of Central and South America were increasingly classed as 'developing', as part of the 'Third World' or more recently as part of the 'global south'. During the latter part of the twentieth century this disparity between a highly developed North America and less developed Central and South America came to play a key role in the development of foreign policies, and increasingly it meshed with the development of world organisations such as the United Nations (UN) and their concern for global development issues. The tensions these disparities generated were exacerbated in Central and South America by the persistence of military or authoritarian rule alongside processes of global integration and development. After the Second World War, the relative insulation of the Americas from broader world political and economic processes was conclusively challenged, as the onset of the Cold War and the development of international business and other economic processes became a dominating feature. The end of the Cold War, in turn, highlighted the importance of democratisation, and thus gave added weight to a process that had been in train in Central and South America since the mid-1980s.

By the 1990s, in consequence, the Americas presented a picture of variety, albeit with certain predominant trends. The structure of power and its projection was unbalanced; the development of regional institutions was extensive but at least potentially in tension with the dictates of power; and the integration of the hemisphere into the global security and economic systems was again profoundly uneven. In terms of foreign policies, there was also a stark contrast between the essentially regional concerns of many countries and the globalisation of US foreign policy.

The foreign policy arena and the challenge of transformation

As noted above, the Americas, as a regional context of foreign policy, have a considerable history. By the 1980s, the trends and tendencies noted earlier were still apparent, but had taken particular forms under the influence of two key processes: the rise and decline of the 'second Cold War' during the early and mid-1980s, and the increasing influence of globalisation. The first of these processes was focused sharply by the posture of the Reagan administration in the US (1980–88), which created increased tensions and defined the US–Soviet confrontation as a global contest (Oye et al., 1983, 1987). For Central and South America, this posture meant that there was an immediate contradiction between domestic political and economic change and international alignment. The most severe examples of this conflict were to be seen in Nicaragua and El Salvador in Central America where domestic civil war was accompanied by external intervention on the part of the US.

The Americas also experienced the force of globalisation – or rather, a tension between regionalisation and globalisation (Smith, 2001a). During the 1980s, there was a persistent and growing attempt to create new mechanisms for regional economic and political cooperation. In the north, this took the form of US–Canada agreements on free trade, leading eventually to the establishment of the North American Free Trade Association (NAFTA). In the south, after the failure of some previous regional cooperation efforts, there was a wave of regional agreements such as those between the Andean Group and the members of MERCOSUR (the 'southern common market').

It was into this situation that the end of the Cold War introduced new regional dynamics and tensions. During the Cold War the US had been the central actor in the Americas, shaping the internal politics, economies and foreign policies of many states in the region. There were some exceptions to this pattern. Cuba under President Fidel Castro had, since the 1960s, relied on its alignment with the Soviet Union, both politically and economically. In the middle of the spectrum, some states had been relatively untouched by the Cold War and of these some (for example, Bolivia,

Colombia, Honduras and Venezuela) were non-aligned in the formal sense. Not surprisingly, therefore, the decline and then the end of the Cold War had a very uneven and often contradictory impact. For all of the countries in the hemisphere, from the US to the tiniest of Caribbean islands, the removal of the 'Cold War overlay' created both new opportunities and new challenges. To take one issue, how was it possible to proclaim non-alignment as a foreign policy strategy in a case where there was no longer a Cold War confrontation in relation to which non-alignment could be defined? Similarly, how could military rulers justify their continued hold-ing on to power if that grasp on power had been justified by the need to defend a country against communism? As a result of such questions there was persistent uncertainty about the relationship between political and economic development and regional security, and a lack of consensus in relation to the 'new security agenda' (Hurrell, 1998).

These changes have meant that all countries in the hemisphere have had to confront problems of 'transition' during the past ten to fifteen years (Dominguez, 1998). In some cases, this transition has been one predominantly of domestic political and economic structures. In other cases, there has also been a dominating need to redefine international roles and orientations. For all countries, there has also been a need to rethink the regional elements of their foreign policies: in Central and South America, the relationship with the US; in North America and particularly in the US the need to reconsider the role played by the country in the political, economic and security dimensions of the 'western hemisphere'. Around this, there has been the pervasive influence of the world economy. This had been felt as long ago as the oil crises of the 1970s, when a number of Central and South American countries suffered severe financial embarrassment as the result not only of oil price rises but also of accumu-lated debts. During the 1980s and 1990s, for many countries in the re-gion, the increased volatility of their linkages with the global economy was a fact of life, and this was brought home in no uncertain fashion by the global financial crises of 1997–98.

The Americas in the post-Cold War era have thus presented a distinct set of foreign policy challenges, but two central features have persisted: the unevenness of the power relations within the hemisphere, and the uneven impact of domestic change and development. The forces of glob-alisation and regionalisation have fed into this mix, to present a complex picture for all foreign policy makers. Although the 'western hemisphere' is home to one of the most venerable state systems in the world, this system has, since the late 1980s, been in a state of flux.

It is in this context that the chapter now undertakes two case studies: of the US and of Brazil. Although both are large countries in 'raw' terms

Table 5.1 A comparison of states in the Americas

State	Population in 2000 (m)	Surface area (thousands of sq. km)	GDP (purchasing power parity) in 1999 (US$ bn)	Military expenditure (US$ m) (year in brackets)
Argentina	37	2,778	367	4,300 (1999)
Bolivia	8.1	1,098	24.2	147 (1999)
Brazil	172.8	8,512	1,050	13,400 (1999)
Canada	31.2	9,976	722	7,400 (1998)
Chile	15.1	757	185	2,500 (1999)
Colombia	39.6	1,141	245	3,400 (1999)
Ecuador	12.9	283	54.5	720 (1998)
Mexico	100	1,972	865	4,000 (1999)
Nicaragua	4.8	148	12.5	26 (1998)
Panama	2.8	78	21	132 (1997)
Paraguay	5.6	406	20	125 (1998)
Peru	27	1,285	116	1,300 (1998)
United States	275	9,363	9,250	276,700 (1999)
Uruguay	3.3	186	28	172 (1998)
Venezuela	23.5	912	182	934 (1999)

Source: Central Intelligence Agency (2000).

(see Table 5.1) each has experienced the challenges outlined above in a very distinct way, and responded with equally distinct policy orientations and initiatives. For the US, as noted earlier, this might be described in terms of the 'politics of predominance'; for Brazil, the 'politics of transition'.

The United States

The challenges of transformation

At the beginning of the 1990s, it seemed to all appearances that the US comprehensively dominated global affairs. It occupied a pre-eminent position in terms of military power, technology, political stability and influence, and global economic reach. Not for nothing was the US described as 'the lonely superpower' during the last decade of the twentieth century (Krauthammer, 1991). That said, the 1990s proved to be a decade of uncertainty and questioning for many Americans. In broad terms, the challenges of the post-Cold War era were as demanding for the US as they were for other states.

The United States was not only involved in the Cold War, it was one of its progenitors, and the Cold War was for many years a central institution of American foreign policy. In a parallel fashion, the US was not only the world's leading economy, it was also the source of many of the institutions and processes which led to the development of the 'Western' economies in the Cold War period (and arguably to the 'underdevelopment' of many countries in the Third World). In many respects, then, the ending of the Cold War could be expected to usher in a period of profound uncertainty. This process, though, must be seen against the background of longer-standing and fundamental aspects of American foreign policy.

One of these long-standing features is the contrast in US foreign policy between 'isolationism' and 'internationalism' (Scott and Crothers, 1998). Given the geographical location and the continental scale of the US, it is perfectly possible to argue that the country can stand aside from the untidiness of the outside world, using its economic and political self-sufficiency as the basis for the construction of a 'fireproof house'. Soviet military power during the Cold War had challenged this assumption, however. With the ending of the Cold War, this threat disappeared but a new sort of challenge confronted US policy makers: in the absence of a Soviet threat, how might they maintain an internationalist outlook in the face of inevitable demands for a retreat and a 'new isolationism'? In addition, a parallel challenge was posed by the predominance of the US in the world economy after the Cold War. Although there were rivals here owing to European economic integration and the dynamism of Japan, the US still stood supreme as a national economic entity. However, this position was not one that fed incentives for a retreat from the world. Indeed, quite the opposite was true, given the increasing development of interdependence and interpenetration in the global economy. The question posed by this state of affairs was not how could Americans use their economic power not to create national self-sufficiency and a 'fortress America', but rather how could the US continue to engage multilaterally in a fashion that was both beneficial to the US and essential to the management of the world economy (Bergner, 1991; Thurow, 1992)?

Alongside this challenge of isolationism versus internationalism, there was another and related question that US policy makers had to confront. Given that the United States' pre-eminence rested fundamentally on its military might, how was that might to be used in the post-Cold War context? The confrontation with the Soviet Union had in many ways simplified the complex calculus of security and military policy, by reducing it to a bilateral contest. In the post-Cold War world, the new diversity of conflicts and the need for rapid and flexible response created a position in which at least some elements of US power were difficult to apply. To take only the most extreme examples, the vast nuclear arsenal possessed by the US was in many respects irrelevant to the type of conflict likely to be encountered in the former Soviet Union, post-Cold War Asia, Africa or indeed Europe. It was arguably more irrelevant still in guarding against the new security threats posed by non-state actors using unconventional terrorist methods (Garden, 2001a).

Related to this basic issue of the use of force, there was another: how were the Americans to reformulate their relationships with their Cold War allies, which had in many case been built on the dominance of the US in the Cold War and which expressed the kind of structural power essential to the exercise of international leadership? Was not leadership a different thing in the diverse and fluid post-Cold War era (Clark and Serfaty, 1991)?

Other challenges faced by the US were not abroad but at home. The consensus in favour of extensive international involvement, which had been maintained throughout the Cold War period, and which had led to a strong emphasis on presidential leadership in foreign policy (Brown, 1994), was not going to be easy to sustain in the new context. We have noted above the tendency towards isolationism in US foreign policy, and this was only likely to be strengthened by the relaxation of Cold War tensions during the 1990s. Given the argument made by many commentators that US foreign policy is primarily a reflection of domestic political needs, policy makers faced a major challenge of domestic adjustment and realignment (Scott and Crothers, 1998). This was given added point by the perception that in the aftermath of the Cold War, the US would be free to concentrate on the needs of the domestic economy – yet, as we have noted, the US economy was more and more dependent on international exchange and the management of interdependence.

A final set of challenges could be described as institutional. Domestically, the mechanisms for making foreign policy had been shaped and moulded by the impact of the Cold War. How were they to be reshaped for the post-Cold War era and amid growing globalisation in the world economy? Internationally, the US had grown accustomed to having its way in many international organisations and being able to shape their rules and operating procedures. In a way, the Cold War had trumped the normal course of events in inter-state relations, in which coalitions and processes of balancing could be mobilised against the potentially dominant power. Would this quasi-unilateral power still be available to the US in the post-Cold War period, and in the management of complex economic and social processes?

The foreign policy debate

The debates about US foreign policy in the post-Cold War period have been shaped, on the one hand, by the types of challenge outlined above and, on the other hand, by the impact of events. They have also been strongly affected by political change in the US itself, and the performance of successive presidencies. In this section, we will outline these elements, before moving on to look at the process and substance of foreign policy.

The challenges we have already outlined were picked up at an early stage in the foreign policy debate. The administration of George Bush senior (1988–92) was at the centre both of the radical transformation brought about by the end of the Cold War and of the turbulence in the global economy which was, in part, its consequence. The result was a curious amalgam of the trends towards isolationism and internationalism already noted. In a series of speeches and policy documents, the Bush administration set out the idea of a transformed international system, a 'new world order' which would rely for its stability not on the bilateral superpower confrontation but rather on the growth of regional and global institutions coupled with the reserve power of the United States as a type of 'global police force' (Mandelbaum, 1991; Pfaff, 1991). The idea of a 'new world order', however, contained a number of important contradictions between the building of new international institutions, the devolution of responsibility for maintaining order at the regional level, and the extremely uneven distribution of military power. The conflict which in many respects epitomised these contradictions was that centred on the Iraqi invasion of Kuwait in 1990. Here the US responded (after considerable domestic debate) to a regional challenge and acted with the support of a wide range of states in both Europe and the Gulf region. Saddam Hussein's defeat, however, led to a reluctant recognition that the American-led military action ('Operation Desert Storm') would have to be followed by a long-term military, economic and political containment of Iraq, something which has subsequently proven to be economically expensive and politically controversial (only the United Kingdom (UK) has, alongside the US, been prepared to police the 'no-fly zones' over Iraq).

The contradictions of the 'new world order' were also apparent from developments in the global economy. The increased mobility of capital and information, brought about at least in part by the development of technologies born in the US, meant that the United States was more than ever before subject to the fluctuations of the broader international economy. As a result, in the late 1980s and early 1990s there was a series of crises centred on the role and status of the US Dollar, in which it was demonstrated that the US simply could not be insulated from international trends.

This formed the context both for the defeat of George Bush in the 1992 presidential election and for the framing of new policies by the Clinton administrations (1992–96 and 1996–2000). President Bill Clinton had come to office on the basis that the key issue was the US economy, and thus in foreign policy terms that the main thrust would be in responding to the challenges of globalisation. The earliest debates in the administration were centred on the need for new commitment to international economic institutions, but at the same time a robust promotion of US national economic interests. The problem was that this only answered half of the challenge. Within months of assuming office, Clinton was grappling not only with the onset of new conflicts in Europe (specifically in the former Yugoslavia) but with the instability of the new Russian regime of Boris Yeltsin and the continuation of challenges in Africa (Somalia most notably). Once again, the debate became one in which the demands of domestic opinion for the 'quiet life' were juxtaposed with the needs of regional and global order (Smith, 2001b).

The net result of these debates was two-fold. On the one hand, the Clinton administration propounded a new foreign policy doctrine of 'engagement and enlargement', in which US engagement with regional issues and matters of world order was linked to the enlargement of the democratic world and to the expansion of international cooperation (Brinkley, 1997). At the root of this doctrine was the perception that the spread of democracy would in itself reduce international conflicts and the demand for US intervention, and that the engagement of the US with processes of reform on a global scale would create a far more robust basis for world order. But at the same time, it expressed the underlying perception that creating a consensus in the US for intervention through the use of military force or other forms of coercion was extremely difficult. The legacy of the Vietnam War was sharp and precluded the deployment of force without the most careful of controls through Congress. As a result, the use of force by the US during the 1990s was only possible in the most clear-cut of situations, where the moral force of arguments for intervention was at least as strong as the practical need to deter or defeat the adversary, and where the risk of American casualties was minimal.

At the same time, the debate about the US role in the world economy continued. The uncertainties of the late 1980s were gradually forgotten as the so-called 'new economy' seemed to make never-ending growth a real possibility. The influence of new technologies was widely seen as the foundation for a new form of US power and status, but this often missed the point that, as a result, the US was more closely integrated into the global economy. Debate thus centred on the ways in which the US could maintain its domestic prosperity while maintaining a commitment to international management and cooperation. In particular, there was a major discussion of the ways in which the US should deal with important multilateral institutions such as the World Trade Organisation (WTO), and with major partners and competitors such as the European Union (EU). The latter in particular was the source of a good deal of tension and recrimination, but this was accompanied by the growth of important institutional arrangements for the management of disputes and the promotion of joint actions (Guay, 2000; Peterson, 1996).

Finally, the US debate was informed by a perception that the regional and the global needed to be balanced and developed in tandem. During the 1990s, there was a partial retreat from direct US intervention in 'western hemisphere' conflicts (see the example of Colombia below), at the same time as there was a move towards increasing cooperation in economic matters, most obvious in the establishment of NAFTA (despite fierce opposition from groups in Congress that resisted the extension of trade privileges to Mexico).

In a way, the foreign policy debate in the US during the 1990s reflected a form of political and foreign policy transition, in which the principles of US foreign policy had to be reformulated to match the challenges of the post-Cold War era – and this seems to be an ongoing process. The coming to power of George W. Bush in January 2001 (the first Republican President for nearly a decade) signalled a further reformulation of principles. This has been marked by a shift away from the multilateralism of Clinton towards a clearer unilateral assertion of American national interests – or what some have claimed is a relapse into traditional, Cold War era security thinking (Daalder and Hill, 2001). In practice, this has meant a more critical attitude towards Russia, the identification of China as the main 'strategic competitor' of the US (with a consequent shift away from Europe and towards the Asia-Pacific region in American defence planning), and an eschewal of some of the cooperative underpinnings of the Clinton doctrine of engagement and enlargement (Kagan, 2001).

The foreign policy process

One of the most frequently used images of US foreign policy making is that of contest and struggle. Another is that of coordination and fragmentation. Both images arise from the ways in which the US constitution allocates responsibility for foreign policy, and from the evolution of American government more generally.

The US constitution, as in other areas, divides responsibility for foreign policy making. The President and the executive branch have responsibility for the operation of foreign policy and diplomacy, but this is subject to significant controls imposed by Congress. For example, in the conclusion of treaties, the President has the power to sign, but only given the 'advice and consent' of the Congress. On matters of armed conflict, the President is nominally Commander-in-Chief but under the 1973 War Powers Act (passed in light of the experience of the Vietnam War) Congress retains significant powers relating to declarations of war and the deployment of American troops. In trade policy meanwhile, the President, and (in this case) the Special Trade Representative have responsibility for conducting negotiations but do so only as a consequence of a Congressional mandate.

There are many other areas in which political control of foreign policy can be and has been contested, to such an extent that at times the constitution seems designed to prevent the US having a foreign policy at all. Major US partners have often found it difficult to work out exactly where and by whom foreign policy is being formulated, and there is built into the system a potential for risk-avoidance and resistance to innovation (Rosati, 1997). This brings us to the second major image of US foreign policy. In contrast to some other countries, the US government has often displayed important tendencies towards fragmentation in the formulation and conduct of foreign policy. Partly this is due to the sheer size and scope of the federal bureaucracy. Indeed, it was on the basis of US foreign policy that the notion of 'bureaucratic politics' was first developed during the early 1970s (Allison, 1971; Halperin, 1974), and during the 1990s and beyond this tendency has been underlined by the increasing complexity of the governmental process in economic as well as in security policies. In any given policy, there might be as many as a dozen agencies centrally involved, and although one will be the nominal lead, this is not necessarily a guide to the policy outcome. In addition to the formal departments of government, there is the apparatus of the White House, in particular the National Security Council and (new under the Clinton administrations) the National Economic Council.

Without going into an exhaustive description of the US foreign policy machine, it is important to note the ways in which the outline given here intersects with the processes of transformation in the foreign policy arena and the policy debates. There has been considerable debate about the ways in which the foreign policy machinery in the US needs reform to match up to the new realities of international life (Scott and Crothers,

1998). For example, in respect of national security policy, there has been a continuous discussion of the role and functions of the State Department and the Department of Defense, as well as of the Pentagon with its responsibilities for military forces. In the area of international trade and competition, there has been a parallel discussion of the ways in which the Department of Commerce might operate as a kind of 'department for international competitiveness' (Borrus and Zysman, 1992).

Around the core of the foreign policy machine, there has been an immense growth of specialised organisations, both within and outside government, pursuing specific areas of policy and acting as lobbies for particular interests. The net result has been a very major diffusion of many areas of international policy making, which in some cases has begun to involve 'sub-central governments' such as those of the states or even some cities (Hocking, 1993, 1999).

The substance of policy

In this section, the focus is on the substance of policy, in three respects: the global context, the regional context and inter-regional relations with major partners and rivals.

Let us first examine the US role in its global setting. We are concerned here to show how the US has responded to the challenges posed by the end of the Cold War and the demands of new types of conflict and co-operation. The disappearance of the Soviet Union in 1991, to be replaced by a set of unstable and in some cases warring states, has been a major shaping force in US policy. How has the US responded? The immediate response was to continue to treat the Soviet Union and then Russia as an 'adversarial partner' with whom major agreements could be worked out. This was particularly the case when it came to the politics of nuclear weapons. Whether or not it was still a 'real' superpower, the Soviet Union and then Russia had a large number of nuclear weapons and sizeable armed forces. So in the early 1990s, the US negotiated a series of arms control agreements with the Soviets/Russians, both on a bilateral basis and in the framework of multilateral institutions. These agreements dealt both with the specific US/Soviet Russian balance (as in the case of the Strategic Arms Reduction or START treaties) and with broader European issues (for example, in the Conventional Forces in Europe [CFE] Treaty). But there was a basic problem in dealing with the Russians as if they were still the Soviets: the Russian capacity to deliver on the agreements was strictly limited, and affected at many points by internal political and other factors.

The disappearance of the Soviet Union had other effects, including perversely a continuing search on the part of the US for new adversaries. This role was occupied for at least part of the late 1990s by North Korea, which was defined as a threat on the basis of its development of new missile technologies, and more generally there was a fear of 'rogue' states and terrorist organisations that might attack the American mainland or use terrorism against US citizens. The attacks on the World Trade Center and the Pentagon by terrorists aboard hijacked American airlines in September 2001 was a dramatic illustration of this threat.

These problems with disarmament and arms control and with perceived new threats were part of the rationale behind US moves from the late 1990s (first under Clinton and more so under George W. Bush) to create a new National Missile Defence – a project that raised sharp concerns in Russia and China and even among America's own allies in Europe because of its promise to create an effective defence for the US but not for them (*Washington Quarterly*, 2000a, 2000b). The more specific threat of terrorist attack, meanwhile, led, after the events of September 2001, to the mobilisation of an American-led 'coalition against terrorism', aimed, in the words of President George W. Bush, at winning the 'first war of the twenty-first century'.

Uncertainty and ambiguity about specific friends and enemies has meant that US foreign policy has been directed towards creating more general frameworks for security and stability. On the institutional front, the US was positively eager in the early 1990s to promote new institutions – or more accurately, new roles for existing institutions (Washburn, 1996). Thus the new activism of the UN in peacekeeping was supported, but not energetically enough to get Congress to authorise the payment of US back dues. One of the episodes in which US foreign policy had its fingers most severely burned during the early 1990s was in Somalia. This intervention, begun under George Bush senior, led eventually to humiliation at the hands of local warlords and to withdrawal, with concomitant effects on future US willingness to intervene where there was the possibility of major casualties.

The UN was also in a sense recruited in the cause of the 'new world order' when it came to the Gulf War in 1990–91. Here, the initial UN concern with regional peace and security was transformed into a US-led multilateral intervention force designed not for peacekeeping but for the fighting of a war. When it came to the former Yugoslavia meanwhile, the interest of the UN in regional peacekeeping and stabilisation could initially be seen by the US as a reason for abstaining from direct involvement, but eventually in 1994–95 the White House became much more actively involved in the promotion of possible settlements and in the use of force against the Bosnian Serbs. In so doing, it ran into constant conflict with the UN Secretary General and some Security Council members (Russia and China notably) who were less keen on the use of coercive force and wanted it linked strictly to UN Security Council mandates and authorisation. This proved a constant irritant to the US and in 1999 it intervened with force against the Serbian regime in the issue of Kosovo, this time without delaying for UN consideration. Here the US placed its faith in the more trusted organisation of NATO as a framework for military action. Two years later the US was to do the same, on this occasion in seeking military support for a mobilisation against the Taliban regime in Afghanistan, which was suspected of harbouring Osama bin Laden, the chief suspect behind the terrorist attacks on the World Trade Center and the Pentagon.

At the same time as the US role in the politics of global security has been evolving and, in some respects, was uncertain (or at least *ad hoc*), there has also been an ambiguity about its role in global economic institutions and what might be termed the 'new agenda' for international bodies. In many trade-related disputes, the US came up against its major allies in Western Europe and the EU (see below), and it was not always clear who had the interests of global trading regulation at heart. Without the US and the EU, no real progress in world trade is possible; but with them, any progress has been marked by continuous disputes and threats of trade wars (Guay, 2000). Likewise, in the area of international monetary policy, the US has sought to get reform through the International Monetary Fund (IMF) and the World Bank (both ironically headquartered in Washington, the US capital), but also was increasingly aware of the fact that European economic and monetary union might create a formidable competitor both in global institutions and in the more limited forum of the G-7 (Group of Seven industrial countries) (Bergsten, 1999).

In both the WTO and other institutions, the US was often concerned and confronted with so-called 'new agenda' items: for example, environmental issues, issues of international human rights and a wide range of social concerns. While in principle supporting the extension of international responsibilities in these areas, the US was often the major obstacle to global agreement. For example, in the aftermath of the Kyoto summit in 1997 on the handling of 'greenhouse gases', the US was unwilling to sign up to the central obligations because of domestic pressures to resist new environmental standards. In another case, the US refused to agree international proposals for an International Criminal Court on the grounds that it might lead to action against US military personnel which would undermine the supremacy of US law (Clinton belatedly signed up in one of the last acts of his second administration).

The general conclusion to be drawn from this review of some issues in the global context is that the US has found it difficult to reconcile the issue of world order with national perspectives, and that there has been a continuing tension between unilateralism and multilateralism in US policy. This links strongly with issues arising at the second level to be discussed here – the regional level. Here, the retreat of old-style communism (except in Cuba) and the democratisation of many countries with a history of military or authoritarian rule meant that the Clinton administration had an opportunity to create a new direction for policy. And indeed, there was an initial commitment to proceed with the building of new institutions on the principle of mutual respect and assistance. The Clinton administrations' focus on economic issues particularly, meant that there was a push to spread the benefits of open market economies among the Central and South American countries, many of which had a tradition of protectionism and state intervention. Thus, the aim of creating a Free Trade Area of the Americas (FTAA) was espoused, building on the more limited regional initiatives previously outlined, and developed through a lengthy set of intergovernmental negotiations (Wrobel, 1998), although on this issue Clinton was unable to get authority from Congress to pursue the initiative. More restricted trade liberalisation was projected with Chile (through membership of NAFTA), but this also was stymied by the lack of negotiating authority. The net result was that during the 1990s, little came of the US governmental initiatives, least of all at the grand multilateral level (Dominguez, 1998). More effective in many cases were either bilateral deals or the activities of private US companies taking advantage of newly-liberalised domestic economies.

Despite the prominence of economic issues, the western hemisphere did not cease to be a security issue for US foreign policy after the Cold War. The disappearance of traditional threats from communism or other political forces was replaced as the decade wore on by the need to counter a new form of security problem – the illegal trade in drugs and the criminal activities that were connected to it. In particular, the Clinton administrations became increasingly entangled with the fortunes of specific regimes in South America who were engaged in a struggle against domestic insurgents (often funded partly from the proceeds of the drugs trade) (Schoultz, 1998). This reached its most extensive level in US relations with Colombia; after increasing entanglement through the late 1990s, the Clinton administration in September 2000 entered into a new and far-reaching commitment which some saw as creating the possibility of a 'new Vietnam'. This was a paradigm case of the 'new security' agenda, with a domestic US problem (the market in illegal drugs) intersecting with a regional security issue (stability in South America) and the fortunes of a specific government (that of Colombia).

The third dimension of US foreign policy substance to be explored here is what has been termed 'inter-regional relations'. As noted in Chapter 2, in the foreign policy arena of the late twentieth and early twenty-first centuries, a major feature is the growth of regional organisations and agreements (see also Smith, 2001a), and this is a trend that US foreign policy has had to accommodate. Indeed, the US has been active in this area for many years and it could be said that the links between the US, the European Economic Community and NATO over the period since 1945 have displayed at least some of the characteristics of inter-regional relations. But for the most part those relations have been shaped by the structural dominance of the US and the exigencies of Cold War confrontation (Peterson 1996; Smith, 2001b). During and since the 1990s there has been a strong need to reorder these inter-regional relations.

This has been particularly apparent in the transatlantic relationships of the US with both the EU and NATO. The deepening of the institutional framework in the EU and the ongoing enlargement of that organisation have been a constant preoccupation of US policy makers. The administration of Bush senior, confronted with the European programme to complete the Single Market during the late 1980s, first feared a 'fortress Europe' and then realised that negotiation could get the US and its companies what they wanted. At the same time, the security implications of the end of the Cold War gave the Bush administration a reason not only to support European economic integration and to conclude a Transatlantic Declaration (December 1990) on the broad framework of relations, but also to respond positively to the development of the EU's Common Foreign and Security Policy after the Maastricht Treaty of 1991. During the mid-1990s the Clinton administration followed through by negotiating successive institutional agreements with the EU. The New Transatlantic Agenda in 1995 laid down principles of relations in more detail and was accompanied by an extensive Action Plan, while in the late 1990s further agreements on specific areas of joint action in regulatory and trade policy were concluded.

There was, though, a residual ambiguity about US policy, especially in the area of security and defence. As already noted, the US had to intervene in the affairs of the former Yugoslavia, at least in part because of the perceived shortcomings of European efforts. The logic of this situation was the need for a greater European contribution to conflict management and a commensurate rebalancing of the defence burdens within NATO towards its European members. Indeed, the so-called European Security and Defence Identity (ESDI) developed within NATO during the second half of the 1990s had been aimed at precisely these purposes. However, while Washington was prepared to endorse ESDI (not least, because it was housed within NATO and, therefore, permitted American oversight of the initiative), it was much less forthcoming when it came to the development after 1998 of a European Security and Defence Policy (ESDP) within the European Union. ESDP created some fears, both in the Clinton and George W. Bush administrations, that the Europeans would be able to go their own way in this vital area of US leadership (Garden, 2001b).

The other major area of development in inter-regional relations concerns the Asia-Pacific region. During the late 1980s, US policy makers had frequently observed that the US was not simply an Atlantic power, and that its trade and other relations with the Pacific Rim were more dynamic than those with Western Europe. In some ways, this was held over the heads of the Europeans as a veiled threat. The end of the Cold War, primarily (though not completely) a European event, diverted attention from this set of choices, but by the middle of the 1990s there was renewed evidence that the US saw economic cooperation (in the shape of the Asia-Pacific Economic Cooperation [APEC]) and even security cooperation (primarily with Japan) as a key area of development (Fukui and Fukai, 1998). Looming over all of this was the shadow of China, whose economic reforms during the 1980s had created the conditions for dynamic growth – and incidentally, a major trade surplus with the US. Under Clinton the need to accommodate Beijing, both in terms of economic relations (and thus for example membership in the WTO) and in terms of broader security concerns was central to US policies. It also presented the US with dilemmas over human rights, which through the actions of US domestic groups became linked with American trade concessions. Only in the later part of 2000 were trade relations with China put on a 'permanent normal' basis, alongside agreement on China's entry into the WTO.

In addition to these essentially economic considerations, American policy in the region has also been driven by long-term strategic calculations. Indeed, this has long been an area of considerable American military engagement whether in the shape of forces stationed in Japan or campaigns in the Korean and Vietnam Wars. During the Cold War period this engagement was shaped by a perceived need to curtail communist influence, be this Soviet- or Chinese-backed. In the post-Cold War period these calculations have applied less. That said, China has continued to be regarded as a regional hegemon and competitor to American interests. Under Clinton, policy towards China was based on engagement in order to manage this challenge. Under his successor, policy has shifted somewhat. Thus, in March 2001, Donald Rumsfeld, the Secretary for Defense in the Bush administration, presented a strategic assessment which suggested that China was to be regarded as America's principal potential adversary and that greater priority, consequently, needed to be given to long-range power projection forces capable of deployment in the Asian-Pacific region (Ricks, 2001).

One obvious conclusion emerges from this review of some major elements in US foreign policy. Compared with the relatively well-defined relationships generated by the Cold War, US policy makers have been confronted with new complexities. Their response to this changing context has often been creative, but equally often uncertain and contradictory. Some key principles of policy have been debated and expounded, but these principles have had to contend with new types of issue and relationship in a world where US primacy does not guarantee effective or coordinated policy. In this context, the meshing of global, regional and inter-regional processes has been a central feature, reflecting in fact the sheer range of US policy concerns and the centrality of the US to geographically wide-ranging processes of transformation. Overall, there can be few clearer illustrations of the ways in which foreign policy at the national level has to contend with a substantially transformed world, and of the complexities to which that gives rise.

Brazil

The challenges of transformation

Whereas for the US, foreign policy has reflected the 'politics of predominance', for Brazil foreign policy has been characterised by what might best be termed the 'politics of transition'. A series of changes both in the domestic and international contexts has created for the Brazilian governments of the 1990s and the 2000s a distinctive set of challenges.

To a degree, these challenges go back to the very origins of Brazilian foreign policy. In common with many other South American countries, Brazil gained its independence (from Portugal) in the early nineteenth century. The road to independence was unique, however. The Napoleonic Wars had led to the exile of the Portuguese monarchy, which had established the capital of its empire in Rio de Janeiro. Independence followed in 1822 upon a declaration of the Portuguese Crown Prince, and until

1889 Brazil was still formally a monarchy. Again, like many other countries in South America, Brazilian independence was qualified by the presence and the increasing dominance of the United States; a combination of the Monroe Doctrine and Brazilian introspection meant that for much of its history Brazil had a relatively unassertive foreign policy. The country was, however, an active participant in international organisations both at the regional level and at the global level (both in the League of Nations and the UN, in which Latin American states were a large and relatively homogeneous grouping) (Calvert, 1994: chapter 7).

The domestic politics of Brazil have been conditioned by three major features: first, the sheer size of the country, which is a federation featuring significant decentralisation of power; second, the demands of development, for a country very rich in natural resources but with great difficulties of infrastructure and communications; and finally, the interaction of the military and politics over a very long period of its history. Together, these features have made Brazil a major developing country, but they have also meant decidedly uneven development across the country as a whole. As a result, the potential of what is by some distance the largest country in South America has been largely unrealised, and Brazil has spent large periods in relative isolation (Wiarda, 1996: 136–41).

The challenge of Brazil as a 'sleeping giant' is thus one that has been confronted almost continuously throughout the history of the country (McCann, 1981; Schneider, 1976). As can be seen from the analysis above, the sources of this gap between potential and performance are both internal and external, and often these have been linked. This was especially the case during the Cold War years when military rule from the mid-1960s to the late 1980s, coupled with the burdens of development, created a situation in which there was a natural tendency to focus on the economic aspects of foreign policy, and on the ways in which this might be expressed through the UN in particular. This has changed somewhat since the end of the Cold War, and there has been an intensification of a number of the underlying challenges facing Brazil.

The foreign policy debate

Since the late 1980s, Brazilian foreign policy has been characterised by the dominance of four interrelated areas of debate. Two of these have been essentially external in origin but with strong internal dimensions: the debate about non-alignment and Cold War, and the debate about regional leadership and integration. Two others have been essentially internal but with significant implications for foreign policy: the debate about militarism and democracy, and the debate about political and economic transition (Calvert, 1994: chapter 2).

In common with most other countries of South America, the Brazilians experienced the tensions between non-alignment and Cold War alignment first as an external force and then as a domestic issue. The structures of domestic politics were, at least in part, a reflection of the ways in which the Cold War was defined. The dominance of the military in politics was in important ways justified by the need for domestic stabilisation and modernisation in the face of a threat from both communism and the US. Although there is debate about the extent to which the US influenced the installation of military rule in Brazil after the coup of 1964, there is no doubt that the military itself came to reflect Brazilian priorities rather than the needs of the US in the Cold War. From the mid-1970s onwards, there was a gradual *abertura* or 'opening up' of the political system, influenced especially by domestic economic needs in the context of the oil crisis and the increasing problem of debt. By the late 1980s, the way was open for the restoration of civilian rule, and for a new constitutional settlement which took place in 1988.

In a sense, then, the political transition in Brazil had begun well before the more dramatic transitions of the late 1980s and early 1990s in Europe or southern Africa. This transition has also affected the other 'externally generated' area of debate about foreign policy: the balance between regional leadership and integration in South America. Latin America in general has seen persistent attempts to foster regional integration since the 1960s, but these have been largely thwarted by two obstacles: the disparities between countries in the region, and related issues of economic and social development. In addition, militarism and authoritarian rule have fostered a tendency towards economic self-sufficiency and related attempts to protect domestic industries and producers. Brazil, on grounds of sheer size and potential as well as the possession of a sophisticated economic and political elite, has been a natural candidate for regional leadership, but this has been contained both by domestic preoccupations and by the lack of strong South American institutional frameworks (Selcher, 1981: chapters 4–6). As we shall see, the balance in this area has changed in recent years, but Brazilian foreign policy is still constrained by the tensions between a desire for economic and political pre-eminence and a felt need for regional institution-building – the latter often also conditioned by the desire for insulation from US foreign policy priorities.

As for the debate about military rule and democracy, this has often been very difficult to disentangle from external influences. As the military began to disengage from politics in the late 1980s, its position was also eroded by the onset of financial and economic crisis. The 1988 election was held in the context of an inflation rate of over 700 per cent, and the governments of the early 1990s proved incapable of stabilising the economy or reducing the endemic corruption that was central to political and economic life (Wynia, 1990: chapter 9). The process of economic and political transition that was in train had clear domestic roots but it was, at the same time, strongly influenced by the impact of the global economy. As the country was gradually stabilised in the mid-1990s, there was an opening up of the country – a liberalisation of the market and of trade policies, and thus a fuller integration into the global economic system. In turn, Brazilian security policy was the subject of debate, with a new consensus arising around the concept of 'sustainable defence' which sought a balance between state security and economic welfare (Fujita, 1998). It appeared that by the late 1990s, the process of transition was effectively irreversible, but this was before the financial and economic crises of 1998 and 1999 (see below).

This discussion seems to confirm that Brazilian foreign policy has been subject to important debates about the stability and development of Brazil itself. The transition from the Cold War to the post-Cold War era, from military rule to civilian rule and the continuing dialogue between leadership and integration in the foreign policy elite has been characteristic of a country in transformation. We shall now explore the extent to which these processes can also be observed in the making of foreign policy itself.

The foreign policy process

Brazil is a long-established state with a sophisticated political, economic and administrative elite. Thus it is to be expected that it would have a sizeable civil and diplomatic service. Indeed, one of the key features of Brazilian government over the years has been the large (some would say excessive) size of the bureaucracy at all levels. The Foreign Ministry has traditionally had a reputation as one of the better run and more effective parts of the government machine, but like foreign ministries in many countries, it has also had to cope with the fact that it is insulated from the political system, and thus relatively unknown or unpopular (Calvert, 1994: 45). The Defence Ministry, on the other hand, was central to the political process during the years of military rule, and was only 'civilianised' in the late 1990s. This meant that its status and links with the ruling elite were arguably more significant and sensitive than those of the Foreign Ministry.

Alongside the fact that the Foreign Ministry was relatively insulated from domestic politics for a long period, it is also clear that when it came to matters of economic development, the Ministry was in a secondary position. The central ministry in many ways was the Ministry of Finance, and the overriding emphasis on economic development and management meant that to a large extent foreign policy was run through the economic and financial apparatus of government (Coleman and Quiros-Varela, 1981). This is true of many countries where the vital national interest is defined as the maximisation of development potential. In Brazil, the fact that presidents rose and fell through economic management or through their relations with the military rather than through the conduct of foreign policy in the narrow sense gave a particular flavour to the conduct of diplomacy throughout the latter parts of the twentieth century (Calvert, 1994: chapter 4; Wiarda, 1996).

This did not mean that the Foreign Ministry was inactive. Both at the inter-American level and more broadly in the context of the UN, there was fertile ground for the making and conduct of Brazilian foreign policy. During the 1970s and 1980s there was a significant expansion of Brazilian representation abroad and of agreements with other countries, particularly in the developing world (Wiarda, 1996). In terms of the diplomatic network available to Brazilian foreign policy makers and the resources on which they could draw for international action, there has thus been a major bilateral as well as multilateral focus.

The broader politics of foreign policy in Brazil have reflected the balance between security and economic development. Owing to either military rule or the influence of developmentalism in the foreign policy context, there has been a tendency for parliamentary debate to focus on these issues at the expense of broader diplomatic considerations. But this is not the whole of the picture, and the growth of new agendas in foreign policy has meant that interest and involvement has grown in a number of key areas. For example, the growth of foreign direct investment in key regions within Brazil has meant a heightened interest in the negotiation of world trade rules and the working of institutions such as the WTO, alongside traditional lending agencies such as the IMF and the World Bank. At the same time, a growing interest in the politics of the environment among both central government and the federal states has created a more intense interest in international environmental regulation. Often, this has become politicised through the activities of both international and non-governmental organisations, who have found fertile ground for their activities over issues relating to the Brazilian rain forests and other sensitive habitats (Kolk, 1998).

The general picture of Brazilian foreign policy processes drawn here is of a relatively insulated 'core diplomacy' focused on the high politics of bilateral and multilateral agreements, but surrounded by a proliferating range of organisations, governmental and non-governmental, dedicated to issues of development, environment and related problems. This is not an unusual picture. But it is very different from the picture of the mid-1980s, when the Foreign Ministry, the Defence Ministry and the Finance Ministry were the key actors and the foreign policy process was effectively fought out between them. Brazil has long had a complex and capable foreign policy machine, but during the past fifteen years it has become increasingly embedded in a more networked and fluid environment.

The substance of policy

At least some of the substance of Brazilian foreign policy can be inferred from the discussion so far, especially in terms of the balance between military, development and diplomatic priorities. In this part of the chapter, we shall undertake a more detailed examination of four key areas: development policy, regional integration, regional leadership and multilateralism. It will be evident as we proceed that the challenges and processes outlined above cut across these policy areas in important and influential ways.

Let us look first at development policy. As already noted, this is central both to the domestic and international politics of Brazilian foreign policy. Prior to the 1990s, there had been a broad tendency to focus development policies on the achievement of self-sufficiency and the nurturing of domestic industries. There were strong elements of protectionism in the system, alongside large-scale government intervention in the economy, particularly in 'strategic' sectors. By the late 1980s, this set of policies was under increasing strain, and was failing to deliver economic growth or stability. When coupled with the broader development of the world economy and the globalisation both of investment and of production and exchange, it seemed that the Brazilian 'model' so much admired in the 1970s had reached the end of the road. A symptom of this was the massive overhang of government debt, exacerbated by the impact of successive energy crises on a country whose natural oil resources were small. During the early 1990s, the picture changed significantly, as the governments of Fernando Cardosa reformed the currency, opened up the economy to foreign participation and successfully generated new sources of energy either through the exploitation of oil and gas deposits or the development of alternatives such as ethanol fuel for automobiles (Wiarda, 1996).

It thus appeared that the Brazilian strategy was one of progressive integration into the global economy, and that this was producing progressive benefits. Two problems qualified this picture, however. First, increasing wealth was very unevenly distributed, both geographically and in terms of social class, across the country. Second, increasing integration brought with it increasing vulnerability (Rezende, 1998). The country was thus a potential candidate for domestic and international instability if things should go wrong. During 1998 and 1999, they did go wrong. A major financial crisis, following on from that of the Asian economies, threatened both the Brazilian currency, the Real, and the broader management of the national economy. Significantly, after a period in which the government attempted to deal with the currency problems through unilateral devaluation, the Real was propped up by a largely IMF initiative (Flynn, 1999).

A major factor conditioning the fate of the Brazilian economy during the turbulence of the late 1990s is the second concern of Brazil's foreign policy – regional integration. During the 1980s and early 1990s, the countries of the 'southern cone' in South America had created a growing organisation for the management of their economies through MERCOSUR whose members are Brazil, Argentina, Uruguay, Bolivia and Paraguay (Phillips, 2000; Tussie, 1998). This had provided the Brazilians not only with a framework within which to carry forward the internationalisation of their own economy, but also with an opportunity to increase their diplomatic influence in the region. When it came to the financial crises of the late 1990s, the MERCOSUR framework was tested almost to destruction, but despite a number of deviations from trade liberalisation and currency cooperation, it held together. The organisation also provided the Brazilians and others with the opportunity to develop a wider and more ambitious range of inter-regional relations, especially through negotiations between MERCOSUR and the EU which promised to produce a substantial liberalisation of trade between the EU and South America (Allen and Smith, 1998–2000). The EU itself had long been one of Brazil's major trading partners and one of the two or three most important markets for Brazilian exports. A key implication of (and motivation for) this diversification of Brazil's foreign economic policies was the desire to reduce reliance on the US and to give a bargaining lever against the US in trade negotiations. In the same spirit, during the 1990s Brazil played a key role in WTO negotiations, particularly in relation to agricultural products and investment rules (Flores, 1997).

The regional integration embodied in MERCOSUR thus interacted strongly with a third area of foreign policy – the search for regional leadership. Brazilian foreign policy has long been characterised by a tension between domestically-generated preoccupations and a more global focus stemming from development concerns and the desire for regional pre-eminence. This tension has not been absent in the 1990s–2000s, particularly as the apparent success of the liberalisation of the Brazilian economy has begun to be translated into political self-confidence and 'weight' among Brazil's neighbours. The need to deal with a number of pressing problems among all South American countries has led to a number of efforts at sub-regional cooperation, both political and economic, but one of the key constraints on all of these has been a lack of energetic leadership. It could be argued that this is a kind of 'automatic limiter' on South American cooperation, since the predominance of any one country is seen as a threat by all. But there is no gainsaying that Brazil is the obvious candidate if there is to be such a predominant power. By the late 1990s, the need to tackle problems of transportation and infrastructure, of the environment and of the illicit drugs trade, created a situation in which it could at least be argued that a new initiative might take off. A Brazilian initiative led in September 2000 to a meeting of twelve South American presidents, in the capital, Brasilia.

In addition to this multilateral initiative, the Brazilians have also been more assertive in dealing with a series of disputes over borders and other issues within the region. A vital component of this policy has been Brazil's more assertive line against American demands (for example, US threats of sanctions against regimes that have shown evidence of backsliding from democracy). The ambitious (and for some dangerous) US plans to support the regime in Colombia against a drug-financed liberation movement has also not been well-received in Brazil. Finally, the FTAA proposal of the Clinton administration (see above) was seen in Brazil as one that ought not to detract from efforts in South America itself towards free trade arrangements (Wrobel, 1998). On all these matters the tone remained one of 'quiet diplomacy' rather than unilateral assertiveness. That said, some may still detect the stirrings of real regional leadership ambitions.

At the same time as developing its regional role, the Brazilian leadership has continued to play an active part in global institutions, this being the fourth main concern of its foreign policy. Successive Brazilian governments have been very keen participants in the UN system, especially in terms of peacekeeping actions and development initiatives. Indeed, Brazil is often talked about as one of the prime candidates for permanent membership of the UN Security Council if that body were ever to be expanded. There is no doubt that from a Brazilian perspective, an active multilateral diplomacy is a primary aim of foreign policy, not least because it again plays a role in the conduct of a broader diplomacy and the diffusion of US influence.

The uneasy relationship between the Brazilians and their northern protectors/exploiters is, in fact, to the fore in areas such as global trade policy, where the Brazilians have played a major role in the coalition of agricultural exporting countries, and have also asserted their position in matters relating to information technology and investment rules. At the same time as Brazil has been keen to balance the US, it also views its northern neighbour as a vital source of investment and of high technology to promote international competitiveness. A similar tension has also been in evidence on environmental issues. Brazil has played a key role in promoting the international politics of the environment, most spectacularly through the hosting of the Rio Summit on environment and development in 1992 and through its continuing drive to balance the demands of fragile habitats against the needs of economic development and national security (Fujita, 1998). The US, however, has proven much less disposed towards these issues.

In summary, Brazilian foreign policy is characterised by an uneasy blend of qualities. The desire for economic internationalisation and economic and social development sits alongside – and often feeds off – the desire for influence at the regional level, and these two, in turn, sit alongside the pursuit of multilateral diplomacy and the search for prestige. This is the substance of Brazilian foreign policy. When coupled with the distinctive range of challenges outlined in the earlier part of this chapter, and with the changing nature of the foreign policy process, it suggests that Brazilian foreign policy has deep roots both in international developments and in the development of Brazilian political and economic life.

Conclusion

At the beginning of this chapter, we identified two contrasting images of foreign policy in relation to the US and Brazil: the 'politics of predominance' and the 'politics of transition'. This characterisation is not, however, straightforward. In important ways Brazil and the US typify both and not just one of these images. The US has had to cope with negotiating the transition between predominance in the divided world of the Cold War and predominance in a much more fluid and complex post-Cold War environment. While it would be wrong to assert that there was no hint of this problem of adjustment before 1990, it is equally clear that the conditions of the 1990s–2000s have placed in stark relief the policy predicaments that have arisen. In the case of Brazil, there has clearly been an important process of domestic democratic transition, with significant implications for foreign policy. But at the same time, this has impacted upon the longer-standing but still unresolved issue of regional predominance in South America.

Tellingly, the policy predicaments and responses of the US and Brazil have been interdependent, in the sense that they have reflected the historical and contemporary linkages between North and South America. But at the same time, they have reflected also the often dramatic unevenness of power relations and institutional development between the component parts of the 'western hemisphere', which create policy dilemmas and policy opportunities for both the weak and the strong. This context of interdependence and unevenness is not unique (consider also the former Soviet Union examined in Chapter 6), but there is no doubt that it gives a specific orientation to the framing of foreign policies in the transformed world of the Americas.

Further reading

The best quick source of reference for US foreign policy developments is the 'Eagle' series of books (see Oye, Rothchild and Lieber, 1983; Oye, Lieber and Rothchild, 1987, 1992; Lieber, 1997). A standard textbook is Kegley and Wittkopf (1996). The best journals are *Foreign Affairs* and *Foreign Policy*. For Brazil the sources in English are rather less plentiful and many of the texts are rather dated. For this reason, the best sources are journals such as *The World Economy*, *Third World Quarterly* and *World Development*. For both countries, the *Financial Times* and *International Herald Tribune* newspapers, as well as the weekly *Economist*, are excellent sources for day-to-day policy developments.

References

Allen, D. and Smith, M. (1998–2000) 'External Policy Developments', in Edwards, G. and Wiessala, G. (eds), *The European Union: Annual Review of Activities*. Oxford: Blackwell, various page numbers.

Allison, G. (1971) *Essence of Decision: Explaining the Cuban Missile Crisis*. Boston, MA: Little Brown.

Bergner, J. (1991) *The New Superpowers: Germany, Japan, the U.S. and the New World Order*. New York: St Martin's Press.

Bergsten, C.F. (1999) 'America and Europe: Clash of the Titans?', *Foreign Affairs*, 78(2), 20–34.

Borrus, M. and Zysman, J. (1992) 'Industrial Competitiveness and American National Security', in Sandholtz, W., Borrus, M., Zysman, J., Cocna, K., Stowsky, J., Vogel, S. and Weber, S., *The Highest Stakes: The Economic Foundations of the Next Security System*. New York: Oxford University Press, 7–52.

Brinkley, D. (1997) 'Democratic Enlargement: the Clinton Doctrine', *Foreign Policy*, 106, 111–27.

Brown, S. (1994) *The Faces of Power: United States Foreign Policy from Truman to Clinton*. New York: Columbia University Press.

Calvert, P. (1994) *The International Politics of Latin America*. Manchester: Manchester University Press.

Central Intelligence Agency (2000) *The World Factbook, 2000*. <http://www.odci.gov/cia/publications/factbook/>.

Clark, M. and Serfaty, S. (eds) (1991) *New Thinking and Old Realities*. Washington, DC: Seven Locks Press.

Coleman, K. and Quiros-Varela, L. (1981) 'Determinants of Latin American Foreign Policies: Bureaucratic Organizations and Development Strategies', in Ferris, E. and Lincoln, J. (eds), *Latin American Foreign Policies: Global and Regional Dimensions*. Boulder, CO: Westview Press.

Daalder, I. and Hill, F. (2001) 'Get Over It, Mr Bush – the Cold War Has Finished', *International Herald Tribune* (24 March).

Dominguez, J. (ed.) (1998) *International Security and Democracy: Latin America and the Caribbean in the Post-Cold War World*. Pittsburgh, PA: University of Pittsburgh Press.

Flores, R. (1997) 'Brazilian Trade Policy and the WTO 1996 Review', *The World Economy*, Special Issue 'Global Trade Policy 1997', 615–32.

Flynn, P. (1999) 'Brazil: the Politics of Crisis', *Third World Quarterly*, 20(2), 287–318.

Fujita, E. (1998) 'The Brazilian Policy of Sustainable Defence', *International Affairs*, 74(3), 577–85.

Fukui, H. and Fukai, S. (1998) 'The Role of the United States in Post-Cold War East Asian Security Affairs', *Journal of Asian and African Studies*, 33(1), 114–33.

Garden, T. (2001a) 'Weapons of Mass Destruction', *The World Today*, 57(10), 5–6.

Garden, T. (2001b) 'Through American Eyes', *The World Today*, 57(2), 7–8.

Guay, T. (2000) *The United States and the European Union: the Political Economy of a Relationship*. Sheffield: Sheffield Academic Press.

Halperin, M. (1974) *Bureaucratic Politics and Foreign Policy*. Washington, DC: Brookings Institution.

Hocking, B. (1993) *Localizing Foreign Policy: Non-Central Governments and Multi-Layered Diplomacy*. London: Macmillan, New York: St Martin's Press.

Hocking, B. (1999) 'Patrolling the "Frontier": Globalization, Localization and the "Actorness" of Non-Central Governments', *Regional and Federal Studies*, 9(1), 17–39.

Hurrell, A. (1998) 'Security in Latin America', *International Affairs*, 74(3), 529–46.

Iriye, A. (1993) *The Cambridge History of American Foreign Relations, Volume III: The Globalizing of America, 1913–1945*. Cambridge: Cambridge University Press.

Kagan, R. (2001) 'The World and President Bush', *Survival*, **43**(1), 7–16.

Kegley, Jr., C.W. and Wittkopf, E.R. (1996) *American Foreign Policy: Pattern and Process* (5th edition). New York: St Martin's Press.

Kolk, A. (1998) 'From Conflict to Cooperation: International Policies to Protect the Amazon Basin', *World Development*, **26**(8), 1481–93.

Krauthammer, C. (1991) 'The Lonely Superpower', *New Republic* (29 July), 23–7.

LaFeber, W. (1993) *The Cambridge History of American Foreign Relations, Volume II: The American Search for Opportunity, 1865–1913*. Cambridge: Cambridge University Press.

Lieber, R. (ed.) (1997) *Eagle Adrift: American Foreign Policy at the End of the Century*. New York: Longman.

Mandelbaum, M. (1991) 'The Bush Foreign Policy', *Foreign Affairs*, **70**(1), 5–22.

McCann, F. (1981) 'Brazilian Foreign Relations in the Twentieth Century', in Selcher, W. (ed.), *Brazil in the International System: the Rise of a Middle Power*. Boulder, CO: Westview Press, 1–24.

Oye, K., Rothchild, D. and Lieber, R. (eds) (1983) *Eagle Defiant*. Boston, MA: Little Brown.

Oye, K., Lieber, R. and Rothchild, D. (eds) (1987) *Eagle Resurgent? The Reagan Era in American Foreign Policy*. Boston, MA: Little Brown.

Oye, K., Lieber, R. and Rothchild, D. (eds) (1992) *Eagle in a New World: American Grand Strategy in the Post-Cold War Era*. New York: Harper Collins.

Peterson, J. (1996) *Europe and America in the 1990s: Prospects for Partnership* (2nd edition). London: Routledge.

Pfaff, W. (1991) 'Redefining World Power', *Foreign Affairs*, **70**(1), 34–48.

Phillips, N. (2000) 'The Future of the Political Economy of Latin America', in Stubbs, R. and Underhill, G. (eds), *Political Economy and the Changing Global Order* (2nd edition). Toronto: Oxford University Press, 284–93.

Rezende, F. (1998) 'The Brazilian Economy: Recent Developments and Future Prospects', *International Affairs*, **74**(3), 563–75.

Ricks, T.E. (2001) 'Rumsfeld Outlines Defence Overhaul', *Washington Post* (23 March).

Rosati, J. (1997) 'United States Leadership into the Next Millennium: a Question of Politics', *International Journal*, **52**(2), 297–315.

Schneider, R. (1976) *Brazil: Foreign Policy of a Future World Power*. Boulder, CO: Westview Press.

Schoultz, L. (1998) *Beneath the United States: a History of U.S. Policy Toward Latin America*. Cambridge, MA: Harvard University Press.

Scott, J. and Crothers, A.L. (1998) 'Out of the Cold: the Post-Cold War Context of U.S. Foreign Policy', in Scott, J. (ed.), *After the End: Making U.S. Foreign Policy in the Post-Cold War World*. Durham, NC, and London: Duke University Press, 1–25.

Selcher, W. (ed.) (1981) *Brazil in the International System: Rise of a Middle Power*. Boulder, CO: Westview Press.

Smith, M. (2001a) 'Regions and Regionalization', in White, B., Little, R. and Smith, M. (eds), *Issues in World Politics* (2nd edition). Basingstoke: Palgrave, 55–73.

Smith, M. (2001b) 'The United States and Western Europe: Empire, Alliance and Interdependence', in McGrew, A. (ed.) *The United States in the Twentieth Century: Empire* (2nd edition). London: Hodder and Stoughton.

Thurow, L. (1992) *Head to Head: the Coming Economic Battle among Japan, Europe, and America.* NewYork: Morrow.

Tussie, D. (1998) 'In the Whirlwind of Globalization and Multilateralism: the Case of Emerging Regionalism in Latin America', in Coleman, W. and Underhill, G. (eds), *Regionalism and Global Economic Integration.* London: Routledge, 81–96.

Washburn, J. (1996) 'United Nations Relations with the United States: the UN Must Look Out for Itself', *Global Governance*, **2**(1), 81–96.

Washington Quarterly (2000a) 'Is Arms Control Dead' (a collection of articles), **23**(2), 173–232.

Washington Quarterly (2000b) 'U.S. National Missile Defence: When and How?' and 'International Perspectives on National Missile Defence' (two series of articles), **23**(3), 79–194.

Wiarda, I. (1996) 'Brazil: the Politics of "Order and Progress" or Chaos and Regression?', in Wiarda, H.J. and Kline, H. (eds), *Latin American Politics and Development* (4th edition). Boulder, CO: Westview Press, 109–43.

Wrobel, P. (1998) 'A Free Trade Area of the Americas in 2005?', *International Affairs*, **74**(3), 547–62.

Wynia, G. (1990) *The Politics of Latin American Development* (3rd edition). Cambridge: Cambridge University Press.

The world wide web

The Brazilian Foreign Ministry can be found at <http://www.mre.gov.br/>
The US State Department can be found at <http://www.state.gov/>

Online US newspapers which carry a wealth of detailed and informed articles on American foreign policy include: the *Washington Post* <http://www.washingtonpost.com/>, the *International Herald Tribune* <http://www.iht.com/frontpage.html> and the *New York Times* <http://www.nytimes.com/>. A large number of think tanks produce online reports on American foreign policy. Among the best are: the Brookings Institution <http://www.brook.edu/>, the Council on Foreign Relations <http://www.cfr.org/p/> and the Woodrow Wilson Centre <http://wwics.si.edu/>. For electronic sources (many in English) pertaining to Latin America (including Brazil) see <http://www.zonalatina.com/Zlpapers.htm>.

6 | The Former Soviet Union: Russia and Ukraine

Mark Webber

Russia and Ukraine are the very embodiment of processes of transformation. Both are 'new' states in the sense that their contemporary standing is a direct product of the collapse of the Soviet Union in 1991. As such they have had to face a number of unique challenges, not least of which has been the fundamental task of defining the very orientation and goals of their foreign policies and accommodating themselves to the new international politics of the former Soviet region. Both states, however, have also brought with them preoccupations of longer standing. This is most obviously the case with Russia – a state which has inherited a good deal of the foreign policy concerns of the Soviet Union and which has (much like its Soviet forebear) sought to pursue a multi-regional, even global, policy that is in keeping with its perceived status as a great power.

Introduction: the emergence of Russia and Ukraine

Russia and Ukraine are direct products of two profound and far-reaching processes of transformation that have marked world politics since the 1980s. The first was the collapse of the Soviet Union in 1991, the multi-national state which had once confined both Russia and Ukraine, along with thirteen other union republics. As a consequence, these states have been affected greatly by the Soviet Union's various legacies, be these political, military, economic or geopolitical.

The second transformation of note is the end of the Cold War, an event which itself owed much to the role played by the Soviet Union in the final act of that 'war'. Innovations introduced by Mikhail Gorbachev – the Soviet leader from 1985 to 1991 – were central to ending East–West estrangement. His pursuit of 'new political thinking' revolutionised the nature of Soviet foreign policy and with it the landscape of international affairs. What had seemed permanent features of international life – the division of Europe into two militarised blocs, the partition of Germany, deadlock in matters of conventional and nuclear disarmament and super-power rivalry in the Third World – were all altered fundamentally in the space of six short years. Under Gorbachev, the Soviet Union began a military withdrawal from Eastern Europe, negotiated the unification of Germany with the other wartime powers, offered concessions that led to major arms control agreements in both the nuclear and conventional spheres, and scaled down its ambitions in the Third World, withdrawing in the process from Afghanistan and promoting political settlements to regional conflicts where previously it had been intent on military solu-tions. These acts had a two-fold impact. First, they created a spirit of compromise and cooperation with the West which formed an auspicious starting point for Russian and Ukrainian foreign policies. But second, they reflected a decline in the Soviet Union's superpower status, something that was to affect Russia's own actual and perceived standing in world politics.

The arena of foreign policy

The governmental and domestic contexts

The foreign policies of Russia and Ukraine, and indeed the other thirteen Soviet successor states, are in some ways similar, affected as they have been by the challenges of post-communist change – the 'triple transition' that has embraced nation-building, state-building and economic restruc-turing (Offe, 1991).

This transition, by no means straightforward even under fortuitous circumstances, has been rendered peculiarly difficult by the long experi-ence of Soviet rule. Take, for instance, the process of nation-building – the creation of a shared or dominant national identity among the population of a state. Here, the Soviet legacy has been particularly profound. Several of the successor states (for instance, Belarus and the states of Central Asia) contain populations with no prior experience of independence and with only a nascent sense of national identity. Others occupy borders that enclose a patchwork of ethnic groups, the result either of arbitrary Soviet nationalities policies (as in the cases of Azerbaijan and Georgia) or Soviet territorial acquisition (Moldova). In these cases, the assertion of a national identity, while aiming to weld together a majority population, has served also to alienate ethnic minorities thereby exacerbating violent civil conflicts. Russia and Ukraine too have faced difficulties. Their political leaderships had been a part of the Soviet communist hierarchy and had played a decisive part in engineering the transfer of power away from the Soviet central authorities in 1991. To give legitimacy to this initial process of separation and then to forge post-communist political consolidation has required the articulation of specifically Russian and Ukrainian notions of national identity and interest. In neither case, however, have such formulations proven straightforward. Ukrainian nation-building has the ostensible advantage of being able to draw upon some experience of independence, most recently in 1917–19. However, it has also had to labour under the weight of long periods of what was, in effect, Russian rule (in its Soviet and, prior to that, Tsarist forms) and has had to deal with the presence of a large ethnic Russian minority. As for Russia itself, its population has experienced a deep confusion. Not only has a peculiarly Russian national identity had to be resurrected (this having been subsumed for decades under the artifice of a Soviet identity), but Russians have also had to cope with the disorienting effects occasioned by the loss of the Soviet Union's International Status (Light, 1996: 36–7).

State-building has been no easier. The domestic dimension of this process – the establishment of internal sovereignty – requires the formation of a coercive apparatus, credible political institutions, and, ultimately, the embedding of a form of governance based not simply on power but on authority and legitimacy. Upon independence few of the Soviet successor states were well prepared for this momentous task. Some of the institutional attributes of statehood (parliaments, government agencies, etc.) did exist but these required restructuring or even abolition having long been conduits of Soviet rule. Where such institutional redesign has occurred (including in both Russia and Ukraine) it has often overlapped with reforms that have introduced a form of democracy. The twin processes of institutional change and partial democratisation, however, have not always been in harmony, and have on occasion given rise to crude institutional competition, unpredictable policy-making routines and an absence of consensus on the ground rules of politics. In such circumstances an imperfect resolution has invariably been found in a considerable concentration of formal political power and decision-making authority around Presidential leaders (Malcolm and Pravda, 1996: 9).

Turning to economic restructuring, here too the successor states have laboured under immense difficulties. The Soviet legacy of inter-republican interdependence has created a seemingly strong imperative for cooperation in areas of energy, transportation, trade and so on. Yet in these fields some successor states have been better blessed by the Soviet inheritance than others. Resource endowments, infrastructure and skilled personnel are unevenly spread throughout the territory of the former Soviet Union (FSU). When coupled with the politically-driven imperative of establishing economic viability, interdependence has tended to give rise not to harmonious economic interactions but rather to friction, competition and strategies of diversification.

The three tasks associated with the triple transition are important not only because they carry obvious domestic repercussions but because they have significant foreign policy implications. Three general phenomena can be noted in this regard. The first is a tendency towards what Robert Levgold (1992: 151–7) has dubbed 'inchoate foreign policies', characterised by conceptual underdevelopment, unpredictability and an uncertain sense of place and purpose in international affairs.

The second relates to the 'war behaviour of newly or partially democratising states' (Snyder, 1996: 22). According to Jack Snyder, democratising states (and, indeed transitional states in general) are much more likely to engage in bellicose foreign policies than either established democracies or even stable authoritarian regimes. The reasons for this are many. 'Pull' factors include the inability of a volatile public opinion, underdeveloped institutions and immature democratic norms to act as constraints on the war making of the state. 'Push' factors, meanwhile, involve the growth of an exaggerated nationalism in the early stages of nation- and state-building, overbidding in foreign affairs by ruling elites in response to the new demands of competitive politics, and the temptation of leaderships to engage in diversionary foreign adventures to compensate populations experiencing the ill-effects of economic dislocation (Snyder, 1996: 24–31). Snyder is careful to point out that the relationship between democratisation and war is a qualified one. Democratisation also has an in-built logic towards more benign foreign policies, for its political (and economic) challenges compel political elites to concentrate on onerous internal tasks, while at the same time providing troubled populations with the safety valve of domestic political participation to voice their grievances. Nevertheless, there is some evidence from among the successor states to support the thesis of war proneness. An undeclared war between Armenia and Azerbaijan, Moscow's military interference in Georgia and Moldova, and periods of high tension between Russia and Ukraine are all suggestive in this regard (Snyder, 1996: 21, 29).

A third and final effect is economic in origin. The general economic plight of the successor states noted above, has forced them to pursue a 'diplomacy of aid' – a search for economic assistance, external investment and market access aimed at assisting the tasks of economic regeneration and market reform (Skak, 1996: 51). Again, there have been variations in the level of enthusiasm with which such policies have been pursued, but even the most autarchic and backward looking of the successor states (notably Belarus) have not eschewed the strategy altogether. Others (including, as we shall see below, Russia and Ukraine), have been more forthcoming.

The international context

As well as the effects upon foreign policy derived from the domestic context, the post-Soviet international context has also had an obvious impact on the foreign policies of the successor states.

One set of effects in this regard concerns the legal and material consequences of the Soviet Union's dissolution. This collapse, as it unfolded during 1991, was met with an increasing sense of unease, particularly among Western states concerned at the consequences of the Soviet Union's withdrawal from international affairs. Such disquiet was partly alleviated by Russia's declared status as a 'continuing state', something that conferred upon it instant membership of international organisations and all the treaty and other obligations formerly borne by the Soviet Union. This seemingly tidy legal process was not, however, trouble free. It occasioned some resentment among the successor states as Russia used its new position to acquire former Soviet assets such as ministries (conveniently located in Moscow, the Soviet and now Russian capital), foreign currency accounts, and embassies and consulates abroad. It also left unresolved how certain commitments were to be met, particularly in the field of arms control, where treaty-limited military assets were not just located in Russia but distributed throughout several states in the FSU.

A second and more lasting consequence of Soviet dissolution was the creation of an entirely new geopolitical space on the Eurasian continent. Upon its formation, this region of fifteen successor states was heralded as a potentially huge source of instability, the equivalent of a 'geostrategic hole' that would be characterised by internal conflicts and inter-state wars (Karaganov, 1992: 122). And, in part, this gloomy scenario has been accurate. Civil wars erupted in Moldova, Tajikistan and Georgia in the early 1990s, and a *de facto* state of war has existed between Armenia and Azerbaijan throughout the post-Soviet period. In addition, less violent disputes have been a common, even defining feature of relations among the successor states. Squabbles over borders, the rights of ethnic minorities, access to resource endowments and the military spoils of the former Soviet Red Army have involved virtually all of the successor states at one time or another.

The disputatious nature of inter-state relations within the FSU has also been apparent in the so far underdeveloped character of multilateral arrangements. The most ambitious of these is the Commonwealth of Independent States (CIS), the intergovernmental body established at the end of 1991 that has come to embrace all the successor states bar the Baltic countries of Estonia, Latvia and Lithuania. This body has failed to live up to the promise inherent in its declaratory statements and treaties. The CIS has been the testing ground for several grand schemes related to military cooperation and economic integration, yet these have developed in a rather erratic and unaccomplished fashion. The CIS has been bedevilled by irreconcilable differences of opinion among its members; there is no shared ideology, common perception of an external threat or agreement on the priorities of economic coordination (Sakwa and Webber, 1999).

More regionally-based forms of cooperation also exist, some more effective and concrete than others. While these have arisen in a myriad of different shapes, two basic arrangements have been evident: first, sub-groups of states with a close link to the CIS proper (as in the case of the Community of Integrated States comprising, upon its formation in March 1996, Russia, Belarus, Kazakhstan and Kyrgyzstan); and second, cooperative structures with no organisational connection to the CIS framework. These include distinct regional bodies embracing respectively the states of the Baltic region and Central Asia, plus more geographically diverse organs such as the 'GUUAM' (Georgia, Ukraine, Uzbekistan, Azerbaijan and Moldova) arrangement, which is defined principally by a common desire among its members to distance themselves from the Russian-dominated CIS.

With the possible exception of the Baltic case, these sub-CIS organisations have developed only slowly. In fact, in the post-Soviet period, the strongest trend among the successor states has been towards the consolidation of bilateral relations, something that has resulted in the establishment of a dense network of agreements and cooperative practices throughout the FSU. In some instances these have complemented CIS and regional mechanisms, but, overall, they have had the effect of supplanting them. On issues such as border recognition, minority rights, and military and economic cooperation, bilateralism has come to be viewed both by Russia and the other successor states as a more reliable method of conducting inter-state business. This situation has pertained both in cases where relations have been amicable (for instance, bilateral ties between Russia on the one hand and Armenia, Belarus and Tajikistan on the other) and in cases of relative friction (as we shall see below, Russia and Ukraine have eschewed the CIS as a forum for reconciling their differences, preferring instead direct negotiations).

The bulk of these bilateral ties have centred on Moscow, something that alerts us to a final, very important characteristic of the FSU region: the preponderant weight within it of one state. Among the successor states Russia stands apart. It is the largest, most populous, best endowed of resources and carries with it the history of centuries of dominance over its immediate neighbours (see Table 6.1). As we shall see below in our

Table 6.1 A comparison of the Soviet successor states

State	Population in 2000 (m)	Surface area (thousands of sq. km)	GDP (purchasing power parity) in 1999 (US$ bn)	Military expenditure (US$ m) (year in brackets)
The Slavs				
Belarus	10.3	207	55.2	156 (1998)
Russia	146	17,075	620.3	4,200 (1998)
Ukraine	49	603	109.5	500 (1999)
The Baltics				
Estonia	1.4	45.2	8	70 (1999)
Latvia	2.4	64.5	9.8	60 (1999)
Lithuania	3.6	65.2	17.3	181 (1999)
Central European				
Moldova	4.4	33.8	9.7	6 (1999)
The Transcaucasians				
Armenia	3.3	29.8	9.9	75 (1999)
Azerbaijan	7.7	86.6	14	121 (1999)
Georgia	5	69.7	11.7	27 (1999)
The Central Asians				
Kazakhstan	16.7	2,717	54.4	322 (1999)
Kyrgyzstan	4.7	198	10.3	12 (1999)
Tajikistan	6.4	143	6.2	17 (1997)
Turkmenistan	4.5	488	7.7	90 (1999)
Uzbekistan	24.7	447	59.3	200 (1997)

Sources: Central Intelligence Agency (2000); Hill (2001).

consideration of Russian foreign policy, these circumstances have not generated an irresistible proclivity towards expansionism, for Russia is at the same time subject to powerful constraints upon its actions. Nonetheless, the imbalance of power has meant that Russia represents at least a potential hegemon. This creates a constant wariness among the successor states of Russia's intentions and has forced upon all of them the task of elaborating strategies aimed at dealing with their powerful neighbour. As the preceding analysis has implied, the response has not been uniform. Some (Armenia, Belarus and Tajikistan) have 'bandwagoned', that is, they have forged a close relationship with Moscow, this being seen as the safest and surest route for the protection of their economic and security interests. Others, for instance the Baltic states, have sought to reorientate themselves as far as possible away from Russia. The remainder (Ukraine included) have followed a more balanced approach – distancing themselves from Russia where their resources and geopolitical position permits, yet when necessary (or unavoidable) maintaining ties to Moscow.

The region of the FSU, then, can be said to exist as an emerging 'international sub-system' (Levgold, 1992: 158). This has not, however, precluded meaningful interaction of the successor states with the wider world. Such a process has, in fact, been far-reaching and is accounted for by five separate factors. First, the looseness of institutionalised cooperation within the FSU itself, something that increases the pull of external diversification. Second, a desire common among new states to obtain recognition of their independent identity through participation in the international community. Third, the proximity of the successor states to other regional sub-systems. Fourth, the deliberate courting of the successor states by regional powers and international organisations. And fifth, the greater incorporation of the successor states into the world capitalist system as a consequence of economic transition.

This five-fold process has given rise to three distinct, sometimes overlapping patterns of interaction. The first, 'internationalisation', simply refers to the legal incorporation of the successor states into international affairs (Motyl, 1991: 6). The peculiar circumstances pertaining to Russia have already been referred to. The other fourteen former Soviet republics, while not enjoying the privileges accorded to Moscow, have experienced a relatively straightforward entry into the world of states. The West, it is true, did lay down in late 1991 certain guidelines by which diplomatic recognition would be conferred. However, these were effectively swept aside once the inevitability of the Soviet Union's demise had become apparent. Recognition thereafter was swift and comprehensive. In parallel, the successor states were also granted membership of both the United

Nations (UN) and the Conference (now Organisation) on Security and Cooperation in Europe (CSCE/OSCE).

The second pattern is regional in nature and refers to relations between the successor states and geographically adjacent countries outside the FSU. In this connection four distinct groupings have emerged, plus the unique case of Russia (Webber, 1996: 110–11). The first is the Baltic states, a group which has considered itself part of the European mainstream, which has cultivated close ties to its Nordic neighbours and which has made a loud claim to membership of both NATO and the European Union (EU). The second group comprises Moldova, Ukraine and Belarus. The latter excepted, this group has aspired to heightened involvement in Euro-Atlantic structures. Geographic proximity and ethnic and territorial issues, however, have also dictated a close attention to Eastern Europe. The Transcaucasian states of Armenia, Azerbaijan and Georgia constitute a third group. These have laboured under fairly concrete geopolitical constraints: isolated from major sea routes (a particular problem for oil-rich Azerbaijan), bounded by influential neighbours (Turkey and Iran, as well as Russia) and occupying an ambiguous position that straddles Europe and Asia. The fourth group, the Central Asian states of Kazakhstan, Kyrgyzstan, Tajikistan, Turkmenistan and Uzbekistan, holds the most distinctively extra-European position of the successor states. Initially considered susceptible to the competing influences of Iran, Turkey and Pakistan, these states have in fact distanced themselves from a specific-ally 'southern' orientation in foreign policy. Many traditional economic and military links to Russia have been retained (especially so in the case of war-wracked Tajikistan). Assisted by ample endowments of energy, Kazakhstan, Turkmenistan and Uzbekistan have also attracted increasing amounts of Western (and, to some degree, Chinese) attention. Fifth is Russia, a state that constitutes a case apart. Its geographic enormity and physical dominance of the Eurasian continent has necessitated a foreign policy that, alone among the successor states, is truly 'multi-regional' in character, sensitive simultaneously to Europe, the Middle East, the Indian sub-continent, China and the Asia-Pacific region (Lukin, 1994: 109).

Finally, the third pattern of interaction refers to important bilateral relationships that depend less on geography and more on an assumed sense of status. Again, Russia is of particular significance. It has attempted to maintain the Soviet Union's position as the principal interlocutor of the US while at the same time seeking privileged positions *vis-à-vis* both Europe and China. Ukraine, for quite different reasons, has also solicited special relationships with Washington and European capitals.

The foreign policy of Russia

The challenges of transformation

Upon its emergence from the Soviet Union, Russia at first sight appeared to be well situated. Gorbachev's foreign policy reforms had rescued Russia from many of the burdens that had long plagued Soviet foreign policy: expensive commitments in the Third World, and a military and political occupation of Eastern Europe that had contributed to military confrontation with the West. Moreover, the relative international amity that prevailed at the point of Soviet dissolution, held out great promise for Russia. With the Cold War at an end and relations with China also substantially improved, the Russian leadership did not have to deal with the scenario that had long preoccupied its Soviet predecessors – global encirclement and nuclear war. In such conditions, Moscow was also presented with the realistic possibility of integrating itself fully into international institutional structures, a state of affairs that meant the testing but nonetheless welcome foreign policy task of securing for itself a position as an equal and not a subordinate member of the post-Cold War order (Kozyrev, 1992).

Alongside these positive aspects, it was clear that the process of transformation had also affected Russia in a more taxing manner. Its geopolitical location, for instance, had been radically altered from that of the Soviet Union. The Gorbachev-initiated withdrawal from Eastern Europe, followed subsequently by the Soviet dissolution, not only gave rise to a diversity of newly assertive states around Russia's borders, it also had the effect of transporting Russian territory away from Europe, in the process highlighting Russia's continued presence in Asia. Indeed, Russia, for all its size as the largest of the successor states, had become a truncated version of both the Soviet Union and Tsarist Russia, occupying a space equivalent to the Russia of the mid-1600s. This attenuation has meant the reversal of a centuries-long historical trend of first Tsarist and then Soviet expansionism. Russia has consequently 'lost' parts of its historic core (Ukraine and Belarus), has been denied easy access to important strategic outlets (the Baltic, Black and Caspian Seas) and has found its westernmost territory, Kaliningrad, separated from the main territory of the Russian state. Taken together, these various challenges have raised important questions pertaining to Russia's foreign policy orientation and, indeed, the very essence of its national identity. Is Russia to define itself as a European or Asian power, or some amalgamation of the two? What is Russia's standing in the international system? Having inherited only the shell of the Soviet Union's superpower status, can Russia still claim to be at least a great power? And how is Russia to act in its adjacent territories? Given that Russian identity had for so long been bound up with the existence of an empire (whether in its Tsarist or Soviet guises), has Moscow been willing or, indeed, able to eschew an imperial role?

The foreign policy debate

The very basic nature of these questions has ensured that debate in Russia on foreign policy has tended, at times, to be both anguished and polarised. The debate was at its most passionate during 1992, the initial, formative year of Russian foreign policy. The position of the leadership at this point, personified by President Boris Yeltsin and his Foreign Minister Andrei Kozyrev, was referred to as 'Atlanticist' or 'Westernist' in orientation. Several reasons account for this stance. In domestic terms, it reflected the political and economic transitions then in full flow. The early democratic aspirations of the Yeltsin leadership and the desire for economic reform and external assistance required cultivation of the West. As Yeltsin explained in February of that year, two primary tasks faced Russian foreign policy: to secure Russia's entry into the 'civilised community' of states and 'to enlist maximum support for our efforts to transform Russia' (Yeltsin, 1992: 70). Westernism, moreover, was also the course of least resistance for an inexperienced foreign policy. Consolidating a sound relationship with the Western states would, Yeltsin explained, be a basis upon which relations could subsequently be built with other states, be these 'in the West or East, Europe or Asia' (cited in Crow, 1994: 1–2). Cooperation, finally, was also calculated to affirm Russian status. Rather than being measured by its ability to stand up to the West, Russia's influence, Kozyrev argued, should best be judged by its willingness to join it in defence of the common principles of democracy, market economics and human rights.

This leadership position did not go unchallenged. In fact, several schools of thought crystallised during 1992. It would be inaccurate to say that these groups were united in their opposition to the Yeltsin/Kozyrev line, ranging as they did from 'patriotic' neo-communists and nationalists at one end of the spectrum to moderate liberals at the other, with moderate conservatives somewhere in the middle (Arbatov, 1997: 136–7). Their positions did, however, offer some common points of attack. The Yeltsin administration's early foreign policy was criticised for: its failure to articulate a clear version of Russian national interests; an absence of initiatives on important issues of post-Cold War international politics (conflict resolution, arms control, the adaptation of international organisations); and, most tellingly, its over-concentration on relations with the West, something that had resulted in the two-fold impression that Moscow was too willing to make unilateral concessions and that it had neglected other important areas of policy, principally in the FSU region.

The severity of these charges meant that throughout 1992 the differences between the leadership and its critics appeared beyond reconciliation. However, during the course of the following year a tentative consensus was reached among elite opinion as the Yeltsin team moved closer to the centre, in the process diluting its initial liberal stance and absorbing positions associated with the moderate conservative outlook (Arbatov, 1997: 143). Several reasons account for this shift. The foreign policy consequences of domestic political competition were noted above as a general phenomenon in democratising states and such dynamics appear relevant in the Russian case. Disillusionment with economic reform and an under-institutionalisation of the Russian political system (apparent during 1992–93 in a series of constitutional clashes between President and parliament, and a volatile party system) fed a heightening of nationalist themes as competing groups sought to win over the loyalty of the electorate. The defining moment in this regard was the elections of December 1993 to the new State Duma (the Russian parliament's lower chamber formed following Yeltsin's dissolution of its predecessor, the Russian Congress of Peoples Deputies). The strong showings of the ultra-nationalist Liberal Democratic Party and the Communist Party of the Russian Federation seemingly indicated to Yeltsin (mindful of his own re-election prospects) the domestic political benefits of a hardened foreign policy. Electoral factors are, however, only part of the explanation. Equally important, Yeltsin calculated that a shift in foreign policy would broaden his political base among influential sections of state and society – industrial managers, the military and security establishments and the government bureaucracy. This would serve to promote domestic stability while also bringing to foreign policy the sense of unity and effectiveness necessary to restore Russian influence abroad (Malcolm, 1994: 28–32). Finally, external factors also had an impact. The initial two years of foreign policy led Yeltsin and Kozyrev, independently, to arrive at a more hard-nosed assessment of Russian interests. In short, the external environment had proven less beneficial than originally supposed. Expectations of substantial Western assistance, of Western sympathy towards Russian security interests, and of 'good-neighbourly' relations with the successor states seemed, from the Yeltsin administration's point of view, to have materialised only in part, thus illustrating the need for a modification of foreign policy (Light, 1996: 84–6).

These various influences contributed to the emergence of a centrist consensus in foreign policy by 1993 (Malcolm, 1994). As articulated in authoritative documents such as the official foreign policy 'Concept' of April, this was built around two central concerns: the active development of relations with the successor states (these were given priority over any other region, including the West) and the maintenance of Russia's great power status (Aron, 1994: 17–34). Taken at face value, these positions certainly suggested a move towards a greater assertiveness in foreign policy and a more questioning attitude towards the states of the West. By the mid-1990s, this trend became even further entrenched. This followed further gains by the communists and nationalists in the parliamentary elections of December 1995, Yeltsin's increasing reliance on symbols of nationalism in order to secure a second term in the 1996 presidential elections and a continued frustration with Western (and particularly American) foreign policy actions (NATO's more interventionist role in Bosnia after 1994 and the increasingly obvious intent of the Alliance to incorporate certain states in Eastern Europe).

Yeltsin's appointment of Yevgenni Primakov as Foreign Minister in January 1996 symbolised an important shift. Primakov, while not eschewing partnership with the West, sought to place Russian foreign policy within a 'multipolar' context. This emphasised Russian's greater engagement with the successor states and centres of regional power other than the US (Europe, China, India, etc.), opposition to the notion that the US should play a special role in global affairs, and the open pursuit of Russian interests even where these contradicted those of the Western states (Simes, 1999: 206–7). These themes were, in turn, incorporated in the official 'National Security Concept' signed into law by Yeltsin in December 1997. As such, this document reflected a 'liberal-statist synthesis' of elite views on foreign policy. This encapsulated both the more assertive demands of the nationalists and other supporters of Russia's claim to great power status (the *derzhavniki*), and the liberal, Kozyrev-type arguments in favour of continued cooperation with the West (Wallander, 1998).

This balance of views was to be revised still further following a marked deterioration of Russia's relations with the West during 1998–99 over issues such as the Kosovo War and NATO enlargement (see below). During the first few months of 2000, three keynote documents were signed into effect by the new Russian President, Vladimir Putin: a new National Security Concept, a revised Foreign Policy Concept and a Military Doctrine (replacing an earlier version adopted in 1993) (the documents are stored at *Johnson's Russia List*, 20 January 2000; 26 April 2000; and 10 July 2000). Although these contained different shades of emphasis (the Military

Doctrine is the most assertive, something that reflects the influence of the General Staff in its formulation), all three reflected a further hardening of attitudes towards the West. The possibilities of cooperation are not denied (this is most obvious in the Foreign Policy Concept), but, equally, the three documents reflect a general predisposition towards a qualified engagement. This is apparent, in what was, by this point, the familiar themes of promoting a multipolar international order, affirming Russia's great power status and upholding far-flung regional priorities. Furthermore, and in a departure from earlier documents, those adopted in 2000 were much more open in listing points of disagreement with the West (and particularly with the US), in naming NATO as a clear threat to Russia's national security (see the National Security Concept), and in making the case for a renewed emphasis on military instruments of defence (the Military Doctrine).

Two qualifications are in order before we leave this overview of the Russian foreign policy debate. First, the positions outlined above have a slightly artificial quality. There is a clear mismatch between Russian aspirations and the material capabilities of the country (something admittedly hinted at in the documents themselves). Furthermore, while these various documents suggest a move towards a coherent view of Russia's place in the post-Soviet, post-Cold War world, they remain statements only, however authoritative. They may well have been departed from in important respects: by key individuals in Russia (Yeltsin in particular struggled to come to terms with the complexities of Russian foreign policy) and by the content of policy itself, which at times has seemed far from systematic.

The second qualification relates to the measure of agreement on foreign policy. Consensus has not been total. While foreign policy discussions since 1993 have not been marked by the almost existential quality that had characterised the early debates, a chasm of difference has remained between the Russian leadership and elements of the political opposition. This has been evident, for instance, in the distance that has separated both Presidents Yeltsin and Putin from the still influential Russian Communist Party. As we shall find in the next section, differences have also lingered among different institutions, both on matters of policy and on the manner in which that policy is made and implemented.

The foreign policy process

A changed international environment, processes of domestic transition and the perceptions of key policy makers correspond to many of the factors outlined in Chapters 3 and 4 as being germane to understanding the nature of foreign policy making and its implementation. Having already alluded to much of this context in preceding sections, here we shall concentrate on a more descriptive account of Russian foreign policy making, focusing on its institutional and political settings.

In a formal sense, the leading institution of foreign policy making in Russia is the office of the President, occupied throughout the period 1991–99 by a single figure, Boris Yeltsin, and thereafter by Vladimir Putin. As well as head of state, the President is also Commander-in-Chief of the armed forces, has direct control over foreign and security-related ministries (the Foreign and Defence Ministries, and the Foreign Intelligence and Federal Border Services), heads and appoints the Security Council, and oversees a presidential administration containing several departments and advisers dealing with foreign policy. Outside of the President's office, the Foreign Ministry has formal responsibility for coordination and implementation. It has also held a key role in formulation through the seconding of personnel to the presidential administration. Other bodies accorded formal foreign policy-related functions include ministries (for instance, those concerned with defence, external economic affairs and cooperation with CIS states), the Prime Minister (who sometimes deputises for the President on foreign trips, takes a keen interest in trade and related issues and who holds a seat on the Security Council) and the Russian parliament (this body reserves the right to ratify or denounce treaties, hold hearings and pass non-binding resolutions on foreign policy issues).

This thumb-nail sketch, with its implicit picture of a neat division of labour among Russian institutions, reflects the constitutional position; it does not necessarily reflect the actual experience of policy making since 1991. This has, in fact, been anything but straightforward.

As with the foreign policy debate noted above, the most turbulent time was the two years immediately following the dissolution of the Soviet Union. This event left an unenviable legacy for policy making. In very general terms, the problem boiled down to one of under-institutionalisation (Checkel, 1995: 44–5). Russia had inherited an unclear Soviet-era constitution and a system of state institutions in considerable disarray owing, first, to the upheavals of the Gorbachev reforms and, second, to the withering away of Communist Party control. Yet the destructive component of political transition took place at a point when its constructive element was at an early stage. Institutional structures and political 'rules of the game' were removed but the nascent Russian state could only act as an inadequate replacement (Wallander, 1996: 211). When combined with the divisive nature of the policy debate itself, this contributed during 1992–93 to a process of foreign policy making and implementation characterised by intense inter-agency competition, an absence of effective coordination and an overall sense of drift and confusion (Crow, 1993).

This rather chaotic situation only began to be addressed seriously in the latter part of 1993. This was assisted by the emerging elite consensus on foreign policy and the general trend towards political centralisation effected by the disbanding of the Soviet-era Russian parliament and the adoption of a new constitution. Other, subsequent developments have also played a role. The armed forces' disastrous campaign in the break-away Russian region of Chechnya in 1994–96, coupled with the demoralising impact of military reform, stripped it of political influence, and thereby diminished the significant foreign policy role it had built up in 1992–93, particularly in policy towards the successor states. The military, while seemingly more in favour with Putin than Yeltsin, has not managed after 1999 to rebuild this influence fully. Indeed, in an act of considerable political symbolism, in March 2001 Putin appointed Sergei Ivanov, a former KGB and foreign intelligence officer, as Russia's first civilian Defence Minister. Moreover, while the political situation in Russia after 1993 could be described as anything but stable, as elections have become more frequent and institutional prerogatives more clearly established, so foreign policy has obtained a more predictable character. This was helped further during Putin's first term in office by a meeting of minds of the executive and legislative arms of government. The perpetual conflict with the parliament which had marked Yeltsin's two terms in office was partly resolved by the outcome of the December 1999 parliamentary elections, which saw a strong showing for centrist and pro-Putin parties.

All of this is not to say that coordination and other problems have been resolved. Foreign policy making and implementation has been complicated by Russia's federal structure and the attempts of some regions to assert their own foreign policy prerogatives (Nunn and Stulberg, 2000). At the centre, meanwhile, since 1993, a number of important bodies have continued to claim a role in foreign policy coordination. These include the Foreign Ministry, the Security Council and specialised bodies of the presidential administration (a Foreign Policy Council was created in 1995 to be replaced some two years later by a presidential Foreign Policy Department). While in practice, the Foreign Ministry has tended to gain the upper hand, this has not eliminated periodic inter-agency confusion even on major issues such as NATO enlargement, relations with the successor states and ties with China (Parrish, 1996).

As for the executive arm of policy, here too problems have been in evidence. In essence, these have a common cause, namely the manner of political centralisation in the office of the President. This courts difficulties associated with policy overload, although these have been partly rectified through the development of bureaucratic capability in the presidential apparatus. More serious have been the adverse consequences of leadership style. In a political system with few effective checks on the executive it is inevitable that personal factors will shape foreign policy. In Yeltsin's case these appeared that much more obvious owing to ill-health, capriciousness in the appointment and dismissal of personnel, and a rumoured tendency towards depression and (prior to a first major heart attack in 1995) heavy alcohol consumption. Certainly, his behaviour was at times embarrassing. Examples also abound of diplomatic disruption caused by extemporaneous presidential initiatives seemingly at odds with the positions of the Foreign and Defence Ministries. Putin, by contrast, has exuded a very different style. More mentally alert and physically capable, his diplomatic appearances have been noteworthy for their air of competence and self-assurance.

The content of Russian foreign policy (i)
Russia and the Soviet successor states: empire restored?

The emergence of consensus in foreign policy noted above, was based partly on a recognition among Russia's political elites of the need to reassert influence among the successor states. This meant a reversal of what has been described as a policy of 'neo-isolationism' during 1992 (Karaganov, 1997: 297). The premises of this early position – that the economic and military interdependencies of the successor states, coupled with their shared experience of post-communism, would ensure amicable and stable relations – soon proved ill-founded. As was noted earlier, the FSU had emerged by the end of 1992 as a region wracked by conflict and dispute.

In response to this situation and the more general influences at work in the foreign policy debate, the position of the Russian leadership underwent a considerable revision. Since 1993 references to the successor states as constituting a zone of Russia's vital national interests have become almost a dogma among the Russian leadership. Yeltsin and Putin, successive Foreign and Defence Ministers and a variety of official policy documents have all elaborated at length the urgency of Russian concerns, and a commitment to bilateral ties and multilateral processes of military and economic integration (notably via the CIS) as a means of pursuing them. Such rhetoric has given rise to the argument that Moscow is intent upon the construction a 'new Russian empire' (Cohen, 1997).

The reality of policy, however, is mixed. On the one hand, plenty of examples can be forwarded as evidence of Russian activism:

■ Russia is the only nuclear power in the region having (during 1992–94) cajoled Ukraine, Kazakhstan and Belarus to abandon the nuclear weapons left on their territories at the time of the Soviet Union's dissolution.

■ Russia has obtained a military presence in a majority of the successor states. In some instances (Armenia, Belarus and Tajikistan), this presence has been welcomed by the host government, in others (Georgia and Moldova) it has followed Russian connivance in the destabilisation of post-Soviet regimes and has been maintained in contravention of international obligations undertaken by Moscow.

■ Russia has emerged as an indispensable diplomatic player in conflict resolution efforts in Azerbaijan (Nagorno-Karabakh), Georgia (Abkhazia and South Ossetia), Moldova (the Dniester region) and Tajikistan. It has also employed peacekeeping forces in all but the first of these states.

■ Russia has promoted its status as a regional economic power. Following an initial flirtation with a policy of subsidisation and monetary union (the 'rouble zone') as a means of encouraging integration, it has since 1993 concentrated on more self-interested economic strategies. These include increases in the price of energy supplies, demands for access to state assets as payment for debts and aggressive bargaining over the exploitation and transportation of energy in the Caspian Sea region and Central Asia.

On the other hand, examples also abound of a certain forbearance in Russian policy:

■ In the Baltic states, Russia had, by September 1994, withdrawn troops inherited from the former Soviet armed forces. This occurred despite constant complaints in Moscow concerning infringements of the rights of local Russian speakers, strong disapproval of Baltic requests for admission to NATO, and unresolved territorial disputes.

■ The Yeltsin and Putin leaderships have given very little support to Russian-speaking secessionist movements in either northern Kazakhstan or the Crimea region of Ukraine.

■ Russia has cooperated with outside powers and international organisations (the UN and the OSCE) in conflict settlement efforts in Azerbaijan, Georgia, Moldova and Tajikistan.

- Yeltsin and Putin have opposed the recreation of the Soviet Union and have respected the legal status of the successor states. Hence, in March 1996 Yeltsin condemned a resolution passed by the State Duma that questioned the legality of the Soviet Union's dissolution in 1991.

Russian policy since 1992, then, has displayed features of both assertiveness and caution. How might one explain this seeming dichotomy? The rhetoric of Russian policy makes it seem beyond doubt that Moscow is intent on influence-building in the FSU. Crucially, however, Russia's reduced capabilities limit its ability to carry through this intention in a comprehensive manner. A forceful, interventionist policy is ruled out by virtue of Russia's over-stretched military (plain to see from the troubled campaigns in the two Chechen wars of 1994–96 and 1999–), while a more benign expansionist policy, one reliant on Russia's role as an economic pole of attraction, has lacked any material foundation in the post-Soviet period. To make matters worse, where Russia has obtained greatest influence, it has tended to be among states which are both weak (Belarus and Tajikistan) and with little to offer Russia. Those states, better positioned economically and politically (the Baltics, for instance) have been among the most determined to diversify their foreign ties and to resist Russian encroachment.

In these circumstances, Russia has tended to pursue a selective engagement. The sheer scale and diversity of the FSU region has required on Russia's part some ordering of priorities and a consequent recognition that it cannot pursue effectively all its interests simultaneously. How Russia has ranked its priorities, however, has tended to vary with time, region and issue. Ukraine was the main concern of Russian policy in 1992–93. During 1993–95, attention shifted to the Transcaucasus owing to regional wars and the proximity of the region to Russia's own internal conflict in Chechnya. In 1996, Belarus moved to the top of the agenda, policy being galvanised on this occasion by the intense debates over NATO enlargement (a Russian-Belarus alliance was posited as one possible response) and the domestic political capital Yeltsin hoped to earn from an appearance of activism in an election year (an agreement on a Russian-Belarus Community was reached in April, just two months before the vote for the Russian presidency). With the resolution of the Chechen conflict in 1996, the winding down of the NATO enlargement debate in 1997 and the short-term gains of an alliance with Belarus exhausted, Russian policy returned thereafter to unresolved issues regarding Ukraine and to trade and energy issues in the Caspian and Central Asian regions.

By the time of Putin's presidency, the emphases of policy had changed once more. Putin came to power with a desire to reinvigorate Russian policy throughout the successor states. This has involved differing approaches. Putin has simultaneously sought to revive the CIS, to entrench important 'special relationships' (notably those with Belarus and Kazakhstan), to woo states such as Uzbekistan and Ukraine which had formerly cold-shouldered Russia, and to pressure certain states, notably Georgia (through the imposition of border controls and cut-offs in natural gas supplies) into loosening their ties with the West (Chinyaeva, 2001).

The content of Russian foreign policy (ii)
Russia and the West: confrontation or cooperation?

Russia's relationship with the West has been likened by one observer to 'a graph, with elevated peaks and low valleys' (Clarke, 1995: 27). Since 1992, Russian policy has travelled from the early Atlanticism of 1992, moving through the reappraisal associated with the centrist consensus and liberal-statist synthesis of the mid-1990s and stabilising during Putin's first term in a balanced position of 'pragmatic minimalism' or 'peaceful coexistence' (Arbatova, 2000).

These alterations have been clearly evident at the rhetorical level. The unstinting references to partnership that were apparent during 1992 have given way to a somewhat more equivocal phraseology in which 'common values' have been given less prominence than the defence of national interests, the delineation of 'zones of vital interest' and the fashioning of a 'strong Russia' (Putin, 2000). In terms of practical policy, however, aspects of cooperation have been significant and enduring. The following four examples provide clear evidence of this:

- Russia, having inherited the obligation to remove Soviet troops from former East Germany, completed the withdrawal in August 1994.

- On nuclear issues Russia committed itself to implementing the 1991 Strategic Arms Reduction Treaty (START) and signed a successor agreement (START II) with the US in 1993. Moscow and Washington have also taken joint actions aimed at removing nuclear weapons from the Soviet successor states, agreed in 1995 to an indefinite extension of the Nuclear Non-Proliferation Treaty (NPT) and in 1996 signed up to a Comprehensive Test Ban Treaty (CTBT). In September 1997 an agreement was signed with the US extending START's implementation period and in April 2000 the State Duma ratified both START II and the CTBT.

- Russia has achieved full membership of a number of Western-oriented organisations (the International Monetary Fund [IMF], the Council of Europe and the Paris Club of creditor countries) and partner or associate status in others (the EU and the World Trade Organisation [WTO]). Since the late 1990s it has also been integrated into the 'Group of Seven' (G7) industrial countries, in the process converting that body into the G8.

- Russia has been a major recipient of multilateral financial assistance provided by Western-dominated institutions, notably the IMF and the World Bank.

Yet these examples ought not to suggest that the relationship with the West has been entirely free of discord. Indeed, in some areas (official contacts with 'pariah states' such as Libya, Iraq and Serbia, involvement in the affairs of some of the successor states, and the use of force in Chechnya) Russia has pursued policies in open defiance of Western criticisms. That said, what is also significant is that in several other, arguably more important areas, disagreement has been tempered by compromise. Consider the following:

- Soviet obligations under the 1990 Conventional Forces in Europe (CFE) Treaty were in 1992 reapportioned to Russia and several other successor states. Moscow subsequently argued that the Treaty required further revision in order to take account of its new security requirements. Despite its reservations on the Treaty, Moscow continued to implement most of its provisions. Following negotiations with the NATO states and other Treaty parties, a comprehensive adaptation agreement was signed in November 1999.

- The dominant European and American roles in resolving the wars in the former Yugoslavia have been resented in Moscow. NATO's bombing of Serb targets during Operation Allied Force in the spring of 1999 led to a period of heightened tension between Moscow and Western capitals. Even so, Russia has proved itself supportive of US-led diplomacy. It backed the Dayton Accords of 1995 which ended the war in Bosnia and was an important diplomatic partner in the search for a political resolution of the 1999 Kosovo conflict. Russian peacekeepers have also operated alongside NATO forces in both Bosnia and Kosovo.

- Moscow has objected strongly to the enlargement of NATO. The Russia–NATO 'Founding Act' signed in May 1997, however, reduced the frictions created by the issue, granting Russia a consultative role in the organisation through the creation of a Permanent Joint Council (PJC) and outlining a lengthy programme of political and military co-operation. Russia suspended its participation in the PJC and froze other links with NATO in protest at Operation Allied Force. These links were gradually restored in late 1999–2000.

■ Russia has criticised American testing of a projected National Missile Defence (NMD) system, claiming it is in breach of the 1972 Anti-Ballistic Missile (ABM) Treaty. The US has taken little heed of these protests, but the Russian case has found a measure of support among governments in Western Europe, including those in France and Germany.

But just how enduring is this pragmatic cooperation likely to be? There are those who suggest that the *rapprochement* with the West is based on a fragile premise, the argument here being that historical and cultural differences and Russia's inevitable craving for great power status will eventually supplant any temporary coincidence of interests (Buszynski, 1996: 70). Indeed, there is much to commend this view. In security matters, despite all the face-saving agreements noted above, a gulf still exists on some fundamental issues. Moscow may have reconciled itself to the inevitability of NATO enlargement but that very act remains unwelcome and suggests to it that European security, as with much else in international politics, is being driven by American interests. Hence, the persistence of Russian proposals to fashion European security by means other than NATO (preferably through a strengthening of the OSCE). These proposals may be unpopular outside Moscow but they are the only means short of force that Russia can use to rehabilitate its influence on the continent (Wyllie, 1997: 74–7).

There are, however, countervailing influences also at work that should help to sustain the more cooperative element of Russian foreign policy. As distinct from the Cold War, relations between Moscow and the West are no longer rooted in ideological rivalry or a presumption (however theoretical) of a major military conflict. They have been embedded in a far more comprehensive network of institutional arrangements than any seen prior to 1992. Furthermore, despite Russia's growing feeling of disillusionment with the West, the attractiveness of cooperation has not disappeared. The West in general, and the US in particular, remain prime sources of trade and investment, necessary interlocutors on the military dimensions of security and the surest guarantors of some sort of respectable international status for Moscow. Russian interests are, by this view, better served by engagement than they are by isolation and confrontation (Webber, 2000b: 222–3).

The content of Russian foreign policy (iii)
Russia: a global role?

Russia's turn away from the 'Atlanticism' of the early 1990s signalled a seeming willingness to adopt a more assertive position far beyond its own borders. Indeed, following a wholesale retreat from areas of the Third World during 1992, Russia began in earnest during 1994 to re-engage states once favoured by the Soviet regime (India and Cuba) and to strengthen ties with states neglected during the Soviet period (South Africa and Israel). This strategy formed an active part of Foreign Minister Primakov's support of a multipolar international order in the mid-1990s and has also been a prominent strand of diplomacy under President Putin.

Much has been made in leadership statements of how these ties reflect Russian status and influence. In reality, however, Russian policy has been limited in scope and effect. It has displayed a strong economic dimension – focusing on bilateral trade, arms sales and, in some instances, attempts to recover Soviet-era debts – but not much more besides. In regional diplomacy Moscow has striven for visibility but has played only an episodic and limited role (for instance, in the Middle East peace process and in negotiations with Iraq and North Korea). As for peacekeeping, the exceptional case of the former Yugoslavia aside, Russia has felt no compunction to emulate Western efforts (in parts of Africa, for instance).

The globalist pretence has also been somewhat belied by the regional foci of Russian policy beyond the West and the successor states. Three echelons of interest can be distinguished; all three are characterised by a close geographic proximity to Russia and the successor states.

The first echelon includes China and the states of Eastern Europe and the Balkans, all of which loom large in Russian history and which retain some bearing on more contemporary Russian concerns. Here, Russian foreign policy has enjoyed mixed fortunes. As regards Eastern Europe, Russia has had to labour under the Soviet legacy of regional domination, something that has continued to alienate it from most of the post-communist states in the region. Moreover, virtually all these states have expressed a strong preference in favour of a Western orientation in their own foreign policies and have actively sought membership of both NATO and the EU. In such circumstances Russia has managed to retain only a lingering influence based on much-reduced economic and military ties.

A similar situation has also pertained in the Balkans. Slovenia, Croatia and Macedonia have no great affinity to Russia. As for what remains of Yugoslavia (Serbia-Montenegro), while this rump state shares some cultural and historical links with Russia, policy in Moscow has, in fact, been determined largely by the vicissitudes of war. Confined to a policy of begrudging cooperation with Western initiatives, Moscow has struggled to retain some semblance of independence and influence in the region. The upshot has been a tortuous balancing act: Moscow, on the one hand, colluding in the international isolation of Serbia while, on the other, attempting to maintain a special relationship with the regime in Belgrade.

Policy towards China has been somewhat more successful. A casualty initially of Russia's Atlanticist orientation, relations with Beijing improved considerably after 1992. By the time of his visit to the Chinese capital in April 1996, Yeltsin was able to declare that there was not a single question upon which the two sides disagreed. The so-called 'strategic partnership' announced during that visit was based on at least three factors: a shared indignation towards American global influence, a common interest in regional stability (for instance, in the Korean peninsula and in Central Asia) and mutually beneficial economic ties. These factors, moreover, reflected concrete movement on the ground in the form of rapidly expanding trade (including the supply of all manner of sophisticated Russian weaponry), demilitarisation along the common border and the settlement of almost all remaining territorial disputes. Yet for all such progress, China has remained a major challenge to Moscow. Numerous irritants have remained in relations (the influx of Chinese migrants to Russia's Far East, Chinese influence-building in Central Asia). Moreover, China's huge population, record of economic growth and regional ambition mark it out as a power on the rise (see Chapter 10). Coupled with a long history of conflictual relations in both the Tsarist and Soviet periods, this has meant the survival of suspicions among the Russian leadership.

The second echelon comprises states such as India, Iran and Turkey, less critical to Russia but worthy of attention owing to their regional influence. These have also proven important because they offer opportunities for Russian exports and because they are germane to Russian policy towards the successor states. Iran provides a good example in all regards. Initially viewed with some scepticism in Moscow, owing to fears of Islamic influence in the Transcaucasus and Central Asia, Tehran has in fact found common cause with Moscow on three crucial issues: the status of the Caspian Sea, a settlement of the civil conflict in Tajikistan and negotiations on Nagorno-Karabakh. Russian suppliers have also been prepared, in the face of American protests, to supply Tehran with submarines and missile and civil nuclear technologies. Differences have occurred, principally over projected land routes for transporting oil and gas extracted from Central Asia, but Iran holds even greater grievances towards the West.

This has worked to Russia's advantage and its relationship with Tehran provides a rare example of successful Russian courtship.

Finally, the third echelon is defined primarily in economic terms. Two states fall within this category: Japan and South Korea. Both are useful trade partners and potentially huge sources of investment in Russia's underdeveloped and under-populated far eastern territories. Of the two, Japan holds greatest weight; it has, however, also proven the more problematic for Moscow. While there are no longer any political obstacles to private Japanese investment (although this has still been at low levels owing to uncertainties about the Russian economic transition), official bilateral aid has been negligible. Japan has also proven the least amenable to Russia's incorporation within the G8 framework. This is a state of affairs that can be accounted for almost entirely by a single irritant in Russian–Japanese relations: the unresolved dispute over the Kurile Islands, territories seized by the Soviet Union in 1945 and claimed by Japan ever since. Despite some early hints by Yeltsin at the possibility of a compromise, Russia has, since late 1992, been unstinting in its reluctance to concede on the issue.

The imponderables of Russian foreign policy

In the post-Soviet period, Russia has aspired towards great power status but has lacked the means to realise such a role. What power and influence it has still remains largely latent, awaiting a revival of its economy, the completion of military reform and the nurturing of post-Soviet statehood. How long this process will take and how successful it will be remain uncertain. A number of observers have argued that Russia is likely to arise in some way from its prostrate position (Brown, 1996: 9), while others have suggested that Russia's decline may be permanent (Snyder, 1999).

However, will the nature of Russia's foreign policy development in years to come be simply determined by the objective resources of economic and military might and political stability? Or, to put it another way, will Russia return to assertiveness and expansionism even if it has the means of doing so? A realist view of international affairs would tend towards the affirmative in answering these questions, as would traditionalist views of Russian history (Pipes, 1997: 65–78). It is also a view encouraged by some of the language of foreign policy emanating from Moscow. Yet there are trends also working in an opposite direction. If political stability is accompanied by democratic reform and if market transition allows for the emergence of a competitive and dynamic Russian economy, then international cooperation and institutionalised integration may prove more natural courses for Russia to pursue. Even with regard to the successor states, where Russia's relative strength and the temptations for interference are greatest, a benign course cannot be ruled out. Of course, Russia will pursue its interests among its neighbours, but 'the cursed dilemma of Russian history' (Aron, 1995: 28) – the choice between a Russia great (one based on the building of empire) and a Russia free – can still be overcome. As Stent and Shevtsova have argued (1996: 104) 'it is a mistake to believe in historical determinism; Russia has changed, and its new domestic system will not necessarily produce a new imperialism'.

The foreign policy of Ukraine

The challenges of transformation

Ukraine is often presented as a state possessing a huge potential, yet labouring under the weight of terrific problems, a duality that has inevitably affected its foreign policy (Moroney, 1998).

In separating from the Soviet Union, Ukraine was bequeathed a number of seemingly significant material advantages. Next to Russia, it was, demographically and territorially speaking, the largest former Soviet republic (comparable on both counts to France). Ukraine had also been an important component of the Soviet economy, accounting for a quarter of Soviet GNP and one-fifth of Soviet agricultural production. These advantages were offset, however, by a comprehensive dependence on the Russian economy (something that was particularly acute in the fields of energy) and an infrastructural obsolescence that required urgent external assistance.

As for the military sphere, on the one hand, Ukraine was a major beneficiary of the Soviet dissolution. Upon independence Soviet assets left on its territory included some 720,000 military personnel, 6,400 tanks, 1,400 fighter aircraft and an entire fleet of the Soviet navy serving the Black Sea. In addition, Ukraine was also home to approximately 14 per cent of Soviet strategic nuclear warheads. In short, these resources rendered Ukraine the largest military force in Europe after Russia and, in quantitative terms, capable of deterring a direct military attack, even one launched by its Russian neighbour (Bukkvoll, 1997a: 86–7). The quality and usefulness of Ukrainian forces were, however, open to question. The majority of its officer corps was Russian, its pattern of deployment oriented towards a coalition war in Europe (a legacy of Cold War military planning) and its running costs well beyond the capacity of the Ukrainian economy. Furthermore, these forces presented Ukraine with formidable foreign policy problems, as we shall see below, shaping its relationship with Russia and the Western powers.

The material legacy bequeathed to Ukraine was, therefore, a liability as well as an asset. The same could also be said of its geostrategic position. Ukraine's pivotal location between Russia and Europe afforded its foreign policy the opportunity to operate in several directions, be this towards Russia and the other successor states, towards the states of Eastern Europe or towards the Euro-Atlantic structures of the West. Yet this situation was not without its problems. Ukraine faced early on the difficult task of striking a balance between these various possibilities and had to face up to the fact that being on the edge of Europe precluded an easy integration into any of the continent's existing political, economic or security structures. It also had to contend with some pressing security issues. Ukraine's inherited land borders measured nearly 8,000 km, bringing it into contact with seven other states: Russia, Moldova, Belarus, Romania, Poland, Hungary and Slovakia. With the exception of Belarus, all had potential cause for territorial claims against Ukraine. These were made that much more worrying by Ukraine's ethnic make-up. About one-fifth of the country's population is ethnically Russian (in the Crimean region constituting a local majority) and compact groups of Hungarians, Romanians and Moldovans reside in Ukraine's western regions.

As this brief survey suggests, the challenges of Ukrainian foreign policy have been determined largely by the manner in which Ukraine emerged as an independent state. Yet central to this entire process was the fact that in breaking from Soviet rule, Ukraine also formally broke with a centuries-long experience of subjugation to Russia. This divorce has been a defining issue in the Ukrainian foreign policy debate.

The foreign policy debate

In Ukraine a foreign policy consensus has been difficult to achieve. Opinion has been divided between at least three schools of thought: nationalist, moderate and leftist (socialist and communist) (Bukkvoll, 1997a: 10–17, 88–9). These shades of opinion correspond to varieties of political parties within Ukraine and, in turn, reflect the ethnic and regional divisions within the country. Nationalist opinion is strongest in the west of the country, whereas leftist opinion is concentrated in the Russian-populated east.

Nationalists argue that Ukraine is naturally a part of Europe from which it has been artificially separated by the long association with Russia. Ukrainian independence, they assert, cannot be guaranteed through a close relationship with Moscow because of Russia's imperial inclinations. In fact, Ukrainian nationalists harbour a sharp sense of grievance at being the victims of rule by Moscow. Under Tsarism, Ukraine experienced the imposition of serfdom and the suppression of its education system and language. The Soviet period had even more harmful consequences. The victims of the famine which accompanied Stalin's enforced collectivisation of agriculture in the early 1930s could be counted in their millions. The longer-term incorporation of Ukraine into the Soviet planning system, meanwhile, was seen to have harmed rather than enhanced Ukrainian economic performance. While both Yeltsin and Putin have distanced themselves from this historical record and professed a respect for Ukrainian independence, others in Russia have been less amenable. Prominent politicians such as Gennadi Zyuganov, the leader of the Russian Communist Party, and Yuri Luzhkov, the Mayor of Moscow, have questioned Ukrainian possession of all or parts of the Crimea and have argued in favour of Ukraine's reintegration into a greater Russia. In this light, Ukrainian nationalists argue that the maintenance of independence is best served by a distancing from Russia and integration with the West and neighbouring countries in Eastern Europe. This, moreover, should be effected with speed, in order to take advantage of the opportunities offered by Russia's transitional weaknesses and before an openly revanchist President assumes power in Moscow.

Leftist opinion, by contrast, has been in favour of close cooperation with Russia and the other successor states. In the case of the Communist Party of Ukraine (CPU) (particularly the membership in the east of the country) this is married to a nostalgia for the Soviet Union and the hope of a communist restoration in Moscow. This group, along with its socialist and agrarian allies, formed the dominant bloc in the Ukrainian parliament following elections in 1994 and 1998.

The differences between the nationalist and leftist positions reflect what F. Stephen Larrabee (1996: 143) has referred to as the 'two conflicting pressures' between which Ukraine is caught: a desire to join European institutions on the one hand and a close economic dependence on Russia on the other. The third, or moderate, position tilts towards a Euro-Atlantic orientation but also seeks to maintain stable relations with Russia. It is encapsulated by the idea of neutrality enshrined in Ukraine's 1990 Declaration of State Sovereignty and has characterised the foreign policy of Ukraine's longest-serving post-communist President, Leonid Kuchma (elected in 1994 and re-elected in 1999).

The delicate balance that neutrality implies, has not, however, been easy to maintain. Under President Leonid Kravchuk (1991–94), Ukrainian foreign policy displayed a preference for relations with the West and a confrontational attitude towards Russia. Although a communist by background, Kravchuk readily adopted a nationalist agenda as a means of boosting his domestic constituency and of distancing newly-independent Ukraine from Russia. This paid some dividends; however, Kravchuk's uncompromising approach courted disapproval not just in Moscow but also in the West. His 'nation-building' foreign policy, moreover, could not detract from a flagging domestic record. Having presided over a catastrophic economic performance, Kravchuk was removed from power in the June–July 1994 presidential elections.

Kuchma was initially felt to be something of a mirror image of Kravchuk and thus, it was presumed, he would be more accommodating to Russia. A career in Soviet space research and rocket manufacturing suggested an awareness on his part of the economic benefits of a close association with Russia, the hub of the formerly integrated Soviet economy. In fact, Kuchma soon emerged as a staunch defender of Ukrainian interests and a vocal sceptic of Russian intentions. This, however, did not led Ukraine towards a total imbalance in its foreign policy orientation. During his two terms in office (Kuchma was re-elected in 1999), considerable efforts have been made to steer the country westwards but, overall, Kuchma has taken the pragmatic view that coexistence with Russia and a level of integration with the West are compatible, not mutually exclusive, goals.

The foreign policy process

The making of foreign policy in Ukraine has shared with Russia a transitional quality; an initial period of uncertainty gradually giving way to more routinised and predictable procedures.

Ukraine entered the post-Soviet period with a political system still nominally regulated by the 1978 constitution. This document, however, was ill-suited to the requirements of political life after communism. With the coordinating role of the Communist Party having been removed, the business of government fell victim to confused lines of authority and institutional competition. Under Kravchuk this constitutional uncertainty remained largely unresolved. Significantly, however, it had a less harmful impact on foreign affairs than on domestic policy. The inherited constitution placed foreign policy within the remit of the President. Kravchuk's own personal interest in foreign affairs (often as a respite from the domestic troubles of economic reform) meant that in the crucial first years of Ukrainian independence important precedents were set in this area. Kravchuk often took personal charge of negotiations with Russia and maintained a high profile on international issues relating to nuclear weapons and European security. His role was boosted further by the establishment of a presidential foreign policy apparatus (headed by a National Security Council) and by the appointment of loyalists to head the nascent Ministries of Foreign Affairs and Defence. Moreover, a potential source of institutional rivalry, the Prime Minister, was largely kept out of foreign policy, and left to concentrate instead on economic issues.

Where Kravchuk did experience trouble was in his relations with the Ukrainian parliament. Formed with a communist majority at the time of its election in 1990, this bloc was diluted during 1991–92. The CPU was temporarily banned in 1991 and a large proportion of its parliamentary membership underwent a nationalist conversion in 1991–92 as a means of adapting to the reality of Ukrainian independence (Bukkvoll, 1997a: 7). The result was a parliament often more vocal in its defence of perceived Ukrainian national interests than the President was himself. On several occasions this proved a complicating factor for Kravchuk, especially, as we shall note in the following section, in the case of nuclear disarmament.

Constitutional uncertainty was one of several criticisms levelled against Kravchuk's period of rule. Kuchma, upon taking power, made clear his desire to strengthen the position of the President and to push through a new constitutional settlement. These objectives were secured with the adoption of a post-communist constitution in June 1996 and constitutional amendments endorsed by a referendum in April 2000. These preserved presidential leadership in foreign affairs as well as codifying the lines of authority flowing from this office to other policy-making bodies. A reduced force, parliament does nonetheless retain some influence. Under the new constitution it reserves the right to ratify treaties signed by the President. Its budget-making powers also have foreign policy implications; the more leftist leaning parliament elected in 1994, for instance, sometimes refused to endorse cuts in social spending, thereby disqualifying Ukraine from IMF credits. The stance of the parliament is significant when its political composition is at odds with the President. This was the case following the election of leftist majorities in 1994 and 1998 (see above). However, the latter dissolved in January 2000 and a majority, pro-presidential coalition of parties was formed.

The content of Ukrainian foreign policy (i)
Squaring up to Russia

Since 1991 Russia has been the primary concern of Ukrainian foreign policy. In protecting its new-found independence, Kiev has had to face Russia from a position of relative weakness. This has resulted in a foreign policy balanced, often uneasily, between self-assertion and compromise. Yet despite these inherent difficulties, Ukraine has achieved some successes. A decade or so after the Soviet Union's dissolution, it is possible to characterise Russian–Ukrainian relations as stable, a marked contrast to the heightened tensions that marked the early post-Soviet years.

One key issue that characterised the earlier, more vexed period of relations was that of nuclear weapons. Having initially declared an intention to become a non-nuclear weapons state, Ukraine subsequently prevaricated over the removal of the strategic nuclear weapons on its territory and it was not until June 1996 that the last warheads were transported to Russia. Ukraine's stance can, in some ways, be read as a foreign policy failure, provoking as it did not just the wrath of Russia but also severely straining relations with the US. It was also generally accepted that the weapons left on Ukrainian territory were of little military value, as the Ukrainian armed forces lacked the wherewithal to either launch or properly maintain them. Yet the delay was the product of concrete strategic and political considerations. Throughout 1992–93, Kiev argued that relinquishing its arsenal should be linked to the provision of financial assistance and security guarantees from the other nuclear powers (Zlenko, 1993: 11–14). In this it was successful. Under the terms of the 'Trilateral Statement on Ukrainian Nuclear Weapons', jointly signed with Moscow and Washington in January 1994, Ukraine received, *de facto*, recognition of its territorial integrity along with nuclear fuel deliveries from Russia. For its part, Ukraine pledged to transfer all its nuclear warheads to Russia. Making good this pledge depended, however, on the Ukrainian parliament ratifying both the START treaty (an agreement to which Ukraine, as a part inheritor of Soviet nuclear forces, had assumed obligations in 1992) and the NPT. Ratification of START did occur in November 1993 but with so many preconditions as to make it meaningless. Personal pleas from President Kravchuk, coupled with threats of economic sanctions from Russia (as well as the US), did, however, persuade the parliament to reverse its position. The START treaty was reconsidered in February 1994 and in November of that year the parliament agreed to accede to the NPT (the following month President Kuchma formally signed the document).

A second major problem in Ukraine's relations with Russia has concerned the status of the Black Sea Fleet (BSF). Located in Ukraine, this remnant of the former Soviet navy has nonetheless been claimed by Russia. The issue has been given an added potency by the fact that the Fleet is headquartered at Sevastopol in the Russian-populated Crimea. As with the nuclear weapons issue, Kiev has sought to wrest from Russia political and economic concessions as a price for an agreement. After five years of negotiation and several interim accords, a 'final', comprehensive package of agreements on the Fleet and related issues was signed in May 1997. This conceded to Russia the right to lease basing facilities (for twenty years) and most of the Fleet's assets. In return, Kiev was allowed to headquarter its own navy in Sevastopol and received settlement of $3 billion worth of debt owed to Russia. Furthermore, the BSF agreements were accompanied by an inter-state friendship treaty that finally confirmed, *de jure*, Russian recognition of Ukrainian sovereignty (Sherr, 1997). This package was, without doubt, historic. It did not, however, remove all sources of friction. It took a further three years of negotiations, for instance, before Ukraine would allow Russia to replace naval aircraft attached to the BSF.

Delimiting the relationship with Russia has also informed Ukraine's approach to the CIS. On the one hand, both Presidents Kravchuk and Kuchma have viewed the organisation with some scepticism, fearful that it might become a mechanism of Russian interference. Ukraine has, therefore, opposed all efforts to create supranational structures of authority within the organisation and has kept its distance from military involvement (it has not, for instance, signed the 1992 CIS Collective Security Treaty). Ukraine has also formed alliances of convenience with Georgia, Moldova and Azerbaijan (states similarly ill-disposed towards both Russia and the CIS), and has been a leading force in the GUUAM grouping (see above). On the other hand, Ukraine has seen some value in the CIS, both as a means of promoting economic cooperation and as a forum for dialogue. Consequently, it has remained within the organisation, albeit in a semi-detached fashion. This stance is exemplified by Ukraine's associate membership of the putative CIS Economic Union.

Turning lastly to bilateral economic issues, here Ukraine has enjoyed only partial success in breaking its dependence upon Russia. Ukraine has diversified its foreign trade (overall trade turnover with Russia has been in decline since the mid-1990s) but this has largely been a consequence of Russian protectionism rather than a deliberate Ukrainian trade strategy. In the critical field of oil and gas supplies, meanwhile, Ukraine has remained tied to Russia. This has not been without certain benefits.

Pipelines which cross Ukraine carry the vast bulk of Russian gas exports to the outside world and this has allowed Ukraine to charge lucrative transit fees. A high proportion of debts built up by Ukraine for its own gas consumption have gone unpaid and local concerns have been involved in siphoning off an estimated 2–3 billion cubic meters of gas from Russian pipelines. The restructuring of overall Ukrainian debt to Russian oil and gas firms, it was estimated in 1997, constitutes a subsidy to the Ukrainian economy worth approximately $700 million per annum (Rontoyanni, 2000: 17). These advantages notwithstanding, Ukraine's long-term dependence on Russia is perceived in Kiev as a source of weakness (energy debts, for instance, were traded in the BSF negotiations) and as an undesirable irritant in relations with Moscow. Ukraine, consequently, has sought to reduce its dependence on Russia through recourse to alternative suppliers such as Iran, Iraq and Turkmenistan and through the development of its own reserves. Neither course, however, has yielded significant results owing to an absence of pipeline and production facilities.

The content of Ukrainian foreign policy (ii)
Ukraine and the West: balancing Russia

Kiev's early concentration on building up relations with the West was based on some solid calculations. These included a desire to establish a diplomatic identity and presence on the world stage, to loosen dependence on the Russian economy, and to solicit outside help to support its external security (Kuzio, 1995: 54–5; Zlenko, 1993: 11). Yet in pursuing these aims the Kravchuk administration faced a serious obstacle in the shape of Western indifference. Although this was partly a consequence of Ukraine's own actions (for instance, a reluctance to initiate economic reform), it also reflected an initial 'Russo-centric' policy in Western capitals. In this context Kravchuk's success lay mainly in winning the West's attention, albeit, as illustrated by the nuclear weapons' issue, in a manner likely to generate tension as much as support.

Kuchma's approach to the West has been based on similar objectives to those of his predecessor. The obvious difference is that Kuchma has been far more successful. This is, in part, a consequence of a growing appreciation among some Western states – the US, Britain and Germany in particular – of Ukraine's strategic significance and its long-term economic and political potential. It reflects also the patient but persistent manner in which the Kuchma administration has set out to persuade the West that Ukraine has a strong case for association with Euro-Atlantic structures.

The successes of Ukraine's Western foreign policy include the following:

- The establishment of a 'distinctive partnership' with NATO. Ukraine was the first successor state to enter NATO's Partnership for Peace programme (and under its auspices has hosted NATO-led exercises on its territory). It has also sent troops to serve in the NATO-led S-FOR and I-FOR contingents in Bosnia and K-FOR in Kosovo. In July 1997 Ukraine signed a special Charter of cooperation and consultation with the Alliance.

- In June 1994 a partnership agreement was signed with the EU; in September 1997 the first Ukraine–EU summit was convened and in December 1999, the EU adopted a 'Common Strategy' on Ukraine. None of these events has moved Ukraine any closer to its aim of full EU membership. However, Ukraine has been granted trade concessions and assistance in the decommissioning of the damaged Chernobyl nuclear facility.

- Ukraine joined the Council of Europe in November 1995, in recognition of the progress the country had made towards creating a constitutionally-based democracy. Kiev's satisfaction was heightened by the fact that its admittance came at a time when Russia was still outside the organisation. The Council of Europe has since criticised Ukraine's political development (for instance, the conduct of the 1999 presidential elections and the 2000 constitutional referendum) but has shown no serious signs of disbarring it.

- Ukraine has become a major recipient of Western financial aid. Since 1996 it has received more bilateral aid from the US than has Russia and has become the third largest recipient of American aid after Israel and Egypt.

There are, however, limits to Kiev's Western orientation. As well as Russian hostility to such a course, these stem also from the reluctance of Western states to embrace Ukraine fully, either because of the woeful performance of its economy (hence, the EU does not consider Ukraine a realistic candidate for membership and the IMF has delayed the disbursement of loans) or from a fear of provoking Russia (hence, NATO has made no indication that Ukraine is likely to be a future member of the Alliance).

The development of relations with NATO illustrates most effectively these tensions. As noted above, Ukraine has developed a concrete partnership with the Alliance and both the Kravchuk and Kuchma administrations have looked upon it appreciatively as an important component of

European security and as a counter to Russian efforts to coerce Ukraine into joining a CIS-based collective defence arrangement. Yet while praising NATO in general terms, Kiev has not made a bid for membership. President Kravchuk and some high-level officials under Kuchma have supported accession in principle, but it has not been an objective of Kuchma himself. This stance stems partly from calculations regarding Russia and also from an awareness that there has not been a consensus in favour of accession within either the parliament, the Ukrainian armed forces or public opinion more generally (Bukkvoll, 1997b: 368–9; Light et al., 2000: 83–5). Kiev has also been rather circumspect in endorsing controversial NATO actions. Operation Allied Force and enlargement into Eastern Europe, for instance, were accepted with qualifications in Kiev, an ambivalence that stemmed from fears that NATO was stoking up trouble with Russia and thus, by extension, complicating Kiev's relations with Moscow (Sherr and Main, 1999).

The content of Ukrainian foreign policy (iii)
Eastern Europe: a bridge to the West

Although often overlooked, an east European direction has been an important component of Ukrainian foreign policy. From Kiev's perspective, relations with the neighbouring states of Poland, Slovakia, Hungary and Romania have been based on three sets of interests. First, a desire to obtain recognition of its identity as an East or Central European nation, both as a means of distancing itself from Russia and as a route to building links with Western Europe. Second, improved relations have been necessary in order to address actual and potential controversies relating to national minorities and territorial claims. And third, in view of Poland and Hungary's accession to NATO and prospects of joining the EU, Ukraine has felt the need to prepare for the eventuality of a new continental dividing line that will run between itself and some of its east European neighbours (Pavliuk, 1997: 347–8).

In seeking to enhance ties with Eastern Europe, Ukraine has registered greatest progress at the bilateral level. Improved relations with Poland have been particularly important in view of a long history of conflict and mistrust (Burant, 1993: 396–7). Cemented by a common appreciation of the latent threat from Russia, these two states have since 1992 undertaken the beginnings of military and economic cooperation. Poland has also backed Ukraine's moves towards Western institutions, being a persuasive voice in favour of Kiev's entry into the Council of Europe. In 1992 Ukraine signed an inter-state treaty with Poland. Similar treaties were also subsequently reached with Hungary (1993), Slovakia (1993) and Romania (1997). These agreements involve a renunciation of territorial claims, something of particular significance in the case of Romania, which had tacitly supported a demand for the return of territories annexed by the Soviet Union in 1940.

Ukraine has been less successful in regional multilateral initiatives. It has put forward its own security proposals. In 1993 Kravchuk suggested the creation of a Central European Security Zone (an idea revived by Kuchma in 1996) and a nuclear-free zone 'between the Baltic and Black Seas'. Neither idea, however, has been well received in Eastern Europe, where they have been viewed as an outgrowth of the Ukrainian–Russian dispute and an unwanted complication in the way of NATO membership (Pavliuk, 1997: 351). Ukraine's approach to political and economic arrangements has been only a little more productive. Ukraine failed in its bid to join the Visegrad Group and has been permitted only observer status, not full membership, in the Central European Free Trade Area (CEFTA). Ukraine has, however, been a member of the Central European Initiative since 1996.

The imponderables of Ukrainian foreign policy

From an unenviable position, Ukraine has achieved much in its foreign policy: a stabilisation of relations with Russia, a strengthening of links with the West and a legitimate place in Eastern Europe. The 'delicate balancing act' (Pedchenko, 1997) that has produced these successes has been played with some skill by Kuchma and his ministers. However, the foreign policy of Ukraine, indeed the very state of Ukraine itself, has been in existence for only a decade. A sound foreign policy based on a clear vision of Ukraine's national interests and embedded in stable bilateral and multilateral relationships has yet to take shape.

In this light, Kiev's attempts to maintain a balance between Russia, the West and its East European neighbours should not be regarded as either the norm or even the likely future of Ukrainian foreign policy. How long it endures will be determined, in part, by developments beyond Ukraine's influence. Thus, his declared commitment to neutrality notwithstanding, Kuchma has let it be known that 'the eventual movement of Ukraine . . . will depend on the behaviour of Russia' (cited in Pedchenko, 1997: 75). Should a more threatening regime emerge in Russia, then Ukraine could abandon neutrality and make a bid for NATO membership (Nabytovych, 1996:

60). Developments away from Russia are also likely to be important. The enlargement of the EU, for instance, to take in some East European states will emasculate CEFTA and prompt Ukraine to deal with its West and East European economic partners within an expanded EU framework. This will, in turn, require Ukraine to build upon the partnership arrangements it has already opened up with the EU.

Possible foreign policy courses are also subject to domestic factors. Politically speaking, much will depend on the outcome of presidential elections given the amount of personal authority the holder of this office exercises in foreign policy. Kuchma may be succeeded by either a leftist candidate in favour of closer relations with Russia or a nationalist more inclined to an unambiguous pitch for integration with NATO, regardless of developments in Russia. Ukraine's long-term international position will also be a reflection of its economic development. Economic reforms have met with little success and foreign investment has been low, owing, in part, to rampant corruption. An inability to correct these deficiencies could threaten continued cooperation with donors such as the US, the EU and the IMF, and reverse the slow reorientation of the Ukrainian economy away from Russia.

Conclusion: Russia and Ukraine – cases apart

The foreign policies of Russia and Ukraine are unlike any other considered in this volume. Consider, first, the context in which the policies have evolved. While it would be true to say that all major states face a transformed world, the international context which Russia and Ukraine have confronted has, uniquely, involved them in the development of an entirely new regional system of international relations. Other regional systems, be these in Europe, the Middle East and elsewhere, may well have changed after the Cold War but they are at least a modification of previous inter-state systems of relations. That in the FSU is quite different, being composed of states whose very existence was either unknown or unacknowledged during the Cold War. The domestic context of policy has also been peculiarly challenging. It is not just Russia and Ukraine which have had to deal with domestic political flux or with the legacy left by a discredited regime. However, what marks these two out is the gravity of change combined with the unique circumstances of their recent emergence through a process of (Soviet) state collapse. This process has not only presented concrete challenges relating to political and economic transition but has raised profound questions relating to national identity; in that identities in Russia and Ukraine are not fixed so the very essence and orientation of their foreign policies has lacked a stabilising anchor. As a result, policy has tended to be dictated more by circumstances and by constraints (both internal and external) than by a clear sense of vision or purpose. Russia and Ukraine have been less the shapers of the post-Cold War international system than shaped by it.

The actual content of their foreign policies also mark out Russia and Ukraine. No other state in this volume has displayed in its foreign policy such a preoccupation with a sense of status as has Russia. The US, China, Japan and Germany may be sensitive on this score, but theirs is a sensitivity that stems from the luxury of being states in the ascendant or in a position of primacy. Status for them is plainly evident in the shape of economic and military prowess and political influence. Russia, however, lacks these attributes; its need to advertise greatness is based less on the reality of power than on the fact of its decline (Adomeit, 1995: 35). As for Ukraine, its foreign policy has been marked by the prominence it has given to presumptions of external threat. While this bears comparison with say Poland and Israel, Ukraine is different in two senses. First, because of its entanglement ethnically, economically and militarily with the source of threat. And second, because it has permitted the transfer of substantial military assets to that source, in the process engaging in one of modern history's few examples of a unilateral renunciation of nuclear weapons.

Further reading

The reader is well served by sources on Russian foreign policy. Useful general surveys include Bowker (1997), Buszynski (1996) and Mandelbaum (ed.) (1998). The edited collections of Baranovsky (1997) and Webber (2000a), while focusing on Russia's relations with Europe, also contain a number of chapters of a more general nature. The journals *Foreign Affairs*, *International Affairs*, *Survival* and *The World Today* regularly carry relevant and respected articles. The literature on Ukraine is thinner but nonetheless significant. Good surveys include Bukkvoll (1997a), Hajda (ed.) (1998) and Kuzio (1995). *The Ukrainian Review* is a good source of detailed articles. Comparative studies of foreign policy in the former Soviet region are few in number but the reader should consult Allison and Bluth (eds) (1998), Skak (1996) and Webber (1996). English language translations of articles in the Russian and Ukrainian press can be found in *The Current Digest of the Post-Soviet Press.*

References

Adomeit, H. (1995) 'Russia as a "Great Power" in World Affairs: Images and Reality', *International Affairs*, **71**(1), 35–68.

Allison, R. and Bluth, C. (eds) (1998) *Security Dilemmas in Russia and Eurasia.* London: Royal Institute of International Affairs.

Arbatov, A. (1997) 'Russian Foreign Policy Thinking in Transition', in Baranovsky, V. (ed.), *Russia and Europe. The Emerging Security Agenda.* Oxford: Oxford University Press/Stockholm International Peace Research Institute, 135–59.

Arbatova, N. (2000) 'Steering Back to a Bipolar World', *Nezavisimaya gazeta* (21 July).

Aron, L. (1994) 'The Emergent Priorities of Russian Foreign Policy', in Aron, L. and Jensen, K.M. (eds), *The Emergence of Russian Foreign Policy.* Washington, DC: United States Institute of Peace Press, 17–34.

Aron, L. (1995) 'A Different Dance – from Tango to Minuet', *The National Interest*, **39**, 27–37.

Baranovsky, V. (ed.) (1997) *Russia and Europe. The Emerging Security Agenda.* Oxford: Oxford University Press/Stockholm International Peace Research Institute.

Bowker, M. (1997) *Russian Foreign Policy and the End of the Cold War.* Aldershot: Dartmouth.

Brown, J.F. (1996) 'Everybody Needs Russia – Including Eastern Europe', *Transition*, **2**(23), 6–10.

Bukkvoll, T. (1997a) *Ukraine and European Security.* London: Royal Institute of International Affairs.

Bukkvoll, T. (1997b) 'Ukraine and NATO. The Politics of Soft Cooperation', *Security Dialogue*, **28**(3), 363–74.

Burant, S.R. (1993) 'International Relations in a Regional Context: Poland and its Eastern Neighbours – Lithuania, Belarus, Ukraine', *Europe-Asia Studies*, **45**(3), 395–418.

Buszynski, L. (1996) *Russian Foreign Policy after the Cold War.* Westport, CT, and London: Praeger.

Central Intelligence Agency (2000), *The World Factbook, 2000.* <http://www.odci.gov/cia/publications/factbook/>.

Checkel, J. (1995) 'Structure, Institutions, and Process: Russia's Changing Foreign Policy', in Dawisha, A. and Dawisha, K. (eds), *The Making of Foreign Policy in Russia and the New States of Eurasia.* Armonk, NY, and London: M.E. Sharpe, 42–65.

Chinyaeva, E. (2001) 'Russia in the CIS: the High Costs of Expansion', *Prism*, **7**(3).

Clarke, D.L. (1995) 'Uncomfortable Partners', *Transition* (1994 in Review, Part II), 27–31.

Cohen, A. (1997) 'A New Paradigm for US–Russia Relations: Facing the Post-Cold War Reality', The Heritage Foundation, *Backgrounder*, **1105**.

Crow, S. (1993) *The Making of Foreign Policy in Russia under Yeltsin*. Munich and Washington, DC: RFE/RL Research Institute.

Crow, S. (1994) 'Why Has Russian Foreign Policy Changed?', *RFE/RL Research Report*, **3**(18), 1–6.

Hajda, L.A. (ed.) (1998) *Ukraine in the World*. Cambridge, MA: Harvard University Press.

Hill, C. (2001) 'How Much Does Russia Spend on Defence?', briefing presented to the Centre for Strategic and International Studies, Washington DC, January 2001 (as carried on *Johnson's Russia List*, 11 February 2001 at <http://www.cdi.org/russia/johnson/>).

Johnson's Russia List (20 January 2000; 26 April 2000; and 10 July 2000), available at <http://www.cdi.org/russia/johnson/>

Karaganov, S.A. (1992) 'Russia I: a Moscow View on the West's Role', *The World Today*, **48**(7), 122–4.

Karaganov, S.A. (1997) 'Russia and the Slav Vicinity', in Baranovsky, V. (ed.), *Russia and Europe. The Emerging Security Agenda*. Oxford: Oxford University Press/Stockholm International Peace Research Institute, 289–300.

Kozyrev, A. (1992) 'Russia: a Chance for Survival', *Foreign Affairs*, **71**(2), 1–16.

Kuzio, T. (1995) *Ukrainian Security Policy*. Westport, CT, and London: Praeger.

Larrabee, F.S. (1996) 'Ukraine's Balancing Act', *Survival*, **38**(2), 143–65.

Levgold, R. (1992) 'Foreign Policy', in Colton, T.J. and Levgold, R. (eds), *After the Soviet Union. From Empire to Nations*. New York and London: W.W. Norton, 147–76.

Light, M. (1996) 'Foreign Policy Thinking', in Malcolm, N., Pravda, A., Allison, R. and Light, M. (eds), *Internal Factors in Russian Foreign Policy*. Oxford: Oxford University Press/Royal Institute of International Affairs, 33–100.

Light, M., White, S. and Löwenhardt, J. (2000) 'A Wider Europe: the View from Moscow and Kyiv', *International Affairs*, **76**(1), 77–88.

Lukin, V.P. (1994) 'Russia and its Interests', in Sestanovich, S. (ed.), *Rethinking Russia's National Interests*. Washington, DC: Centre for Strategic and International Studies, 106–15.

Malcolm, N. (1994) 'The New Russian Foreign Policy', *The World Today*, **50**(2), 28–32.

Malcolm, N. and Pravda, A. (1996) 'Introduction', in Malcolm, N., Pravda, A., Allison, R. and Light, M. (eds), *Internal Factors in Russian Foreign Policy*. Oxford: Oxford University Press/Royal Institute of International Affairs, 1–32.

Mandelbaum, M. (ed.) (1998) *The New Russian Foreign Policy*. New York: Council on Foreign Relations.

Moroney, J.D.P. (1998) 'The Lack of Determinacy in Ukraine's Foreign and Security Policy', *The Ukrainian Review*, **45**(4), 3–14.

Motyl, A.J. (1991) 'Russian Hegemony and Non-Russian Insecurity: Foreign Policy Dilemmas of the USSR's Successor States', *The Harriman Institute Forum*, **5**(4), 1–11.

Nabytovych, I. (1996) 'Ukraine–NATO–Russia: the Search for Sides in the Trilateral Relationship', *The Ukrainian Review*, **43**(4), 55–60.

Nunn, S. and Stulberg, A.N. (2000) 'The Many Faces of Modern Russia', *Foreign Affairs*, **79**(2), 45–62.

Offe, C. (1991) 'Capitalism by Democratic Design? Democratic Theory Facing the Triple Transition in East Central Europe', *Social Research*, **58**(4), 876–92.

Parrish, S. (1996) 'Chaos in Foreign-Policy Decision-Making', *Transition*, **2**(10), 30–3, 64.

Pavliuk, O. (1997) 'Ukraine and Regional Cooperation in Eastern Europe', *Security Dialogue*, **28**(3), 347–61.

Pedchenko, V. (1997) 'Ukraine's Delicate Balancing Act', *Transitions*, **4**(3), 72–6.

Pipes, R. (1997) 'Is Russia Still an Enemy?', *Foreign Affairs*, **76**(5), 65–78.

Putin, V. (2000) 'Vladimir Putin's Open Letter to Russian Voters', *Izvestiya* (25 February).

Rontoyanni, C. (2000) 'Building the Wider Europe. Ambitions and Constraints in Russia's Policies towards Belarus and Ukraine', The Glasgow Papers, **3**, Institute of Central and East European Studies, University of Glasgow.

Sakwa, R. and Webber, M. (1999) 'The Commonwealth of Independent States, 1991–1998: Stagnation and Survival', *Europe Asia Studies*, **51**(3), 379–416.

Sherr, J. (1997) 'Russia–Ukraine *Rapprochement*?: the Black Sea Fleet Accords', *Survival*, **39**(3), 33–50.

Sherr, J. and Main, S. (1999) 'Russian and Ukrainian Perceptions of Events in Yugoslavia', Conflict Studies Research Centre, Royal Military College, Sandhurst, <http://www.ppc.pims.org/Projects/csrc/F64-js-compl.htm>

Simes, D. (1999) *After the Collapse. Russia Seeks its Place as a Great Power*. New York: Simon and Schuster.

Skak, M. (1996) *From Empire to Anarchy. Postcommunist Foreign Policy and International Relations*. London: Hurst and Company.

Snyder, J. (1996) 'Democratisation, War and Nationalism in the Post-Communist States', in Wallander, C.A. (ed.), *The Sources of Russian Foreign Policy after the Cold War*. Boulder, CO: Westview Press, 21–40.

Snyder, J. (1999) 'Russia: Responses to Relative Decline', in Paul, T.V. and Hall, J.A. (eds), *International Order and the Future of World Politics*. Cambridge: Cambridge University Press, 146–54.

Stent, A. and Shevtsova, L. (1996) 'Russia's Election: No Turning Back', *Foreign Policy*, **103**, 92–109.

Wallander, C.A. (1996) 'Ideas, Interests, and Institutions in Russian Foreign Policy', in Wallander, C.A. (ed.), *The Sources of Russian Foreign Policy after the Cold War*. Boulder, CO: Westview Press, 207–18.

Wallander, C.A. (1998) 'The Russian National Security Concept: a Liberal-Statist Synthesis', Program on New Approaches to Russian Security, Policy Memo No.30 at <http://www.fas.harvard.edu/~ponars/memos.html>

Webber, M. (1996) *The International Politics of Russia and the Successor States*. Manchester and New York: Manchester University Press.

Webber, M. (ed.) (2000a) *Russia and Europe: Conflict or Cooperation?* Basingstoke: Macmillan.

Webber, M. (2000b) 'Conclusion: Russia and Europe – Trajectories of Development', in Webber, M. (ed.), *Russia and Europe: Conflict or Cooperation?* Basingstoke: Macmillan, 210–26.

Wyllie, J.H. (1997) *European Security in the New Political Environment*. London and New York: Longman.

Yeltsin, B. (1992) *Diplomaticheskii vestnik*, **4–5**, 70–2.

Zlenko, A. (1993) 'Ukraine and the Nuclear Dilemma', *NATO Review* **41**(4), 11–14.

The world wide web

The Russian Foreign Ministry can be found at: <http://www.mid.ru/>. Ukraine's Foreign Ministry is at: <http://www.mfa.gov.ua>. Developments in Russian foreign policy can be tracked on Johnson's Russia List at: <http://www.cdi.org/russia/johnson/default.asp>. The web site of Radio Free Europe/Radio Liberty at: <http://www.rferl.org/> contains a wealth of links that provide detailed information on both Russia and Ukraine. The Programme on New Approaches to Regional Security (PONARS) carries numerous short articles on Russian foreign policy and can be accessed at: <http://www.fas.harvard.edu/~ponars/>.

7 | The New Europe: Germany and Poland

David Allen and Mark Webber

Germany and Poland occupy pivotal positions in Europe and the foreign policy challenges each has faced have been profound and in some senses revolutionary. Germany (or more properly prior to 1990 the Federal Republic of Germany and the German Democratic Republic) was a state which typified the Cold War – it was divided into east and west, owed split allegiances to NATO and the Warsaw Pact and was on the frontline of the military build-up between the Soviet bloc and the Western alliance. Since 1990 the country has been unified and foreign policy, while embedded within a firm multilateral framework (defined by NATO and the EU), has reached out to the former communist bloc. Poland, meanwhile, has effectively switched sides. Once a sizeable military contributor to the Warsaw Pact, it has, following the collapse of that body (and the subsequent dissolution of the Soviet Union), turned towards an unashamedly Western orientation. This saw Poland join NATO in 1999 and has taken it close to EU membership. Poland, however, retains a significant appreciation that policy towards its eastern neighbours ought not to be neglected and that the east European regional context remains important. This has meant the pursuit of what might be described as a 'multi-directional' foreign policy.

The foreign policy arena and the challenge of transformation

Europe is at the very heart of the transformation of international politics that is the central focus of this text. It was in and over Europe principally that the Cold War was shaped and fought and it was in Europe that it came to an end. Between 1945 and 1989 Europe was divided between East and West creating two interacting sub-systems of international relations.

The states of Europe were subjected to 'superpower overlay' (Buzan et al., 1990: 36–41) to such an extent that their broad foreign policy orientation was essentially fixed by their geographic position. European states were either part of the Soviet-dominated Eastern bloc, the American-dominated Western bloc or they were neutral. The Cold War system severely restricted the foreign policy options that European states could select because a change of political orientation was ruled out by the stalemate imposed by the two superpowers, who came to fear that any change would rapidly escalate into a full-scale nuclear confrontation. This harsh reality was most graphically illustrated in 1968 by the attempt of Czechoslovakia to liberalise its communist system and the consequent armed intervention by the Soviet Union.

The European state system can be traced back to the Treaty of Westphalia of 1648. It is one based upon the primacy of state sovereignty and as such its core principle has spread throughout the wider international system. The sanctity attached to state sovereignty has not, however, meant the principle has always been observed and so consequently within Europe there is a long history of attempts to develop a system of 'order'. Throughout the eighteenth and nineteenth centuries European states sought to uphold order by pursuing an informal balance of power policy designed to prevent any one state predominating in the system. Here, states were free to change alliances in their search for either dominance or self-preservation, something that placed a premium upon diplomatic skills and well-crafted foreign policies. Great Britain often played the balancing role among several great powers and while this policy eventually succeeded in defeating Napoleon's attempt to dominate Europe and deterred others from attempting domination throughout the nineteenth century, it eventually broke down in the early twentieth century in the face of German ambition.

The discredited balance of power system was abandoned with the stalemated peace of 1918 (following the First World War) and was replaced by an attempt to institutionalise a system of collective security under the aegis of the League of Nations. Non-participation by the United States (US) and an apparent weakness in the face of German, Italian and Japanese aggression in the 1930s led to a belated return to the balance of power with first of all Britain and then others intervening to oppose Hitler's bid to dominate Europe. A further attempt at a more 'realistic' global system of collective security was then created with the United Nations (UN), headed by a Security Council dominated by the five victorious powers, three of whom were European (the Soviet Union, Britain and France). In Europe, however, the defeat of Germany left a vacuum which was contested by the Western Allies on the one hand and on the other by the Soviet Union. At the end of the Second World War the Nazi empire was broken up and the Westphalian state system revived by the conquering allies. Everywhere European states were either restored or reinvented but under the heavy ideological influence of the victors. The Western Allies sought to create viable liberal democracies while the Red Army's successful thrust into eastern Europe resulted in the imposition of communist systems in the states that they occupied. By 1947 Europe was deeply divided both geographically and ideologically.

The states of Europe thus found themselves restored but in a unique foreign policy environment, forced to belong to one of the two competing alliance structures established by the US and the Soviet Union or to accept perpetual neutrality. In this context any adjustments had to take place within the alliances rather than between them. In Cold War Europe there could be no question of a European state changing sides or choosing either to renounce or to adopt a policy of neutrality. At the centre of this divided Europe lay Germany – itself divided, initially into zones of occupation, but eventually into two separate states: the German Democratic Republic (GDR) and the Federal Republic of Germany (FRG).

During the Cold War many European states found themselves host to the military forces and thus the political influence of the two superpowers. These forces were formally present to guarantee the territorial integrity of their hosts but they were also clearly present in order to maintain the established regimes. Such was the longevity of the Cold War that the two competing systems in Europe became 'institutionalised'. In the East the Soviet Union consolidated its economic and military domination by the creation of the Council for Mutual Economic Assistance (CMEA) and the Warsaw Pact respectively. In the West there was a more varied pattern of institutionalisation. Military affairs were dominated by the North Atlantic Treaty Organisation (NATO) in which the US, as the military hegemon, was always *primus inter pares* despite the nominal equality of all Alliance members and decision-making arrangements based on unanimity. The degree of integration was low, with each NATO member state retaining national forces and attempting, where possible, to preserve national systems of arms procurement. Attempts by groupings of West European states to work together in the defence field were frustrated by disagreements about whether the objective of such cooperation was to reinforce NATO or to prepare for its replacement, and by nervousness about the likely US reaction to European defence initiatives. For its part, the US remained ambiguous about European efforts; anxious to preserve the dominant position that NATO guaranteed it but equally determined that the Europeans should pull their weight in the competition with the Soviet Union. On the economic front, encouraged and supported by the US, the West Europeans sought to consolidate their market economies and liberal democracies by creating institutions such as the European Community (EC), the European Free Trade Association (EFTA) and the Council of Europe. As the Cold War developed, the EC gradually evolved into the European Union (EU) and became the dominant European organisation, adding new members and new tasks, including cooperative political and military ambitions, to its successful economic achievements. Before the end of the Cold War most West European states sought membership of, or association with, the EU, implicitly accepting a set of membership criteria which excluded the so-called non-democratic Eastern bloc countries. Those within the states of Eastern Europe who aspired to membership of the EU and NATO knew that this would only be possible after a transformation of the Cold War system in Europe – a transformation which few believed before 1989 would be possible without a full-scale nuclear confrontation between the US and the Soviet Union.

While the foreign policy options for the states of Cold War Europe were restrained, there remained nonetheless some room for manoeuvre. Each bloc had its non-conforming members. Within NATO France sought to make a virtue of its resistance to US influence by expelling Alliance forces from its territory and refusing to integrate its military into NATO command; Norway and Denmark found space to prevent the deployment of nuclear weapons on their territory; and Greece and Turkey often seemed to be preparing to go to war against one another rather than to meet their joint Alliance obligations to fight together. Within the Soviet bloc, meanwhile, Romania under Nicolae Ceaucesçu was an awkward partner and successfully refused to allow Warsaw Pact troops on to its territory.

Other dynamics also blurred the edges of the Cold War divide. There was, for instance, some contact between the two blocs and this was a process that eventually played its part in the transformation of the European system. In this regard, the relationship between the two Germanys was always special. In the mid-1970s, pioneered by West Germany's pursuit of an *Ostpolitik* aimed at reconciliation as a basis for peaceful coexistence, a period of *détente* was inaugurated in Europe. This was symbolised by a significant pan-European gathering in Helsinki at the Conference on Security and Cooperation in Europe (CSCE) in 1975.

Participation in the CSCE suggested a European system of international relations that stretched geographically from Vancouver to Vladivostock, involving as it did all the states of Europe (with the sole exception of Albania) and the two extra-European superpowers (the US and the Soviet Union) as well as Canada. The CSCE 'process' continued after this initial conference and, in a sense, illustrated the changing nature of the foreign policy agenda in Europe. Because of its pan-European character and because the US expressed little real interest at the outset, the

CSCE was never a straightforward NATO–Warsaw Pact negotiating forum. This presented a number of European states with considerable scope to 'escape' the constrictions of deliberations dominated by the two super-powers. Moreover, the initial CSCE conference was effectively organised into three 'baskets', dealing with economic, politico-military and socio-cultural agendas that reflected and subsequently encouraged a growing range of contacts between the two sides of Europe. Considerable emphasis was placed on what became known as the 'low politics' of economic and social exchanges as well as the more familiar 'high politics' of defence and diplomacy. On the Western side, it was the EC rather than NATO that provided the coordinating mechanisms, especially over economic matters. On the other side, the fact that the Warsaw Pact was not the prime basis for organising coordination ensured that the East European states were able to pursue, within obvious limits, foreign policy positions that reflected their individuality rather than exclusively the demands and positions of the Soviet Union.

While the CSCE was important during the 1970s and 1980s, we have already noted the increasing significance also of the EC. Here, the European member states engaged in a growing network of multilateral diplomacy that gradually transformed their relationship into one that was 'domestic-ated' or civilised to the extent that the threat or the actual use of force between member states became unthinkable. Not only had the EC states transformed their foreign policy relations with one another, they had also begun to work together, first of all over external economic relations but later over traditional foreign and security policies, to develop, alongside their national policies, collective European stances towards the outside world. All member states had to deal with an expanded foreign policy agenda which, within the EU, meant that most aspects of domestic politics acquired an international dimension. This led to a perception of foreign policy as essentially a coordination problem. In many European states the need for a separate foreign ministry and diplomatic corps began to be questioned as more and more domestic government representatives became involved in international business and as more and more contacts between European governments and societies were direct and no longer exclusively conducted through diplomatic channels.

Throughout the Cold War the ultimate destiny of the EC remained contested, with some anticipating the eventual development of a United States of Europe and others determined to see the EC as a means of preserving the individual states – the European 'rescue' of the state. On the Eastern side of the Iron Curtain the picture was very different; there was little scope for distinct national foreign policies and individual East European states gained little experience of multilateral diplomacy, despite the existence of the Warsaw Pact and CMEA. The East European states essentially implemented external policies determined within their one-sided bilateral relationship with the Soviet Union, a relationship of control which operated at both the governmental and party level.

The features of the Cold War system sketched out above did suggest a degree of stability and certainty. As the Cold War wound down in the late 1980s–early 1990s some feared that these characteristics would be replaced by considerably more disruptive influences (Meirsheimer, 1990). The sudden collapse of CMEA, the Warsaw Pact and the Soviet Union itself in 1991 seemed to bear this view out. In the West there was a similar concern about the likely future of military structures – surely with the end of the Soviet threat NATO had lost its *raison d'être* (Corterier, 1990)? However, this was not how the future of the EC was viewed. While the organisation was, to a certain extent, a child of the Cold War inspired by a fear of the Soviet Union, there was also a sense in which it was felt it had been set free to pursue a more ambitious agenda once these influences were no more. The formal transformation of the EC into the EU with the Maastricht Treaty on European Union in 1992 symbolised this shift. At the same time, the EU became an increasingly powerful magnet for the former communist states, and by 1992, once it was clear that NATO would survive, a similar force was also exerted by the Alliance. Thus one of the major challenges of the transformation, once the Warsaw Pact and CMEA had rapidly disappeared, was the ability of the 'triumphant' Western organisations to adapt their practices in order both to survive the end of the Cold War and to enlarge their memberships (Croft et al., 1999). For the applicant states, meanwhile, the need to meet the membership criteria laid down by the organisations such as the Council of Europe, the EU and NATO could be used domestically to support and sustain the transformation process.

The end of the Cold War, therefore, meant the arrival of a number of new and inexperienced states in an environment where many of the old certainties were under challenge. While there was much talk of the need to create a new 'architecture' to underpin an emergent European order, it was not clear who would take responsibility for leadership. Who, in other words, would be the prime architect (Hyde-Price, 1992)? It might reasonably have been assumed in the early 1990s that the two former superpowers would take something of a back seat now that their contest was over. Maybe the US would concentrate more of its attention on the Pacific Rim and maybe Russia, as the successor to the Soviet Union, would be diverted by the burden of its internal transformation. Although an early attention focused on the ongoing CSCE and its eventual formalisation from 1995 as the Organisation for Security and Cooperation in Europe (OSCE), it also soon became clear that the EU and NATO would be the most important focal points and, moreover, that their own development both in terms of membership and task would continue to be significantly affected by the policies of the US. As the EU's drive for enlargement faltered in the mid-1990s, NATO's took off, with the result that Poland, the Czech Republic and Hungary became full members of the Alliance in 1999 without having any real idea about when they might attain entry into the EU.

While some states, like Germany, appeared to have little difficulty anticipating a Europe organised into a complex web of overlapping but essentially complementary organisations, others worried about a potential rivalry between the EU and NATO. When the EU, from the late 1990s, sought to develop a defence and security competence, the states within the Euro-Atlantic system found themselves in a rather familiar situation, with some worrying about a duplication of effort between NATO and the EU, some arguing that a European defence identity would undermine NATO and others that it would enhance the Alliance. Ongoing debates over NATO enlargement (who should be admitted after Polish, Czech and Hungarian entry and when?) also caused strains both within the Alliance itself and with a Russia that had never resigned itself to the loss of Moscow's influence in Eastern Europe. Thus a decade or so after the end of the Cold War the very real influence of the US and the potential influence of Russia remained a significant aspect of European affairs.

While it was the states of Eastern Europe and the former Soviet Union that faced the biggest challenges of transformation, it was also the case that the end of the Cold War impacted upon the way that the West European states operated, even though their political and economic systems remained much the same as before. It was noticeable that in Western Europe governments seemed to be relatively weaker than they had been before – in a number of states the bipartisan consensus on foreign policy goals began to be challenged and everywhere public opinion began to exert more influence on an area of policy that previously had been notable for its immunity to the vagaries of domestic politics. By way of example, it was apparent that from the early 1990s onwards the governments of both EU member states and of would-be member states found themselves increasingly at odds with their electorates over EU matters. The EU in particular was built from the top down – it is an edifice constructed by 'strong' governments which, until the Maastricht Treaty, were secure in the knowledge that if they could agree matters between themselves their publics would follow suit. However, the ambitious nature of the Maastricht Treaty provoked hostile reactions in a number of states even though the governments had pronounced themselves quite satisfied with it. Similarly, when the Norwegian and Swiss governments decided that EU membership was desirable, it was their publics rather than their fellow European governments who rejected their suggestions. One obvious consequence of this has been the much weaker EU treaties agreed at Amsterdam in 1997 and at Nice in 2000 – treaties negotiated by uncertain governments constantly looking over their shoulders to see how their proposals were going down at home. An interesting feature of post-Cold War Europe is that the operation of European institutions has become much more difficult, and this is made worse by difficulties within domestic government that are especially apparent in the 'transformed' states (see the Polish case study below).

There is another sense in which the states of Europe have come under challenge in recent years. As well as facing domestic challenges to their foreign policy judgements, the central governments of the European states find themselves increasingly assailed from both above and below as the European system has evolved from one dominated by 'sovereign' states to one increasingly characterised by multi-level forms of governance. There has always been pressure to transfer decision-making power from the national to the European level and this has often given rise to controversies over whether such transfers represent a challenge to, or rescue of, the European state. However, the post-1989 period has been characterised also by a growing demand for power to be devolved downwards to new states or to regional and local levels within existing states. At first this was most apparent in the eastern part of the continent as the Soviet Union, Czechoslovakia and Yugoslavia all rapidly broke up, but there has also been a significant pressure for decentralisation in Western Europe too, with the EU often providing a rationalising frame of reference. In a number of West European states there are territorial groups pressing either for devolved power or for independence. The Scots, the Bavarians, the Wallonians, the Basques, the Italian supporters of the Northern League and others all argue for their viability as separate units with the EU. In Switzerland – previously a model of multilingual harmony – most French-speaking Swiss would like to join the EU while most German-speaking Swiss would rather not. The EU publishes a map of the 'Europe of the Regions' with some pride but few have given much thought to the impact of further devolution and a further weakening of the present national governments on the management of international relations in Europe. It is possible that the transformation of the actors in the European system may continue with a continuous growth in the numbers of those who claim the right to exist as separate identities and thus to pursue 'foreign' policies towards one another.

It is, of course, too early to make definitive judgements about the nature of the European context within which its states seek to design and implement their foreign policies both individually and collectively. At the start of the period of transformation all the actors in the European drama found themselves, to a certain extent, overwhelmed by events. In 1991 alone, the Gulf War was fought, a coup was mounted against Soviet leader Mikhail Gorbachev, the Soviet Union itself disintegrated and wars broke out in Yugoslavia as that state began to break apart. In those early years of change many hasty decisions were taken, promises made and expectations raised, all of which suggested that foreign policy machines were struggling to cope.

Furthermore, the pressure for adjustment in Europe has taken place within a global setting which itself has experienced great change. Attempts to 'manage' Europe overlap with efforts to come to terms with the broader challenge of globalisation, for instance, leading to arguments as to whether further European integration is best seen as a defence against such global pressures or a means to better facilitate them. Hence, as so often in the past, developments in Europe seem to be merely a more extreme version of what have to be seen as global trends. Within the new Europe, economies are more integrated, societies more interdependent, the traditional boundaries between the domestic and the foreign more confused, and notions of security more complex than in any other part of the international system.

In Europe the major threats to the way people live no longer predominately arise from the threat or use of military force by one state against another – violent threats have become internalised so that it is no longer whole societies who are challenged but minorities within them (Waever et al., 1993). This presents some problems for an international system based on the notion of sovereignty and the related assumption that it is wrong to interfere in the domestic affairs of others. Most of the challenges to the well-being of European citizens (which can no longer be taken to be the same thing as the well being of European states or their governments), be these related to the environment, health, crime, migration, drugs and so on, require some form of collective intervention if they are to be managed. Europe's security challenges can, in the main, no longer be confronted by physically defending national boundaries or deterred by the threat of retaliation. Ukraine's neighbours cannot hope to prevent another Chernobyl by either exploding one of their own nuclear reactors or passing a law banning the passage of radioactive wind across their territories. Similarly, the states of Europe cannot prevent an influx of migrants from the east and south by physically closing its borders – wherever they may lie.

As the 'new Europe' moves into its second decade the challenge to its foreign policy makers remain enormous and most of the important questions continue to be unresolved. There is as yet no firm agreement about the functional or geographic boundaries of Europe and hence about the eventual membership (or role) of either the EU or NATO. If, for instance, NATO retains defence as its core concern, then it will always exclude Russia, but if the Alliance becomes more of a collective security organisation, then Russian membership will become imperative. The Euro-Atlantic connection also remains important but increasingly uncertain. The degree of concern shown in the foreign ministries of Europe about the replacement of Bill Clinton by George W. Bush in 2001 suggests that huge significance is still attached to the role of the US in Europe.

As the challenges posed within the new Europe multiply, the more helpless and leaderless the European states might appear to be. Yet for all this, these same European states have demonstrated resilience in the face of uncertainty. This may at times have appeared comic (the boast that 'the hour of Europe' had arrived with EU efforts at resolving the Yugoslav crisis during its early stages) but, as we shall see in the case studies below, an image of hapless Europeans pursuing bumbling foreign policies is belied by other more polished and determined efforts.

Germany

The challenges of transformation

For Germany the end of the Cold War was accompanied by an event of momentous historic importance, namely the unification in October 1990 of the FRG and the GDR. This represented a massive change both to the nature of the German state, which was now much bigger but also poorer on a per capita basis, and to its geopolitical position (see Table 7.1). Almost at a stroke Germany's situation changed from being 'a frontline state between two hostile alliance systems [. . . to] a country at the heart of [. . . a] continent aspiring to become "whole and free"' (Hyde-Price, 2000: 105). However one defined the ultimate boundaries of the new Europe, the new Germany was central. The inclusion of the former GDR meant that once the Soviet Union had broken up Germany was entirely surrounded by states which were in or aspired to be in either the EU or NATO or, in most cases, both. Holland, Belgium, Luxembourg, France, Switzerland, Austria, the Czech Republic, Poland and Denmark were all allies and partners who looked to Germany for leadership and support

Table 7.1 A comparison of European states

State	Population in 2000 (m)	Surface area (thousands of sq. km)	GDP (purchasing power parity) in 1999 (US$ bn)	Military expenditure (US$ m) (year in brackets)
Albania	3.5	28.7	5.6	42 (1999)
Austria	8.1	84	190	1,700 (1998)
Belgium	10.2	30.5	243.4	2,800 (1999)
Bulgaria	7.8	110	34.9	379 (1999)
Czech Republic	10.2	78.8	120.8	1,200 (1999)
Denmark	5.3	43	127.7	2,800 (1998)
Finland	5.1	337	108.6	1,800 (1998)
France	59.3	547	1,370	39,800 (1997)
Germany	82.8	356	1,860	32,800 (1998)
Greece	10.6	132	149	4,000 (1998)
Hungary	10.1	93	79.4	732 (1999)
Ireland	3.8	70	73.7	732 (1998)
Italy	57.6	301	1,200	23,300 (1999)
Netherlands	15.9	41.5	365	6,900 (1998)
Norway	4.5	386	111.3	3,100 (1998)
Poland	38.6	312	276.5	3,200 (2000)
Portugal	10	92	151.4	2,400 (1997)
Romania	22.4	237	87.4	650 (1996)
Slovakia	5.4	48.8	45.9	332 (1999)
Sweden	8.8	450	184	5,000 (1998)
Switzerland	7.2	41	197	3,100 (1998)
Turkey	65.6	779	409	6,700 (1997)
United Kingdom	59.5	244	1,290	36,884 (1997)
Yugoslavia (Serbia/ Montenegro)	10.6	102.3	20.6	911 (1999)

Source: Central Intelligence Agency (2000).

and who presented no direct physical threat. The military threat that the Soviet Union had presented first of all receded as Soviet troops withdrew or planned to withdraw from Eastern Europe and was further diminished by the collapse of the Soviet Union itself. All of this meant that the German people were faced with an enormous cost – of paying for the integration of the former GDR and compensating Moscow for troop withdrawals. It was expected that the so-called 'peace dividend' of reduced defence expenditure would partly compensate for this.

Although the end of the Cold War and the unification of Germany had been the stated objective of all of Germany's allies in NATO and the EU, not all of them initially responded positively when it actually happened. Germany found itself once again faced with the problem of adjusting to changes that it was not responsible for in a manner that reassured its neighbours. France and Britain in particular exhibited signs of distress and worried aloud that Germany might exploit its new position and break free of the multilateral obligations that had so clearly restrained it during the Cold War (Cole, 1993). The new Germany therefore had to reassure those around it, to the East as well as to the West, that no new threats might arise from its transformed situation. An additional problem arose from France's concerns about the possibility of Germany slipping from the restraints represented by the EU. As on a number of previous occasions, France worried about a dilution of the EU through enlargement and argued for a deepening of integration among the existing members before any consideration of adding new members. Germany, on the other hand, was concerned both to reassure its Western partners and to offer encouragement and assistance to its newly 'liberated' Eastern neighbours. Britain presented less of a challenge in this respect. It followed the logic that a wider EU would mean a weaker one, and for this reason supported enlargement apparently unconcerned that this might lead to Germany's escape from the EU's entangling clutches.

The new situation also challenged Germany's relationship with the US and with first the Soviet Union and then Russia. While it was clear from the very beginning that Washington would support German unification unconditionally and support NATO membership for a united Germany, it was also clear that the US expected Germany in turn to play a more proactive role in international relations. George Bush's call to Germany to be his 'partner in leadership' in the construction of a new world order implied a changed role for Germany and the outbreak of hostilities in the Gulf in 1991 meant that the new challenge soon became a reality. With Russia, Germany faced the historically familiar problem of trying to forge a sound relationship that did not, in turn, arouse the concern of neighbours in Eastern Europe, fearful of the old notion of German and Russian spheres of influence. Furthermore, the Germans were only too well aware of the need to maintain Moscow's goodwill following the difficult international negotiations that preceded unification.

The transformation of Europe meant that Germany was now a 'normal' state but this meant that all sorts of expectations were raised externally about how it should or would behave. It could be argued that if West

Germany had had a foreign policy limited to the search for a state, the new Germany looked a little like a state in search of a foreign policy. During the Cold War, German governments and German public opinion had become accustomed to life in the international system and to defining their external ambitions and interests always in a multilateral context. It was by no means clear that either were ready to make the adjustments that seem to be required and expected of them (Maull, 1990). Indeed, it was debatable even whether the German people were unanimously enthusiastic about unification. Following the division of the country after the Second World War, Germany had been described as two states but one nation. Soon after unification, as the cost of eliminating the enormous differences between Germany's eastern and western halves became apparent, it became possible to describe it as one state and two nations. One immediate challenge arose over the siting of the capital of the new Germany. Bonn, the capital of the FRG, retained its attractions for those who wished Germany to remain as a relatively inactive participant in international politico-strategic affairs. If Germany was to remain primarily an economic actor, then Frankfurt would remain the real centre of German power, but for others Germany's new situation and geography meant that the capital would eventually have to revert to Berlin, despite the memories of Germany's past that this would revive.

The foreign policy debate

During the Cold War there was little real debate in the FRG about the broad lines of foreign policy. For a time during the 1950s and 1960s, the political Left expressed doubts about the compatibility of Chancellor Konrad Adenauer's enthusiasm for integration into Western multilateral institutions with the objective of eventual reunification. Some outside, meanwhile, often worried that West Germany would one day accept neutrality as the price of unification (an option that the Soviets constantly offered). This concern was expressed particularly strongly at the time of the FRG's pursuit of *Ostpolitik* in the late 1960s and 1970s, but it soon became apparent that a better and more constructive relationship with the East was not an alternative to Western integration but a complement.

There was also little debate within the FRG about how the then EC should develop. In this regard, there had always been an enthusiasm for both a widening and deepening of the Community as well as a willingness to accept that West Germany would be a substantial net contributor to the Community budget. Furthermore, the FRG had little difficulty reconciling its multiple membership of several institutions in the Euro-Atlantic system, whereas for the British and the French there so often seemed to be choices to be made between a NATO or EU orientation.

Many analysts believed that the FRG's foreign policy stances during the Cold War could best be understood as a product of Germany's geopolitical position and of its semi-sovereign status. They thus predicted that if Germany's position were ever to change, then so too would Germany's foreign policy (Meirsheimer, 1990: 6–7). The idea that Germany might go 'back to the future' was one that Chancellor Helmut Kohl was determined to reject by his insistence on maintaining Germany's multilateral, pacifist, and pro-integrationist stance (Meiers, 1995). There was, in fact, a solid domestic consensus inside Germany for an absolute rejection of the past and, in particular, of the Third Reich. This underpinned Germany's enthusiasm for a decentralised system of government at both the national and European level and gave rise to a rejection of militarism as a form of power projection and a commensurate emphasis on political instruments of foreign policy. In this sense, Germany was defined as a 'civilian power' (Maull, 1990). These were not short-term, shallow views, pragmatically held as the result of a specific situation. They were deeply imbued into modern German thinking and so a significant change in foreign policy orientation was never really on the cards. Rejection of the past also gave powerful support to those who argued both before and after 1989 for a policy of active reconciliation towards those states which had been most severely affected by German excess in the past – initially Israel and France, and later Poland and Czechoslovakia (Feldman, 1999).

Several years after 1989, the 'shadow of the past' still hung over the German foreign policy debate. Justifying German reluctance to send forces to parts of Europe in the mid-1990s, Kohl claimed that such movements were politically sensitive owing to local memories of actions carried out by Nazi soldiers during the Second World War. Of course, over time, generations pass and memories fade, and it is perhaps this that explains the gradual shift in the German debate that began to look more like a significant change once Kohl and his generation of Germans had withdrawn from power. In this sense, it could be argued that the real foreign policy debate in Germany only really began with the departure of Helmut Kohl and the formation in October 1998 of a coalition between the Social Democratic Party (SPD) and the Greens under the leadership of Chancellor Gerhard Schröder (Maull, 2000).

However, the beginnings of the debate were, in fact, there already in the early and mid-1990s. True, under Helmut Kohl, Chancellor for the decade either side of 1989, there was a remarkable continuity of German foreign policy: Kohl was not prepared to consider any serious alternative to the commitment to multilateralism that had characterised German foreign policy during the Cold War. It was this continuity that Kohl could point to in order to reassure those who most feared the power of a unified Germany. But Kohl's reluctance to consider any serious change did not rule a consideration of alternatives among German politicians and foreign policy analysts, and at least five options could be identified in the debate over German foreign policy (Hellmann, 1997; Janning, 1996). First, Germany could push for a further deepening of European integration, consolidating its relationship with France and with the US within NATO. On the other hand, Germany might prioritise its relationship with the emerging democracies of Eastern Europe, seeking enlargement of the EU and breaking free from the restraints of the Franco-German bilateral leadership of an EU limited to Western Europe. This strategy implied a German willingness to accept a leadership role within an enlarged and perhaps more diverse and less restrictive EU. Third, there were those who argued that a strategic bilateral partnership with the US was the most attractive option for a Germany that might seek to loosen its multilateral ties and pursue a more individualistic foreign policy. The opposite to this third position was the possibility of seeking a strategic partnership with Russia – the classic Eastern option that relied heavily on Russia being both willing and able to cooperate and which was likely to arouse the ire and anxiety of Germany's neighbours. Under this option, Germany and Russia would become even bigger trading partners, with Germany exchanging technology and advanced consumer goods in return for Russian raw materials. Finally there was the option that some had feared during the Cold War, of a Germany seeking to profit from its 'civilian' status by acting as a neutral politico-military power and concentrating on the exploitation of its economic might.

These alternatives suggest a debate not just about the orientation of German foreign policy, but also about its style. It was argued, for instance, that if Germany did stick with the broad lines of its Cold War foreign policy, it would be hard to avoid firm definitions of German interest within multilateral frameworks. In other words, there was an expectation that Germany would now play more of a leadership role, that it would accept more responsibility for its undoubted power and influence (Bluth, 1995). This expectation had some very practical consequences. Would Germany define its interests and positions before it attended multilateral meetings rather than wait to adopt the views of the majority as had so often been the case in the past? How would Germany react to the demands of those within the EU and NATO who wanted it to exploit more fully the full range of its potential foreign policy tools? And how would these expectations be received among German public opinion?

Another aspect of this debate concerned the use of force. At a time when the use of force was becoming increasingly more urgent for NATO members, Germany was compelled to ponder the relevance of its predisposition against military measures. In fact, political opinion in Germany had been moving towards a more permissive position on this issue throughout the 1990s, largely in response to a perceived need to act in the former Yugoslavia. By the time of NATO's Operation Allied Force against Serbia in 1999 a clear majority of the German electorate supported German participation in air strikes even if this meant German casualties (Maull, 2000: 10).

This, in turn, illustrated that given the momentous changes that had occurred with the end of the Cold War and unification, there was a very real sense in which the foreign policy debate had widened out to embrace German society as a whole. Indeed, with so many options and so many external pressures it was inevitable that the German public would begin to take more of an interest than before in foreign policy. As well as the issue of military force, this was manifest in the reaction to the Maastricht Treaty (albeit less spectacularly than in France and Britain) and grew into a concern about the combined costs of unification and further support for European integration, particularly as it now involved the subsuming of the much-prized German Mark into a single European currency. German foreign policy makers found themselves in a similar position to their counterparts in other West European states – increasingly forced to consider public opinion at home and abroad, leading to pressure to develop the means to prosecute public as well as governmental diplomacy. It was notable that at his last significant meeting of the EU European Council in Amsterdam in 1997 even Helmut Kohl was forced to curb his integrationist instincts for fear (justified as it turned out) that he would be punished by the German electorate.

The foreign policy process

When Germany was unified in 1990 the foreign policy apparatus of the GDR was absorbed into that of the Federal Republic, leading to an immediate increase in the numbers of diplomatic personnel and foreign delegations. During the 1990s these figures have been steadily cut back such that the German Foreign Ministry and diplomatic service is about the same size now as before unification. This is the case even though it has nearly 20 million more German citizens to represent and even though the proliferation of 'new' states in Europe has led to an increase in the number of external missions.

Germany is similar in many ways to France, Italy and the UK in that it is one of just a few European states which attempt to maintain world-wide representation with embassies and missions in almost every state in the world. Unlike in Britain and France, however, there seems to be less resistance in Germany to ideas of rationalising the external representation of the EU member states, either by developing joint embassies and collective representation or, more dramatically, by empowering the EU to undertake more representational work through its own network of delegations. The Germans have always been impressed with the fact that while the EU member states have a total of 40,000 diplomatic personnel organised in fifteen foreign ministries and 1,500 overseas missions, the US has just 15,000 diplomats, a single State Department and 300 overseas missions. When the Soviet Union broke up into a number of independent states it was Germany that suggested that the EU might provide a suitable framework for joint embassies to these new states and it was the British and the French who rejected the idea out of hand.

In addition, the foreign policy process in Germany has had to adjust to two other elements of transformation in recent years. First of all, like all European states, it has had to organise itself increasingly for both multi-lateral and bilateral diplomacy, covering an enormously expanded foreign policy agenda. This has involved an increasing number of 'domestic' departments in Germany's foreign business, something that, in turn, has led to problems of coordination and to arguments concerning the proper role of the German Foreign Ministry in shaping and implementing policy.

The second element concerns the particular nature of Germany's political system. Germany has a fragmented federal system of government which has always had problems in coordinating policy towards the outside world. Post-war Germany has lacked strong institutions capable of exercising central control – the Chancellor's office has not developed a foreign policy role to the extent that this has occurred either in the Prime Minister's office in the UK or the Elysée Palace in France. Certainly during the Cold War period, it could be said that the German system was not set up for a foreign policy designed to identify and pursue German national interests. It was an ideal system for pursuing cooperative policies within a multilateral context in which others took the lead, but it was less useful in identifying and pursuing specifically German objectives. Given the different set of expectations of Germany in the post-Cold War period, this is a system that has had to change. As the EU becomes more diverse in both membership and task, then there will be more and more areas where others, in particular new members from the north and east of Europe, will look to Germany for a lead. Within NATO the hegemonic power of the US may not be as available as before either to set the agenda for military considerations or to provide the solutions to problems that involve the use of military power. If this results in the EU developing its own military dimension, then, while the onus for sustaining progress will primarily remain with Britain and France, Germany too will be required to make its contribution and to develop its own stances on the use of force for a whole range of new tasks such as humanitarian intervention, crisis management and peacekeeping. In 1994 the German Constitutional Court removed the formal legal obstacles to the *Bundeswehr* operating militarily outside of the NATO area but the fact remains that Germany is at present institutionally not capable of planning military activity outside of the NATO framework (Longhurst, 2000). Put simply, Germany has entered the new period in European affairs without the foreign policy apparatus to support its changed status as a significant power and to meet the expectations of its partners that it will begin to act as such.

It must also be remembered that Germany has been governed by coalitions for most of its post-1945 existence. This has usually resulted in a situation whereby the Foreign Ministry has been held by the junior alliance partner – either the Free Democrats or, more recently, the Green Party. Despite this there have been few examples of serious political differences interfering with the established bipartisan consensus on foreign policy (even during Operation Allied Force this consensus was largely maintained). Coalition politics does, however, have its effects. It was perhaps no accident that the Free Democrat Foreign Minister, Hans Dietrich Genscher, was generally more multilateralist in orientation than Kohl and that the Green Foreign Minister, Joschka Fischer, had to expend considerably more political energy in persuading his party of the necessity of air strikes during Operation Allied Force than did Schröder in relation to his.

The substance of foreign policy

As already noted, during the Cold War German foreign policy was essentially multilateralised within the comforting frameworks of NATO and the EU (and its predecessors). With regard to the former, the FRG was, in the main, a cooperative partner. NATO was seen as essential to German interests, not only as a defensive alliance but also as a forum in which German rearmament could occur without reviving historical suspicions on the part of France and Britain. Tellingly perhaps, the FRG was willing in the mid-1980s to allow the US deployment of Pershing II intermediate nuclear weapons on its territory as part of a NATO strategy of responding to Soviet SS-20 deployments in Eastern Europe.

Within the EU, meanwhile, the FRG showed considerable enthusiasm for the process of European Political Cooperation (EPC) and, after 1993, the Common Foreign and Security Policy (CFSP). Outside the multilateral framework, the FRG was an active supporter of its economic, financial and trading interests but exhibited little interest in either unilateral political initiatives or the management of the world political order that so obsessed the other major powers in the system. The FRG, like Japan, was the ultimate 'free rider' in the Cold War era, enjoying and prospering in the stability that the politico-military efforts of others produced.

The one major unilateral initiative that the FRG did pursue was the development from 1969 onwards of *Ostpolitik*, a focus on the communist countries to its East to counter-balance its Western orientation. This was a policy that meshed well with the American and West European concern with *détente* during the 1970s. However, unlike the US, West Germany sought to continue to promote cordial relations with the Soviet Union even during the downturn in East–West relations occasioned by the so-called 'second Cold War' of the early 1980s.

The challenge of the post-1989 period was even more demanding. Even if the FRG was to continue to resist attempts to make it define and pursue national interests in the traditional ways of a great power, it did have to face up to the changed environment of multilateralism. Where once the FRG's coordination reflex led it to go straight to the EU or NATO in order to define its position on whatever was the crisis of the day, post-Cold War Germany has found that it is expected at a minimum to have a position and preferably to be prepared to take some leads. In other words, the definition of German interests is now required to shape multilateral deliberations rather than to emerge as a result of them.

Events during 1990–91 proved a watershed in this regard. The first event of note was the Gulf War, which broke out almost at the point of unification. Germany's response here was fairly traditional, offering unquestioning diplomatic and financial support for the American-led military operation but exhibiting an unwillingness to participate in the operation itself, pleading the Basic Law as a constitutional barrier to any German military activity outside the NATO area. Nevertheless, German planes did support the humanitarian activities in Turkey and Iran designed to assist the Kurds, and after the Gulf War German mine-removal teams were active in the Arabian Sea removing Iraqi mines.

The second event at this juncture was the outbreak of hostilities in the former Yugoslavia. Here, Germany acted in a seemingly much more robust fashion. It unilaterally recognised Croatia and Slovenia in December 1991 and thereby forced the rest of the EU member states to take a similar decision in order to preserve European diplomatic unity. However, this has to be seen as an exception to Germany's otherwise rigid adherence to multilateralism and can be explained less in terms of an increasingly strident Germany and more in terms of domestic politics. Whatever the motives, the step did amount to a German lead and one with considerable consequences, signalling as it did the effective end of 'Yugolsavia's existence as a sovereign state' (Crawford, 1995: 1).

Following the watershed of 1990–91, Germany has moved towards more activist positions. However, the pattern exhibited in 1991 over the former Yugoslavia has been rare; Germany has sought to remain within the boundaries of consensus. This is clear from a consideration of its position on military intervention. What Germany has done since 1991 is move inch by inch towards getting itself in a position of near normality on involvement in NATO or other international operations. The constitutional barriers were removed by the 1994 decision of the Constitutional Court, enabling German troops to take part in the NATO-led Intervention Force (IFOR) and the Stabilisation Force (SFOR) in Bosnia. Even prior to this decision, German air force personnel flew in NATO AWACs aircraft patrolling various Bosnian no-fly zones and, in the Adriatic, German naval vessels participated after 1992 in the supervision of the NATO/Western European Union (WEU) embargo of Yugoslavia. German forces have also achieved a degree of integration with French and Spanish forces in the Eurocorps. More spectacularly, and as a sign of further progress, in 1999 during the Kosovo campaign German armed forces went into action against another sovereign state for the first time, controversially without the cover of a UN resolution. Once the air-bombing campaign was concluded the Eurocorps provided the headquarters staff for KFOR (the Kosovan Intervention Force) for a short period. In October 1999 a German general, Klaus Reinhardt, was appointed to command KFOR.

Away from Europe, and perhaps in pursuit of its ambitions to achieve the status of permanent membership of the UN Security Council, German planes and ground forces participated in the UN-led operation in Somalia (UNOSOM 11) in 1992–94, German officers were sent to Georgia as part of the UN observer mission (UNOMIG) and the German air force flew many aid-bearing missions in Rwanda in 1994. A German contingent was also sent to East Timor in 1999 as part of the Australian-led UN peacekeeping force. These examples notwithstanding, Germany cannot be said to have embraced military operations with any great enthusiasm, it remains an essentially pacifist country, with as many young Germans absenting themselves from military service as those participating, but over the last decade the shift in governmental attitude is clear and the movement is all in one direction (Hyde-Price, 1999).

The war in Kosovo broke out during the German presidency of the EU Council of Ministers and serves to illustrate a number of distinctive features of German foreign policy in a transformed Europe. First, as already noted, Germany managed to overcome its military reticence and both fully support and participate in the NATO bombing campaign, although there were signs that the German government would have experienced some difficulties had President Milosovic not surrendered and had British Prime Minister Tony Blair been successful in persuading the Americans to use NATO ground forces in a peacemaking, as opposed to a peacekeeping, role. While one would have expected Helmut Kohl to support NATO military action, it was of some significance that the Green/SPD coalition with Joschka Fischer as Foreign Minister was prepared to adhere to the NATO line. Many commentators observed that the new German foreign policy establishment was now prepared to countenance the use of force as legitimate and to take more seriously the role of Germany 'in the reshaping of Europe' (Hyde-Price, 1999: 15).

Despite supporting the military campaign, the German foreign policy elite were also anxious to pursue diplomatic channels both in search of a peace settlement and in search of a long-term solution to the problems of the area. To this end, Germany was instrumental in trying to use the UN to engage the attention of the Russians and to encourage the Americans to take Russian involvement in any solution seriously. The peace settlement that was eventually achieved owed much to German diplomacy. The Germans, however, went much further and in April 1999 also initiated plans for a Stability Pact for Southeastern Europe which was designed to use the essentially civilian attractions of the EU to persuade the states of former Yugoslavia to alter their behaviour towards one another and towards minorities within their territories. The German-inspired plan went way beyond the role that the EU had assumed in Bosnia (paying for and supervising reconstruction) and instead offered the attraction of prospective membership of the EU to the states of Albania, Bosnia, Croatia, Macedonia and the Federal Republic of Yugoslavia (Serbia-Montenegro) so as to extend the zone of civilised international interactions to an area which had previously, with the exception of Slovenia, been regarded as beyond the pale (Friis and Murphy, 2000).

The war in Kosovo also gave rise to the Anglo-French initiative to create a Common European Security and Defence Policy (CESDP), transferring the 'Petersberg' tasks from the WEU to the EU and creating a European Rapid Reaction Force to work both within NATO and 'where NATO chooses not to be engaged' outside the NATO framework. This development has been received with apparent equanimity inside Germany – despite plans to further reduce defence expenditure – although it has the potential to raise some difficult choices for Germany in the future, especially if the EU decides to take military action in the face of American opposition.

On the bilateral front, there have also been some significant changes in German policy. First of all, Germany has sought to develop close links with both the Soviet Union and latterly Russia. Partly this arose out of the delicate negotiations that were required to confirm Soviet acceptance of German unification and membership of a unified Germany within the NATO structure. Germany, immediately thereafter, had to ensure the orderly return of former Soviet troops from the former GDR and in the longer term has sought to promote Russian stabilisation. Russia is viewed pragmatically as a major trading partner and investment opportunity and, from a more historical perspective, as a partner/rival to Germany in the shaping of European order, given their status as Europe's two largest states (Höhmann et al., 1998: 24–5).

Elsewhere in the former communist bloc, Germany's relations with Poland have been equally significant. In the early 1990s these carried a certain historical baggage. Polish distrust of Germany was deep-rooted, not least owing to its treatment during the Second World War. An important early step was taken in November 1990 with the signing of a German–Polish treaty which confirmed the border between Poland and a now unified and enlarged Germany. In June of the following year Germany and Poland signed a treaty on good neighbourliness and cooperation, which symbolically marked what has been described as 'an historic reconciliation between the two age-old enemies' (Terry, 2000: 11). Thereafter, German strategy has been based on a realisation of post-communist Poland's role as a pivot between the Euro-Atlantic community of NATO/EU and the former communist states of Europe (including Russia and Ukraine) and a consequent need to integrate it fully into a stable multilateral framework (Hyde-Price, 2000: 216–18). As a result, Germany has been a champion of Polish entry into both NATO and the EU.

In 1989 and 1990 Germany relied heavily on its special relationship with the US and its growing relationship with Soviet leader Mikhail Gorbachev but considered itself to be badly let down by its other two special partners – Britain and France – which for different reasons expressed some disquiet at the prospect of German unification. As the 1990s progressed, however, there has been a growing recognition in both London and Paris of German weight in European affairs and with this a recognition that the balance of influence increasingly favours Germany. This has been most apparent in the relationship with France, particularly so following the disappearance from the political stage of President François Mitterrand and Chancellor Helmut Kohl in the latter half of the 1990s. This is a relationship that had been based on forty years of active reconciliation and which was best expressed in Franco-German leadership of the EU. Most observers began to question the continued vitality of this relationship at the time of the Treaty of Amsterdam in 1997, but the change was most apparent later, during the negotiations at the end of 2000 which led to the Treaty of Nice. Nice seemed to mark a sea-change in the Franco-German relationship – it certainly marked the end of the French domination of the relationship and the end of easy Franco-German solutions to the problems of European integration. Much of the business at Nice revolved around a significant dispute between the large and the small states of the EU over voting rights in an enlarged Union. This in some ways meant Germany lining up alongside France, but it also led to talk of a 'European directory' of Germany, France and the UK, with Germany accorded a grudging respect by France as an equal rather than junior partner.

Ten years after unification, most of the German government had been moved from Bonn to the new capital Berlin (83 per cent of the Foreign Ministry has been so transferred) and many pointed out the irony of the *Bundestag* (the German parliament) holding its first session in the new capital in the shadow of the war in Kosovo in April 1999. Germany is now a 'normal' state. It is now possible inside and outside Germany to talk of German interests without fear that this is indicative of past historical misdemeanours. Yet while Germany is more willing to exercise its own priorities in foreign policy, it has continued to do so within a multilateral institutionalist setting that places a high value on the notion of responsibility and the desirability of preserving ideas of collective security and collective international morality. The EU and its CFSP continue to be the main framework for consideration of Germany's international outlook and Germany has chosen to subsume some of its economic and financial power into the EU via Economic and Monetary Union and the single currency. German military engagement has to be seen against a background of 'civilian' power and Germany does not share with the same enthusiasm Anglo-French ambitions to create a viable EU security force.

Perhaps the power that Germany most effectively demonstrates at present is the power of example. Germany is an attractive model for those who would seek to develop further the EU around the notions of federalism and subsidiarity. Moreover, German ideas about the desirability of moderation, of consensus and of collective international responsibility may well turn German foreign policy and German foreign policy making into an attractive role model for the developing democracies of Eastern Europe.

Poland

The challenges of transformation

Poland is a country which has been wrenched over centuries by developments on the European continent. In the late eighteenth century it was divided between Prussia, Russia and Austria. Independence was regained after the First World War, but Poland disappeared from the map once more in 1939 following partition between Nazi Germany and the Soviet Union. Following the Second World War, Poland was resurrected, albeit with a shrunken population (caused in part by the almost total elimination of its Jewish population during the Holocaust), a different territory (parts of Poland were incorporated into the Soviet republics of Ukraine, Belorussia and Lithuania and Poland gained land to the west in what had been part of Germany), and a position firmly within the Soviet sphere of influence.

In light of this record of suffering, the euphoria which greeted the removal of communism in 1989 and, in tandem, the retreat of Soviet power, was tempered initially by a sense of realism and caution. Some compared Poland's position in 1989 to that of 1918. Then, the newly-independent Poland found itself surrounded by unstable and soon-to-be expansionist neighbours and with a population, some 30 per cent of whom represented national minorities from bordering states. This precarious position had resulted in a war with Soviet Russia in 1920, German invasion in 1939 (the ostensible trigger of the Second World War in Europe) and the German-Soviet partition. However, the catastrophes visited upon Poland during this period had the long-term effect of actually making the Polish state a more viable entity. The state that emerged after the Second World War was one with a clearly Polish national population. The German minority in the west was effectively driven out after 1945, while the Lithuanians, Belarussians and Ukrainians returned 'home' to their host republics in the Soviet Union.

It was this potential for statehood that was eventually released by the events of 1989. In 1989, unlike in 1918, Poland at least began its fully sovereign existence as an established viable state. A further legacy which had to be overcome, however, was that of subordination to Moscow. During the post-war period of Soviet domination Poland's freedom of manoeuvre was slight. Membership of the Warsaw Pact legitimised the stationing of Soviet and other Eastern bloc forces on Polish territory and membership of the CMEA effectively tied Poland to the Soviet economy. Sewn up economically and militarily, Poland was also politically controlled through the Polish United Workers' Party (PUWP). This ruling organisation did on occasion try to establish some freedom of manoeuvre from the Soviet communists but ultimately was subordinate to a Soviet 'party line'. This was evidenced most dramatically in 1980–81 when martial law was declared in Poland under the leadership of General Wojtech Jaruzelski. In the face of an upsurge of domestic protest at communist rule, Jaruzelski acted following signals from Moscow that unless a 'Polish solution' was found to the political troubles, then the Soviet Union would intervene in a manner similar to its military interventions in Hungary in 1956 and Czechoslovakia in 1968 (Mastny, 1999).

With the break-up of the Soviet Union in late 1991 Poland found itself next door to three new and potentially unstable states in the shape of Belarus, Lithuania and Ukraine, not to mention the run-down Russian enclave of Kaliningrad (Burant, 1993). To its west lay the newly unified Germany and to the south Czechoslovakia (which would itself divide into the Czech and Slovak Republics after November 1992). The challenge for Poland in this early post-Cold War period was to try to find a balance between at least four distinct European groupings of states – the Western states organised in NATO and the EU, fellow former communist states of Eastern Europe (particularly Hungary and the Czech Republic), a number of former Soviet republics, and lastly the special case of Russia – the Soviet Union's 'continuing state'. In meeting this challenge, Poland had few signposts to follow given that during the previous forty-five years it had enjoyed no effective foreign policy autonomy owing to its position in the Soviet bloc. This long-term subordination, moreover, imposed other more particular challenges, what Curt Gasteyger (1991) has referred to as 'de-Sovietization, renationalisation and demilitarisation'. The first of these entailed the overcoming of a foreign policy which, for decades, had been formulated (at least in public) through a Soviet-inflected Marxist-Leninist vocabulary. The second meant the pursuit of a foreign policy independent of Soviet influence and a consequent need to articulate the goals of a national interest. The third, meanwhile, required ridding Poland of its military subordination to the Soviet-dominated Warsaw Pact and, as part of this, negotiating and overseeing the removal of Soviet troops from its territory.

To add to these challenges, Poland (along with a number of other former communist states) entered after the Cold War a kind of 'grey zone' or 'security vacuum' between the states of the EU and NATO on the one hand, and Russia and the states of the former Soviet Union on the other. This was an area characterised by a 'lack of international structure[s], uncertain democracies, weak economies, ethnic strife, and potentially troublesome neighbours' (Frost, 1993: 37). As the history of Poland testifies, it was also a region defined by a certain 'in-betweeness' – one 'between East and West, between the Germans and the Russians', potentially subject to the 'intersection of spheres of influence' and, historically, of only minor concern to the other European powers and the US (Medvedev, 1998: i–ii).

As well as its external setting, Poland's foreign policy situation has been affected by processes of domestic transformation. The termination of communist rule in 1989 had been relatively seamless. A government led by the former anti-communist trade union movement 'Solidarity' was formed in September 1989 and in November of the following year Solidarity's leader, Lech Walesa, replaced Jaruzelsi as President. This process occurred without bloodshed or Soviet resistance, and with the compliance of the PUWP. At the forefront politically in Eastern Europe (Poland saw the first non-communist Prime Minister in the region) it was also an economic path-breaker, launching the programme of 'shock therapy' reform in 1990. For Poland to sustain its democratic transformation and the development of a market economy required internal procedures and institutions capable of independently interacting with the regional, European and international systems to which it became exposed with the retreat of Soviet power. Democratic states are expected to plan, decide upon and implement their foreign and security policies in a certain way acceptable to the international community. Market economies are by definition interdependent in the globalised international political economy and are perforce required to recognise the rules of international economic conduct and to participate in their development. The institutions and procedures required to run the foreign and security policies of a dependent communist state with a controlled economy would not be adequate for a transformed Poland operating in a transformed Europe.

The foreign policy debate

There is a sense in which there has never been much of a foreign policy debate within Poland because the broad lines of Polish foreign policy, both during the communist period and afterwards have been determined primarily by external factors and by the realities of Poland's geopolitical position. Among the opposition to the communist regime and among exiles there was consideration of the role that Poland might play should the communist system ever be overthrown and there was always an assumption that, for Poland, political and economic security outside of the communist system could only be found in alliance with the states of Western Europe and in particular with the support of the US. During the Cold War these groups did not view neutrality between the two blocs as an attractive alternative for Poland. It is true that for a brief period after 1989, when Poland was still uncertain of both the reception it would receive from the West and of the long-term prognosis for political developments in the Soviet Union/Russia, forms of pan-European security provision (exemplified by the CSCE) did appeal to Poland's new political elites. This position reflected also a sense of gratitude among Polish one-time dissidents for the assistance the CSCE had given to exposing the human rights deficiencies of communist regimes. During the early 1990s, therefore, Poland (along with neighbours Hungary and the Czech Republic, and the then German Foreign Minister Hans-Dietrich Genscher) championed the cause of strengthening the CSCE in order that it play a more robust role in conflict prevention, confidence-building measures and peacekeeping (Switalski, 1995: 28). Complementing this pan-Europeanist position was the notion that Polish foreign policy ought to be multi-directional, giving equal attention to Russia, the East European regional context and relations with the Euro-Atlantic states (Terry, 2000: 11–17).

An important shift in emphasis was soon to occur, however. The emergence of a more assertive foreign policy in Russia during 1993 (see Chapter 6), the first tentative moves by both NATO and the EU towards the idea of enlarging their memberships to include former communist states, and the waning potential of regional East European initiatives such as the Visegrad Group, combined to shift Polish foreign policy in a decisively westward direction. This, in fact, confirmed what had already emerged as a strong theme in Polish foreign policy discourse – the idea of a 'return to Europe'. This was a theme with considerable historical resonance (and popular support), suggesting as it did Poland's integration within the mainstream of European institutions, politics and economics, and thus a route to resolving the country's centuries-long vulnerabilities (Wiskie, 1999: 138).

It also reflected more immediate and pragmatic considerations. As Prime Minister Hanna Suchocka (1993) explained, Poland's 'European perspective' was driven by an awareness of burgeoning security problems on the continent, not least the worsening conflicts in the former Yugoslavia and certain Soviet successor states (hence the stated desire to join NATO), and by a need to entrench political and economic reform (something that would be guaranteed through membership of the EU).

Entry into NATO and the EU, thereafter, became an abiding objective of Polish foreign policy. Speaking in March 1998, Polish Foreign Minister Bronislaw Geremek (1998) listed nine 'task[s] of priority importance'. First and second were accession to NATO and the EU respectively. This was followed, thirdly, by the development of bilateral relations with the US, Germany, France and the UK; fourth, the cultivation of constructive links with Russia and Poland's other neighbours; fifth, the promotion of regional cooperation, down to the ninth priority, which was the maintenance of favourable ties with the Polish diaspora. This list indicated a continuation of sorts of Poland's multi-directional foreign policy, but it was quite clear which direction took precedence.

The foreign policy process

Poland has a semi-presidential system of government and in the early years of transition the President had reserved powers of appointment with regard to the Foreign and Defence Ministers and in the pursuit of foreign policy. That said, in the period to 1997 a lack of constitutional clarity existed on the processes of foreign policy decision-making. Under the constitution adopted in 1997 the power of appointing the Foreign and Defence Ministers was removed, but the President has, nonetheless, remained a powerful voice in Polish foreign affairs. President Aleksander Kwasniewski (elected in 1995 and re-elected in 2000) has played a very active role in Poland's pursuit of both NATO and EU membership, in fostering good relations with Ukraine and in outlining the terms for sending the Polish armed forces abroad (Millard, 2000: 54–5).

Between 1989 and 2001 Poland has had ten governments and nine Prime Ministers yet has managed to maintain a relatively consistent and coherent foreign policy. This reflects the existence of a clear consensus about the broad lines of this policy, something in turn dictated by the external exigencies of Poland's position – the need to balance new relations with the West with satisfactory dealings with both fellow East Europeans and the former Soviet republics. There are other reasons also why domestic politics has been kept at a distance from foreign policy. Poland has no territorial disputes with its neighbours and it has no significant minorities from neighbouring states living within its territory, nor any significant irredenta apart from the 80,000 Poles who live in the Czech Republic. Poland would appear to have no immediate enemies or irredentist causes, therefore, which might have served as causes for domestic political mobilisation. The only real exception to this happy state of affairs is the increasingly controversial nature of entry into the EU. While domestic political opinion has generally favoured this as a goal of foreign policy, the sheer difficulty of negotiating accession, as well as the attendant need to restructure important economic sectors such as steel and agriculture, has led to some disillusionment among parliamentary and public opinion (Cirtautus, 2000).

Negotiations with the EU have also highlighted another interesting aspect of Polish foreign policy making, namely a problem of coordination. As with other accession countries, Poland has had to coordinate accession negotiations and preparations across a wide range of ministries given that the so-called 'structured dialogue' on entry involves consideration of a whole host of domestic arrangements. This, moreover, has occurred at a time when Polish ministries (including the Foreign Ministry) have experienced considerable organisational and personnel changes consequent upon post-communist adaptation. Poland has experienced some problems, both in recruiting competent civil servants and diplomats and managing the process of weeding out the least acceptable officials and politicians from the communist period. Poland's dealings with both the EU and NATO have revealed a lack of experience and expertise in the processes of multilateral diplomacy, but the learning curve is steep and the Poles have received quite a bit of help in the shape of training from both the British and German diplomatic services.

One significant group that might have been expected to cause some problems in the shaping of foreign policy is the Polish military. This, however, has not been the case to date. The new post-communist governments decided against a big purge of the pre-1989 officers and opted instead for a gradual removal of the more unbending supporters (mainly elderly) of the old regime. Civilian control was easily established and a big incentive for the military in this regard was the requirements of NATO membership. Not only did this promise a more interesting future for the military, but it also provided an opportunity for it to be more effectively integrated into Polish foreign policy. The armed forces, consequently, underpinned Poland's NATO application (and its formal accession in March 1999). In pursuit of (and consequent upon) membership, the Polish military has been an active participant in NATO's Partnership for Peace (PfP) programme, it has participated in NATO-led peacekeeping in the Balkans and has developed bilateral military ties with NATO states (notably

Germany) and other states of the region (including Russia, Lithuania and Ukraine) (Pastusiak, 1998).

What institutional restraints there are on Polish foreign policy makers are increasing redolent of practices in established democratic states. Poland has experienced its fair share of bureaucratic politics and institutional 'turf-battles'. It is also worth noting that the parliament (through its committee system) has attempted to foster an effective process of foreign policy scrutiny and has the ability to ratify or abrogate international treaties (Sanford, 1999). Furthermore, the constant need to deal with most other European states within a set of new multilateral institutions has impacted back on Poland. Polish diplomats are in constant contact with the diplomatic machines of the established Western democracies, especially via the CFSP procedures of the EU and through a variety of NATO consultation processes, and this, in turn, has affected their working methods and outlook.

The substance of foreign policy

During the initial post-communist period, Poland's main foreign policy preoccupation was the Soviet Union. Not until the middle of 1991 were the Warsaw Pact and CMEA formally dissolved, and the last Soviet/Russian troops did not leave the country until October 1992. The dissolution of the Soviet Union at the end of 1991 did provide a sea-change in the relationship with Moscow. The heritage of mistrust on the Polish side which hung over the relationship was not totally removed with the emergence of an independent post-communist Russia, but it did provide the opportunity for a new beginning based on what at the time appeared a genuine commitment towards partnership and cooperation on the part of Russian President Boris Yeltsin. The fruits of this were soon apparent. Yeltsin agreed to release historical documents relating to past Soviet complicity in Polish events and in May 1992 a Polish–Russian Treaty of Friendship was signed.

Relations with Russia have not, however, been plain sailing. Poland has expressed concern at the presence of large military forces in the Russian enclave of Kaliningrad (sandwiched between Poland and Lithuania). Controversies have also arisen over trade (Poland relies for a large part of its energy on Russian oil and gas supplies) and espionage (Poland expelled nine alleged Russian spies in January 2000). The main bone of contention, however, has been Polish membership of NATO, something which has strained relations since the mid-1990s.

Poland made clear its desire to join NATO as early as 1992 and in July 1994 its individual PfP programme was inaugurated, geared towards integration of the Polish armed forces into the Alliance. At this juncture

NATO itself remained cautious on enlargement. However, a turn in American thinking during the second term in office of Bill Clinton galvanised the Alliance and in July 1997 Poland was invited to open accession talks. Along with the Czech Republic and Hungary, it was formally admitted in March 1999. Polish membership benefited hugely from German and American support, as well as the more obvious benefits that Poland offered to the Alliance in terms of its geostrategic location and the size and experience of its armed forces (Dutkiewicz and Lodzinski, 1998).

Since accession, membership has imposed certain conditions upon Polish defence policy (in terms of reform and integration into NATO military structures) and foreign policy. Alliance membership permits states to retain formal foreign policy independence (decision making in NATO is intergovernmental and based on consensus) but this operates within a culture of deference to the major NATO states (the UK, Germany, France and particularly the US). In this respect, Poland has adopted a generally Atlanticist line. This was evident during NATO's Operation Allied Force against Serbia in the spring of 1999. This was a campaign backed by the President, government and Prime Minister and broadly supported by the Polish public and parliamentary opinion. Such a stance was, in part, a reflection of the close relationship with the US and in part a consequence of the fact that Poland would have found it politically impossible to take a critical view a matter of two weeks after joining the Alliance (Gebert, 1999).

Poland has had less immediate success in its goal of joining the EU, although in many respects this is a more difficult organisation to join than NATO, requiring as it does the meeting of very stringent social, economic and political criteria. In December 1991, Poland signed a Europe Agreement with the EU which declared that Poland's ultimate goals was membership of the Union. In April 1994 Poland submitted a formal application for membership and subsequently set the year 2003 as the point by which it hoped this would be achieved (Komorski, 2000). In pursuit of its goal, Poland has reoriented trade away from Russia and its former CMEA partners, has implemented sweeping economic reform (privatisation, for instance) and in 1998 introduced much stricter border controls with its eastern neighbours (notably Ukraine).

The difficulty of accession notwithstanding, Poland is generally regarded as a 'front-runner' for membership among the former communist states. Opinion within the EU has generally been supportive of Polish accession, although there is some disquiet within both the European Commission and the member states at the condition of Polish agriculture, the coal and steel industries, and the impact of Polish nationals seeking employment in neighbouring EU states such as Germany. Poland and the EU opened accession negotiations in March 1998. In February 2001, during a meeting of the so-called 'Weimar Triangle' of Germany, France and Poland, the French President, Jacques Chirac, and German Chancellor Schröder, while offering no timetable to Poland, suggested that it would be 'impossible to discount' the country from the first group of new East European members (Busse, 2001).

The priority accorded to NATO and the EU has not meant a neglect of other directions in Polish foreign policy. The rift with Russia over NATO membership notwithstanding, Warsaw considers dialogue with Moscow a crucial necessity. Also to the East, relations with Ukraine, Belarus and Lithuania have loomed large. In dealing with these states, however, Poland has faced a dilemma. The imperative of joining the EU has placed a limit upon favourable relations. This is of particular concern with regard to Ukraine. New Polish border controls have impacted adversely upon Ukraine and Poland has also signalled its willingness (as part of its obligations to NATO) to station nuclear weapons and foreign troops on its soil. Although NATO has shown no desire to act upon this, such a signal has strained relations with a Ukrainain political leadership, which is fearful that any militarisation of the region will increase attempts by Moscow to reabsorb Ukraine into a Russian sphere of influence (Wolczuk, 2000: 148).

These issues are unlikely to be easily resolved. Arguably, Polish membership of NATO and its prospective accession to the EU will mark it out as a clearly Western-oriented state and one less inclined towards the preferences of its Eastern neighbours. That said, the historical legacies that influence Poland, coupled with its position as a bridge to the East, will continue to instil some sensitivity towards Moscow and particularly Kiev (indeed, this is a foreign policy position which the EU/NATO states of Western Europe are happy to encourage). Its ability to perform this function will, in the long term, be enhanced by the fact that Poland is increasingly acquiring the status of a regional leader. Not only has its status been boosted by joining NATO (hence states such as Lithuania now look to it for support in their own bids for accession), but it is a state with some presence in regional bodies such as the Council of Baltic Sea States, the Central European Free Trade Area and the Central European Initiative, and in pan-European organisations such as the OSCE (where Poland held the rotating position of Chair-in-Office in 1998).

Conclusion

The foreign policies of all European states have had to confront far-reaching challenges over the last decade or so. In Europe's western half, the challenges facing Germany have in many ways been the same as those of others in the region (and comparable in scale to those of the United Kingdom and France). This has involved a reorientation towards emerging security threats, a restructuring of ministries dealing with foreign policy (and related areas of defence and security), an increasing preoccupation with issues of trade, commerce and other socio-economic concerns, and the 'Europeanisation' of foreign policy consequent upon the growing international role of the EU. In other senses, however, German foreign policy has a somewhat special quality owing to, first, the consequences of unification and, second, geographic location – Germany is fully integrated in its Western direction and to its east it borders states seeking to emulate such integration. In the first decade of the twenty-first century German foreign policy can be regarded as having met these challenges with some degree of success. This, moreover, has occurred in such a fashion that Germany remains (despite some of the presentiments offered at the time of unification) a respected and responsible power in Europe. As Hyde-Price (2000: 223) has argued,

> [t]he dominant values, norms and principles of late modern Germany are those of a mature liberal-democracy, firmly embedded within the structures of a pluralistic security community. Germany's national identity and its dominant foreign policy role conceptions are those of a normal *Zivilmacht* [civilian power], committed to the shaping of [a] pan-European cooperative security order buttressed by enlarged Euro-Atlantic structures.

As for Poland, certain parallels exist with its German neighbour. It too has navigated the challenges of transformation with some success and has emerged as a state with an increasingly important geopolitical position in Europe, a position it has dealt with rather adroitly. Of course, the challenges are also, in many ways, very different, owing to Poland's communist past, its proximity to the former Soviet Union, belated membership of NATO and present status outside the EU. It is in dealing with these challenges that the merits of Polish foreign policy will be judged in the long term.

Further reading

Useful accounts of German foreign policy include Baring (ed.) (1994), Bluth (2000), Hyde-Price (2000) and Katzenstein (ed.) (1997). The journals *Aussenpolitik* (available in both English and German), *German Politics*,

German Politics and Society and *International Affairs* regularly carry relevant articles. As for Poland, surveys of its foreign policy in the post-Cold War period can be found in Cordell (ed.) (2000), Prizel, Nitze and Michta (eds) (1995) and Terry (2000). The journals *Communist and Post-Communist Studies, Europe–Asia Studies* and *Journal of Communist Studies and Transition Politics* carry a lot of material on both Poland's domestic and foreign policies.

References

Baring, A. (ed.) (1994) *Germany's New Position in Europe: Problems and Perspectives.* Oxford: Berg.

Bluth, C. (1995) 'Germany: Defining the National Interest', *The World Today*, 51(3), 51–5.

Bluth, C. (2000) *Germany and the Future of European Security.* Basingstoke: Palgrave.

Burant, S. (1993) 'International Relations in a Regional Context: Poland and its Eastern Neighbours – Lithuania, Belarus, Ukraine', *Europe–Asia Studies*, 45(3), 395–418.

Busse, N. (2001) 'Poland Promised Swift EU Accession', *Frankfurter Allgemeine Zeitung* (27 February).

Buzan, B., Kelstrup, M., Lemaitre, P., Tromer, E. and Waever, O. (1990) *The European Security Order Recast. Scenarios for the Post-Cold War Era.* London and New York: Pinter.

Central Intelligence Agency (2000) *The World Factbook, 2000.* <http://www.odci.gov/cia/publications/factbook/>.

Cirtautas, A.M. (2000) 'Enlargement as Seen from the East: Poland', *East European Constitutional Review*, 9(4), 70–6.

Cole, A. (1993) 'Looking On: France and the New Germany', *German Politics*, 2(3), 358–76.

Cordell, K. (ed.) (2000) *Poland and the European Union.* London: Routledge.

Corterier, P. (1990) '*Quo vadis* NATO?', *Survival*, 32(2), 141–56.

Crawford, B. (1995) 'Domestic Pressures and Multilateral Mistrust: Why Germany Unilaterally Recognised Croatia in 1991', *German Politics and Society*, 13(2), 1–34.

Croft, S., Rees, G.W., Redmond, J. and Webber, M. (1999) *The Enlargement of Europe.* Manchester: Manchester University Press.

Dutkiewicz, P. and Lodzinski, S. (1998) 'The "Grey Zone". Poland's Security Policy since 1989', in Dutkiewicz, P. and Jackson, R.J. (eds), *NATO Looks East.* Westport, CT, and London: Praeger.

Feldman, L.G. (1999) 'The Principle and Practice of "Reconciliation" in German Foreign Policy: Relations with France, Israel, Poland and the Czech Republic', *International Affairs*, 75(2), 333–56.

Friis, L. and Murphy, A. (2000) ' "Turbo-Charged Negotiations": the EU and the Stability Pact for South Eastern Europe', *Journal of European Public Policy*, 7(5), 767–86.

Frost, H.E. (1993) 'Eastern Europe's Search for Security', *Orbis*, 37(1), 37–53.

Gasteyger, C. (1991) 'The Remaking of Eastern Europe's Security', *Survival*, 33(2), 111–24.

Gebert, K. (1999) 'Splintered Unity: Polish Politics and the Crisis', *East European Constitutional Review*, 8(3), 56–60.

Geremek, B. (1998) 'Address of the Minister of Foreign Affairs Bronislaw Geremek on the Main Lines of Poland's Foreign Policy in 1998', speech to the Polish parliament available at http://www3.itu.int/MISSIONS/poland/geremek4.htm

Hellmann, G. (1997) 'The Sirens of Power and German Foreign Policy: Who is Listening?', *German Politics*, 6(2), 29–57.

Höhmann, H.-H., Meier, C. and Timmermann, H. (1998) 'Russia and Germany in Europe: Recent Trends in Political and Economic Relations', *Journal of Communist Studies and Transition Politics*, 14(3), 24–57.

Hyde-Price, A. (1992) 'Future Security Systems for Europe', in McInnes, C. (ed.), *Security and Strategy in the New Europe*. London: Routledge, 37–58.

Hyde-Price, A. (1999) 'Berlin Republic Takes to Arms', *The World Today* (June), 13–15.

Hyde-Price, A. (2000) *Germany and European Order. Enlarging NATO and the EU*. Manchester and New York: Manchester University Press.

Janning, J. (1996) 'A German Europe – a European Germany? On the Debate over Germany's Foreign Policy', *International Affairs*, 72(1), 33–41.

Katzenstein, P. (ed.) (1997) *Tamed Power: Germany in Europe*. Ithaca, NY, and London: Cornell University Press.

Komorski, S. [Polish Ambassador to the UK] (2000) 'The Accession of Poland to the European Union', *European Foreign Affairs Review*, 5, 131–7.

Longhurst, K. (2000) 'The Reform of the German Armed Forces: Coming of Age?', *European Security*, 9(4), 31–44.

Mastny, V. (1999) 'The Soviet Non-Invasion of Poland in 1980–1981 and the End of the Cold War', *Europe–Asia Studies*, 51(2), 189–211.

Maull, H. (1990) 'Germany and Japan: The New Civilian Powers', *Foreign Affairs*, 69(5), 91–106.

Maull, H. (2000) 'German Foreign Policy, Post-Kosovo: Still a "Civilian Power?" ', *German Politics*, 9(2), 1–24.

Medvedev, S. (1998) ' "Zwischeneuropa": Historic Experiences, National Views and Strategic Alternatives'. Helsinki: The Finnish Institute of International Affairs, *Working Paper*, 6.

Meiers, F.-J. (1995) 'Germany: the Reluctant Power', *Survival*, 37(3), 82–103.

Meirsheimer, J.J. (1990) 'Back to the Future. Instability in Europe after the Cold War', *International Security*, 15(1), 5–56.

Millard, F. (2000) 'Presidents and Democratization in Poland: the Roles of Lech Walesa and Aleksander Kwasniewski', *Journal of Communist Studies and Transition Politics*, 16(3), 39–62.

Pastusiak, L. (1998) 'Poland on Her Way to NATO', *European Security*, 7(2), 54–62.

Prizel, I., Nitze, P.H. and Michta, A.M. (eds) (1995) *Polish Foreign Policy Reconsidered: Challenges of Independence.* Basingstoke: Macmillan.

Sanford, G. (1999) 'Parliamentary Control and the Constitutional Definition of Foreign Policy Making in Democratic Poland', *Europe–Asia Studies*, 51(5), 769–97.

Suchocka, H. (1993) 'Poland's European Perspective', *NATO Review*, 41(3), 3–6.

Switalski, P. (1995) 'An Ally for the Central and Eastern European States', *Transition*, 1(11), 26–9.

Terry, S.M. (2000) 'Poland's Foreign Policy since 1989: the Challenges of Independence', *Communist and Post-Communist Studies*, 33(1), 7–47.

Waever, O., Lemaitre, P. and Tromer, E. (1993) *Identity, Migration and the New European Security Order.* London: Pinter.

Wiskie, B. (1999) 'Poland's Long Desired Return to Europe', in Marácz, L. (ed.), *Yearbook of European Studies*, 11, Amsterdam and Atlanta, GA: Rodopi, 131–49.

Wolczuk, R. (2000) 'Ukrainian–Polish Relations between 1991 and 1998: from the Declaratory to the Substantive', *European Security*, 9(1), 127–56.

The world wide web

The German Foreign Ministry can be found at: <http://www.auswaertiges-amt.government.de/www/de/index_html>. Poland's Foreign Ministry is at: <http://www.msz.gov.pl/english/indexang.html>. Developments in Poland can be followed through 'Poland Today' at Central Europe Online at <http://www.centraleurope.com/polandtoday/> and through the variety of online publications concerned with Poland offered by Radio Free Europe/Radio Liberty via <http://www.rferl.org/>. The German newspaper *Frankfurter Allgemeine Zeitung* is available (in both German and English) at <http://www.faz.com> and provides authoritative articles on German foreign policy.

8 Sub-Saharan Africa: Nigeria and South Africa

Denny Morgan and Mark Webber

Nigeria and South Africa both constitute middle-ranking powers. Their foreign policies have little global consequence, but closer to home these states have a considerable influence. This chapter considers these two states within their regional settings – respectively west and southern Africa. It also takes a broader view of the continental setting and the domestic economic and political conditions which have affected the foreign policies of African states, Nigeria and South Africa included.

Introduction

In certain respects, sub-Saharan Africa (SSA) might be said to have been little affected by the transformation of world politics. Long-term trends very much in evidence through the decades of the 1960s, 1970s and 1980s have persisted beyond the watershed years of the late 1980s. The end of communism and the Cold War thus did little to change either SSA's economic dependence within a globalising economy, the general condition of marginality within the global economic and political order or the preoccupation of many of its regimes with domestic security. These continuities are undeniable. However, alongside them important changes have nonetheless occurred over the last decade or so. Certain issues have fallen by the wayside (the causes of independence and liberation are no longer as relevant with the end of colonialism and apartheid, and few regimes now couch their foreign policies in ideological language) and foreign policies have become much more tempered by what Shaw and Nyang'oro (1999: 237–8) have described as a 'sober, realistic mood' focused on unwelcome and intractable issues such as debt, economic structural adjustment, and conflict prevention and resolution. This realism springs from difficulties experienced in the national (political and economic), regional and global contexts of the foreign policy arena. It is these that we shall explore first before turning to a consideration of two case studies based on Nigeria and South Africa.

The arena of foreign policy

The political context

No understanding of the domestic context of the foreign policies of the states of SSA would be possible without taking into account the peculiar nature of statehood within the region. The history of the state in Africa is a remarkably short one. In all but a few cases the organising principles of the state only impeded upon the continent with the arrival of European colonial rule and the territorial partition of the late nineteenth century. Yet despite its shallow roots, the state was seized upon as the form of rule following the process of decolonisation that began in earnest in the late 1950s. Colonial jurisdications became the basis of Africa's independent states and the assumption was widely held that these new states would take on the domestic features of longer-established states elsewhere: unquestioned physical control over a defined territory, an administrative presence throughout that territory and the allegiance of its bordered population.

Upon independence, however, few of Africa's states could be said to have enjoyed a sound basis for the development of these characteristics. The absence of national communities, an underdeveloped administrative capability, arbitrary political boundaries and a scarcity of social and economic resources marked out most of them. In this setting many African states have been states in name only, juridically recognised as such by the international community, but in the internal sphere lacking many of the 'empirical' qualities commonly associated with state viability (Jackson and Rosberg, 1986).

The fragility of the state in SSA has, in turn, had several long-term political consequences. A first concerns a general tendency towards forms of authoritarian government (whether in the form of military, single-party or personalist regimes), something which has had few compensatory benefits. The claim often made by authoritarian governments that theirs is a form of rule necessary to impose order has been belied in SSA by a tendency towards endemic instability. Why this should be so reflects the fact that most states in Africa have proven unable to cope with the sectional nature of African societies. They have, in fact, developed in a partial manner, as the instruments of aggrandisement by particular ethno-linguistic or other status groups, rather than as autonomous mediators of conflict and the ostensible upholders of a common good. In such circumstances political conflict has arisen, either because disaffected groups have sought to capture state power for their own particular ends (military coups), or have attempted to establish their own forms of statehood (through secession and civil war). The long-term effect has been a cumulative undermining of state viability throughout SSA. Combined with factors we shall explore below (mounting economic difficulties and alterations in the pattern of external assistance), this had resulted, by the early 1990s, in crises of a profound quality. According to one estimate, by that point up to half of Africa's states were in serious or maximum danger of collapse (Zartman, 1995: 3), a situation involving not merely the removal of an incumbent government but the dissolution of the very infrastructure of rule itself. In its extreme form – as in Rwanda, Somalia, Liberia and Sierra Leone – this was accompanied by widespread violence.

The foreign policy implications of the conditions outlined above are considerable. Political instability results in foreign policies that are erratic, while the general tendency towards sectional, authoritarian rule leads to policies premised not so much on the pursuit of a national interest as on the short-term concerns of a particular regime, group or individual (Metz, 2000: 11). In such an environment, the policy-making process tends to be heavily influenced by individual leaders and groups such as the military and business elites, and rarely by press, public or political opposition (Wright, 1999b: 6). The precariousness of rule, moreover, imposes definite limits on action. This may take the extreme form of leaders being unable to leave their country for fear of being replaced or, more prosaically, the tailoring of external policies to domestic requirements. The latter, a commonplace in the foreign policies of all states, has assumed an urgent tone in SSA. Here foreign policy has, in Clapham's (1996a: 60) words become the 'politics of state survival', geared towards simply acquiring the resources 'to maintain the domestic political structure'.

This brief survey has, admittedly, painted a rather bleak picture of politics in SSA and at least three qualifications are in order. First, a necessarily brief treatment requires generalisation and the reader should be aware that a true picture of African politics is in fact one of considerable diversity. Second, and a connected point, the instabilities highlighted above have not applied uniformly. Throughout SSA there are notable cases of long-term stability (Botswana and Tanzania), the reconstruction of political life following murderous interludes (Uganda) and recent cases of relatively successful democratisation (Ghana). Third, one should avoid the temptation to regard politics in SSA as somehow exotic and unusual. The case can be made that its multiple conflicts simply reflect the particular historical juncture African states are at, one comparable to Europe during its own violent and war-ridden periods of state formation. The only difference is the speed of historical evolution. A process which in Europe took centuries has in Africa been telescoped into a few decades (Herbst, 1996/97: 130).

Bearing these qualifications in mind, it is appropriate to consider at this point the question of how typical of the general trends outlined above are Nigeria and South Africa, the two case study states of this chapter.

Taking Nigeria first, since obtaining independence from the British in 1960, this state has enjoyed very little stability or continuity of rule. In a forty-year period it has had three civilian republics, a short-lived interim national government and eight military leaders (six of whom seized power through *coups d'état*) (Table 8.1). It has also witnessed a full-scale civil war (1967–70) and periodic outbreaks of violence based on regional, religious and ethnically-based grievances.

Throughout this turbulent history, Nigeria has managed to maintain some democratic features: a free press, trade unions and political associations, and a relatively independent judiciary and professional civil service. The country has also periodically enjoyed a flourishing party system (albeit one restricted and sometimes manipulated during periods of military rule) and has maintained a federal system (one, in fact, that has been amended

Table 8.1 Nigerian regimes since independence

Years	Head of state	Type of regime
1960–66	Tafawa Balewa	Civilian
1966	J.T.U. Aguiyu Ironsi	Military
1966–75	Yakubu Gowon	Military
1975–76	Murtala Muhammed	Military
1976–79	Olusegan Obasanjo	Military
1979–83	Shehu Shagari	Civilian
1984–85	Muhammadu Buhari	Military
1985–93	Ibrahim Babangida	Military
1993	Ernest Shonekan	Mixed
1993–98	Sani Abacha	Military
1998–99	Abdulsalam Abubakar	Military
1999–	Olusegun Obasanjo	Civilian

on several occasions to accommodate ethnic and regional diversity). Yet for all this, what are commonly regarded as the bases for democracy (and also for long-term political stability) are largely absent in the country. In particular, Nigeria lacks national unity. The state that emerged upon independence was an essentially artificial creation, composed of over 250 ethnic groups (four of whom are demographically dominant: the Hausas, Fulanis, Igbos and Yorubas) and three sets of religions (Islam, Christianity and traditional beliefs). Loyalties are usually attached to these groups before they are to the notion of a Nigerian nation. Politics in the country has consequently been largely determined by these cleavages, something that has prevented the emergence of any sense of elite cohesion and consensus on political, economic or foreign policy priorities. The military, which has claimed to stand above such division, has pursued inclusive policies up to a point. However, where this really matters – at the level of national leadership – politics has remained dominated by sectional calculations.

While Nigeria in many ways typifies political development in SSA, the same cannot be said of South Africa. In contrast to the vast number of states in the region, South Africa has, in effect, experienced two processes of decolonisation: the first involving the end of British dominion status in 1934 and the second (during the first half of the 1990s) the dismantling of the apartheid system of white minority rule. This almost unparalleled process (only Rhodesia/Zimbabwe bears comparison) has left the country with some unique political legacies and challenges. First and foremost, South Africa has had to embark upon a sensitive process of national reconciliation, one designed not simply to accommodate the white population, but also to prevent the alienation of portions of the black majority (of which the Zulu population and its political manifestation the Inkatha Freedom Party is the most significant). However, in relative terms, South Africa is in an advantageous position, not because it lacks ethnic diversity, but rather because its ruling party, the African National Congress (ANC), has historically eschewed ethnicity as a basis of political mobilisation.

In the midst of this process of belated nation-building, post-apartheid South Africa has also had to address a restructuring of the state administration. In comparison with other African states, South Africa is well endowed in this regard, yet it still faces the challenge of reorganising a state which under apartheid was oriented heavily towards internal security needs and advancing the lot of the white minority. It is at present too early to judge the long-term success of any such reorganisation and, in particular, whether it can be undertaken avoiding the sorts of corruption and abuses of power noted in the case of Nigeria. Some have warned that the dominance of the ANC (it convincingly won parliamentary elections in 1994 and 1999 and has provided both of the post-apartheid period's two Presidents, Nelson Mandela and Thabo Mbeki) may augur a quasi-authoritarian single-party state (Southall, 1998). What is instructive, however, is the facilitating influence presented by South Africa's democratic potential. Paradoxically, the denial of many political rights to the black majority during the apartheid period had the effect of encouraging a democratic culture by stimulating political organisation and strategies of opposition. South Africa consequently entered the post-apartheid period with a vibrant civil society embracing a free press, political parties, trade unions, and politically and socially conscious religious organisations. Democratic values are also said to be well entrenched within the ANC's leadership (Chettle, 1997: 72). The survival of democracy does, however, also depend on several other contingencies, not least the economic fortunes of the country (see below) but also the manner in which social challenges such as an appalling blossoming of crime and the problem of HIV and AIDS are tackled (Grimond, 2001).

The economic context

Just as political conditions frame the context of foreign policy, so too do economic factors. It is obvious, for instance, that states with considerable economic resources and/or successful records of growth will possess the wherewithal to pursue active foreign policies. By the same token, those lacking such resources will be denied much international influence and will necessarily be constrained in their foreign policy choices. The states of SSA have generally fallen into the latter of these two categories.

The economic predicament of SSA is immediately apparent from a consideration of a few basic statistics. According to World Bank figures, the overall rate of economic growth in SSA has been the lowest of any region in the world (Clapham, 1996b: 809). Although gross domestic product (GDP) has grown by an annual average of some 3.4 per cent since 1961, this is only barely above the rate of population expansion. When this is taken into account, per capita GDP actually declined by an annual rate of 1.5 per cent during the 1980s and early 1990s. This trend was reversed during the mid-1990s. However, projections for per capita growth for the period 1997–2006 remained low, at just 1 per cent per annum (Sparks, 1998: 10).

This general trend does, of course, conceal considerable variation both in terms of resource endowments and actual economic performance. The region as a whole is poor. According to the World Bank (1997: 214) nine of the world's ten lowest income countries are situated in SSA and Mozambique holds the unfortunate place as the planet's poorest state. Yet alongside this poverty, several states possess abundant natural and physical resources and a few have relatively successful rates of economic growth. South Africa and, to a lesser extent, Nigeria fall within this group and it is to a consideration of their economies that we now turn.

Taking Nigeria first, on paper it appears something of an economic giant in Africa. Since 1973 it has been the continent's largest producer of petroleum and since 1990 of rubber. It also possesses Africa's largest deposits of natural gas and is richly endowed with agricultural resources. These assets have ensured that Nigeria is the second largest recipient of foreign private investment in SSA (South Africa is the largest). Yet for all this potential, the country remains economically underdeveloped. Although the second largest national economy in SSA, its GDP was, in 1993, just three-quarters the size of the Republic of Ireland, one of Western Europe's smallest economies (Clapham, 1996b: 810–11). The World Bank estimated in 1997 that Nigeria's per capita gross national product (GNP) had shrunk from over $1,000 in 1980 to just $240 by 1997, making it the world's nineteenth poorest state.

There is no single explanation for Nigeria's economic malaise. As with the continent's broader economic problems, opinions differ as to the source of economic trouble (see below). What is clear is that in the Nigerian case a rich endowment has been squandered. Revenues from the petroleum sector, the basis of the modern Nigerian economy, have been misdirected into inappropriate infrastructural projects or diverted by corruption and the demands of clientalist politics. A misplaced reliance on this product has also left the country open to fluctuations in the price of oil. Having benefited from the oil price-boom of the 1970s, Nigeria over-extended itself financially and by 1997 held external debts of $34.7 billion, the servicing of which was equivalent to some 40 per cent of export earnings.

The position of South Africa is far more favourable than that of Nigeria. The country is unusually well-endowed, possessing all manner of minerals (with especially large amounts of diamonds and gold), SSA's most developed industrial sector (which produces the same value of manufactured goods as the rest of SSA countries combined) and some of the world's richest fishing grounds. In sum, South Africa contains the largest economy in SSA (accounting in 1994 for 36 per cent of total SSA GDP) and the region's second largest GNP per capita (behind oil-rich Gabon).

Clearly ahead in relative terms, the South African economy has nonetheless suffered certain problems of its own in recent decades. The average annual rate of growth of GDP, for instance, declined from 5.7 per cent in the period 1960–70 to just 1.5 per cent in the period 1980–90 and a negative rate of −0.5 in 1990–93. This decline reflects a certain structural weakness of the economy in the shape of the high percentage of exports accounted for by gold (hence a certain vulnerability to contracting bullion prices). Political factors, however, were also partly to blame. Political instability resulted in a net outflow of foreign investment after 1980 and international sanctions affected some markets, for instance coal exports. It was against this economic backdrop that the ANC took office in 1994. In the years since, the economy has performed at a moderate level. Net foreign direct investment grew after 1994 (albeit at levels lower than the comparable economies of Brazil and Argentina) and GDP growth was resumed (albeit at an annual average rate during the 1990s lower than that of the 1970s). The lifting of sanctions during the early 1990s also permitted a growth of exports and a return of South Africa to international lending institutions. Further, the election of the ANC in 1994 created the conditions for an expansion of economic ties with the southern African region. These positive aspects have, in part, been overshadowed by the slowness of social reforms, and the high unemployment and poverty rates among the black population. Yet what is significant in the current context is the avoidance of the economic crises typical of many other SSA countries. As we shall see below, this has allowed South Africa to maintain its position as a regional economic hegemon.

Sub-Saharan Africa in the international system

The states of SSA are generally regarded as of only peripheral significance in the international system of states, whether this is measured in economic, strategic or political-diplomatic terms.

The first of these – SSA's lowly economic status – is apparent in terms of the region's small percentage shares of global GNP, trade, commercial bank lending and private capital flows. Some of the reasons for this state of affairs have already been touched upon above. In addition, SSA's structural position within the global economy is worth highlighting. In this connection, the region is usually characterised as being in a position of dependence, economically subservient, that is, to the more developed economies of the industrialised world. The manner in which such dependency operates is a highly controversial subject (Sparks, 1998). Many African scholars, large numbers of non-governmental organisations (NGOs) and certain interested international bodies (for instance, the United Nations' (UN) Economic Commission for Africa) tend to regard the condition as essentially iniquitous, a post-colonial means of economic exactitude whereby SSA states are held subordinate by virtue of protected markets, unfairly depressed commodity prices, debt servitude, and the imposition of economic directives by Western-led international financial institutions (IFIs) such as the World Bank and the International Monetary Fund (IMF). Others tend to see SSA's international economic relationships in a somewhat different light. The consensus opinion of Western governments and IFIs holds that SSA's economic problems have been largely self-inflicted, the consequence of domestic policy failure, poor governance and a long-term unwillingness to adapt to global market conditions. As a consequence, prescriptions for economic recovery have tended to emphasise the need for change in the domestic sphere rather than any fundamental innovations by the Western economies themselves (debt forgiveness, increases in official aid).

Standing back from the debate, what is clear is that SSA has undoubtedly been disadvantaged by certain external trends that have been beyond its capacity to influence. Some of these relate to the manner in which the international economy has altered in recent years. The move towards 'post-industrial' production of technologically advanced manufactures has by-passed the region, which lacks a developed scientific-technological base and skilled work force. Similarly adverse has been the movement towards regional economic integration and the concomitant development of trade blocs. This is of particular significance with regard to the European Union (EU), which has historically been SSA's largest export market. Although all SSA countries (with the partial exception of South Africa) are linked to the EU by virtue of the Lomé Conventions that date back to 1975, the trade preferences of these arrangements have not prevented a long-term decline in SSA's share of EU imports. This drop reflects, in part, the reduced demand for Africa's primary products, but it can also be attributed to the EU's own restrictive practices, notably in the agricultural sphere. Trade concessions granted in the 1995 amended (fourth) Lomé Convention, have generally been regarded as too piecemeal to reverse this decline (Parfitt, 1996: 63).

An event even further from African influence has been the end of the Cold War and the attendant collapse of communism in Eastern Europe and the Soviet Union. This has been economically significant in that it has meant, first, a termination of the Soviet aid budget and, second, an increased competition for resources as former communist states have emerged as more attractive propositions for Western governments, lending agencies and investors. To these factors one should also add a growing frustration among both donors and lenders at the paucity of tangible results from their earlier commitments. Thus, while some resource-rich states (Nigeria and South Africa included) have managed to maintain relatively favourable levels of external funding, for SSA as a whole, the 1990s were characterised by reductions in official development assistance, stagnant levels of concessionary lending and a falling share of foreign direct investment (Olsen, 1997: 299; Riddell, 1999: 313).

As for its strategic location, here SSA occupies a somewhat ambiguous position. Certainly by traditional criteria (military potential, the possession of strategic commodities and the ability to project a threat) the states of the region occupy a largely unimportant position in the international order. During the period of the Cold War, however, this marginality was partly masked by a willingness of the superpowers (and others such as Cuba and France) to interfere in the affairs of the continent.

This manifested itself in at least two ways. First, through the temporary elevation of the region's strategic relevance, either as a source of bases in peacetime and as a strategic resource in global conflict scenarios. Such calculation prompted an interest in certain littoral states (Angola, Ethiopia, Kenya and South Africa) or, in the case of Zaire, those that commanded a central geographic position in SSA. Second, a willingness on the part of Washington and Moscow to provide favoured regimes (and, in some cases guerilla movements), with unconditional economic and military assistance. This was not only wasteful from an economic point of view, serving quite often to prop up notoriously corrupt regimes rather than further local developmental needs, but also contributed to a militarisation of the region, thereby ensuring that local conflicts were more bloody and prolonged than would otherwise have been the case. This type of situation was particularly striking during the 1970s and 1980s and was played out to dramatic effect in both the Horn of Africa (the 1977 Ogaden War) and in southern Africa (most injuriously in the shape of prolonged warfare in Angola).

Given the manner in which the Cold War helped determine the strategic position of SSA, its end has had far-reaching effects. No longer material in a global competition for influence, the region's significance to outside powers has diminished considerably with only the Horn and Kenya retaining any real strategic value owing to their proximity to the Middle East and Persian Gulf. This strategic marginalisation, moreover, has occurred even though the end of the Cold War has brought to prominence other issues relating to SSA (drug trafficking, migration, the spread of infectious diseases, environmental degradation and the exploitation of oil) that also hold security implications for both Europe and the United States (US) (Metz, 2000). The difference between these and the defining issues of the

Cold War, however, is that they have tended to be viewed from outside more as problems than as opportunities, consequently generating less powerful incentives for outside engagement (Clapham, 1996a: 257). Particularly telling in this regard is the issue of conflict resolution. This has remained a central issue in SSA, for even though the aggravating effects of competitive superpower intervention and militarisation have been removed, the more basic, internal roots of civil conflict have endured. That said, the enhanced post-Cold War potential of external efforts to mediate these conflicts has not been fully realised. With few direct strategic or economic incentives, external involvement has been driven by less concrete (and more easily exhaustible) humanitarian and political concerns. This has resulted in a variety of conflict resolution efforts (the UN-backed American military presence in Somalia in 1992–93, the unilateral French deployment in Rwanda in 1994, financial and diplomatic support for UN operations as far apart as Mozambique, Angola and Liberia, and the African Crisis Response Initiative [ACRI] – a military aid programme sponsored jointly by the US, France and Britain). But overall, these efforts have tended to be temporary, sometimes poorly executed and generally lacking the robustness and enthusiasm that has been reserved for other areas of crisis, such as the former Yugoslavia, that are of greater strategic significance to the West (Stremlau, 2000).

SSA's political and diplomatic marginality, finally, is also easy to gauge. This is apparent in at least two senses. First, the states of the region have very little say in crucial decisions of a global character, even when these have an impact on African states themselves. This is most apparent in the fora of IFIs but also in global institutions such as the UN Security Council and the World Trade Organisation (WTO). SSA states, consequently, have merely reacted to, rather than helped to shape the post-Cold War international order. Second, they have been forced under external influence to adapt their own political systems. The somewhat unique case of apartheid South Africa aside, these pressures are fairly recent in origin. In part, they have an economic rationale: the World Bank and IMF came to recognise during the 1980s that structural adjustment policies were best implemented by governments enjoying broad popular support and effective political institutions. These institutions have consequently incorporated political conditions (usually under the rubric of 'good governance') into their loan packages and these have also been taken up by bilateral donors such as the US, the United Kingdom and, to a lesser degree, France. More overt political considerations have also applied. During the Cold War, the authoritarian complexion of a regime mattered far less to the West than its anti-communist credentials. With the Cold War's demise, however, the perceived political shortcomings of these African states have become less tolerable, while the self-confidence of Western states (particularly the US) in imposing upon them preferred political values has increased (Clapham, 1996a: 193–8).

Despite the picture painted here, the notion of marginalisation can be a little misleading. Africa may not present a major voice in world politics or the international economy but it is thoroughly enmeshed in these spheres and in others by virtue of its ongoing trade and assistance dependencies, the movement of its populations outside the continent (notably to Europe), the penetration of private foreign actors (aid organisations, security companies, mercenaries, criminal mafias, etc.) and what Bayart (2000: 239) has described as 'the self-proclaimed right [of Western governments] to influence the course of events [in Africa]'. Thus, Bayart continues, it is 'appropriate to speak not of marginalisation . . . but rather of an aggravation of dependence'.

A further qualification needs to be made by reference to the variations that have occurred between states in SSA. While the features of marginalisation may serve as a general picture, it remains the case that not all its features fit uniformly and that specific states have, by virtue of their own particular strengths, been able to moderate its effects. As we shall see in more detail in this chapter's case studies, this is certainly the case with South Africa, although much less so with Nigeria. It should also be borne in mind that the entire notion of marginalisation is relative. SSA may well be peripheral in global terms and secondary to the calculations of outside powers, but for SSA states themselves, their own locality is not peripheral but central. For this reason it is worth considering the regional setting of foreign policy in SSA.

SSA as a regional system

Few attempts have so far succeeded in welding together patterns of institutionally-framed cooperation that embrace the entire SSA region. In this respect SSA and, indeed, Africa as a whole, is typical of many Third World areas, but is in marked contrast to the extensive institutionalisation which characterises Europe. This state of affairs is plain to see when one considers what is the longest-standing and perhaps the best-known of Africa's regional organisations, the Organisation of African Unity (OAU). This body has operated as the framework for what, on paper, appear to be several ambitious schemes of cooperation, and, in some respects, it has been successful. Since its foundation in 1963, the organisation has been able to make a claim to comprehensive membership, no mean feat in a continent of over fifty states. It has also helped to define some of the enduring principles of African affairs through its opposition to apartheid and colonialism, and its commitment to the territorial integrity of states (something, crucially, that entailed a recognition of colonial borders as the basis for African statehood and helps explain the rarity of inter-state wars in SSA). Yet these political achievements aside, in other regards the record of the OAU has been rather modest. In the period prior to the end of the Cold War, the organisation provided very little material support to its proclaimed causes of liberation, enjoyed a mixed record in the area of crisis management and had virtually no effect in tackling SSA's growing economic problems (Clapham, 1996a: 110–13). The reasons for this indifferent performance are not difficult to discern given the size, political diversity, and the generally dependent and impoverished nature of the OAU's membership. During the 1990s and 2000s the OAU has had to reorientate itself. With the completion of decolonisation and the end of apartheid, its attentions have turned to unresolved issues of socio-economic development and crisis management. Its ability to tackle these issues, however, has not necessarily improved.

The problems of the OAU are in large part those of scale. As many observers have pointed out, a continental framework is inappropriate for the states of SSA in that their foreign policy interactions are normally carried out within the confines of groups of neighbouring states (Clapham, 1996a: 117). Even a state such as Nigeria, which has at times displayed aspirations towards continental leadership, is preoccupied more with its immediate regional setting. Localism of this sort is a reflection, partly, of the limited capacities of SSA states but corresponds also to patterns of African regional diversity. The African continent is clearly divided between an Arabic-speaking north and the geographic bulk of Black or sub-Saharan Africa. This latter region, in turn, is sufficiently diverse to be broken down into several sub-regions: west Africa, southern Africa, central Africa, the Horn and so on. For our purposes the first two of these are the most significant.

Taking west Africa first, this region has several defining features. It is, to begin with, a somewhat heterogeneous area comprising some sixteen states overlain across a multiplicity of ethnicities, cultures and nations, and divided by contrasting colonial experiences (at the hands of the French, British and Portuguese). It is also a region divided by inter-state rivalries. The Francophone states of Senegal and Côte d'Ivoire (occasionally egged on by France itself) have traditionally looked with suspicion upon Anglophone Nigeria and Ghana, and all four of these states have, at times, competed in playing a leadership role in the region. Disputes have also arisen over frontiers, refugees and migrant populations and the harbouring of dissident forces by one state targeted against another.

Differences are also obvious in terms of indices of territorial size, economic power and demographic strength. As Table 8.2 makes clear, Nigeria enjoys, on paper, a dominant position by these criteria.

Such heterogeneity, however, has not prevented efforts towards cooperation based on the exigencies of proximity and the considerable transnational movements of population and communication which occur in the region. These have, however, had limited success. The existence of two competing intergovernmental organisations with overlapping memberships (the Economic Community of West African States [ECOWAS] and the Francophone West African Economic and Monetary Union) and the tensions caused by Nigeria's lead position within the first of these, has tended to stymy regional economic integration.

A further feature of the region concerns its proclivity for violence. Although inter-state wars have been both rare and short-lived, civil wars

Table 8.2 A comparison of the states of west Africa

State	Population in 2000 (m)	Surface area (thousands of sq. km)	GDP (purchasing power parity) in 1999 (US$ bn)	Military expenditure (US$ m) (year in brackets)
Benin	6.4	113	8.1	27 (1996)
Burkina Faso	11.9	274	12.4	66 (1996)
Cameroon	15.4	475	31.5	155 (1999)
Côte d'Ivoire	16	322	25.7	94 (1996)
The Gambia	1.3	11	1.4	1 (1997)
Ghana	19.5	239	35.5	53 (1999)
Guinea	7.4	246	9.2	56 (1996)
Guinea-Bissau	1.3	36	1.1	8 (1996)
Liberia	3.1	111	2.8	1 (1998)
Mali	10.6	1,240	8.5	49 (1996)
Mauritania	2.6	1,026	4.9	41 (1997)
Niger	10	1,267	9.6	20 (1996)
Nigeria	123.3	924	110.5	236 (1999)
Senegal	10	197	16.6	68 (1997)
Sierra Leone	5.2	72	2.5	46 (1997)
Togo	5	57	8.6	27 (1996)

Source: Central Intelligence Agency (2000).

have been protracted and noted for their ferocity. Four such wars have marked the region: in Nigeria (1967–70), Liberia (1990–96), Sierra Leone (1991–) and, on a somewhat smaller scale, Guinea-Bissau (1998–99). All but the first of these has occurred against the post-Cold War backdrop of lowered incentives for extra-African military involvement and conflict settlement efforts (see above). The lead role in their resolution has, consequently, been taken by regional bodies such as ECOMOG (the military Monitoring Group of ECOWAS), something that, in turn, has facilitated the projection of Nigerian influence.

Moving to the southern African region, this constitutes some eleven states diverse in historical background and political and economic complexion. Dominating the entire region, however, is South Africa itself. This dominance is a product, first, of preponderant economic, demographic and military strength (see Table 8.3) and, second, geographic location. During the apartheid era, South Africa's hegemonic position was used to great effect in destabilising the majority of neighbouring countries which were sympathetic to the cause of the ANC. The end of apartheid has had the effect of abruptly terminating such strategies and of bringing a relative peace to the region (although for reasons unique to Angola, civil conflict has continued). One consequence of this is that South Africa, uniquely in its history, no longer faces any obvious military threat to its security.

Table 8.3 A comparison of the states of southern Africa

State	Population in 2000 (m)	Surface area (thousands of sq. km)	GDP (purchasing power parity) in 1999 (US$ bn)	Military expenditure (US$ m) (year in brackets)
Angola	10.1	1,247	11.6	1,200 (1998)
Botswana	1.5	582	5.7	61 (2000)
Lesotho	2.1	30	4.7 (1998)	not available
Malawi	10.3	118	9.4	17 (1997)
Mozambique	19.1	802	18.7	72 (1997)
Namibia	1.7	824	7.1	90 (1998)
South Africa	43.4	1,221	296	2,000 (2000)
Swaziland	1	17.3	4.2	23 (1996)
Tanzania	35.3	945	23.3	21 (1999)
Zambia	9.5	753	8.5	76 (1997)
Zimbabwe	11.3	391	26.5	127 (2000)

Source: Central Intelligence Agency (2000).

During the apartheid period South Africa was also fairly shameless in its exploitation of regional economic dependencies. Lesotho, Swaziland and Botswana, for instance, were, through their membership of the Southern African Customs Union (SACU), put in service of South African development needs, while the economic fortunes of Mozambique and Malawi were intimately linked to the employment of large portions of their work force in South Africa. Even though they have been obscured by talk of a regional 'peace dividend' and economic revival, these inequalities have survived beyond apartheid. South Africa possesses by far the largest, most industrialised and most outwardly-oriented economy. Regardless of the complexion of the government in Pretoria, the country has consequently retained an ability to exercise regional economic dominance. This may, though, have benevolent consequences as South Africa has shown a willingness to engage in regional economic projects.

The foreign policy of South Africa

The challenges of transformation

South Africa in many ways exemplifies the processes of transformation that have attended world politics since the 1980s. Inside the country, a fundamental political shift has occurred with the removal of apartheid. This has not quite created a new state, but it has certainly meant the establishment of new regime – a new party in power, a newly-enfranchised electorate, and a whole new agenda of politics. Outside, similarly, South Africa faces a fundamentally altered environment, both in terms of the regional southern African setting and the manner in which South Africa is perceived by other states and international organisations. The period of international isolation that marked the apartheid era has essentially ended.

The change of regime in South Africa has thus meant a fundamental reappraisal and reorientation of foreign policy. The preoccupations of the apartheid regime – the fear of a communist-backed onslaught against white minority rule, the consequent desire to weaken (if necessary by force) its regional neighbours and an eschewal of an African orientation in favour of a tacit alliance with Western states – are all now largely irrelevant. Yet while a break is clearly evident, certain continuities are also discernible both in terms of the South Africa's 'existing commitments (and) traditions of state behaviour in international society' (Spence, 1998:

157) and the 'foreign policy' the ANC pursued while in exile during the apartheid years. South African foreign policy is also conditioned by how the state is perceived by others. The removal of apartheid has made a difference to these views, but a certain wariness remains, particularly among South Africa's neighbours, for South Africa's regional stature remains unaltered. All of these factors exercise a constraining influence upon what the 'new' South Africa can do in foreign affairs.

In order to illustrate the challenges of change we will here consider three major issues that have confronted South Africa. These relate to South Africa's international reintegration, the search for a guiding set of ideas and principles for the conduct of foreign policy, and foreign policy making and implementation.

The reintegration of South Africa into international society was an initial and symbolically very important aim of the ANC-led Government of National Unity (GNU) which assumed power in 1994. Mandela, in his inauguration speech, pointed out that the country would no longer suffer the ignominy of being the 'skunk of the world' and during that year South Africa established (or re-established) diplomatic relations with some forty-nine states, bringing the total to 162 – most of the states of the world. It also made an emotional return to international organisations. After a twenty-year absence, South African representatives took their seats at the UN General Assembly in May 1994 and re-entered the Commonwealth in June (having been absent for thirty-three years). During the summer months South Africa also joined, for the first time, the Non-Aligned Movement, the OAU and Southern African Development Community (SADC). This process marked a real achievement for what has been dubbed South Africa's 'diplomacy of reintegration'. By the end of 1994 it had become a full participant in the international community with many new avenues for the pursuit of foreign policy (Muller, 1996). The process did, however, present certain problems. These relate partly to the need to accommodate and organise a whole new range of activities (something we shall return to when we consider foreign policy making) and partly to the awkward choices that a state may face when opening diplomatic relations (South Africa was forced, for instance, to sever the ties it had inherited with Taiwan for the sake of opening relations with China).

The second issue that has confronted South Africa is perhaps the most fundamental of all: the need to lay down a coherent framework of ideas and principles to guide its foreign policy. Although it could be argued that simply responding to pressing regional issues (migration, trade, transport, etc.) or the imperatives of the transition (economic regeneration) could have sufficed as guides to action, there was a feeling that the post-apartheid state ought to stake out a far more principled position in its foreign policy – one that reflected the political achievements of national reconciliation and political progress at home. Translating this into a workable set of ideas, however, has not proven easy and during the first two years of the GNU, South Africa's foreign policy was frequently criticised for a 'lack of conceptual and operational clarity' (Evans, 1996: 263).

This state of affairs has been rendered that much more challenging by the need to balance ideals with the realities of foreign policy – a contradiction between morality and pragmatism, in other words. Handling this contradiction has been a defining feature of South African foreign policy. Insofar as the ANC-led government did have a set of proclaimed ideals upon taking power, these oriented, in large part, around the centrality of human rights issues in foreign policy (Mandela, 1993: 87). Actual policy content, however, has not always comfortably reflected these fine ideals. South Africa has, for instance, established and maintained ties with regimes with dubious human rights records such as Indonesia and Sudan, and has reneged on pre-1994 pledges to support movements of self-determination in Western Sahara (claimed by Morocco) and East Timor. This stance, in part, reflects the debt of gratitude the ANC feels it owes to states which supported it during the apartheid period and also the desire to safeguard lucrative trade relations (van der Westhuizen, 1998: 449).

On occasion South Africa has veered towards the moral high ground. However, this too has brought its problems. Responding to death sentences imposed upon Ken Saro-Wiwa and other Ogoni activists in Nigeria in 1995, South Africa initially pursued a cautious diplomatic strategy. The links that Nigeria and the ANC had forged in the anti-apartheid cause and Mandela's moral stature proved, however, insufficient to persuade the Nigerian military junta to rescind the sentences. Mandela then issued a call for full-scale sanctions against Nigeria, only to be rebuffed by most African states (the OAU rejected the plea as 'not an African way to deal with an African problem') (Vale and Maseko, 1998: 272).

Arms sales have also given rise to controversy. Significantly, the GNU decided not to disband South Africa's state-controlled arms industry (Armscor) but did pledge, in a 1995 defence white paper, that its arms trade would be conducted in accord with a respect for human rights (O'Brien, 1996: 63). Indeed, the personal intervention of Mandela has prevented arms deliveries to Turkey and Rwanda. Yet the economic advantages of these sales are highly prized (in 1994 weapons exports were the second biggest export earner in South Africa) and since 1994 South Africa has provided arms to lucrative buyers such as the United Kingdom, the US and France. Economic motives, however, have led to some controversial deals. South Africa has reportedly sold surveillance equipment to Algeria and in 1997 prompted protests from the US and Israel over a provisional arms deal with Syria (the sale was subsequently suspended).

Turning to the third challenge of change, that of policy making and implementation, here too South Africa has faced some far-reaching developments. To begin with, the Department of Foreign Affairs (DFA) has had to be reorganised, a process that reflects the enlarged scope of South Africa's foreign policy activities. In parallel, the DFA has also been subject to an affirmative action programme that has sought to recruit and promote greater numbers of female and non-white personnel and has seen a large expansion of its overseas missions. These changes have not been without problems. The DFA has had to operate within tight budget constraints (resulting in the closure of a number of missions from 1998) and the personnel shake-up has been politically controversial (Muller, 1999: 18–27).

Foreign policy making has also been affected, to some degree, by the new democratic dispensation in South Africa. Issues formerly closed to parliament and public because of censorship or emergency provisions are now subject to greater scrutiny. The initiation of popular elections has also meant that foreign policy issues have been given a much broader airing. Such debate is, however, subject to the ANC's dominant position in government. This has not prevented opposition parties, think tanks and NGOs criticising its foreign policy, often quite severely (for instance over arms sales, and the Ken Saro-Wiwa episode). However, it has meant that it is within the ANC itself that the more influential foreign policy debates are to be found (Evans, 1996: 263). Personal and bureaucratic positions within the ANC-led government have also been of some importance. In the period 1994–99, foreign policy oversight increasingly drifted away from the DFA towards the offices of President and Vice-President, although the replacement in June 1999 of Foreign Minister Alfred Nzo by Nkosazana Zuma did partially reverse this trend.

Outside these changes there do, however, lie certain continuities with the past. The business community, in the guise of powerful firms such as Anglo American and De Beers, can still exert a significant influence when foreign policy is concerned with issues of trade and investment (Cooper, 1998: 723–4). Further, despite the importance of the political executive in both the apartheid and post-apartheid periods, an inter-agency competition for influence over foreign policy has continued, involving not just the DFA but the Defence Department, the Department of Trade and Industry, and the Department of Safety and Security (O'Meara, 2000).

Finally, it is also worth noting some changes in the instruments of foreign policy. Throughout the 1970s and 1980s South Africa's was a foreign policy that relied heavily on military force (notably in respect of the subjugation of its neighbours) and unconventional instruments (espionage, the assassination of exiled political opponents, black market trading, etc.). These instruments are, with a few exceptions (see the Lesotho case below), no longer needed by a post-apartheid South Africa (Muller, 1996: 14).

The content of South African foreign policy (i) South Africa and Africa

Africa has been a central concern of South Africa's foreign policy. An ANC policy document prepared just before the 1994 elections suggested that in government the organisation would dedicate its foreign policy 'to helping to ensure that Africa's people are not forgotten or ignored by humankind'. Some three years after the elections the theme persisted. In widely noted remarks, the then Deputy President, Thabo Mbeki, spoke of an 'African Renaissance' and his own African identity, something that appeared to reinforce the ANC's commitment to the continent (Vale and Maseko, 1998: 273–4).

This priority had at least five sources: (i) the obvious fact of geography (South Africa is inescapably part of Africa); (ii) a desire to repay some of the support given to the ANC by African nations in the apartheid period; (iii) cultural importance and a sense of black consciousness (a theme of Mbeki's); (iv) South Africa's regional weight; and (v) a desire to reverse the neglect of Africa by the apartheid regime.

South Africa's post-apartheid involvement in Africa has not, however, been straightforward. A clear tension has existed between the aims and the means of policy. The domestic demands of economic and social restructuring, for instance, have limited the amount of economic assistance that South Africa can provide (in 1995 South Africa cancelled debts owed to it by Namibia and has provided loans and credits to Zimbabwe) and have resulted in a hard-nosed attitude towards regional organisations (South Africa has demanded a renegotiation of the revenue sharing provisions of SACU). Similarly, while both Mandela and Mbeki have suggested a South African role in regional peacekeeping, no formal deployments have yet transpired. This is a state of affairs that reflects not just the intrinsic dangers of the missions themselves, but also the fact that the South African military still lacks the appropriate expertise and has undergone a fundamental restructuring consequent upon budgetary cuts and the integration of military cadres from the ANC's armed wing (Spence, 1998: 162). The organisational problems this has entailed were well illustrated by a South African military intervention in Lesotho in May 1998. Ostensibly aimed at putting down a revolt by junior Lesotho officers against the established government, the exercise was soon after described as 'a botched affair' which created an image of South Africa as 'a heavy handed, and not particularly efficient, exponent of military power politics' (Hamill, 1998: 23).

A further tension stems from the emergence of strains with African states. The very rhetoric of South Africa's African vocation has been met with some suspicion by some who feel it reflects a more down-to-earth promotion of regional leadership. The lack of enthusiasm for Mandela's calls for sanctions against Nigeria and the fact that a number of African states voted against Cape Town's submission to stage the 2004 Olympic Games are both reflective of this (Vale and Maseko, 1998: 284). More practical issues have also emerged. Both Lesotho and Swaziland have raised territorial claims against South Africa; oil-producing Angola has been resentful of South Africa's preference for Persian Gulf suppliers; and bordering states such as Mozambique, Zambia, Zimbabwe and Botswana have complained at South Africa's tough stance on the movement of migrants.

Two areas of policy illustrate well the African direction of South Africa's foreign policy and some of the attendant problems. The first is conflict prevention and mediation. Since 1994, South Africa has been keen to promote regional peace, and on several occasions Mandela, Mbeki and others have personally taken up the role of mediator. In some instances, this has proven a success. Mbeki (when Deputy President) helped persuade the Mozambican opposition movement Renamo to rejoin the electoral process in 1994 and that same year a joint South Africa/Botswana/Zimbabwe initiative helped resolve a constitutional crisis in Lesotho. In 1999 Mbeki, in concert with the Zambian President, Frederick Chiluba, helped to persuade rebel movements in the Democratic Republic of Congo (DRC [formerly Zaire]) to sign a cease-fire agreement as a prelude to a UN peacekeeping deployment. On other occasions South African efforts have been somewhat less productive. An earlier diplomatic intervention in Zaire in 1997 failed to broker a peaceful exit for the then ruling Mobutu regime and in all, South African diplomacy in the DRC has led to strained relations with Zimbabwe, Angola and Namibia, all of which intervened militarily in the country in the late 1990s–early 2000s. Quiet diplomacy also proved less than successful in Zimbabwe where during 2000 Mbeki failed to dissuade Zimbabwe's President, Robert Mugabe, from sanctioning violent seizures of white-owned farms.

The second area concerns regional organisations. Since 1994 South Africa has voiced its support for the role of such bodies in promoting regional security, economic development and democratic reform. They have also been viewed as a means by which South Africa can reconnect itself with African affairs. As noted above, South Africa has joined the OAU and SADC (South Africa was also elected chair of the latter for the period 1996–99). It was also a moving force in the creation in 1995 of the Association of Southern African States and has retained its membership of SACU. It is a moot point, however, how much more powerful these bodies are following the demise of apartheid. Issues of regional integration remain hostage to conflicts of economic and political interest among their members. SADC illustrates these contradictions well. Since 1994 its members have reached a number of ambitious agreements on free trade, the establishment of a regional peacekeeping force, transport and energy integration, and so on, but in practice little has materialised (Simon and Johnston, 1999). Given South Africa's regional preponderance, its full participation is a key to the success of such projects. Its own domestic priorities have, however, rendered it a reluctant burden-carrier of integrationist efforts, and certain states (notably Zimbabwe and Angola) would, in any case, be wary of a South Africa that did take such a course.

The content of South African foreign policy (ii) External economic relations

The ANC-led GNU came to power in 1994 dedicated to an ambitious programme of economic reconstruction and social redistribution. Promoting domestic economic revival has subsequently become a driving force of foreign policy. In pursuing this aim, South Africa's economic strategy has been conditioned by what Trevor Manuel, the first ANC Finance Minister, referred to as 'taking stock of the disciplines of the global economy' (*Financial Times*, 1997: i). Reflecting these considerations, prior to 1994 the ANC leadership had divested itself of many populist economic commitments (for instance, a commitment to wholesale nationalisation) and in government has pursued largely orthodox measures such as privatisation and prudent budgetary policies. In the external economic sphere, these have been paralleled by incentives to foreign investment, export-led growth and trade and currency liberalisation.

Involvement in the global economy is, however, an exacting process for any state, and South Africa too has experienced some difficulties consequent upon its fuller economic reintegration. South Africa's adherence to provisions of the General Agreement on Tariffs and Trade and the WTO, for instance, has been rationalised as promoting the international competitiveness of the South African economy, but in the short term it has posed a threat to jobs in the formerly protected sectors of agriculture and mining. South Africa is somewhat better situated in its relations with the IMF. Unusual for an African state, South Africa's level of foreign indebtedness is very low, a consequence, in part, of the drying-up of lending to the apartheid regime in the 1980s. With the removal of apartheid, drawing rights have been restored and South Africa has been keen to maintain healthy relations with the IMF in order to secure access to its funds should they be required. Both South Africa's Reconstruction and Development Programme (1994–96) and the Growth, Employment and Redistribution Programme (1996–) were in line with IMF policy prescriptions. Relations, however, have not been trouble-free. In August 1997 the IMF was critical of the South African Reserve Bank for its interventions to protect the value of the Rand.

Another example of the problems of reintegration is provided by South Africa's relations with the EU. These ties are of fundamental significance, for the EU states constitute South Africa's major sources of trade and foreign investment. With the inauguration of the GNU in 1994 there was considerable expectation in South Africa that these links would develop further through the provision of development assistance, a preferential trade regime and incentives for investment. South Africa was not permitted to accede to the Lomé Convention (on the grounds that it was not, in certain respects, a developing country) but did gain partial membership under a special protocol adopted in April 1997. South Africa has also benefited from ongoing foreign investment and in 1997 the EU launched a Programme for Reconstruction and Development in South Africa. Problems have arisen, however, over trade. A bilateral free trade agreement was finally signed in October 1999 but only after four years of negotiation. The agreement itself outlined a liberalisation of some 90 per cent of bilateral trade over a twelve-year period but within weeks of its signing was nearly scuppered by a dispute over the labelling of South African beverages.

The content of South African foreign policy (iii)
South Africa: a middle-ranking power?

By the straightforward criteria of economic and military capability, and the size of its population, South Africa would seem fit the category of a 'middle power' (van der Westhuizen, 1998: 436). Such a status, however, also depends upon influence and interests. South Africa clearly possesses both of these in its own regional environment, but to what degree has it engaged in a wider, even global, role?

The post-1994 leadership has voiced some aspirations in this direction. Shortly before assuming the office of President, Mandela suggested that South Africa should play a leading role in the global promotion of the values of democracy, justice and peace (Mandela, 1993: 87). President Mbeki, meanwhile, speaking in February 2000, referred to South Africa's 'obligation . . . to contribute to the construction of a better world for all humanity' (cited in Muller, 2000). South Africa has also sought to heighten its international profile. South Africa played a leading role in 1995 in the negotiations over the extension of the Nuclear Non-Proliferation Treaty and has been a fairly active participant in both the Commonwealth (hosting the organisation's summit in 1999) and the Non-Aligned Movement (hosting its summit in 1998).

The ANC-led government has also made much of its self-declared African vocation (see above). At the rhetorical level at least, this suggests not just the promotion of issues of development, democracy and stability within Africa itself, but also the staking out of an African agenda in world affairs. Here South Africa would assume the role of the continent's voice on issues such as debt, trade and economic marginalisation. Its keen interest in the reform of the UN, the case it has made for a permanent seat in any enlarged UN Security Council and its chairing during 1996–2000 of the United Nations Conference on Trade and Development reflect the possibilities of such a role.

One should bear in mind that a globalist vision belies some very immediate and specific South African interests. As we saw in the previous section, the fortunes of the South African economy (and thus, by extension, the domestic economic and political programme of the ANC-led government) are intimately linked to its trading position and its attractiveness as a source of foreign investment. South Africa has consequently been very active in courting Western states. Mandela and Mbeki's numerous visits to Western capitals, as well as involving the normal pomp and circumstance of a state occasion, have entailed considerable lobbying and commercial activities by a variety of South African economic delegations. The itinerary of other tours – to East Asia and Latin America, for instance – have also, according to Muller (1999: 29), been 'aimed at furthering the economic interests of South Africa'.

South Africa's pursuit of a globalist position has involved it in the maintenance of a range of activities, not all of which sit comfortably together. This is illustrated particularly well by South Africa's relations with the US. Since 1994, the ANC-led government has considered close relations with Washington as a priority, not least for economic reasons. Yet relations have not always been smooth. The two are often direct competitors in world arms markets and South Africa's desire to pursue friendly relations and/or dialogue with 'rogue' states such as Iraq, Libya and Cuba has led to criticism in Washington. Pretoria meanwhile, has been unhappy at the paucity of American economic assistance to South Africa and the lack of support it has attracted in Washington on issues such as debt forgiveness in Africa and a refashioning of the IMF and World Bank (Stremlau, 2000: 129–31).

The imponderables of South African foreign policy

Views of South Africa often veer between a heady optimism that stems from the momentous political transition of the 1990s and apocalyptic scenarios of political, economic and social collapse. What is not in doubt is the scale of the transformation that has occurred within the country. This is a process that has far from run its course. There are some signs of long-term stability – it is probable that an ANC-dominated government will be in power for the foreseeable future and the country has already made a relatively smooth transition towards a post-Mandela leadership, even though this has brought to an end the 'Mandela magic' which South Africa was able to exploit in its dealings with foreign states (Muller, 1999: 27).

One should be careful, however, in attributing too much to the sway of individuals in foreign policy. Far more important has been the overall change of the domestic political regime and the manner in which the 'new' South Africa has dealt with an outside world that is fundamentally different from that which preoccupied its apartheid predecessors. In these regards perhaps the overriding theme has been economic, a theme particularly visible given the lowered saliency after apartheid of traditional military-security concerns. This is a theme, moreover, that clearly links both the domestic and external spheres. The compelling demands of South Africa's economic restructuring and associated programmes of social redistribution have had, and will long continue to have, a clear impact on foreign policy. This may at times be tempered by less concrete impulses relating to the moral and Africanist dimensions of policy, but it appears that even these have increasingly been viewed in a pragmatic light. This is what Mandela has called 'democratic realism', a desire to promote democracy in southern Africa not simply because it is a just cause, but also because it promotes regional stability and thus stability in South Africa itself (Stremlau, 2000: 128).

The foreign policy of Nigeria

The challenges of transformation

With one in four Africans living within its borders, Nigeria's foreign policy merits some attention. Nigeria has suffered from what has been described as 'outward-directed growth' – a colonial legacy of external dependency and the internal, sometimes divisive, effects of federalism. The challenge of post-Cold War change for Nigeria then has involved sustaining some important post-independence continuities. It has pursued both global and regional roles commensurate with 'medium-power' status, but at the same time foreign policy formulation and orientation have been influenced by an ongoing quest for nation-building and the projection of a specifically Nigerian identity in international affairs.

Since 1963, official responsibility for Nigeria's foreign policy making has rested with the Ministry of External Affairs. The operation of this ministry has, however, been consistently compromised by the command structures of military governments and the pivotal role played by Presidents and Prime Ministers. Prior to 1990, the strategy of Nigeria's foreign policy was principally determined by the authoritarian and personalised over-sight of strong military leaders such as Olusegun Obasanjo and Ibrahim Babangida. This reflected an elite reluctance to countenance political opposition or to democratise, something which, in turn, attracted increasing Western censure. In May 1999 Nigeria transformed its military regime into a civil administration, with Obasanjo elevated to the position of civilian President.

Nigeria's federal structure has also been important. Fears at the centre that Nigeria's regions (particularly in the south) might unite to challenge the power of the federal government have meant a jealous guarding of foreign policy prerogatives. In practice, however, the regions have executed their own 'foreign policy' actions in certain spheres (entering into economic arrangements with outside.states, for instance). The upshot has been occasional foreign policy confusion and the lack of a single Nigerian voice. Finally, Nigeria has been slow to develop a culture of *prior*, inclusive consultation. Civilian structures for foreign policy debate (the Nigerian

Institute for International Affairs and the Nigerian Institute for Policy and Strategic Studies) have had little impact, and foreign policy agenda setting in political parties or the National Assembly has proven difficult (Gambari, 1991). That said, this state of affairs has changed following Nigeria's recent moves towards democracy and a parliamentary system, and political and civic groups have since exercised a telling influence on some aspects of Nigeria's foreign policy.

The transition to civilian rule in the late 1990s notwithstanding, the outlook for Nigeria has been widely reported as bleak, owing to endemic economic weakness and political fragility. These are long-standing issues for Nigeria and have presented it with uncomfortable foreign policy implications in the shape of managing indebtedness and relations with foreign lenders since at least the late 1970s. In this light it is possible to argue that the end of the Cold War has been only one among many influences on the country's foreign policy (Bach, 1999: 115). Indeed, there are perennial concerns of Nigerian foreign policy which have very little to do with this watershed. Nigeria has long aspired to the role of sub-regional hegemon and motor of west African economic integration, and it has sought also to mark itself out more widely as a middle-ranking power of influence in bodies such as the UN General Assembly and the OAU. That said, the agenda of Nigeria's foreign policy has, in certain respects, undergone something of a sea-change since the late 1980s. The Cold War commitment to non-alignment has become a much less relevant issue and Nigeria has been able to take advantage of a diminution of French interest in regional west African affairs. Here, its priority continues to be regional economic integration, but increasingly accompanied by 'human security' concerns, including peacekeeping, environmental degradation and the management of relations with multinational companies.

In order to unpack Nigeria's adjustments to, and expectations of, a transformed world the following sections consider three concentric circles of its foreign policy concerns: west Africa, sub-Saharan Black Africa, and the external economic and political relations of military rule and democratisation.

The content of Nigerian foreign policy (i)
Nigeria in west Africa: a regional hegemon?

As already noted, west Africa is a region in which Nigeria enjoys a natural regional predominance. This has provided a facilitating context for an influential, sometimes assertive, foreign policy. This is a policy which has aroused some suspicion among Nigeria's neighbours, not least when it has involved military intervention (as in the cases of Liberia and Sierra Leone) or territorial disputes (as with Benin, Cameroon and Chad). That said, Nigeria's policy has been characterised by a temperate 'good neighbourliness'. Moreover, this has been welcomed in some respects in the region given the spate of civil wars there and the palpable disinclination of the US and European powers (the British intervention in Sierra Leone notwithstanding) to involve themselves in local security crises. Leadership, in other words, has been seemingly as much required *of* Nigeria as sought *by* it.

In the main, Nigeria's foreign policy stance towards west Africa has been reflected in an unfailing commitment to political and economic integration played out principally through Nigeria's active participation in ECOWAS. Nigeria was a prime mover in the creation of this organisation in 1975 viewing it as a hedge against undue European influence exercised through the Lomé arrangements and as a political investment designed to avoid the balkanisation of west Africa. These were essentially long-term considerations and there were few, if any, short- or medium-term economic gains to be had. In fact, Nigeria subsequently contributed sizeable amounts of aid to its neighbours and bore the brunt of criticisms for the failure of ECOWAS throughout the 1980s to match its own rhetoric of economic integration (apparent in continuing low levels of intra-west African trade).

Nigeria has unfailingly encouraged and supported the incremental institutionalisation of ECOWAS. In the wake of the Community's failure to meet its goal of a single west African market by 1990, Nigeria backed efforts to reactivate the Community with a 1993 treaty revision. Under Article 1, ECOWAS duly became an official pillar of the African Economic Community (AEC), established by the Abuja Treaty of 1991. Nevertheless, after 1994 ECOWAS fortunes declined, largely due to its Francophone members' interest in a parallel initiative formed in January of that year – the West African Economic and Monetary Union – and widespread economic and political instabilities to which Nigeria was also prone. In an effort to mitigate its Anglophone isolation, Nigeria's military leader, Sani Abacha, took on the chairmanship of ECOWAS in 1996, determined to salvage the organisation, despite unpaid contributions by other member states estimated at US$53 million. At the 1996 ECOWAS summit he promised 'an intensification of . . . regional structural transformation' and the implementation of an ECOWAS Minimum Agenda for Action which entailed concrete steps towards the free movement of persons, goods and services. Also included was a commitment to establish a regional parliament, along with moves towards a single currency with the establishment of Ecobank and the West African Clearing House. Further, although its treaty does not make explicit provision for a common foreign policy, ECOWAS has developed a sufficiently large bureaucracy to design and implement one – a potential not lost on Nigeria. Indeed, it is this potential, built into the provision of a Defence Protocol included in the 1993 revised treaty, that has given rise to some of Nigeria's most assertive post-Cold War foreign policy initiatives under the auspices of ECOMOG.

ECOMOG has been seen as a kind of spin-off from the economic imperatives of regional cooperation. However, for Nigeria, concerns for security have been as prominent in its approach to the west African sub-region. For most of the 1990s ECOMOG found itself enmeshed in damage limitation and regional peacekeeping initiatives in two civil wars – first in Liberia and then in Sierra Leone. But it was war in the former that marked the entry of Nigeria into serious regional peacekeeping. From the onset of the Liberian crisis, Nigeria spearheaded, financed and led the ECOMOG interventions, providing six of ECOMOG's seven commanders in the field and 70 per cent of men and matériel (Howe, 1997: 152).

Nigeria's ready assumption of the lion's share of these political and economic costs was impressive but unsurprising. In early 1990, as the Liberian crisis escalated, a need to contain regional knock-on effects overrode reservations among some of Nigeria's ECOWAS neighbours concerning the Nigerian lead role. As for Nigeria itself, its involvement in Liberia was triggered by four eventualities: first, a close personal relationship between Babangida and the Liberian President Samuel Doe; second, American refusal actively to intervene; third, spiralling refugee flows into Sierra Leone, Ghana, The Gambia, Guinea, Côte d'Ivoire and Nigeria itself; and fourth, the lack of any OAU initiative (Osaghae, 1998: 268). Babangida was apparently prepared to deploy Nigerian troops against the anti-Doe forces of Charles Taylor's National Patriotic Front of Liberia from the outset but was persuaded to adopt a more diplomatic approach and go through ECOWAS to broker between Doe's government and rebel forces. Nigeria accordingly convened the Standing Mediation Committee – an ECOWAS inner circle mandated to act in dispute and conflict settlement. But divisions among its members over how best to deal with the Liberian crisis effectively emasculated it.

In the event, Nigeria offered logistical support for an interventionist force mandated to monitor any agreed cease-fire. This initiative was not welcomed by all in ECOWAS (Côte d'Ivoire was a notable dissenter). The OAU, however, supported Nigerian recommendations to deploy a military force, and these gained a UN seal of approval on the back of American support. What were effectively Nigerian peacekeeping forces duly landed in the Liberian capital Monrovia in August 1990 to conduct what ECOMOG sources described as a 'defensive offensive'. Its subsequent deployment has generally been regarded as positive insofar as it contained the fighting and helped create conditions for negotiations and elections which helped end the conflict (Omach, 2000: 79). That said, Nigeria's role within ECOMOG was contentious. Charles Taylor, not surprisingly, questioned ECOMOG's impartiality and Zimbabwe flatly refused to place troops under the *de facto* command of a Nigerian military dictatorship. At home, meanwhile, Nigeria's intervention was portrayed as unnecessarily complicating Nigeria's relations with its neighbours and as a huge drain on Nigeria's resources at a time of domestic economic crisis (Osaghae, 1998: 269). Others, however, did see some longer-term benefits both to Nigeria and to the west African region. ECOMOG's Liberian adventure helped to legitimise Nigeria's regional role, provided a political boost to ECOWAS and established a precedent for a muscular African (as opposed to extra-continental) response to regional crises.

The precedent set by Liberia was soon followed by a subsequent involvement in Sierra Leone. The latter had, in fact, been prey to civil war since 1991 and an ECOMOG force of Nigerian peacekeepers (along with troops from Ghana, Guinea and Mali) had been stationed there since June 1997 following the overthrow of the Nigerian-backed regime of President Ahmad Kabbah. ECOMOG played a decisive role in restoring Kabbah to power in March 1998 and the subsequent twelve months saw ECOMOG defend the Kabbah regime militarily. However, Nigeria's commitment to Sierra Leone was both expensive (costing it up to US$1 million a day) and increasingly unpopular at home. Obasanjo's election as Nigerian President in May 1999 saw the coming to power of a leader much more attuned to the voices of parliament and domestic public opinion, and he set about an immediate withdrawal of the ECOMOG contingent (an act facilitated by the Lomé agreement reached between Kabbah and Sierra Leonian rebel forces in July) – although some 3,000 remained behind as part of a UN peacekeeping force (Adebajo and Keen, 2000: 9–10).

Despite obvious costs, Nigeria's sub-regional potential has been enhanced rather than eroded by its leadership of ECOMOG. One significant consequence has been to raise Nigeria's international profile. Thus, during a visit to Lagos in April 2000 US Secretary of Defense William Cohen signalled American support for continuing Nigerian leadership of west African peacekeeping by resuming military assistance suspended during the period of the Abacha regime.

Further, Nigeria has shown that it can act cooperatively to provide an 'African solution to an African problem'. This suggests that Nigeria, in terms of security policy at least, may not be as impotent as more pessimistic assessments of Africa's marginalisation might suggest. However, while Nigeria's regional interventions in west Africa have broadly demonstrated a hegemonic status, its role in SSA more broadly is much less assured.

The content of Nigerian foreign policy (ii)
Nigeria in Black Africa: destined to lead?

Since independence Nigerian foreign policy has been premised on the claim that Nigeria has somehow been destined to lead Black Africa. Acclaimed as 'Africa's equivalent to Brazil, India, or Indonesia' (Maier 2000), the country's foreign policy formulations have referred to Nigeria's 'manifest destiny' and its role as 'champion of Africa' (Osaghae, 1998: 29; Wright and Okolo, 1999: 119). This is a view that persists despite Nigeria's troubled post-independence development. As the *Economist* (15 January 2000) magazine has argued, 'many [Nigerians] believe that their country is a superpower which just happens to have lost its way; that with better leadership Nigeria will quickly become a beacon for Africa'.

As a consequence of its considerable oil resources, Nigeria has at times seemed close to attaining its continental ambitions. The buoyancy of the Nigerian economy during the 1970s permitted the country to extend its largesse to other African states and liberation movements. Nigeria supplied oil at concessionary rates, provided relief to drought-stricken countries, and furnished technical and financial support to a range of states (both in ECOWAS and outside that organisation). Much later, in 1987, Nigeria launched the Technical Aid Corps scheme. Intended as a kind of peace corps, it involved the secondment of Nigerian professionals to provide expertise in legal, business, education and health-care fields to any interested African country – all entirely at the expense of the Nigerian government.

This economic 'spray diplomacy' was, however, contingent on the strength of the petro-Naira and thus a slump in oil prices during the 1980s severely curtailed Nigeria's quest for pre-eminence in SSA. Protracted domestic turmoil, meanwhile, drained political will for such a role and by the mid-1980s the country's economic self-interest had led it into confrontation with its neighbours. In January 1983, Nigeria precipitately expelled several million migrant workers, contrary to the spirit and the letter of ECOWAS. Such action caused much hardship for significant numbers of the Ghanaians, Chadians and Benois who were compelled to leave, while the subsequent closure of Nigeria's borders with Benin and Niger, in a (vain) attempt to stem smuggling, damaged further the economies of Nigeria's neighbours and with it Nigeria's image.

These moves notwithstanding, by the Cold War's end Nigeria had still managed to sustain a foreign policy characterised by a strident pan-Africanist, anti-apartheid rhetoric and a degree of influence throughout SSA. Nigeria was a prominent backer of the anti-colonial cause in Angola and Rhodesia (Zimbabwe) in the 1970s, and during the 1980s provided significant support for SWAPO of Namibia and for the ANC. Its anti-apartheid credentials, moreover, gained Nigeria a place in the Eminent Persons Group, set up by the Commonwealth in 1986 to mediate in the political crisis in South Africa.

In the post-Cold War period, Nigerian foreign policy has been deprived of its anti-apartheid and anti-colonial themes and so, at the continental level, Nigeria has fallen back on its long-standing commitment to the OAU as a visible symbol of its pan-Africanism. Nigeria accordingly hosted the June 1991 OAU summit, at which Babangida was installed as OAU Chairman and Nigeria proved instrumental in achieving a consensus on the establishment of a Conflict Resolution Department. But perhaps the most significant achievement of that year was the formation and ratification of the AEC (see above) – a 'common market' initiative presaged by ECOWAS and the Lagos Plan of Action formulated at Nigeria's instigation back in 1980, that set a thirty-four-year timetable for the integration of African states' economies. It looked a promising start to a new era in which the marginalisation of Africa might be reversed under the OAU's auspices.

Support for the OAU has, however, taken a heavy financial toll. In light of the previously incurred costs of supporting South African, Namibian and Zimbabwean liberation movements, Babangida's chairmanship was criticised within Nigeria as an extravagance. Babangida's public demands that reparations be paid to African states by the former colonial powers were, predictably, ignored, leaving Nigeria almost obligated to make compensatory 'donations' in order to promote and maintain its image. As the 1990s progressed, domestic coffers, already bled by rampant corruption, were further depleted as Abacha allegedly bankrolled the electioneering of favoured candidates in Benin and Ghana. According to former security adviser, Ishmael Gwarzo, just before Abacha's death in 1998 some US$250 million was to have been taken to the OAU summit, earmarked for distribution to those African heads of state Abacha wanted to influence. Such revelations indicate the high price paid in the search for continental influence.

The limits of Nigerian influence have also been apparent in the military sphere. While Nigeria's military role in west Africa has been significant, this has translated poorly into initiatives of continent-wide relevance. In light of the success of the American-led Gulf War coalition in 1991, the OAU did propose a similar arrangement, fronted by Nigeria, to deal with African crises – a designated 'African High Command'. The operational-isation of this force has, however, proven elusive, owing to rivalries among Africa's more influential states, capability deficiencies and the difficulties of harnessing African militaries to function under civilian control. Nigeria's commitment has also been contingent upon the development of the ACRI initiative (see above). America has been keen for Nigeria to participate in ACRI, and this was the focus of US President Bill Clinton's visit to Nigeria in August 2000.

The development of African peacekeeping – like other continental initiatives – has come to depend increasingly on cooperation between Nigeria and SSA's other major power, South Africa. From Nigeria's per-spective, once the apartheid regime had been removed, policy swiftly evolved towards support for the new ANC-led regime. Ironically, the trans-ition in South Africa focused greater attention on Africa's other auto-cratic regimes and, as part and parcel of this, led to increasing criticism of Abacha's Nigeria by Nelson Mandela. Relations soon deteriorated once Mandela took up the cause of sanctions against Nigeria following the controversial execution of Ogoni activists in Nigeria in 1995 (see above).

With the passing of the Abacha regime relations with South Africa warmed, and although the two countries could be presented as long-term rivals in Africa, the line pursued by both Abubakar and Obasanjo has been to present South Africa as a complement to Nigerian efforts towards regional security and economic integration. As part of this Nigeria has made a strong case for the inclusion in the UN Security Council of two permanent seats for Africa – for Nigeria and possibly South Africa.

These more contemporary themes have not entirely filled the vacuum left in Nigerian foreign policy by the passing of the anti-apartheid and anti-colonial causes. It was around these that Nigeria had enjoyed a certain credibility in SSA. Nigeria's calls for a new international economic order have not been an effective alternative rallying cry and sound somewhat *passé* in an era of competitive globalisation. That Nigeria has retained influence, despite the disappearance of some of its long-term foreign policy planks, says much for its acquired status. Even so, the anticipated benefits of its 'manifest destiny' have failed to materialise and its 'Cold War capital' has been steadily eroded. Beyond west Africa, Nigeria's projection of influence has been marginal, leaving it open to accusations of showman-ship rather than dynamism.

The content of Nigerian foreign policy (iii)
Nigeria in the world: international politics and economic realities

Nigeria's more globally-oriented foreign policy has tended to revolve around two overriding economic factors: the reliance on oil and its derivatives as the single most important trading commodity (accounting for over 90 per cent of foreign currency earnings) and the rigours of structural adjustment demanded by external lenders. Both factors reflect Nigeria's vulnerable externally-oriented economy and its essential dependency on Western powers and institutions.

Nigeria's preoccupation with economic diplomacy has mostly consisted of negotiations aimed at debt rescheduling and the procurement of foreign investment and additional credit lines. On the oil front, Nigeria remains hostage to Western technology as well as Western markets for oil export revenues. In an effort to mitigate this dependency, in 1987 Nigeria spearheaded the founding of the African Petroleum Producers' Association (APPA), with the objective of promoting cooperation in oil and petrochemical research and technologies. But Nigeria derived little benefit, as APPA's twelve member states found their different interests hard to reconcile. Consequently, Nigeria has sustained its more important commitment to the Organisation of Petroleum Exporting Countries (OPEC), although it has done so in a balanced fashion. It remained neutral during the Gulf War and, unlike radical OPEC members such as Libya and Iraq, has maintained relatively amicable relations with Israel.

This position did not, however, compensate for the deterioration of relations with Western states owing to the reluctance of Nigeria's military regimes to democratise throughout much of the 1980s and 1990s, and the country's image as endemically corrupt and the source of large-scale drug trafficking. It was the Ogoni issue, however, that set the seal on Nigeria's ostracisation. The Ogoni demand for revenue sharing, environmental protection and the devolution of political power in a principal oil-producing region presented a major challenge to the military's control of Nigeria's oil-based political economy. The Nigerian government's repression of Ogoni activists led, in turn, to a range of international measures, including economic sanctions, aid cancellation and a US embargo on direct flights. The EU restricted diplomatic access and Nigeria was expelled from the Commonwealth. In response, Abacha criticised outsiders for interfering in Nigeria's internal affairs and sought to rally support from fellow 'pariahs' such as Libya and Iraq. This strategy proved of little benefit. Nigeria's debt and trade dependencies have determined a need to retain at least respectful relations with states such as the US, Britain, Germany and France.

This state of affairs is captured also by Nigeria's experience of structural adjustment. The oil boom of the 1970s and early 1980s, as noted above, had been largely wasted in Nigeria owing to misdirected expenditure and corruption. The upshot has been a massive balance of payments deficit. Despite a mini-boom around the time of the Gulf War, by the end of 1991 Nigeria had become the largest sub-Saharan debtor state. Nigeria's efforts to diversify its exports thereafter failed badly and, by the mid-1990s, the country was forced to fall ever more into line with World Bank and IMF-prescribed structural adjustment policies. These have proven controversial. Under Obasanjo, Nigeria has resisted the establishment of a resident IMF mission within the Finance Ministry and Central Bank (a requirement set by the UK for debt rescheduling) and the Nigerian military has balked at demands for reduced defence spending as a condition of renewed lending. Obasanjo, meanwhile, has conducted a global campaign for Nigeria's debt cancellation. In December 2000 the Paris Club of international creditors agreed to reschedule US$23.4 billion and Obasanjo in turn lauded this as evidence of Nigeria's 'democracy dividend'. Additionally, some US$200 billion of stolen public funds has been tracked down and arrangements for their repatriation are proceeding. Most were in the late Abacha's Swiss bank accounts.

As these examples illustrate, Nigeria has, under civilian rule, attracted a certain belated sympathy for its economic plight. Of no small significance in this regard has been an upturn in relations with the US in the late 1990s. Ever conscious of the need to diversify energy supplies away from the Middle East and Persian Gulf, the US has long seen Nigeria as a potentially important economic partner. During Bill Clinton's second term, the US re-engaged with Nigeria in a flurry of high level, high profile visits, culminating in that of the President himself (see above). The material benefits, however, have been few and as the twentieth century closed Nigeria's economic prospects seemed once more to be at the mercy of two perennials – the implementation of structural adjustment and the vicissitudes of the international oil market (although by 1999/2000, the long-term decline in price had been reversed, thus boosting significantly Nigeria's oil earnings).

By 2000 Nigeria was supposedly entering the third stage of its 'Vision 2010' programme – an optimistic wish-list that pledges to transform Nigeria into a 'united, industrious, caring and God-fearing democratic society . . . [while] creating Africa's leading economy' (para 4) but which recognises that 'all is not well with Nigeria's external image' (para 73). Post-Cold War, Nigeria has seemingly lost much diplomatic leverage in its relations with the West and external lending agencies. Nigerian foreign policy has consequently been characterised as essentially reactive to these intrusive externalities. But this tells only a partial story, one located in the outermost circle of Nigeria's foreign policy. In the regional and continental circles, Nigeria's story can be read as more positive (if not always more successful) in that it has involved real choices and a degree of influence over the course of events (Wright and Okolo, 1999: 130).

The imponderables of Nigerian foreign policy

Nigeria's foreign policy has, in many ways, certain fixed features – the pursuit of leadership in African affairs, for instance. However, the foreign policy challenges which Nigeria has faced have shifted over time. Concerns with pan-African unity and the promotion of anti-colonial and anti-apartheid causes are now a thing of the past. In their stead, Nigeria has found itself sucked into ever more taxing issues relating to regional conflict management and economic cooperation, and diplomatic balancing among the often fractious community of states in SSA. Beyond the continent, matters have also been far from easy. Economic mismanagement, compounded by the uncontrollable vacillations of the international market in oil products have meant that Nigeria's promising economic resources have not been translated into either domestic economic prosperity or international economic influence. In foreign policy terms, this has meant a constant thematic preoccupation with the vagaries of economic dependency and a day-to-day process of negotiation with external creditors over the management of Nigerian indebtedness.

These problems, already difficult enough, have not been rendered any easier by Nigeria's proclivity for political instability, corruption and military rule. It could well be argued that this is a pattern of government that has assumed a certain air of normality. However, the major imponderable when looking at Nigeria is whether or not this pattern will change (in the direction of stable, secure and well-intentioned civilian government) or whether it will continue (in the manner of constant military–civilian interludes, long-term political turmoil and economic decline). Either route would give rise to certain foreign policy similarities, if only because pressing regional and external economic concerns would remain unaltered. That said, these two routes do imply foreign policy differences. The most recent period of civilian rule suggests a moderation of regional military involvement and a seemingly greater willingness to knuckle down to domestic economic priorities and the strictures of external creditors.

Conclusion

African foreign policies labour under some particularly trying circumstances. In this sense, the transformation of world politics detailed in this volume has made little difference. Whether during the Cold War or after, the essential condition of African states has remained the same: marginal and dependent. The relative positions of South Africa and Nigeria are more favourable than say Mozambique, Sierra Leone or Somalia, but even these, the two most powerful states of SSA, enjoy a lowly position in international affairs. There is very little evidence to suggest that this will change for international economic, military and political structures of power do little to favour these states. In these circumstances, the regional and continental settings will continue to be crucial. This is true of all states, but more so in Africa given that it is only really in these settings that influence can be purposively pursued and demonstrated in the long term. Beyond these settings, the challenges of foreign policy will continue to be the maximisation of access, the cultivation of sympathy and the championing of causes which might make some difference to domestic predicaments, particularly in the economic field. The evidence of this chapter suggests that in these respects, South Africa has achieved more than has Nigeria.

Further reading

There is a growing literature on the contemporary foreign policies of both Nigeria and South Africa. The interested reader should consult the relevant chapters in Harbeson and Rothchild (eds) (1995) and Wright (ed.) (1999a). In addition, Osaghea (1998) is useful for Nigeria while Carlsnaes and Muller (eds) (1997) provide a comprehensive (but now a little dated) overview of South African foreign policy. Journal articles are plentiful and one should consult *African Affairs*, *The Journal of Modern African Studies* and *Third World Quarterly*. The magazines *West Africa* and *Africa Confidential* are useful for following events. A very good analysis of the international relations of the African continent is Clapham (1996a).

References

Adebajo, A. and Keen, D. (2000) 'Banquet for Warlords', *The World Today*, 56(7), 8–10.

Bach, D.C. (1999) *Regionalisation in Africa: Integration and Disintegration*. London: James Curry.

Bayart, J.-F. (2000) 'Africa in the World: a History of Extraversion', *African Affairs*, 99, 217–67.

Carlsnaes, W. and Muller, M. (eds) (1997) *Change and South African External Relations*. Johannesburg: Thomson.

Central Intelligence Agency (2000) *The World Factbook, 2000*. <http://www.odci.gov/cia/publications/factbook/>.

Chettle, J. (1997) 'After the Miracle. Can South Africa Be a Normal State?', *The National Interest* (spring), 64–75.

Clapham, C. (1996a) *Africa and the International System. The Politics of State Survival*. Cambridge: Cambridge University Press.

Clapham, C. (1996b) 'Governmentality and Economic Policy in Sub-Saharan Africa', *Third World Quarterly*, 17(4), 809–24.

Cooper, A.F. (1998) 'The Multiple Faces of South African Foreign Policy', *International Journal*, LIII(4), 705–32.

Economist, The (2000) 'Here's Hoping A Survey of Nigeria, 15 January.

Evans, G. (1996) 'South Africa in Remission: the Foreign Policy of an Altered State', *The Journal of Modern African Studies*, 34(2), 249–69.

Financial Times (1997) 'Survey: Investing in South Africa' (25 March).

Gambari, I. (1991) *Political and Comparative Dimensions of Regional Integration: the Case of ECOWAS*. Atlantic Highlands, NJ: Humanities Press.

Grimond, J. (2001) 'Africa's Great Black Hope: a Survey of South Africa', *The Economist* (24 February).

Hamill, J. (1998) 'From Realism to Complex Interdependence? South Africa, Southern Africa and the Question of Security', *International Relations*, 14(3), 1–30.

Harbeson, J.W. and Rothchild, D. (eds) (1995) *Africa in World Politics: Post-Cold War Challenges*, Boulder, CO: Westview Press.

Herbst, J. (1996/97) 'Responding to State Failure in Africa', *International Security*, 21(3), 120–44.

Howe, H. (1997) 'Lessons of Liberia: ECOMOG and Regional Peacekeeping', *International Security*, 21(3), 145–76.

Jackson, R. and Rosberg, C.G. (1986) 'Sovereignty and Underdevelopment: Juridical Statehood in the African Crisis', *The Journal of Modern African Studies*, 24(1), 1–31.

Maier, K. (2000) *The House Has Fallen. Midnight in Nigeria*. Lagos: Public Affairs.

Mandela, N. (1993) 'South Africa's Future Foreign Policy', *Foreign Affairs*, 72(5), 86–97.

Metz, S. (2000) *Refining American Strategy in Africa*. Carlisle, PA: Strategic Studies Institute, US Army War College.

Muller, M. (1996) 'South Africa and the Diplomacy of Reintegration', University of Leicester, Diplomatic Studies Programme, Discussion Paper, 16.

Muller, M. (1999) 'South African Diplomacy and Security Complex Theory', University of Leicester, Diplomatic Studies Programme, Discussion Paper, 53.

Muller, M. (2000) 'South African Economic Diplomacy in the Age of Globalisation', paper presented to the International Studies Association, 41st Annual Convention, Los Angeles. <htttps://www.cc.columbia.edu/sec/dlc/ciao/isa/mum01/>.

O'Brien, K.A. (1996) 'Regional Security in Southern Africa: South Africa's National Perspective', *International Peacekeeping*, 3(3), 52–76.

Olsen, G.R. (1997) 'Western Europe's Relations with Africa since the End of the Cold War', *The Journal of Modern African Studies*, 35(2), 299–319.

Omach, P. (2000) 'The African Crisis Response Initiative: Domestic Politics and Convergence of National Interests', *African Affairs*, 99, 73–95.

O'Meara, D. (2000) 'Reinventing a Regional Superpower? Theoretical Issues in the Analysis of South African Foreign Policy after Apartheid', paper presented to the International Studies Association, 41st Annual Convention, Los Angeles. <htttps://www.cc.columbia.edu/sec/dlc/ciao/isa/omd01/>.

Osaghae, E.E. (1998) *Crippled Giant: Nigeria since Independence*. London: Hurst and Company.

Parfitt, T. (1996) 'The Decline of Eurafrica? Lomé's Mid-Term Review', *Review of African Political Economy*, 67, 53–66.

Riddell, R.C. (1999) 'The End of Foreign Aid to Africa? Concerns about Donor Policies', *African Affairs*, 98, 309–35.

Shaw, T. and Nyang'oro, J.E. (1999) 'Conclusion: African Foreign Policies and the Next Millennium: Alternative Perspectives, Practices and Possibilities', in Wright, S. (ed.), *African Foreign Policies*. Boulder, CO: Westview Press, 237–48.

Simon, D. and Johnston, A. (1999) 'The Southern African Development Community: Regional Integration in Ferment', The Royal Institute of International Affairs (London), Southern Africa Study Group, Briefing Paper, 8.

Southall, R. (1998) 'The Centralization and Fragmentation of South Africa's Dominant Party System', *African Affairs*, 97, 443–69.

Sparks, D. (1998) 'Economic Trends in Africa South of the Sahara, 1998', *Africa South of the Sahara 1999*. London: Europa Publications, 10–17.

Spence, J.E. (1998) 'The New South African Foreign Policy: Incentives and Constraints', in Toase, F.H. and Yorke, E.J. (eds), *The New South Africa. Prospects for Domestic and International Security*. Basingstoke: Macmillan, 157–68.

Stremlau, J. (2000) 'Ending Africa's Wars', *Foreign Affairs*, 79(4), 117–32.

Vale, P. and Maseko, S. (1998) 'South Africa and the African Renaissance', *International Affairs*, 74(2), 271–89.

van der Westhuizen, J. (1998) 'South Africa's Emergence as a Middle Power', *Third World Quarterly*, 19(3), 435–55.

World Bank (1997) *World Development Report 1997*. Oxford: World Bank/Oxford University Press.

Wright, S. (ed.) (1999a) *African Foreign Policies*. Boulder, CO: Westview Press.

Wright, S. (1999b) 'The Changing Context of African Foreign Policies', in Wright, S. (ed.), *African Foreign Policies*. Boulder, CO: Westview Press, 1–22.

Wright, S. and Okolo, J.E. (1999) 'Nigeria: Aspirations of Regional Power', in Wright, S. (ed.), *African Foreign Policies*. Boulder, CO: Westview Press, 118–53.

Zartman, I.W. (1995) *Collapsed States: State–Society Relations and Restoration of Legitimacy and Authority*. Boulder, CO: Lynne Rienner.

The world wide web

The Nigerian Federal Government can be found at: <http://www.nigeriagov.org/info.htm>. The South African Foreign Ministry can be found at: <http://www.gov.za/ministry/foreign.htm>. The web site of the African National Congress is at: <http://www.anc.org.za/>. A rich source of news from around the continent is available at: <http://allafrica.com/>.

9 | The Middle East: Iran and Israel

Anoushiravan Ehteshami

The Middle East is a region in which war or the threat of war has become commonplace. It is also a region riven with animosity – most obviously that which divides Israel from its Arab neighbours. These characteristics have survived the end of the Cold War and thus there is a good deal of continuity apparent in regional foreign policies. That said, the end of the Cold War did also mark an important watershed both for the region and for the two states considered here – Iran and Israel. This chapter will argue that the demise of the Cold War was, in fact, only one of a number of changes that have impacted upon the states of the region; all, however, have posed foreign policy challenges and have, as a consequence, given rise to debate and efforts at policy adaptation.

Introduction

For the best part of two hundred years, the Middle East region (defined here as encompassing the Arab world and thus parts of north Africa and the Persian Gulf region, in addition to Iran, Israel and Turkey) has been one of the main playgrounds of outside, largely Western powers. The slow demise of European imperial influence in the aftermath of the Second World War might have signalled the end of outside intervention in this region, had it not been for the onset of the Cold War, which itself began with the 'Azerbaijan crisis' on Iran's northern border with the Soviet Union in 1946. For the next fifty years, the superpowers were to regard the Middle East as a prize in their strategic calculations.

Since the dawn of civilisation the region's location – at the crossroads of Africa, Asia and Europe – has made it important to large and small powers alike, from the empires of the East to the imperial powers of the

West. The opening of the Suez Canal in 1869, which transformed maritime travel between Europe and Asia, added to European interest. The region's other riches also encouraged European intervention and rivalries. This resulted in a series of confrontations between the Ottoman Empire and its European adversaries, and finally in the collapse of the former and the direct or indirect colonisation of large parts of the region in the course of the nineteenth and early twentieth centuries. But what added to the Middle East's importance in the twentieth century was oil, which was found in abundance in the Persian Gulf and in parts of north Africa.

In the strategic context of the Cold War, moreover, the region's geopolitical importance provided an added incentive for the superpowers to increase their role and presence. The Middle East's geopolitical importance was underwritten by several factors: first, its proximity to Soviet territory. This put Iran on the 'frontline' (it was the only Middle Eastern country bordering the Soviet Union), gave birth to the Cold War concept of the 'southern tier', and eventually led to the creation of the Central Treaty Organisation in the 1950s and Turkey's membership of NATO in 1952. Throughout the Cold War, Turkey (which grew into NATO's largest army in the 1970s and 1980s) remained the only NATO country with a maritime and land border with the Soviet superpower.

Second, in search of supremacy, the superpowers found themselves sucked into the area's inherently unstable inter-state and intra-state structures, with significant consequences for both. In the region's greatest conflict, that between the Arabs and Israel, for example, the Soviet Union emerged as the key ally of the nationalist/radical Arab states while the United States (US) championed Israel. In more than three major wars between Israel and its Arab neighbours, the two superpowers rushed to the aid of their own side and threatened the escalation of what was essentially a regional conflict into a major conflagration between the world's greatest powers.

Third, unlike earlier European interventions, the superpowers during the Cold War no longer had the option of advancing their interests through territorial domination. Without the ability to dominate directly, the superpowers' preferred option evolved into alliance-building with local powers. The strategy was based on the simple Cold War concept of denial to the enemy and securing support for the prevailing superpower. In geopolitical terms, this strategy required the Soviet Union to cross the 'southern belt' along its western Asian border and attempt to penetrate the Middle East through alliances with anti-imperial, nationalist and leftist forces. By the 1950s the nationalist wave in the region was also favouring Moscow, which speedily set about establishing close relationships with several Arab states.

By the early 1970s, Moscow could count a score of Arab countries and actors as allies or 'partners' (Algeria, Egypt, Iraq, Libya, Syria, South Yemen, the Palestinian Liberation Organisation [PLO], other radical Palestinian groups, and many left-leaning revolutionary organisations). The United States' position, on the other hand, was more defensive during this early nationalist wave. It did, however, build close links with the region's three non-Arab powers (Iran, Israel, Turkey) and support the more traditional and conservative Arab states (Jordan, Morocco and Saudi Arabia).

Both superpowers underpinned their regional alliances with close military, security and diplomatic support, something that added to regional rivalries and helped to further militarise an already unstable regional system. These Cold War relationships in turn affected, and in many instances shaped, the foreign policy options as well as foreign relations of the Middle Eastern states. Moreover, although the Middle East states' developmental strategies were not directly shaped by the Cold War, the fact that much of the credit lines and the technical support systems for economic development were in the hands of the two global Cold War blocs meant that they had little option but to cut their developmental cloth to the size of external support available. This said, the corporatist strategy of import-substitution industrialisation was widely followed in the Middle East, by both the pro-Western (Iran, Turkey) and pro-Soviet (Egypt, Iraq, Syria) states, as well as the more independent regional players (Algeria, Tunisia).

The Middle East in the twentieth century

The history of the modern Middle East began in the late nineteenth century, but became recognisable in its current form in the wake of the rise of the territorial state across the regional system in the twentieth century. Broadly speaking, the Middle East states' relations with each other, as well as those with the rest of the world, were shaped by six sets of forces: nationalism, the Arab–Israeli conflict, war, oil, political Islam, and the influence of external powers.

Nationalism

Looking at each of these forces in turn, Middle East nationalism (which took four forms: Arab, Iranian, Turkish and Zionist) grew in power from the early twentieth century, but only patchily. What Mustafa Kemal Atatürk and his reformist, modern-leaning and secularist 'Young Turks' accomplished in post-Ottoman Turkey in the 1920s was soon copied by others. Iran's first technocratic nationalist leader, Reza Khan, is a case in point. Not only did this young military officer actually model himself on Atatürk, his state policies and reforms also closely mirrored those of the new Turkish republic. Arguably, these two leaders' nationalist drive, which was based on state-building and unashamed copying of Western practices, actually created the modern state in their respective countries. Many of the institutions and systems which they put into place still survive and flourish to this day. Indeed, their influence is still felt in both contemporary Turkey and Iran. In Turkey, for instance, Atatürk's vehement secularism remains a main plank of the modern state and the basis of many of its policies.

Elsewhere in the region, nationalist sentiments, which had been awakened in the late nineteenth century, were inflamed by the Ottoman Empire's demise early in the twentieth century. In the 1920s, 1930s and 1940s Syrian, Lebanese and Egyptian intellectuals were openly adopting nationalism as an ideology and a political tool. But it was not until 1952 in Egypt that Arab nationalism burst on to the scene as a major political force. The 'Free Officers' ouster of the Egyptian monarchy opened the way for a surge of Arab nationalist sentiments across the region. There were three primary driving forces of Arab nationalism. First, the perceptible decline in European power in the region (nationalists saw the European retreat from the Arab world as a historic opportunity). Second, the establishment, with Western help, of the state of Israel in Palestine in 1948 and the 1948–49 Arab–Israeli war – in which Arabs from across the region participated, including Egypt's Colonel Nasser and several of his associates. This event, more than any, radicalised the Arab youth of the 1950s and 1960s and pushed to the edge the precariously-placed pro-Western Arab regimes. Third, the Arab masses and the impatient young officers were increasingly influenced by the spread of nationalist ideologies from non-Arab lands and liberation struggles elsewhere in the Third World, which were being fanned by the Soviet Union and China.

By 1954, when Colonel Gamal Abdel-Nasser finally took full charge of the new Egyptian republic, his reputation and popularity had reached every corner of the vast Arab world. Before too long, his message began to weaken the existing structures in other Arab states or territories and provided the hammer for the destruction of the ruling political elites. In Syria, a country which had been ready for revolution since the 1930s, Nasser's sympathisers took power in the late 1950s. In Iraq, the British-installed monarch was overthrown in 1958 and the new radical republican regime attempted to join hands with Syria and Egypt.

But it was the 1956 Suez campaign, a war waged on Egypt by the Anglo-French-Israeli trio, which acted as a major catalyst for the radicalisation of Arab nationalists. It encouraged anti-imperialist sentiments in the Arab world, added pan-Arabism to the agenda and encouraged superpower interest in the context of the brewing Cold War.

The fourth nationalist wave was that of Zionism, which was born in Europe in the late nineteenth century and enjoyed considerable following among Ashkenazi Jews across Europe. This new socialist-leaning force provided the ideology for the construction of a new Jewish state in Palestine, something which became a reality in May 1948, after several bloody encounters between armed Jewish groups and the local Arab inhabitants of the area and Britain (which was mandated by the international community to look after Palestine). Like the Middle East's other nationalisms, Zionism was also a secular ideology, aspiring towards the creation of a modern and Western-style state. Naturally, it too has played a major part in the region, providing on the one hand the necessary tools for Israel's founding fathers to build a new Jewish state in the heart of the Arab and Muslim worlds and, on the other, the logic for Israel's regional policy and outlook.

Thus, all four types of nationalism have played a major part in the shaping of the region and the behaviour of its state-actors. It is important to underline, however, that these forces had been unleashed before the onset of the Cold War, and that the Cold War merely provided them with a new and more dynamic backdrop. Although some of these nationalisms have become jaded with age and their relevance superseded by events, they nonetheless provide a living reminder of a fundamental force that helped shape the Middle East during the Cold War era.

The Arab–Israeli conflict

The second decisive force in the modern history of the region has been the Arab–Israeli conflict, which grew from a localised conflict between Palestinian Arabs and settler Jewish groups in the 1930s to an inter-state war in 1948. From its birth until the early 1980s, Israel fought five wars with one or more of its Arab neighbours (in 1949, 1956, 1967, 1973 and 1982). To say that this conflict shaped the politics of the region for over fifty years is no exaggeration. Not only did it determine the nature of the

Israeli state and its rapid militarisation, it also dictated the pace of intra-Arab relations and dominated the domestic agenda in the majority of the Arab countries in the Levant. Causing major casualties across the board, changes to territory, and to economic vibrancy of the warring parties, the Arab–Israeli conflict was one issue in which the superpowers openly attached their colours to the mast of their allies and provided extensive material and diplomatic support for their own side. It should not be very surprising, therefore, that the end of the Cold War left a clear impression on the conduct of this conflict.

Another significant aspect of the conflict was the way in which it gave birth to another specific nationalist movement in the region, that of Palestinian nationalism, which grew from a small revolutionary core in the mid-1960s to become the most important pan-Arab issue in the 1970s and 1980s. By 1987 secular Palestinian nationalism had more or less abandoned its violent anti-Israeli tactics of the previous two decades and had begun to develop roots in the 1967 Israeli-occupied Palestinian territories, ushering in one of the most significant civil disobedience campaigns of the post-war period. The 1987–91 period of Palestinian uprising in the Occupied Territories, the *Intifadah*, firmly established the Palestinian peoples' claims to national rights, such as sovereignty and territory; but it also gave birth to a new force among the Palestinian communities, that of political Islam.

War

While the Arab–Israeli conflict was the Middle East's main zone of conflict between 1945 and the end of the Cold War, it was not by any means the only cause of major wars in the region. Indeed, by the late-1970s (by which time Israel and Egypt had signed a peace treaty – the 1978/79 Camp David Accords) the scope for another major Arab–Israeli war had been considerably reduced.

Since the 1950s, however, other wars have erupted in the Middle East. In the early 1960s Egypt and Saudi Arabia conducted proxy war in the Yemen; in the 1970s and 1980s, Lebanon, with the active involvement of some regional powers, tore itself apart; and, last but not least, Iraq and Iran spent what effectively became the last decade of the Cold War engaged in a major war (1980–88).

Collectively, these wars have been responsible for the raising of regional tensions and the redrawing of the strategic map of the region. What is most striking, however, about the region's only other major war outside the Arab–Israeli theatre during the Cold War – the Iran–Iraq War – is the fact that the superpowers did not line up behind the competing camps. For a range of reasons, neither superpower wanted revolutionary Islamic Iran to triumph in the war and spread its influence more widely. Still, the war lasted for eight years, resulting in an estimated one million casualties and economic damage to the tune of US$900 billion. The greatest irony of this war was that by the time the parties accepted a UN-brokered cease-fire in July 1988, neither combatant could claim that it had achieved any of its declared war aims, even though both still claimed victory.

Iraq's dissatisfaction provided the basis for further instabilities in the Persian Gulf, which finally manifested themselves in the Iraqi invasion of Kuwait in August 1990 and the West's debilitating war against the occupy-ing power between January and March 1991. This was the post-Cold War era's first major regional conflict and it provided the occasion for the dawn of the so-called 'New World Order'. By the end of Operation Desert Storm, Kuwait had been liberated and Iraq had effectively been destroyed as a major regional power. It can be claimed with some justification that this conflict did more to change the dynamics of the region in broad political and strategic terms than the ending of the Cold War itself. The Kuwait crisis provided the basis for the redefining of the Middle East regional system, removing as a powerful variable the radical Arab pull, finally freeing Arab regimes from the pressures of pan-Arabism and en-abling them to base policy on their own, more narrowly defined, national interests without recrimination. It also opened the way for a dialogue between the main parties still engaged in the Arab–Israeli conflict. It was, therefore, not surprising that the Kuwait war was soon followed by the ground-breaking Madrid talks in October and November 1991 on the Arab–Israeli peace process. In a region where symbolism still matters, the Madrid talks were co-sponsored by both the US and the Soviet Union. As history would have it, the Arab–Israeli peace talks of late 1991 were to be the last major international initiative in which the Soviet Union took part.

Oil

Much of the interest in the Middle East since the start of the twentieth century has been based on the presence of oil in abundant quantities in parts of the Persian Gulf and north Africa. As oil has been a strategic commodity from the outset, no major power has been able to ignore its geopolitics. Thus, the main consumers of oil, the Western powers, have felt compelled to protect the Western-leaning oil producers of the region and to defend the free flow of oil through the Strait of Hormuz. Another reason, particularly since the early 1970s, for outside interest in the stability of the oil states has been the sheer amount of capital that oil exports have generated. To put the magnitude of oil-generated wealth in some perspective, while the total income of the member states of the Organisation of Petroleum Exporting Countries (OPEC) was an impressive US$37.1 billion in 1973, it had gone up to US$143 billion in 1977 and reached a staggering US$285.9 billion in 1980. In the Gulf, the states of the Arabian Peninsula, some of them very small in terms of population and size, reaped huge profits from their oil exports. Kuwait, for example, with fewer than one million inhabitants, increased the value of its oil exports from US$3.5 billion in 1973 to US$8.9 billion in 1974, peaking at US$18.9 billion in 1980. In 1980, Saudi Arabia, with a population of around 14 million, amassed nearly US$110 billion from its petroleum exports.

Oil, therefore, has provided one of the key defining contours of the Middle East region, shaping the political economy of many of its states since the late 1960s, pulling the Western powers into the waters of the Persian Gulf, and, in a globalised economy, tying the fortunes of these so-called 'capital-surplus' oil-exporting countries to the economic performance of the main consumers – the Organisation for Economic Cooperation and Development (OECD) countries (particularly the European Union (EU), Japan and the US). In strategic terms, too, oil (and access to it) became an important feature of the Cold War.

Political Islam

The 1979 Iranian Islamic revolution (symbolised by the return from exile of Ayatollah Khomeini) was the high mark of a movement which had been growing across the region for the best part of the twentieth century. The Iranian revolution ended the reign of a pro-Western and secular regime in a large, well-placed and strategically important Middle Eastern country. Inevitably, therefore, its ripples were to be felt across the region despite the fact that this revolution had occurred in a non-Arab and Shia-dominated country. Like other revolutionary regimes, Tehran was determined to encourage the growth of its brand of ideology and to 'export' it wherever possible. Islamist movements in other Muslim lands began receiving support from Iran's new revolutionaries and many Arab groups were to find sanctuary in the country.

The forces of revolutionary Islam were also fanned by local resistance to the Soviet occupation of Afghanistan after the 1979 invasion of that country. For ten years, Western military and security agencies trained and supplied these Islamic fundamentalists, helped in getting Muslim volunteers to the battlefields of Afghanistan, and turned a blind eye to the growth of a widely anti-secular and anti-Western network of radical Islamists across west Asia and north Africa.

Iran's revolution and the Afghan War, however, were manifestations of a long tradition of Islamist politics in the region, which, in the twentieth century, had begun in Egypt in the 1920s (with the rise of the famous Muslim Brotherhood movement) and had spread to every corner of the regional system by the late 1980s. In 1980, one group assassinated the Egyptian President (Anwar Sadat); in 1982 Syrian forces put down an Islamist challenge; in the late 1980s the Palestinian Hamas and Islamic Jihad organisations unleashed terror on the Israeli population and took on the secular Palestinian groups; and, throughout the 1980s Lebanese Islamist groups attacked Western targets in that country, took Westerners hostage and started a military campaign against the Israeli occupation forces. By the end of the 1990s, although some Islamist forces had managed to enter mainstream politics (in Jordan, Kuwait, Morocco, Sudan, Turkey, Yemen), political Islam as a whole – the so-called revivalist movements – had not quite managed to shed its violent streak. In Afghanistan, Algeria, Bahrain, Egypt, Libya, Israel, Saudi Arabia, Sudan and Yemen, radical Islam continued to engage in violent activities.

Influence of external powers

As mentioned at the outset, outside forces have played a major part in the birth and development of Middle Eastern states, as well as in shaping the environment in which these states have operated. Since Napoleon's intervention in Egypt in the late eighteenth century, European powers have been an important part of the Middle East's make-up – its politics, socio-economic development and external orientation. It was the European powers who took control of significant areas of the region from the nineteenth century; it was they who brought about the demise of the Ottoman Empire and shared its spoils in the early twentieth century; and it was the same set of European powers who carved new states from territories under their control.

But in the second half of the twentieth century, the nature of outside intervention changed somewhat. As a penetrated regional system, the

Middle East, for all its active internal dynamics (nationalism, the Arab–Israeli war, radical Islam, etc.), was by the 1950s subject to the influence of strategically-driven calculations made by the world's two superpowers. The superpowers' calculations and strategies not only directly affected the politics of the region, but also the environment in which the local forces were taking shape. For over a generation, the Cold War was the framework of the Middle East's regional system, from North Africa in the west to the borders of the Soviet Caucasus and Central Asia.

The Cold War created a loosely controlled environment for Middle Eastern regional actors to function within. For all its inconsistencies and tensions, the Cold War had at the very least given the region a degree of forced organisation, even 'organised chaos'. Its ending exposed the Soviet allies to new pressures, threatened to remove the special privileges of the pro-US allies, and lifted the curtain on internal political and economic processes. Thus, the sea-change in the international system, which followed the end of the Cold War and the collapse of the Soviet Union, created the necessary conditions for a new period of dynamic change in the Middle East.

The arena of foreign policy and the challenge of transformation

With the Cold War behind us, we can now begin to consider the types of force which are shaping the contemporary Middle East region. Although the issue of superpower influence is still being debated by scholars, it will be argued here that the end of the Cold War has caused a real and perceptible change in the nature of regional relations and, perhaps more crucially, in the behaviour and calculations of the Middle East's key regional actors, two of which form our case studies in this chapter. For those states such as Iran, Israel, Turkey and Syria, which had either developed a dependence on Cold War relations or had found themselves on Cold War fault-lines, its passing created major challenges. For the others, the changes in the region's strategic geometry also made certain foreign and domestic policy adjustments more or less inevitable.

The end of the Cold War was, however, only one important factor in a range of changes which have swept the arena of foreign policy in the Middle East. Broadly speaking, the most important of these are: the impact of globalisation; structural economic difficulties; the development of an EU presence, particularly around the Mediterranean basin; deepening sub-regionalism; the fading away of unifying issues (pan-Arabism, the demise of the secularist radical camp in the Arab world, opposition to Israel, support for the Palestinian cause); political instability in the Arab world, fuelled by high levels of militarisation and the unaccountability of ruling regimes; problems associated with political succession and transfers of power; and, finally, political Islam emerging as a divisive rather than a unifying force.

In foreign policy terms, these challenges have left key Middle Eastern actors with serious problems to overcome. Looking at some of the issues more closely, globalisation (as an economic, political, information, and socio-economic force) has caught many Middle Eastern states unawares. At first, the instinct of republics (Egypt, Libya, Iran, Syria, Tunisia, Yemen) and monarchies (Jordan, Morocco, Saudi Arabia) alike was to shield themselves from the winds of change fanned by this process. They attempted to control satellite and Internet access, distanced themselves from the World Trade Organisation, fought off pressures for structural economic reform, restricted foreign investment, tried to shackle civil society and avoided political reform. Over time, however, many of these states have learnt to adapt to powerful globalising forces and have tried to realign their domestic economic and foreign policies accordingly. Globalisation has not brought about political homogenisation. In terms of regime type and domestic policies, the states of the Middle East remain highly individualistic, even where they share the same problems.

Globalisation has, however, accentuated the evolution of sub-regionalist tendencies (which had been growing also partly thanks to the collapse of the Soviet empire, the vertical and horizontal growth of the EU, and the fracturing of the Arab order in the course of the Kuwait crisis) and, since the end of the Cold War, Middle Eastern states have been forced to develop a more focused foreign policy and a sharper definition of the national interest. Today, in the Arab world, 'the national' refers more to the imperatives of the territorial state than the pan-Arabist dream of a single boundary-less Arab nation living within one large political entity. The Arab states and their non-Arab counterparts have had little alternative but to respond to these external pressures. So, the North African Arab states have developed their European links, have signed new association agreements with the EU, their main economic partner, and have accepted the principles of the 'Barcelona' round of EU–Mediterranean discussions. Indeed, as virtually every southern and eastern Mediterranean country has now been sucked into some kind of EU-led

Mediterranean initiative, they increasingly, though perhaps unconsciously, have prioritised this direction of policy over their perceived interests in the 'interior' – the Middle East region as a whole.

At the other end of the Middle East region, Iran and Turkey have revitalised their historic links with the Islamic states of the former Soviet Union (Azerbaijan, and the states of Central Asia) and have been instrumental in expanding the remit and operations of the Economic Cooperation Organisation (ECO), which now includes all these states plus Afghanistan and Pakistan. Turkey has also established a Black Sea grouping. In the Persian Gulf in the meanwhile, the six-state Gulf Cooperation Council (GCC), founded in 1981, has continued to intensify its activities and is increasingly acting as the overarching body for the Gulf's conservative monarchies.

The end of the Cold War has also encouraged a de-radicalisation of the region, a trend which the Islamists have tried to buck, but with little success at the state level. De-radicalisation of foreign policy has in turn encouraged pragmatism. From revolutionary Islamic Iran to radical Ba'athist Syria and maverick Libya, we see a tangible shift in behaviour. Tehran has opened up to the EU and the West in general (see below); Syria has openly held talks with Israel and the US; and Libya has departured from its radical policies of the past, denouncing state terrorism, handing over the bombing suspects of Pan Am flight 103, and opening up its economy (including the strategic oil sector) to European and Far Eastern direct investment.

This de-radicalisation has introduced new and exciting opportunities for cooperation as well, as is evident from the emergence of closer ties between Iran and Saudi Arabia, Libya and Egypt, Israel and Jordan, but it has failed to remove the problems associated with regional rivalries. Thus, Iran and Israel remain rivals, so too do Syria and Turkey. In the Arab world also the 'core actors' (Iraq and Syria, for instance) remain locked into competitive structures and continue to search for ways of dominating the Arab agenda.

Where Islamic fundamentalism has played a part in the politics of the region, it has had to adopt a territorial bias to its endeavours. Pan-Islamism, rather like pan-Arabism before it, has proved unable to create a sustainable international and intra-Islamic structure. But, at the practical level, Middle Eastern states have had to respond to the challenge of political Islam, which they have done through suppression, cross-border cooperation and the introduction of major reforms. To increase regime survivability, some Arab states have responded to the challenge by increasing the Islamic content of their public policies and sometimes their Islamic rhetoric as well. But in foreign policy terms, even where the Islamists have managed to gain access to the levers of power (as in Turkey in 1997) or have amassed influence in the legislature (as in Jordan, Kuwait and Yemen) they have been unable to effect a significant change in the external orientation of the state.

Though posing an undeniable challenge of sorts to their secular-leaning counterparts, the region's overtly Islamic states – Iran and Saudi Arabia and, on its periphery, Sudan, Afghanistan and Pakistan – can hardly be said to be providing incentives for the further Islamisation of the Middle East either. For one thing, these Islamist states do not act in unison and are very different from each other. The two Arab states of Saudi Arabia and Sudan are hardly alike and the three non-Arab Islamist states share little with each other. Furthermore, the five do not form a cohesive unit of pan-Islamic states, they do not share each other's Islamic ideologies and some even find themselves in open conflict and competition with the others. Moreover, no single state has been able to secure a hegemonic position which might have helped lead the group as an effective front. Thus Islamism at the state level has been directionless and an ineffective intra-regional force for political change. Early post-Cold War fears of an all-powerful *Pax Islamica* emerging from the Middle East region to replace the force of international communism in international affairs have proven to be unfounded (Huntington, 1993).

The states of the Middle East have thus had to operate within a complex regional and international environment. To shed more light on the arena of foreign policy and the challenge of transformation, the remainder of the chapter will explore the foreign policy of two very different states, Iran and Israel. Iran is home to one of the world's oldest civilisations, dating back to at least 600 BC. Though invaded and occupied by many powers over the ages, it has been successful in protecting its core and assimilating the invader. Never a colony of the European powers, it was, until the nineteenth century, a serious Asian rival of Russia, the Ottoman Empire and Britain. In the course of the twentieth century, Iran managed to recover from its costly encounters with Russia, the Ottomans and Britain, and grew into a powerful regional actor with hegemonic ambitions in the Persian Gulf. Following a mass-based revolution, however, the state changed direction in 1979 and became the world's first revolutionary Islamic state. Its foreign policy slogan was 'neither East nor West'. With some 69 million people, it is the most populous Muslim state of the Middle East and one of its biggest geographic entities. It enjoys an advantaged geopolitical location and benefits from substantial natural resources, including huge hydrocarbon reserves.

Table 9.1 A comparison of the states of the Middle East region

State	Population in 2000 (m)	Surface area (thousands of sq. km)	GDP (purchasing power parity) in 1999 (US$ bn)	Military expenditure (US$ m) (date in brackets)
Egypt	68	1,001	200	3,280 (1996)
Bahrain	0.63	0.6	8.6	318 (1999)
Iran	65.6	1,648	347.6	5,780 (1999)
Iraq	22.6	434	60	not available
Israel	5.8	20.7	105	8,700 (1999)
Jordan	5	98	16	608 (1998)
Kuwait	2	17.8	45	2,500 (2000)
Lebanon	3.5	10.4	16.2	500 (1998)
Oman	2.5	212	19.6	1,600 (1999)
Qatar	0.74	11	12.3	816 (2000)
Saudi Arabia	22	2,149	191	18,100 (1997)
Syria	16.3	185	42.2	1,000 (1997)
United Arab Emirates	2.3	92	41.5	2,100 (1999)
Yemen	17.4	482	12.7	414 (1999)

Source: Central Intelligence Agency (2000).

Israel, by contrast, is a very new Middle Eastern state. Despite the deep roots of Judaism in the Middle East and earlier Judaic empires, there was no separate Jewish state in the region until the middle of the twentieth century. Indeed, although the state crafted in 1948 may have owed its culture and social ethos to Judaism, it was not a religious-based state by any means. Israel is the region's main immigration-based country. It is small in terms of population (just 6 million inhabitants, 19 per cent of whom are non-Jews) and size, and is the region's only Jewish (indeed non-Muslim-dominated) country. It has been at war with its neighbours more than any other Middle Eastern state, has a large and powerful military machine, yet is the region's leading democracy and economy. It has few natural resources to speak of, but enjoys the benefits of a highly innovative and educated labour force and a sophisticated business community. It is the Middle East's only nuclear weapon state and a major recipient of American military and economic aid. By virtue of its origins and immigration-based population growth, Israel is a multifaceted polity, with increasingly apparent cleavages over the state's identity, outlook and regional orientation.

The foreign policy of Iran

The challenges of transformation

The end of the Cold War brought to the fore the importance of the 'three Gs' in Iran's foreign relations: geopolitics, geostrategic vulnerabilities, and globalisation. Iran is still trying to make sense of the systematic changes that took place with the end of the Cold War, and in this endeavour is struggling to find its natural place in the increasingly interdependent and globalised international system. Since the late 1980s, Tehran has had to respond to systemic changes around it, and has been compelled to function as much as possible within the new international system, which is characterised by the demise of the Soviet Union and the emergence of the US as the undisputed extra-regional power in the Middle East. In addition, the ethnic resurgence that has characterised the post-Cold War period has not been looked upon favourably in Iran. Fears that secessionist movements within the country and on its borders could be used by outside powers to destabilise the Iranian regime have struck a chord with Islamists and nationalists alike.

The foreign policy debate

At least two schools of thought about the new international system have prevailed in Iran (Ehteshami and Hinnesbusch, 1997). One school welcomes the changes which have occurred in the international system since the late 1980s. Due to the end of the Cold War and of strategic competition between Moscow and Washington, Iran can emerge as a more independent and powerful regional power. In the absence of superpower pressure, Tehran is left free to create a new regional order in which it holds the balance of power. In the new situation, power derived from a combination of the Islamic revolution, a sound and pragmatic foreign policy, combined with the country's energy resources will, it is argued, enhance Tehran's ability to more fully influence regional developments. Proponents of this school also argue that continuing competition between the US, the EU and Japan over the resources of the Persian Gulf and Caspian Sea will inevitably generate new rivalries which, with careful planning, Tehran will be able to exploit.

The second school views the end of the Cold War and the demise of the Soviet Union with concern: Iran can no longer rely on the tried and tested strategy of the negative balance between Washington and Moscow. With the superpower competition now effectively over, Iran has become less valuable strategically to the superpowers. It has no value to the West in terms of 'containing' the Soviet threat. Moreover, as there appears to be no external threat to US interests in the Middle East, Washington, it is felt, will increase its pressure on states like Iran which manage to function outside its sphere of influence. Even in Central Asia and the Transcaucasus, Washington is determined to 'freeze' Iran out of its emerging markets and strategically important energy pipeline routes. Elements in this school also maintain that it is wrong to assume that in the new world order, the energy needs of the Western countries will lead to competition over control of these resources. Far from competing for control, the West will unite to prevent the monopolisation of these resources by any local power unfriendly to the West.

Actual Iranian foreign policy in the post-Cold War era has been based around the notion of 'both North and South'. Iranian strategy has focused on exploiting rifts between the US, its European allies and Japan over regional and international economic issues as a way of blunting the US-imposed sanctions on the country. The post-Cold War order has tended to encourage, and Tehran has taken advantage of, the trend towards the 'region-alisation' of the international system by developing such organisations as the ECO and the Tehran-based Caspian Sea Organisation. Iran has also attempted to improve its relations with states like Syria in the Middle East and to deepen its ties further afield with China, North Korea, Russia, and lately India, Greece and Georgia. Iran, in short, has been developing links with both the 'North' and the 'South' poles of the international system.

The foreign policy process

For much of the 1980s, various factions and centres of power within the clerical establishment took advantage of many opportunities to advance their own interests and to implement their own foreign policy agendas. This was particularly visible in relation to the Arab world. The radical camps were in constant search of the vehicles for exporting the Islamic revolution and concluding alliances with Islamist movements in the region. In the first decade of the Iranian Republic, the struggle between the so-called moderates or pragmatists and the radicals was a determining element of the policy process.

Factionalism and institutional competition has been rife and an important feature of the post-revolution Iranian political system. The factions themselves are rather fluid, and as they are normally comprised of a variety of tendencies and blocs built around powerful personalities, they tend to act as fronts and as such do not always function as a single entity. Since August 1989 and the constitutional reforms of that year, a 'presidential centre' has been created at the heart of the executive power structure of the republic (Ehteshami, 1995). But this institutional change has not ended intra-elite power politics in the system. Indeed, policy making has been characterised by the growth of a number of consultation circles at various levels of decision making.

That said, certain important centralising tendencies have been evident. The constitutional reforms brought into being a National Security Council, controlled by the President and his staff. This body has become the nerve centre of policy making in Iran and is, as such, the key body where foreign policy is debated. Under the reformed constitution, the Foreign Minister reports directly to the President who heads the Council of Ministers. Thus, implementation of foreign policy initiatives through the Foreign Ministry is also monitored through the President's office. While the legislature (the Majlis) is constitutionally barred from interfering in the executive's foreign policy-making process, this body does discuss foreign policy issues and its members are often heard making pronouncements on regional and international matters. Furthermore, they do try to influence the direction of foreign policy through legislative committees and not infrequent contacts with foreign dignitaries.

Ayatollah Khamenei, the 'Leader' (Faqih) of the Islamic Republic since 1989 is an opponent of the radical factions but is himself a 'conservative' in Iranian political terms, favouring a reasonable distance between Iran and the West and opposing 'Westernisation' of Iranian society (Bakhash, 1995). He frequently speaks about the cultural invasion of the country by the US-led Western powers. Such perceptions do have an impact on Tehran's foreign policy but not enough to dislodge or derail its pragmatic orientation. The presidency is the key foreign policy maker, and both post-Khomeini Presidents (Hashemi Rafsanjani [1989–97] and Mohammad Khatami [1997–]) have favoured Iran's integration in the international system and have been supportive of efforts to improve the country's relations with the outside world.

In short, since 1989, the presidential office has emerged as the main foreign policy-making organ of the state. However, the President's foreign policy decisions are not made in isolation from other power centres and in this regard the role of the Faqih, the Majlis and the Council of Guardians are all extremely important in the Iranian foreign policy-making process. The Faqih is the individual whose support is crucial in the implementation of foreign policy decisions. He can and does make public statements in endorsement of decisions, thus providing justification for the President's foreign policy initiatives and diffusing direct criticism of his administration.

Not unlike other states, the Iranian Foreign Ministry's role in the policy process and that of the Foreign Minister are also significant. The ministry tends to be engaged in implementing policy and providing the public face for the rest of the world. Another important factor influencing contemporary Iranian foreign policy is public opinion, which is shaped by open debate in the press and disseminated by a relatively free and large media machinery. Numerous newspapers and periodicals discuss foreign policy issues and involve in their discussions virtually all the core opinion makers from within the political establishment, as well as increasingly influential individuals from the world of academia and slowly-emerging semi-independent think tanks.

The content of Iranian foreign policy

The post-1990 changes in Iran's geopolitical environment have not meant that ideology and strategic ambition have been completely displaced. Iran's leaders have asserted, however, that the Republic's strategic ambitions cannot be realised without the country's economic renewal. By the same token, a weak economic base in the globalised economic system has increasingly been viewed by many Iranian leaders as a recipe for further peripheralisation. In broad terms, the country's foreign policy has come to tally with its economic priorities. The main feature in this regard can be observed in a behavioural change towards moderation and a consequent *realpolitik* towards Iran's neighbours and the European powers.

But, while it is true to say that Tehran has been redefining its priorities in the post-Cold War era, it would be unrealistic to expect it to have foregone its Islamic profile only for the sake of economic gain. One only has to consider Iran's successful involvement with the Islamic Conference Organisation since autumn 1997 to realise this. It is also true, however, that in practice since the early 1990s Iran has chosen to prioritise the resolution of domestic problems (economic reconstruction and the strengthening of civil society and the rule of law) over long-term ideological foreign policy posturing (Bakhash, 1998).

By the late 1980s, therefore, the early 'rejectionist' strategy of post-revolution Iran had given way to a foreign policy of accommodation. This did, however, have its limits. Although close contacts between Tehran and its Arab friends were maintained after 1988, the *rapprochement* in Syrian–Egyptian relations in 1990, and the success of the Saudi–Syrian-sponsored

Taif agreement for Lebanon raised the prospects of a re-emergence of the same tripartite alliance between Egypt, Saudi Arabia and Syria which had existed in the mid-1970s. The danger from Tehran's perspective was that the presence of such an Arab alliance could only lead to the marginalisation of Iran's regional role. While in the 1970s Iran under the Shah had been relatively successful in containing the influence of this alliance in the Persian Gulf sub-region, in the absence of the same resources at its disposal, latter-day Iran clearly could not do likewise. It had no diplomatic relations with Saudi Arabia or Egypt at that time, and it could offer few incentives to Syria to resist the lure of Saudi oil and petro-dollars and Egyptian diplomatic clout.

For Iran, the Iraqi invasion of Kuwait in August 1990 marked a new watershed. The invasion immediately raised Iran's profile and highlighted its significance as a regional player, but it also raised regional tensions and provided the catalyst for the return of Western powers to the Gulf sub-region, thus weakening Tehran's ability to shape the policies of the GCC and forge ties with the Gulf sheikhdoms based on collective action. Iran's position during this crisis was in sharp contrast to the interventionist and adventurist policies of the initial post-revolution period. Thus, in 1990 Iran stood on the side of the West and in favour of the restoration of Kuwait's sovereignty. It did not, however, support US-led military intervention. Neutrality in this conflict gave Tehran a large measure of flexibility in its foreign relations. It gave it scope to deal with Iraq as well as the anti-war Arab forces, while its insistence on the reversal of the Iraqi aggression and an unconditional Iraqi pull-out brought it closer to the anti-Iraq Gulf monarchies. Its restraint and neutrality also obtained for Iran renewed diplomatic relations with Jordan, Tunisia and Saudi Arabia, and some constructive contacts with Egypt and Morocco.

The isolation of Iraq in the region and the active role of Arab armies in the defence of Kuwait brought with it renewed pressures to address the Middle East's most serious problem, the Arab–Israeli conflict. For Iranian diplomacy, the Madrid process was a minefield. Not only did it threaten to subsume Syria in a Western-oriented peace agreement with Israel, but it effectively excluded Iran from an unfolding post-1990 regional order and seemed to confirm an Israeli strategy of encirclement. Tehran was concerned that the emergence of new agendas between Israel and the Arab states and the Palestinians left no room for Iranian involvement, bar in opposition to the whole process. Iran readily adopted such a role on the grounds that the Madrid process was US-inspired and that it was designed to rob the Palestinians of their rights in favour of Israel's regional ambitions and aspirations. Also, Tehran's overtly Islamic profile did necessitate its formal opposition to the peace process on religious grounds.

Also problematic for Iran was the way in which the peace process was sucking in Iran's Gulf Arab neighbours, and thus adding to Tehran's sense of isolation and loss of influence in the Persian Gulf sub-region. This sense of diminishing influence was heightened after 1993 when many GCC states (Oman and Qatar particularly) opened direct channels of communications and trade talks with Israel. Nonetheless, Tehran's declared strategy towards the peace process was one of non-intervention; it would not endorse the process, but neither would it stand in its way.

One of the most crucial and interesting developments in Iran's foreign policy was marked by the presidential election victory of Hojjatoleslam Khatami in 1997. Khatami's foreign policy has reinforced the non-ideological trends already apparent, but it has also gone further, preaching compromise, the rule of law and moderation. Indeed, this phase in Iran's foreign policy can suitably be characterised as a drive for moderation. It has been symbolised by Khatami's overtly non-confrontational approach to foreign policy, the President's declared aim of establishing a 'dialogue of civilisations', and attempts at reaching an 'understanding' with the West (including the US). Khatami and his policies have captured international headlines and have kept Western governments deeply interested in developments in Iran. During his first term in office he made scores of overseas trips and visited no less than ten countries, more than any other Iranian leader since the revolution. His travels took him to such non-traditional destinations as Italy, France, Germany and Saudi Arabia, as well as China, Syria and several Central Asian countries. This policy does, however, have its limits. The Iranian leadership has made no moves towards an unfreezing of relations with the US or Israel. This is a state of affairs that reflects historical antipathy, cultural distance and a lingering sense that the US and its closest ally in the Middle East continue to pose an existential threat to the Islamic revolution (Kemp, 2000).

With regard to the Persian Gulf, clearly Iran's pro-GCC strategy has borne some fruit, as seen by its successful courting of Saudi Arabia since 1996. The two countries' Defence Ministers have met on several occasions since 1996 and Iranian naval vessels have visited the Saudi Red Sea port of Jeddah, arguably the country's most strategic maritime facility. But Tehran still regards Saudi Arabia as an ideological rival, in Central Asia and elsewhere in west Asia, as well as a close ally of the US. Saudi Arabia is also conscious of the latent threat Iran poses to its interests in the Persian Gulf and beyond, but has been keen, nonetheless, to develop a friendship with the pragmatic Iranian leadership and to carve for itself the role of a mediator in Iranian–American exploratory discussions.

The foreign policy of Israel

The challenges of transformation

Israel started life as a potential ally of the international socialist movement and the Soviet Union, but soon found itself in dispute with Moscow and moving closer to the Western camp. First loosely allied to France, it was not until the mid-1960s that it strengthened its relations with the US. By the end of the Cold War, Israel had managed to lodge itself as the United States' most important ally in the Middle East. Israel had positioned itself not only as a bastion against Soviet expansionism, but also as a pro-Western bulwark against Arab nationalism and political Islam. It portrayed itself as the protector and defender of Western interests in an unstable and strategically important region.

Thanks to its already strong regional position, Israel was one of a handful of Middle East countries able to capitalise on the opportunities presented by the end of the superpower deadlock in the Middle East. In the first place, it realised that the end of the Cold War and of Soviet cover for Arab states had left it in a stronger regional position, particularly as its Soviet-dependent counterparts had swiftly lost access to weaponry as well as diplomatic support. Second, in the course of the Madrid peace process, Israel took full advantage of Arab divisions and new regional realities to negotiate with some of its Arab neighbours without compromising any of its own strategic or political assets. Third, the end of the Cold War and the start of the Arab–Israeli peace process enabled Israel to circumvent the Arab boycott, begin to rebuild links with Third World countries across the world and to develop new links with other powerful regional actors in Africa and Asia. The end of the Cold War, in other words, created the conditions for Israel to break down the political barriers to its international legitimacy, and these crumbled further following the start of the peace talks in Madrid in 1991 (Klieman, 1994: 98).

The end of the Cold War and the Arab–Israeli peace process thus allowed Israel to broaden its foreign policy horizons and to raise its sights from its immediate environment to view and explore the bloc-free international system. In the course of the 1990s Israel was able to move away from a foreign policy that was essentially defensive and concerned with damage control to one of international integration. As Murphy (1996: 90) observed in the mid-1990s, 'Israel is already taking advantage of the peace process to leap into the globalization pool and swim'.

The foreign policy debate

Since the founding of the Israeli state, Israel's foreign policy debate has been dominated by security issues and strategic concerns. During the Cold War and the height of the Arab–Israeli conflict much of this debate and government energies more generally were concerned with bolstering Israel's security and survival. Security concerns, in turn, encouraged Israel's reliance on its military and the strengthening of the alliance with the US. The US–Israeli alliance not only provided access to sophisticated American arms and military equipment, but also cash (in terms of direct military and economic aid in excess of US$3 billion per annum) for Israel's economy and military machinery. From the 1970s, moreover, the relationship with the US also provided Israel with an extensive security umbrella. In the 1990s this led to the joint development of the Arrow anti-missile missile and a host of other less high profile industrial-military research projects.

The close links between the two countries, however, have not always been trouble-free and Washington has had to balance its security relations with Israel against its broader interests in the Arab world (oil supplies, markets for its goods and services, etc.). Set against these interests, the Israel–US alliance was indeed seen as a liability by some influential quarters in Europe and the US. Writing in the mid-1980s, Steinberg and Spiegel (1987: 27–8) suggested that influential American voices 'still see Israel's policies as a major detriment to US security concerns in [the Middle East] – as impediments to Washington's ability to safeguard oil supplies and to preserve close relations with sympathetic Arab states'. It was partly in response to these criticisms and partly due to Israel's correct reading of the regional dynamics of the Cold War that it presented itself as a bulwark against the Soviet Union and a deterrent to Moscow's ambitions in the Middle East. By attaching itself to the superpower struggle, Israel successfully delinked its liabilities as an isolated and unwelcome regional actor from its value as a powerful force against Soviet expansionism. Not surprisingly, therefore, Tel Aviv's foreign policy debate for the best part of the 1948–89 period was dominated by Israel's relationship with the United States and the Cold War order. So although ultimately Israel was to be a beneficiary of the end of the Cold War, the collapse of the Soviet challenge to the US supremacy in the region filled Israel with some trepidation about its 'special relationship' with the remaining superpower and its ability to present itself as a defender of Western interests.

It was only when push came to shove in the region – as it did during the 1990/91 Kuwait crisis – that Israel's special role in the Middle East was put to the test. During this essentially inter-Arab crisis, Israel proved to be part of the problem rather than the solution. Washington soon learnt, and was told as much, that the only way to muster a war coalition from Arab ranks to challenge Iraq's aggression would be to exclude Israel from the conflict. As Shlaim (1994: 77) has put it: 'Here was a conflict which threatened America's most vital interests in the region and the best service that Israel could render to her senior partner was to refrain from doing anything. Far from being a strategic asset, Israel was widely perceived as an embarrassment and a liability.' Thus, despite the fact that some forty surface-to-surface Iraqi missiles were to land on its territory during the war, Israel remained firmly on the sidelines of this major security crisis. Under direct pressure from the US, this became the first time in Israel's history that a direct military attack on the Jewish state was to go unanswered.

More broadly, Israel, not unlike Iran, also had to face up to the strategic implications of the dawn of a new international era for its regional role. Some in Israel welcomed the access to the rest of the world that the end of the Cold War and the Arab–Israeli peace process were clearly and visibly producing. More diplomatic contacts went hand-in-hand with more trade and investment deals, travel, etc. This path was expressly advocated by the premiership of Yitzhak Rabin. As Rabin put it to the Israeli parliament, the Knesset, in 1992, Israel faced real opportunities in the post-Cold War era: 'We have got to rescue ourselves from that pervading sense of isolation gripping us for the better part of a half-century. We must join the worldwide movement towards peace, reconciliation and cooperation, for otherwise we shall be left behind, standing alone at the station platform' (quoted in Klieman, 1994: 106).

Others in Israel, however, feared that 'normalisation' could bring an end to Israel's uniqueness as the international system's only Jewish/Zionist state, and threaten its very identity as a religious-based polity. Engagement with the rest of the world could also encourage Israel to withdraw its security shield and to downgrade its military prowess, which it had so painstakingly created in the first forty years of its existence. Moreover, by the end of the Gulf War in the spring of 1991, elements within the Israeli establishment were openly debating the proposition that 'both conventional and unconventional Arab state capabilities pose a military threat to the existence of Israel in the absence of a broad regional peace framework' (Inbar, 1993: 151). The need for a change of tune and attitude was being recognised at several levels of decision making, including the powerful military establishment.

More profoundly, the end of the Cold War and the start of the Arab–Israeli peace process in the early 1990s compelled the Israeli establishment to consider overhauling the long-standing Ben Gurion doctrine (named after Israel's first Prime Minister) of reliance on military superiority and the eschewal of serious efforts at political reconciliation with Israel's Arab neighbours (Heller, 2000–1: 21–2). The review of the doctrine resulted in the development of links with several Arab countries (Jordan, Qatar, Oman, Kuwait, Tunisia, Morocco, in particular) following the breakthrough in the peace process with the Palestinians in 1993 (see below). At the same time, however, Israel deepened its relationship with non-Arab Turkey, upgrading it to a close military-security partnership. Under their joint military pact, for instance, the armed forces of the two countries train and exercise together, use each other's territory, exchange military and intelligence know-how and technologies, and try to develop joint approaches to threats to their security. For Israel, the relationship has resulted in the Israeli air force being able to use Turkish airspace for training and intelligence-gathering operations on Iran, Iraq and Syria, military sales and substantial upgrading contracts for the Turkish armed forces.

In summary, some of the key themes in the Israeli foreign policy debate have concerned how to maintain, develop or enhance:

- the close Israeli–US alliance and the flow of US funds;

- Israel's superior military power in the Middle East region;

- its nuclear deterrence against a new mood and international desire for disarmament and regional confidence-building measures;

- the state's security through a more active carrot-and-stick policy in relation to the Arab countries surrounding it;

- links with the Soviet successor states;

- a useful role for itself as a guarantor of Western interests against another perceived threat – the spread of Islamic fundamentalism and Islamist political violence – and closer links with such pro-Western countries as Turkey whose regional role had been enhanced after the end of the Cold War and the collapse of the Soviet state.

The foreign policy process

Naomi Chazan (1991: 83) has argued that Israel's international relations and its foreign policy making have been moulded by three domestic factors: '(1) the structure and composition of political institutions; (2) social differentiation and the concern of specific groups; and (3) the substance of political debates and their relation to fundamental ideological concerns.' She goes on to say that 'Israeli responses to external stimuli are filtered through a domestic political lens which operates according to its own distinctive rules'. These rules seem to have been drawn up around the workings of Israel's political system, the immigrant nature of the state, and its highly divisive political party structures. Israeli foreign policy process is sharpened by two further points: first, the way that Israel's proportional representative political system gives the balance of power in the supreme legislative and political body, the Knesset, to the smaller fringe parties; and, second, the significant role that public opinion plays in foreign policy making and debate. With regard to the latter, it is worth noting that security continues to play a paramount role in the public's mind. As Stephen Zunes (1999: 108) has suggested: 'The overriding sentiment among the Israeli public regarding its foreign relations is that of fear. While the actual threat to Israel's survival posed by its Arab neighbours has been and continues to be exaggerated, there is no question that there have indeed been powerful forces in the Middle East which have sought the destruction of the Jewish state.' Underwriting all this, of course, is the Jewish people's keen sense of history and their place in the world.

In the 1990s and beyond, these key domestic factors have continued to shape Israel's foreign policy, but Israel's domestic setting has been changing fast. The influx of large numbers of immigrants from the Soviet Union/ Russia (200,000 in the 1970s and as many as 800,000 between 1989 and 1998, which now accounts for around 12 per cent of Israel's electorate) has had a decisive effect on the country's political map and its orientation. So much so that it is said that 'it was the immigrant vote that put Yitzhak Rabin in power in 1992, Binyamin Netanyahu in 1996, and Ehud Barak in 1999. Because of their sheer numbers, it has become almost axiomatic that whoever carries the Russian-speaking vote will carry the election' (*Jerusalem Post*, 20 December 1999, cited in Perezt and Doron, 2000: 269). Added to this powerful factor is the parallel problem of the growing divisiveness of the Israeli polity and society since the end of the Cold War and its splintering into special interest political organisations. Special interest politics tends to dilute the consensus about what are core issues in the national debate and prevents the emergence of consensus-based politics on key foreign policy and security issues.

On another level, the fragmentation of the foreign policy debate at the institutional level has been encouraged by constitutional changes introduced in 1992. These have meant that at national elections the electorate chooses the Prime Minister separately from the candidates for the 120-seat Knesset.

What this democratic exercise means in practice is more confusion at the policy debate level, for the vote for the Prime Minister 'could be guided by broad strategic considerations, the second [for the Knesset members] by more parochial interests' (Peretz and Doron, 2000: 266). As has been observed, the introduction of a two-ballot procedure could easily result in the voters undermining the position of the 'chief executive', the Prime Minister, 'by electing a divided Knesset capable of subverting the government' (Peretz and Doron, 2000: 273).

In addition, the preoccupation with Israel's national security at all levels of society has meant that the military and the other security forces have continued to play a direct role in Israel's foreign policy making (Jones, 2001). The peace process and the end of the Cold War have not measurably reduced the role of the security establishment in policy making. Foreign policy, with its security trappings, is still very much a domestic, that is to say a national, security issue and is internal to the workings and priorities of the ruling coalition. The contrast between Israel's main governments in the 1990s–early 2000s (respectively, the Labour-led government of Yitzhak Rabin, the Likud-led government of Benjamin Netanyahu, the Labour-One Israel government of Ehud Barak and the Likud-led government of Ariel Sharon) over Israel's priorities in the region and relations with the Arab world alone testifies to the continuing importance of the national-political in the country's foreign policy making. In this regard, the role of the Prime Minister, who has a team of foreign policy advisers at hand, the cabinet and the defence and security establishments in shaping foreign policy remain paramount, far outweighing that of the Foreign Ministry, the Knesset or other institutions of the state.

The content of Israeli foreign policy

Until the election of Ariel Sharon in 2001, successive Israeli governments have, since 1990, made the peace process a priority, even though they have differed over their interpretation of the process itself, its content and desired outcomes. Pursuit of peaceful relations with neighbouring Arab countries has been a first major change in Israel's traditional strategy of encirclement through alliance with non-Arab neighbours.

Israel's post-Cold War foreign policy can be viewed in the context of two important orientations. The first is Israel's place in the Middle East region and, associated with this, its relations with its Arab neighbours. The second, and one that Israel has pursued with some vigour, has been Israel's place in the wider community of states.

With respect to its regional relations, as already noted, it was a fresh crisis well beyond its own borders in Kuwait that changed the regional landscape forever. From Israel's perspective, while this crisis tested its security doctrine to the limit, it nonetheless resulted in the weakening of one of Israel's main Arab detractors, Iraq. Furthermore, the crisis, by shuffling the geopolitics of the Middle East region and fragmenting the Arab order, created other opportunities for Israel to exploit.

It was in this changed environment that peace with neighbouring states became a strategic aim of Israeli governments from the early 1990s. This involved a process of consolidating Israel's own military superiority while also trying to reach out diplomatically to its immediate neighbours. In retrospect, one can argue that having secured a lasting peace treaty with its greatest Arab enemy (Egypt) in 1979, Israel had to wait for a transformed regional and international environment, and endure considerable American pressure to boot, before striking another peace deal with an Arab neighbour. Israel had to pursue its negotiations through its less favoured route of the multilateral groups of the Madrid process, but it never abandoned its policy of bilateral negotiations either, which bore fruit in 1993 and 1994.

As it happened, the next Arab neighbour after Egypt to reach an agreement with Israel happened to be the Palestinian neighbour within. The September 1993 Declaration of Principles signed by Premier Rabin and the PLO Chair, Yasser Arafat, in Washington seemingly opened the door for a peaceful settlement of the Palestinian–Israeli conflict. The 'land for peace' formula, which had become the Rabin government's main negotiating tactic with its immediate neighbours, provided the basis of the discussions with the Palestinians. Although the 'Principles' failed to translate into a peace treaty, their signing nonetheless provided sufficient momentum for Israel to break down the barriers of sanctions and diplomatic isolation. Thus, soon after the September Declaration Israel signed a peace treaty with Jordan and entered into direct negotiations with Syria. More importantly still, it also managed to open new channels of communication with non-frontline Arab states, making considerable progress in developing links with several Gulf Arab and north African states. Beyond the region, the peace process with the Palestinians, whose liberation had been a major Third World cause for decades, helped in the rehabilitation of Israel and its diplomatic overtures towards the traditionally non-aligned countries, which takes us to the second orientation of Israeli foreign policy.

With relations with its neighbours on a firmer footing, Israel used the peace process as a launching pad for its diplomatic machinery to reestablish the country not only as a dominant regional actor but also as an active international player with a growing and sophisticated economic system. It sought better relations with India and the countries of Southeast Asia, closer links with China, commercial links with Russia, improved trading conditions with the EU, a presence in the emerging post-Soviet republics of the Caucasus and Central Asia, a strategic partnership with Turkey, a more active presence in sub-Saharan Africa, and, last but not least, a continuation of the comprehensive military-security partnership with the US. In the space of just ten years, it managed to attain several of these goals. Putting the political and diplomatic shortcomings of the 1996–99 Likud government aside, Israeli governments have been remarkably successful in using the country's economic prowess as a diplomatic tool to open or widen access to Asia, Africa and Latin America.

One final area of foreign policy concern has been Israel's relations with an increasingly culturally distinct diaspora. Israel would like to see this community as an external pillar of support for the country, but this community, particularly that based in the US, is itself divided over religous-cultural issues and is unable to speak with one voice over the direction and evolution of the Jewish state. These tensions in the diaspora get transmitted to Israeli society, complicating the state's relations with the diaspora communities.

Conclusion

As a highly penetrated regional system, it was inevitable that the Middle East would be affected by the winds of change blowing at the international level. The end of the Cold War and the new dynamics of the international system left an almost immediate, but lasting, mark on the region. After the Kuwait crisis the Arab–Israeli dispute became subject to negotiations sucking in, in the process, virtually every party to the dispute. While the Arab–Israeli conflict is still far from a final settlement, other issues continue to complicate the political dynamics of the region. Iraq entered the new century as a pariah state languishing under the most stringent international sanctions regime introduced by the United Nations. Political crises of different types also continued to linger. Old patriarchs – the Emir of Qatar, King Hussein of Jordan, King Hassan of Morocco, President Assad of Syria – either through death or pressure, have vacated their positions of power. The new leaders have not only had to balance the forces already at play at home, but also to defend the interests of the state they inherited. This is before they could even begin to think about putting their own stamp of authority on the country. This has proved hard to do in some places and remarkably easy in others. With the exception of Syria, which has proved to be a rare case of hereditary presidency, in that the son of the late President was quickly sworn in as the Republic's new President in the summer of 2000, the monarchies have best managed the process of transition. When looking beyond these countries at the rest of the Arab world, however, the process of elite change is anything but over.

On another level, the forces of globalisation and Western pressures for economic reform have pushed Middle Eastern states towards the adoption of wide-ranging economic liberalisation programmes and some radical restructuring exercises, largely following policies that Egypt tried to make fashionable under its *infitah* (openness) strategy as long ago as the mid-1970s. We are likely to feel the impact of these reform strategies only in twenty or thirty years' time. In the meantime, the states of the region are likely to continue to struggle against taxing domestic pressures while also trying to swim with the flow of globalisation. A difficult task indeed, even for the most robust of the region's elites. As has been shown, our two case studies are not exempt from these general pressures.

It is ironic that the two Middle Eastern states, Iran and Israel, which have for some time, and for very different reasons, prided themselves on being different and unique, are today anxious to be no more than 'normal' states, ready to get on and integrate fully with the international community. They are both less ideological today in their approaches to international relations and are seeking, again in very different ways, to benefit from the internationalisation of trade and investment opportunities. So perhaps, in the final analysis, the pressures to conform and to adapt, and the instinct to explore the opportunities that the end of the Cold War and increasing globalisation have brought will be the most enduring legacy of the world transformed – the world of a single, borderless, economic system and footloose industries.

Another irony is that all the while that Iran and Israel have been introducing positive domestic reforms, and at the same time trying to come to terms with the realities of a changed regional and international environment, they have proceeded to demonise each other and to think of the other as the main regional rival. It is likely that even when the dust finally begins to settle on the Arab–Israeli dispute, Iran and Israel (both non-Arab states), will continue to see each other as regional competitors and will play out their respective geopolitical games either on the torn fabric of the Arab order or the unstitched west Asian borderlands of the former Soviet Union. If nothing else, the end of the Cold War and the progress of the Arab–Israeli peace process has given the two countries a much larger arena in which to test their hegemonic instincts and challenge their rival's regional interests. The world may have been transformed but the pursuit of the 'national interest' in the Middle East remains a potent force and an ever-present and dynamic variable of this regional system.

Further reading

The literature on Iranian and Israeli foreign policy and foreign policy making is large and growing. In the case of Iran, a good starting point is Calabrese (1994). A number of foreign policy-related edited volumes commemorating the first decade of the Islamic Republic were published in the early 1990s. The best of these include Ehteshami and Varasteh (eds) (1991), Esposito (ed.) (1990), Keddie and Gasiorowski (eds) (1990) and Rezun (ed.) (1990). Other useful publications which focus on the broader linkages between foreign policy and domestic politics and regional relations include Ehteshami (1995), Fuller (1991) and Ramazani (1986).

Because of the primacy of the national security debate in Israel and the dominance of defence as a focus of attention, material on Israel's foreign policy is more diverse and fragmented than in the case of other Middle Eastern countries. Still, a good starting point on the country's foreign policy is Flamhaft (1996) followed by Levi-Faur, Sheffer and Vogel (eds) (1999). On linkages between Israeli politics and its foreign policy, Karsh and Mahler (eds) (1994) is useful. A good historical study is Bialer (1990). Jones and Murphy (2001) have produced the most comprehensive recent study of the Israeli state and its external affairs.

Such journals as *Foreign Affairs, Survival, Middle East Journal, British Journal of Middle Eastern Studies, Middle Eastern Studies,* and *International Journal of Middle Eastern Studies* often contain topical and relevant articles on the Middle East region, including in-depth studies of both Iran and Israel.

References

Bakhash, S. (1995) 'Iran: the Crisis of Legitimacy', in *Middle Eastern Lectures*, 1, Tel Aviv, Moshe Dayan Centre for Middle Eastern and African Studies, 99–118.

Bakhash, S. (1998) 'Iran since the Gulf War', in Freedman, R.O. (ed.), *The Middle East and the Peace Process. The Impact of the Oslo Accords.* Gainesville, FL: University Press of Florida, 241–64.

Bialer, U. (1990) *Between East and West: Israel's Foreign Policy Orientation 1948–1956.* Cambridge: Cambridge University Press.

Calabrese, J. (1994) *Revolutionary Horizons: Regional and Foreign Policy in Post-Khomeini Iran.* Basingstoke: Macmillan.

Central Intelligence Agency, *World Factbook, 2000.* <http://www.odci.gov/cia/publications/factbook/>.

Chazan, N. (1991) 'The Domestic Foundations of Israeli Foreign Policy', in Kipper, J. and Saunders, H.H. (eds), *The Middle East in Global Perspective.* Boulder, CO: Westview Press, 82–126.

Ehteshami, A. (1995) *After Khomeni. The Iranian Second Republic.* London: Routledge.

Ehteshami, A. and Hinnebusch, R.A. (1997) *Syria and Iran: Middle Powers in a Penetrated Regional System.* London: Routledge.

Ehteshami, A. and Varasteh, M. (eds) (1991) *Iran and the International Community.* London: Routledge.

Esposito, J.L. (ed.) (1990) *The Iranian Revolution: Its Global Impact.* Gainesville, FL: Florida International University Press.

Flamhaft, Z. (1996) *Israel on the Road to Peace: Accepting the Unacceptable.* Boulder, CO: Westview Press.

Fuller, G. (1991) *The Centre of the Universe. The Geopolitics of Iran.* Boulder, CO: Westview Press.

Heller, M.A. (2000–1) 'Israel's Dilemmas', *Survival*, 42(4), 21–34.

Huntington, S. (1993) 'The Clash of Civilizations?', *Foreign Affairs*, 72(3), 22–49.

Inbar, E. (1993) 'Strategic Consequences for Israel', in Barzilai G., Klieman, A. and Shildo, G. (eds), *The Gulf Crisis and its Global Aftermath.* London: Routledge, 146–59.

Jones, C. (2001) 'Israeli Foreign Policy: the Past as Present?', in Hinnebusch, R.A. and Ehteshami, A. (eds), *Foreign Policies of Middle Eastern States.* Boulder, CO: Lynne Rienner.

Jones, C. and Murphy, E. (2001) *Israel: Democracy, Identity and the State.* London: Harwood Academic Press.

Karsh, E. and Mahler, G. (eds) (1994) *Israel at the Crossroads. The Challenge of Peace.* London: British Academic Press.

Keddie, N.R. and Gasiorowski, M.J. (eds) (1990) *Neither East nor West: Iran, the Soviet Union, and the United States.* New Haven, CT, and London: Yale University Press.

Kemp, G. (2000) 'Iran: Can the United States Do a Deal?', *The Washington Quarterly*, 24(1), 109–24.

Klieman, K. (1994) 'New Directions in Israel's Foreign Policy', *Israeli Affairs*, 1(1), 96–117.

Levi-Faur, D., Sheffer, G. and Vogel, D. (eds) (1999) *Israel: the Dynamics of Change and Continuity.* London: Frank Cass.

Murphy, E.C. (1996) 'The Arab–Israeli Peace Process: Responding to the Economics of Globalization', *Critique: Journal of Critical Studies of the Middle East*, 9, 67–91.

Peretz, D. and Doron, G. (2000) 'Sectarian Politics and the Peace Process: the 1999 Israel Elections', *Middle East Journal*, 54(2), 259–73.

Ramazani, R.K. (1986) *Revolutionary Iran: Challenges and Responses*. Baltimore, MD: Johns Hopkins University Press.

Rezun, M. (ed.) (1990) *Iran at the Crossroads: Global Relations in a Turbulent Decade*. Boulder, CO: Westview Press.

Shlaim, A. (1994) 'Israel and the Conflict', in Danchev, A. and Keohane, D. (eds), *International Perspectives on the Gulf Conflict 1990–91*. London: Macmillan, 59–79.

Steinberg, G.M. and Spiegel, S.L. (1987) 'Israel and the Security of the West', in Braum, A. (ed.), *The Middle East in Global Strategy*. Boulder, CO: Westview Press, 27–46.

Zunes, S. (1999) 'Israeli Foreign Policy in the Era of *Pax Americana*', in Dorraj, M. (ed.), *Middle East at the Crossroads. The Changing Political Dynamics and the Foreign Policy Challenges*. Lanham, MD: University Press of America, 107–46.

The world wide web

The Iranian Foreign Ministry can be found at: <http://mfa.gov.ir/>. The Israeli Foreign Ministry can be found at: <http://www.mfa.gov.il/mfa/home.asp>. For news updates, see the English-language *Jerusalem Post* at <http://www.jpost.com/>, the *Iran Weekly Press Digest* at <http://www.neda.net/iran-wpd/> and the *Tehran Times* at <http://www.netiran.com/dailynews.html>. For a wealth of links pertaining to the international politics of the Middle East region, see The Harry S. Truman Research Institute for the Advancement of Peace, The Hebrew University of Jerusalem at <http://atar.mscc.huji.ac.il/~truman/mideastlinks.htm>.

10 East Asia and the Pacific Rim: Japan and China

Alan Collins

East Asia and the Pacific Rim is a region that at once epitomises both the trans-formed agenda of world politics (the increased attention to external economic preoccupations) and the remnants of older, often Cold War, concerns (territorial disputes and the lingering influence of overt ideology). This chapter focuses on how these concerns have manifested themselves in the foreign policies of the region's two key states: China and Japan. The analysis thus focuses closely on foreign economic relations and more traditional security issues, as well as con-sidering the nature of policy making.

Introduction

At the beginning of a new century East Asia is beset with uncertainties regarding a host of different issues. These encompass problems as diverse as territorial disputes, economic upheavals and challenges to political ideo-logies. In addition, there is the prospect of a power vacuum developing because, combined with the collapse of the Soviet Union and the con-sequential reduction of Moscow's influence, there is a perception that the United States' (US) military presence in East Asia will contract. It is a power vacuum that a hesitant Japan is seen to be ill-equipped to fill, but one which could be occupied by an economically and militarily resurgent People's Republic of China (PRC). Although it is evident that the US will remain interested in East Asian affairs (see Chapter 5), it is the relation-ship between Japan and China that will bear much of the responsibility for maintaining stability in East Asia. It is the foreign policy apparatus and goals of these two states that will therefore concern this chapter. However, before an examination of their foreign policy processes can be undertaken it is necessary to examine, if only briefly, the complexity of East Asia to appreciate the environment in which these two states conduct their relations.

The arena of foreign policy and the challenges of transformation

While the Cold War division of Europe is becoming a distant memory, in East Asia the division of Korea and a continuing American military presence mean that remnants of the Cold War still exist. The provocative behaviour of the communist regime in North Korea (which includes the firing of a ballistic missile over Japan during August 1998 and an exchange of naval fire in June 1999 with South Korea over fishing rights in the Yellow Sea) makes Northeast Asia particularly troublesome for stability in the wider region. Other disputes which have their origins in the early years of the Cold War, and remain problems, include a Russian–Japanese dispute over ownership of the Kurile Islands and, vying with Korea for East Asia's top hotspot, China's determination to reunite with Taiwan. China has also laid claim to the Diaoyu/Senkaku Islands (also claimed by Japan) and a collection of islands in the South China Sea, the ownership of which is disputed by a number of Southeast Asian states. Indeed, China's determination to see the return of lost territory is seen by many as indicating that China is not only a rising great power, but one dissatisfied with the status quo.

To add fuel to these burning issues, the region is slowly coming to terms with the aftermath of an economic crisis. This brought to an end the seemingly enduring Suharto regime in Indonesia, exposed the inadequacies of the large conglomerates (*chaebols*) in South Korea, and exacerbated the failings of the Japanese banking system. The reverberations of the economic crisis will continue to be felt for some time to come, with Japan's economy, which was already struggling after the collapse of its 'bubble' economy in 1990, not expected to show growth until 2001. Indeed, it has been suggested that 'Japan's recession is likely to be the longest, and the most severe, in any industrial country since the Great Depression' (Dibb et al., 1999: 8). Economic considerations also have a part to play in the rise of China. Despite confident talk of China's growing economy, the scale of the changes the Chinese Communist Party (CCP) are embarking upon – in essence it is seeking to replace the inefficient state-controlled enterprises with those able to compete in a global market – are likely to create much pain before gain. This pain can be witnessed in rising unemployment figures (12 million in March 1998), unprecedented protests against the authorities and the closing of failing banks, such as the Hainan Development ment Bank in June 1998.

The regimes of East Asia, and most especially Southeast Asia, are also faced with demands for political change. In Southeast Asia these demands have been encapsulated in the clarion call of *reformasi* which overthrew Suharto in Indonesia in 1998 and which spread to Malaysia, resulting in riots and accusations of cronyism directed against Mahathir Mohamad's ruling party, the United Malays' National Organisation (UMNO). Although UMNO won the Malaysian national election of 29 November 1999, the majority the government enjoyed was reduced, with the main beneficiary being the opposition Islamic party, Parti Islam Se-Malaysia (PAS), which gained twenty seats in parliament.

Indonesia witnessed its first presidential election in the post-Suharto era in October 1999, when Abdurrahman Wahid, an Islamic cleric of fragile health, was the surprising victor. Megawati Sukarnoputri, widely tipped to win the election and replace the incumbent President, B.J. Habibie, became Vice-President. The extent to which Indonesia will emerge as a democratic state is still unknown. There are promising signs, of which the removal of the armed forces chief, General Wiranto, is the most tangible, but there are also concerns that Wahid's style resembles a form of 'benign Suhartoism' (McBeth, 2000: 18–19). The acceptance of the August 1999 independence referendum in East Timor, and the establishment of a National Commission on Human Rights to investigate abuses committed against civilians there during Indonesia's brutal occupation between 1974 and 1999, while important steps in distancing Indonesia from its Suharto past, also carry the danger of encouraging secessionist demands in Aceh and Irian Jaya, and raise the prospect of a military *coup d'état*.

In China there have been some grounds for optimism with regard to political reform. In early 1998, a number of publications appeared noting the value of democracy and the need to implement political reform in order to achieve economic success. Researchers at the Chinese Academy of Social Sciences were also commissioned by the CCP to examine the operation of presidential and democratic systems throughout the world. However, subsequent developments have cast doubts about the likelihood of political reform. By the end of 1998 the CCP was cracking down on dissidents with the would-be founders of the China Democracy Party, Xu Wenli and Wang Youcai, being sentenced to thirteen and eleven years in prison respectively. The end of the twentieth century has witnessed the CCP banning a quasi-religious movement, the Falun Gong, and sentencing its members to between seven and eighteen years in prison. Apparently the CCP regards the Falun Gong as a challenge to its legitimacy (Lawrence, 1999: 16–17). The prospects of political reform have not been entirely quashed; there remains an open attitude to criticism directed at state corruption, as epitomised by the publications from the Chinese Academy of Social Sciences and Premier Zhu Rongji's annual report to the National People's Congress in March 2000 (Gittings, 2000: 17).

Elsewhere in East Asia, political demands for a response to the economic crisis have taken place within the established political architecture. Nevertheless, even here the effects of economic repression have had a dramatic affect. Having experienced one-party rule since 1955, the Japanese political landscape experienced considerable transformation in the 1990s. The dominant Liberal Democratic Party (LDP), which controlled the Japanese parliament (Diet) with sizeable majorities, lost the 1993 election and fared badly in the 1998 election as the Japanese electorate vented its frustration at the government's inability to resurrect the economy. In 1993 the LDP lost its majority in the Diet's upper house (House of Councillors) and a broad grouping of opposition parties took over and formed the Hosokawa and Hata governments. The collapse by mid-1994 of these administrations and the inauguration of a new electoral system resulted in a new opposition party, the New Frontier Party (Shinshinto). The New Frontier Party, though, had a short lifespan and was dissolved at the end of 1997. The more conservative elements formed the Liberal Party (LP), while others forged a new coalition with the recently formed Democratic Party of Japan (DJP). The July 1998 upper house election produced a stinging defeat for the LDP. It lost seventeen seats, its worst ever performance in an upper house election, and it failed to capture a single seat in major cities such as Tokyo, Osaka and Nagoya. The main beneficiaries were the DJP and the Japanese Communist Party, and with no overall majority the LDP was forced to seek coalition partners. By the end of 1998, the LDP and LP formed a coalition, and on 5 October 1999 the New Komeito Party joined the LDP–LP coalition to form a ruling coalition that held more than 70 per cent of the seats in the Diet's lower house (House of Representatives) and more than 50 per cent of the seats in the upper house. In May 2000 the Japanese Prime Minister, Keizo Obuchi, died (following a severe stroke in April) and was replaced by Yoshiro Mori. In the lower house election of that June Mori's LDP party lost thirty-eight constituencies, and although the coalition government lost sixty-four seats, it still retained its overall majority.

As for the wider region, the East Asia of the early 1990s witnessed the emergence of international institutions concerned with economic and security matters. The Asia-Pacific Economic Cooperation (APEC) conference was created in November 1989, while the Association of South East Asian Nations (ASEAN) Regional Forum (ARF) was founded in July 1993 in Singapore. The first meeting of the ARF was in Bangkok in July 1994. The emergence of a multilateral approach to achieving goals in the region is new, and while these bodies are very much in their infancy, they do provide the great powers – chiefly the US, China and Japan, but also Russia and India – with an opportunity for dialogue and, by treating the ARF as a supplement to their bilateral relations, the norms developed in this multilateral setting could provide the basis for crisis management and conflict prevention (Acharya, 1999: 98–9).

East Asia is, therefore, a region in transition and the relationship that emerges between China and Japan will be instrumental in determining the region's future stability. The chapter will now examine each of these states in turn. Japan is the first case study. Here, the focus will be on Japan's regional leadership qualities. In the second case study China's attempts to maintain good regional relations while also pursuing irredentism will be the focus.

Table 10.1 A comparison of the states of East Asia and the Pacific Rim

State	Population in 2000 (m)	Surface area (thousands of sq. km)	GDP (purchasing power parity) in 1999 (US$ bn)	Military expenditure (US$ m) (date in brackets)
Brunei	0.336	5.7	5.6	343 (1998)
Cambodia	12.2	181	8.2	85 (1998)
China	1,262	9,561	4,800	12,600 (1999)
Indonesia	224.7	1,900	610	1,000 (1999)
Japan	126.5	181	2,950	42,900 (1999)
Laos	5.6	236	7	77 (1997)
Malaysia	21.8	330	229	1,200 (1998)
North Korea	21.6	122	22.6	3,700 (1998)
Philippines	81	300	282	995 (1998)
Singapore	4.1	6.2	98	4,400 (1999)
South Korea	47.4	100	625.7	9,900 (1999)
Taiwan	22.1	36	357	8,000 (1999)
Thailand	61.2	514	388.7	2,075 (1998)
Vietnam	78.7	329	143	650 (1998)

Source: Central Intelligence Agency (2000).

The foreign policy of Japan

Japan exists on the periphery of East Asia, not just in terms of geography but also culturally, and this helps us to understand why Japan has closer ties to the West than other Asian countries. Indeed, Japan has used this position to portray itself as a bridge between Asia and the West.

Existing on the periphery does not mean that the Japanese have been unaffected by Asian culture. Indeed, Asian ideas and practice have influenced Japan's political systems. Rather, it means that there has existed for the Japanese the option to 'quit Asia' and adopt Westernisation. It was a decision the Japanese took in the mid-nineteenth century, and which consequently transformed Japan in a period of forty years into a major international actor as epitomised by the formation of the Anglo-Japanese alliance and the Japanese victory in the Russo-Japanese War in 1904–5. Not only did this war enhance Japan's international status, but it also led Japan to engage in a westward policy of colonisation, which, with its victory over the Russians, began with the occupation of the Korean peninsula.

The Japanese occupation of Korea and then its expansion into China damaged Japan's international credibility and its Asian identity. Japan increasingly found itself isolated; it was not acceptable to Asia or to the Western world. By the late 1930s, Japan chose to impose its own order on Asia – the Greater East Asia Co-Prosperity Sphere – thus replacing its Westernisation approach with that of Asianism (Shibusawa, 1997: 25–36).

With defeat in 1945, Japan was an international pariah, the defeated enemy of both the West and Asia. Since 1945 Japan's foreign policy has reflected the deep psychological scars that a sudden rise and fall in power in only one hundred years can bring. Despite emerging during the Cold War as an economic success story, Japan has fought shy of adopting a lead role in East Asia. Feeling neither comfortable with being Asian nor Western, and conscious of the grievances felt world-wide towards it because of atrocities committed during the Second World War, Japan has been willing to follow in the wake of the US. With the end of the Cold War it was thought Japan might emerge from behind the US to throw off the 'free-rider' label and adopt the role of navigator. This case study will provide an examination of Japan's foreign policy apparatus before looking at its leadership potential in the economic and security fields.

The foreign policy process

Graham Allison's seminal work on decision making during the Cuban Missile Crisis of 1962 emphasises organisational processes and bureaucratic politics in understanding foreign policy decision making (see Chapter 3.). This is particularly apt for understanding Japan's foreign policy apparatus. Allison notes that the standard operating procedures and routines adopted by organisations in order to undertake their tasks, and the infighting that occurs within and between bureaucracies, profoundly influences the state's decision-making process (Allison, 1971). Japanese foreign policy is conducted by a myriad of organisations that include a plethora of government ministries, the Japanese private sector, and what Kent Calder (1997) refers to as 'para-public' bodies. The poor levels of coordination within and between these bodies help to explain Japan's lack of decisiveness in decision making in the foreign policy arena.

The key foreign policy government ministries are the Ministry of Foreign Affairs (MFA), the Ministry of International Trade and Industry (MITI) and the Ministry of Finance (MOF). The accelerating internationalisation of Japan's economy during the 1980s led to a number of domestic ministries also becoming involved in Japan's foreign policy making: the Ministry of Posts and Telecommunications (MPT) was one of the first, and it has since been joined by the Ministry of Transportation (MOT) and the Ministry of Education (MOE). Although the MFA is the most actively involved in dispensing Japan's foreign policy functions, the small size of its staff in comparison to MITI and MOF, plus MITI and MOFs' control over Japan's economic relations, ensures that understanding Japanese foreign policy entails appreciating the interaction between these ministries, as well as the other ministries and non-governmental agencies (Calder, 1997: 3, 8–9). For example, within the MFA there are nine bureaux with either geographical or issue responsibilities. One of these issue bureaux is focused on economics and yet it is the International Finance Bureau at MOF that, among other things, coordinates G7/G8 summits, while the staff of the International Economic Section within the Commercial Policy Bureau of MITI provides the support for trade negotiations at these summits. MITI's role in Japan's trade and investment in North Korea has also afforded it a role in Japan's foreign policy approach towards the Pyongyang regime (Hughes, 1999: 180).

The key actors within these ministries are *Kacho* (directors of divisions under bureaux). It is the *Kacho* at the different ministries who are responsible for coordination with other ministries. The ability of *Kacho* to influence and persuade a counterpart is not only dependent upon their expertise, but also their political connections. The perception that *Kacho* have strong political connections to a vice minister or powerful bureau director can lead inter-ministry coordination to 'rapidly degenerate from rational policy decision making into pressure politics, thereby ushering in a form of bureaucratic politics centred around Kacho' (Ahn, 1998: 48). The level of expertise between ministries can be hotly disputed, with MITI officials often claiming economic expertise and MFA officials claiming they are from the only ministry that can speak for Japan's economic and security interests. The importance of an economic issue to Japanese society often favours the *Kacho* from MITI or MOF, since these *Kacho* are able to harness the activities of a number of interest groups. It is only when the issue centres on a core societal value, such as nationalism or pacifism, that an MFA *Kacho* can use the public's support as leverage over his counterpart.

Japanese foreign policy therefore entails appreciating the competitive interchanges between the various ministries – Calder (1997: 15) refers to the relationship between MITI and MFA as an 'on-going turf war'. This competitiveness can be seen in the suspicion that communication between the ministries is not as comprehensive as it could be. When the Prime Minister meets a head of a foreign government, MFA officials are the only ones present during the informal meetings. An MFA official will brief other ministerial officials but, Ahn (1998: 50) notes, 'the "veracity" of the briefing often comes under suspicion because the MFA's attempts to "shed the best light" on itself are well known to other ministries'.

The result of this suspicion is that ministries such as MITI and MOF use their own independent channels of communication via para-public institutions. There is a wide range of these institutions, some are financially tied to the ministries while others have a greater degree of autonomy. These institutions allow ministries such as MITI and MOF to operate in areas that the ministries themselves cannot. MITI has the most extensive network of para-public institutions, the best known being the Japan External Trade Organisation (JETRO) which promotes trade activities and houses MITI officials on secondment. It is, for instance, via JETRO that MITI monitors the progress of the 1995 Korean Peninsula Energy Development Organisation (KEDO) Treaty aimed at overseeing the building of light-water nuclear reactors in North Korea. Ministries have also established 'think tanks' which sponsor international conferences and engage in research projects. MOF has established the Japan Centre for International Finance, while the MFA has created the Japan Institute of International Affairs.

Although other ministries do have their independent channels of communication, the MFA exercises exclusive control of official communication from overseas. This can, and does, cause inter-ministry coordination problems because of the MFA's lack of openness. During the Gulf War in 1991 the US requested assistance from Japan in the form of transportation ships. The ministry in charge of establishing a plan and the guidelines underpinning Japan's assistance was MOT. The initial MOT plan stipulated that the ships would not engage in the transport of weapons, munitions or military personnel and that the ships would be ordinary cargo ships. When a MOT official gave the Finance Minister a briefing of the plan, he was surprised to learn that it had always been intended that the ships would transport military personnel and munitions, and when the plan was nearing implementation, it appeared that roll-on roll-off ships had been requested. With this new information MOT officials demanded to see the communication from the Japanese Embassy in Washington detailing the US request. MFA officials grudgingly yielded and the cable read, '[H]igh-level US officials have made it clear that Japan's cooperation is needed in the area of transporting military personnel and materials, and a dispatch of roll-on roll-off ships will be particularly appreciated' (Ahn, 1998: 51). Not only does this help us to understand why MITI and MOF have their own private forms of communication, but it also reveals the bureaucratic politics inherent in the workings of Japan's foreign policy making.

With Japan's rise in the world economy there was an expectation that Tokyo would play a proactive role in determining the agendas of such bodies as the G7/G8 and the World Trade Organisation (WTO). However, the type of central executive authority that exists in the US, or the United Kingdom (UK), is missing in Japan. The Japanese Prime Minister's Office (*kantei*) has a small staff comprised of individuals on secondment from the ministries. In 1986, during Yasuhiro Nakasone's premiership, there were structural changes made to the *kantei*, including the creation of the Cabinet Councillors' Office on External Affairs and the Cabinet Security Affairs Office. However, these structural changes have failed to galvanise the *kantei* into an equivalent of the White House staff that exists in the US. In comparison with other great powers, the decision-making and leadership qualities of Japan's Prime Minister are therefore conspicuous by their absence.

A picture of Japan's foreign policy apparatus can thus be discerned. With a weak executive the decision making arises out of the bifurcated relationship of MITI/MOF and the MFA, with occasional appearances from other ministries, that can best be described as partisan.

In addition to the official policy-making apparatus, Japanese foreign policy is also influenced by the role of private business organisations. The best known of these is the Federation of Economic Organisations, or *Keidanren*. During the 1970s *Keidanren* was involved in Japan's development projects in the Amazon Basin and Mexico, and throughout the 1990s it encouraged liberal trade policies, especially in the area of agriculture. When official relations between Japan and another state are nearing a nadir, these private business organisations can help to prevent a further decline. For example, within a week of the collapse of the Clinton–Hosokawa summit in 1994, the chairman of the US National Economic Council, Robert Rubin, met with Japanese participants in the US–Japan Business Council. Calder notes that this meeting was 'an important step in arresting an escalation of confrontationist sentiments on both sides of the Pacific' (Calder, 1997: 19).

The examination of Japanese foreign policy will now turn to a consideration of Japan's foreign economic and security policies. The first will focus on Japan's economic development strategy and the creation of APEC, and the second on Japan's key security relationship with the US, including its bid for a permanent seat in the United Nations Security Council (UNSC). The key question in both sections is Japan's ability and willingness to assume the mantle of leader. In view of Japan's weak executive and the sectionalist and partisan attitude of the ministries, plus Japan's unease over its self-identity (is it Asian or not?), it is not difficult to appreciate that Japan has failed to assume the role of leader. Indeed, references to Japanese foreign policy coalesce around phrases such as incremental or even vacillating, rather than bold and decisive. The changing political climate since the 1990s noted earlier has only further exacerbated this state of affairs.

The content of Japanese foreign policy (i) Japan's foreign economic relations

Although Japan's economy has strengthened since the end of the Second World War, Japan's emergence as the leader of East Asia's economic development during this period has been more implicit than explicit. Part of the explanation can be found in the bureaucratic infighting of the MFA and MITI, but there is also the constraining effect of Japan's war record and Japan's uncertainty regarding its identity as an Asian state. In addition, by shielding its domestic market from the exports of other countries, Japan has essentially prevented the emergence of a Yen bloc, which would be a clear indication of its leadership position. Japan's economic weakness in the 1990s also undercut its leadership potential at a time when the prospects of Japanese leadership looked promising.

This account of Japan's foreign economic relations will begin with an examination of its economic policies, before examining its political role in the evolution of APEC. In its economic relations it will be argued that a Yen bloc has not emerged because Japan has failed to become the leader of its own 'flying geese' theory of development.

Akamatsu Kaname constructed the flying geese theory during the 1930s and 1940s. It divides states into their different stages of development with those at the advanced stage being the leaders and the others the followers. According to the theory, through international trade the undeveloped state would find its economic system unable to compete with the leader and consequently its economy would fail. In time though, the practices of the leader's economy would be copied by the undeveloped state and it would thus follow the leader's path to economic development (Korhonen, 1998: 22–3).

At the fourth Pacific Economic Cooperation Council (PECC) in April 1985 in Seoul, Japan's Foreign Minister, Okita Saburo, presented the flying geese theory in English at a major international conference. Korhonen claims that, 'Okita's position, and the forum at which his speech was presented, meant that the theory was no longer purely academic, but an expression of Japanese foreign political ideology with respect to the Pacific region' (Korhonen, 1998: 138). Throughout the 1980s the flying geese theory of development gained momentum, and as the 1980s drew to a close Japan had, with its technical prowess, emerged as the recognised Asian leader with the Asian Newly Industrialised Economies (ANIEs) of Taiwan, South Korea, Hong Kong and Singapore, then the ASEAN members, and finally China, following behind. By the mid-1990s the flying geese theory of development was widely regarded as lying behind the East Asian miracle (World Bank, 1993; UNCTAD, 1993: 131).

This Asian recognition of Japanese economic leadership was manifest in Malaysia's 'Look East' policy of the 1980s. Malaysian Prime Minister, Mahathir Mohamad, had throughout the 1980s downgraded relations with Britain and the Commonwealth in favour of Japan and South Korea. In his 'Look East' policy, Mahathir called for a replacing of Western influence with the more relevant development strategies of Japan and South Korea. Mahathir's preference for Japanese leadership led to his call for an East Asia Economic Group (later called a Caucus – EAEC) in which Japan would play a prominent part.

At the end of the 1980s Tokyo appeared to have the potential to take on the responsibilities of a great power that its economic growth had bestowed upon it. Japan, however, proved reluctant to play this role. Japan's failure to act as a leader can be seen in its trading relations with its 'followers'. While Japan has exported capital and technology – and Japan's foreign direct investment (FDI) in the ANIEs and ASEAN states has been very significant – it has imported very few advanced products from Asia. With the exception of China, between 1985 and 1992 Asian countries witnessed an increase in their trade deficits with Japan. In 1995 Singapore's Senior Minister, Lee Kuan Yew, posited Japan's leadership specifically over the issue of trade liberalisation. He argued that Japan needed to set a good example by opening up its markets, given that Japan absorbed only 12 per cent of exports from East Asia compared to 22 per cent from America (Chin, 1997: 115). Japan, though, has shielded its market from the ANIEs and ASEAN members, and where Asian exports have succeeded in the Japanese market the government has succumbed to domestic pressure to block their import. This occurred in the case of South Korean knitwear exports when the Japanese promptly forced South Korea to accept voluntary export restraints. Unless Japan is to become a significant importer of Asian manufactured goods a Yen bloc will not emerge. The stagnation of its economy in the 1990s (real growth of GDP averaged a mere 1 per cent between 1992 and 1999) however has further limited its ability to assume a leadership position.

The failure to liberalise its trading policies and the stagnation of its own economy are the key reasons behind Japan's inability to emerge as the region's explicit economic leader (Funabashi, 2000–1: 73–8). However, to appreciate fully Japan's lack of decisive leadership it is necessary to examine the evolution of APEC.

The impasse in the Uruguay Round of the General Agreement on Tariffs and Trade (GATT) provided a conducive political environment to establish an Asian economic multilateral venture. This venture began with the so-called 'Hawke initiative', named after the Australian Prime Minister, Bob Hawke, who in January 1989 proposed the establishment of a consultative body for regional cooperation to sustain the economic development of the Asia-Pacific region. Hawke's proposal presented Japan with a problem. By referring to the Western Pacific, Hawke had, at least by implication, excluded the US. With Japan's Prime Minister Takeshita Nobura's attention focused on a domestic corruption scandal, the response was made by the ministries. The MFA initially opposed the initiative because it excluded the US, and because there was a suspicion that it was actually a MITI idea. The MFA only concurred when the Australians assured them that it was an Australian idea, that foreign ministries would be involved, and the US and Canada would be invited to attend.

In November 1989 at Canberra, the US, Canada, South Korea, New Zealand and the ASEAN members joined Australia and Japan for a ministerial meeting of Trade and Foreign Ministries. The involvement of both foreign and economic ministries pitted the MFA and MITI against one another. Indeed, according to Yamagami Susumu, who acted between 1990 and 1993 as a coordinator of the ministries' Pacific policies: 'Different ministries presented at various times quite differing policy lines. Japan could demand double representation in committees, and Japan might even need two separate chairs at dinner tables' (cited in Korhonen, 1998: 162). Such infighting between the MFA and MITI not only highlights the difficulty of determining the direction of Japan's foreign policy, but it also explains why Japan would struggle to take a leadership role in Asia's economic relations.

The importance of domestic matters also impinged on Japan's ability to take a proactive role. With APEC focusing on trade liberalisation, including agricultural trade, no Japanese Prime Minister was going to anger influential groups in the countryside. 'For domestic audiences', Korhonen (1998: 165) asserts, 'Japanese leadership had to appear as if it was [not] only following a general trend, but dragging its feet whenever possible.'

The APEC process gained momentum in the 1990s with the third APEC Ministerial Meeting in 1991 adopting the Seoul Declaration, and US President Bill Clinton attending the Seattle meeting in 1993 and thereby elevating APEC to summit level. Japan hosted the seventh APEC Ministerial Meeting at Osaka in November 1995 and once again it was the MFA and MITI that took centre stage. With it being the fiftieth anniversary of the ending of the Second World War, Prime Minister Tomiichi Murayama's main foreign policy task was apologising for Japan's war crimes, which left the ministries to co-chair the conference. Both ministries were able to cooperate and this probably reflected the nature of the task at Osaka. The direction APEC was going to take had already been established through the Seoul Declaration, and Clinton in 1993 and Indonesia's President Suharto in 1994, had given the process leadership and impetus. At Osaka therefore decisive leadership was not required. The bureaucrats at MITI and the MFA needed to only guide the APEC process forward. They produced the Osaka Action Agenda, a document of over a hundred pages, which rested on the pillars of trade liberalisation, investment and economic cooperation agreed at Seoul.

APEC continues to meet annually and it has slowly evolved into an institution, with a small secretariat established in Singapore at the 1992 Ministerial Meeting. The membership is diverse; it currently has twenty-one members, each having its own foreign and economic policies. Consequently, APEC statements tend to be declarations of intent, such as achieving free and open trade and investment by 2010 and 2020, rather than detailed policy statements. Although APEC receives much criticism in the media for doing little to solve the problems of the 'real world', if the number of informal APEC meetings is anything to go by, at the beginning of the twenty-first century the organisation appears to be in good health.

The story of APEC highlights the failure of Japan to take an economic leadership role. It was Clinton who provided the impetus and Suharto who provided the Asian perspective. Japan's reluctance to assume the mantle of leader was also captured in its ambivalence towards the EAEC proposal noted above. The EAEC excluded the US and would have elevated Japan to the position of economic leader, but Japan was not prepared to cut itself off from the US. This reflected not only the fruitful Japanese–US relationship that had developed since 1945, but also Japan's uncertainty over its identity. Throughout the early 1990s Japanese leaders therefore spoke of an Asia-Pacific region, not the Western Pacific, and consistently supported APEC. The EAEC proposal has consequently withered and died.

The content of Japanese foreign policy (ii) Japan's security relations

At the beginning of the 1990s there was a prospect that Japan would emerge as a political heavyweight, directing the development of security relations as Cold War security dynamics subsided. Japan, as it has done in the economic field, has failed to assume this role. The key in any discussion of Japan's security foreign relations is Tokyo's relationship with Washington.

At the end of the Second World War Japan was given a new constitution, a constitution that has been labelled the 'Peace Constitution' because of Article 9. This states that the 'Japanese people forever renounce war . . . and the threat or use of force as a means of settling international disputes . . . in order to accomplish this aim . . . land, sea, and air forces, as well as other war potential, will never be maintained' (quoted from Bessho, 1999: 15). This pacifist article has been interpreted to mean that Tokyo can maintain a Japanese Self-Defence Force (JSDF), which was created in 1954, but Japan cannot deploy troops overseas. The advent of the Cold War led the US to strengthen its relationship with Japan and to identify it as a member of the Western industrialised democracies. Thus the US aided Japan's membership of GATT in 1955, the UN in 1956 and the Organisation for Economic Cooperation and Development (OECD) in 1964. In the security field this strengthening relationship was codified in the 1951 US–Japan Security Treaty that commits the US to the defence of the country.

The 1951 Security Treaty remains the cornerstone of Japan's security foreign relations. During the Cold War Japan's defence policy altered to give the JSDF a greater, if still limited, role. In 1981, for example, Japanese Prime Minister Zenko Suzuki agreed to assist in the protection of sea lanes 1,000 nautical miles west of the US pacific island of Guam and north of the Philippines. In the 1990s the relationship was further strengthened and Japan's role gradually increased. In 1996 the 'US–Japan Joint Declaration on Security', signed by Japanese Prime Minister Ryutaro Hashimoto and US President Clinton, elaborated on areas of cooperation in the alliance. Essentially it defined the extent of joint US–Japanese cooperation in military exercises and UN peacekeeping and humanitarian operations, but it also led to a revision of the 1987 'Guidelines for US–Japan Defence Cooperation'. These revisions, which were completed in September 1997, list forty items of cooperation that are concerned with 'situations in areas surrounding Japan' and, among other tasks, include ensuring the effectiveness of economic sanctions, the use of Japanese facilities by the US military, rear-area support (supply, transportation, etc.), surveillance and minesweeping. As the threat of missile attack from North Korea has become an increasing concern, so Japan has taken an interest in the US plans to deploy a Theatre Missile Defence (TMD) system in Asia. In January 1999 Tokyo earmarked US$ 8 million for TMD research and development.

However, in the early 1990s the continuing relationship between the US and Japan was not necessarily a foregone conclusion. With the Cold War over, the US wanted to reduce its overseas force deployments. In early 1990 Richard Cheney, the US Secretary of Defense, announced that 5,000 troops would be withdrawn from South Korea and in 1992 the Pentagon called for a 25 per cent reduction in overall military strength in East Asia. The US withdrawal of forces in the region, coupled with the growing perception that Japan should take a more proactive role in world affairs, led Japan to take a number of further steps in the security field.

One such step was the establishment of an Asian equivalent to the Organisation on Security and Cooperation in Europe (OSCE). In July 1991 the then Foreign Minister, Taro Nakayama, gave a speech at the ASEAN-Post Ministerial Conference (ASEAN-PMC) in Kuala Lumpur, proposing the creation of a security and political framework for dialogue under the auspices of the ASEAN-PMC. Although the idea was initially rejected by the ASEAN members, Nakayama's proposal was influential in the establishment of the ARF two years later by ASEAN. According to Michael Leifer (1996: 24), this Japanese initiative was not designed to assume a more prominent regional role for Tokyo. Rather, because of the concerns regarding the reduction of US military strength in the

Asia-Pacific, Nakayama's initiative was intended to enhance Japanese security by 'encouraging a new structure of regional relations that would perpetuate US military engagement'. Indeed, Japan's security approach throughout the 1990s has been one of steadily seeking to influence the direction of Asian security while also keeping the US engaged in the region.

In view of Asia's past experience of Japanese assertiveness, it is not surprising that Japan preferred a multilateral rather than a unilateral approach to Asian security affairs. Japan's wartime record still causes concern among some Asian states and thus statements calling for a greater Japanese role were unlikely to fall on receptive ears. This sensitivity to its Asian neighbours, coupled with Tokyo's aspirations for a permanent seat on the UN Security Council, also helps to explain Japan's involvement in UN peacekeeping.

Japan has, at least since the 1970s, sought a permanent seat on the Security Council. In the aftermath of the Cold War, and specifically the Gulf War of 1990/91, the Japanese desire has become much more forthright. The Gulf War highlighted that in order to be a world power, Security Council permanent membership was extremely important. Japan was not a member of the Security Council when Iraq annexed Kuwait, and thus it was not privy to the discussions taking place at the top diplomatic table. This hindered its ability to take a proactive policy, and it was subsequently criticised for being hesitant in providing financial assistance to Operation Desert Shield and Operation Desert Storm.

In 1997 the Japanese linked the issue of permanent Security Council membership to their UN assessed contribution. Although Japan has a strong case for permanent status – and along with Germany it does attract much sympathy for its position among UN members because of its financial contribution – the provisions stipulated in Article 23 of the UN Charter make changing the composition of the Council difficult to attain. In order to restructure the Security Council there has to be nine affirmative votes cast by the Security Council members, including the permanent five, plus a two-thirds majority in the General Assembly. These difficulties aside, the issue of reforming the Security Council remains on the UN's agenda and, along with Germany, Japan is widely regarded as a permanent member in waiting.

The Gulf War not only reinforced Japan's desire for permanent membership of the UNSC, it also revealed that Japan would have to be able to support UN operations with military forces. Japan's financial contribution to the UN of US$13 billion was not likely to receive the same merit as those states that were putting their own people's lives at risk to defend Kuwaiti sovereignty and uphold a key provision of the UN Charter. Japan was thus faced with the difficulty of balancing the need to take an active role in supporting UN operations through the provision of troops (not causing alarm among its neighbours in the process) while also working within its own restrictive constitution.

In 1992 Japan passed the International Peace Cooperation Law which enables Japanese forces to participate in UN peacekeeping operations. Since 1992, Japan has contributed to the United Nations Angola Verification Mission II (UNAVEMII), the United Nations Transitional Authority in Cambodia (UNTAC) and the United Nations Operation in Mozambique (ONUMOZ) in 1993–95, the United Nations Observer Mission in El Salvador (ONUSAL) in 1994, the Rwanda refugee relief activities in 1994, and the United Nations Disengagement Observer Force (UNDOF) in the Golan Heights in 1995–96 (Soeya, 1998: 221).

The early 1990s thus witnessed, albeit in an incremental manner, the emergence of proactive Japanese policies in the security field. This reflected both a greater desire to make its economic strength equate to political influence on the world stage, and also the concern that the US could not be relied upon to continue providing Japan with a security guarantee in the aftermath of the Cold War. However, the strong Japanese–US relationship, while not untroubled, has endured in the post-Cold War era and this reflects, on the one hand, a shared security concern over North Korea and, on the other, a common objective of forging a *modus vivendi* with China (Funabashi, 2000–1: 81–3).

For the Japanese, the concern with China during the Cold War was not so much to contain the spread of communism, but rather to prevent China from imploding. Since the *rapprochement* between the US and China in the early 1970s, Japan has sought to achieve this by supporting China's economic modernisation, and thereby generate domestic stability. Thus when economic sanctions were imposed on Beijing after the suppression of the pro-democracy supporters in Tiananmen Square in June 1989, it was Japan's Prime Minister, Toshiki Kaifu, who was the first G7 leader to visit China in August 1991. In April 1992 President Jiang Zemin visited Japan, and in October 1992 the first ever visit by the Japanese emperor to China took place.

However, developments since 1992 have caused a worsening of relations and in August 1995, in protest at Chinese nuclear testing, Japan decided for the first time in its history to suspend grant aid to China. Throughout the 1990s China's growing assertiveness over territorial disputes, particularly in the South China Sea and Taiwan, and of more immediate concern to Japan, the Diaoyu/Senkaku Islands, has raised worries about Chinese ambitions in the region. The proclamation of the 1992

Law on the Territorial Waters and their Contiguous Areas, the seizure of Mischief Reef in 1995 and the use of military exercises to intimidate the Taiwanese voters in March 1996, have indicated that China is prepared to use military force for political purposes. Japan's response has been to strengthen its ties with the US, hence the revisions to the 1987 guidelines noted above, but it has not yet designated China as a threat. The change in attitude towards Beijing is, however, unmistakable. Whether this will naturally lead to a conflictual relationship depends upon whether China emerges as a responsible great power or one seeking to alter the status quo. To know this, and to determine who is influencing Chinese foreign policy, we need to examine China itself.

The foreign policy of China

Any understanding of China's foreign policy must begin with an appreciation of the historical baggage that influences Chinese decision making, and specifically the lessons learnt by the Chinese from the 'Century of Shame'. This began with China's defeat in the Opium War of 1840–42, it included the failed 'Boxer Rebellion' of 1900, the defeat at the hands of the Japanese in 1894–95 and the invasion of China by the Japanese in 1937, and it came to an end with the founding of the People's Republic of China in 1949. This period is known as one of shame because prior to the nineteenth century China perceived itself to be the political and cultural centre of the world, the 'Middle Kingdom'. With the most sophisticated civilisation in the world, China's neighbours were not equals and were instead expected to show deference to the Chinese emperor through the tribute system. The tribute system entailed foreign dignitaries acknowledging China's superior status by performing the 'kow-tow' ceremony (prostrating themselves before the emperor) and providing gifts. In return these tributary states received Chinese trading privileges and benefited from access to Confucian culture. Those states that did not belong to the tribute system were simply regarded as barbarians.

Internally, China was, and still is, a vast, populous and multi-ethnic country that meets the criteria for being a weak state. The central government of the Qing Dynasty had perennial worries regarding internal rebellions and ultimately these were to bring the dynasty to an end in 1912. The most serious of these internal challenges to the central government was the 1850–64 Taiping Rebellion that resulted in 20 million deaths. It was not uncommon for these internal rebellions to coincide with external threats, leading to the Chinese belief that internal disorder increases China's vulnerability to foreign attack. For the Chinese, therefore, it was no coincidence that the Japanese seizure of Manchuria in 1931 and the invasion of China six years later, coincided with the civil war raging between Mao Tsetung's communists and the Kuomintang forces of Chiang Kai-Shek.

The civil war resulted in victory for the CCP on China's mainland, but Chiang's Kuomintang forces fled to Formosa (Taiwan) and declared themselves the legitimate rulers of all China with the establishment of the Republic of China. Until Taiwan is reunified with China, the legacy of China's century of shame will remain. Denny Roy (1998: 13) notes three lessons the Chinese have learnt from this period: first, foreign powers want to weaken and exploit China; second, the Chinese must never leave themselves vulnerable to foreigners; third, the world has not adequately acknowledged the great injustices done to China nor given China due respect for being a great civilisation. It is possible to add to these lessons the Chinese perception noted above that domestic disorder invites an external threat.

During the Cold War, China's foreign relations evolved from hostility, via *rapprochement*, to engagement with the capitalist Western powers and, in particular, the US. In line with Marxist thinking, there was a presumption in Beijing that conflict in world politics was unavoidable because of the imperialist ambitions of the capitalist states. It was also assumed that because socialism would triumph over capitalism, the capitalist states would be a threat to China. It is not, therefore, surprising that the Chinese viewed the US involvement in the Korean civil war with unease. This unease was seemingly borne out when US forces (under a UN mandate) invaded North Korea in the autumn of 1950. When these troops approached the Yalu River, Chinese 'volunteers' entered the fray and pushed the American forces back to the original North–South demarcation line along the 38th parallel.

Confrontational relations between China and the US were also evident in Washington's refusal to allow the CCP to represent China on the UN Security Council, and the Taiwan Straits crises of 1954–55 and 1958 which confirmed that the US would support the Kuomintang regime in Taiwan. However, with the split in the Sino-Soviet camp in the early 1960s creating a Soviet enemy to its north, by the early 1970s *rapprochement* with Washington was looked upon favourably in Beijing. The improving relationship with the US took a further step forward when Mao's death in 1976 brought a backlash against his economic policies and cultural radicalism. With Deng Xiaoping's subsequent rise to power, China gained a leader who placed economic engagement with the West as the key to economic prosperity. Although relations with Washington throughout the 1980s were not without their problems, they were much improved from their 1950s version. However, by the end of the 1980s the wave of democratisation that had brought down the communist regimes in the Soviet Union and elsewhere in Europe was creating domestic disorder in China. The suppression of the pro-democracy demonstrators in Tiananmen Square in June 1989 was a clear sign that while China may have opened its doors to capitalist economic practices, it was not so open to its political ideology. The remainder of this case study will focus on Chinese foreign policy during the first decade of the post-Cold War era, but before that it is necessary to examine the apparatus of Chinese foreign policy making.

The foreign policy process

There are two parallel government structures operating in China: the Party and the state. It is the former that holds real power. The highest Party organisation is the Politburo (Political Bureau) Standing Committee and below this, the full Politburo and the Central Committee. The most powerful state organisations are the National People's Congress, which is the legislative body, and the State Council, which has the executive function. The State Council, much like the Party's Central Committee, is both large and unwieldy so the main decision making occurs in the smaller State Council cabinet. Of some importance also is the Foreign Affairs Leading Small Group (FALSG) of the CCP Central Committee. This oversees the implementation of decisions taken at the Politburo Standing Committee. The two main state bodies that influence the direction of China's foreign policy are the Ministry of Foreign Affairs (MFA) and the People's Liberation Army (PLA). Party and state structures are interlocked, with leaders at the highest levels being members of both.

Under Deng's leadership, and the opening of China to international trade, China's foreign policy apparatus underwent important changes. The increase in international contacts enhanced the policy makers' knowledge of the outside world and increased the number of decision makers involved in foreign policy discussions. This generally led to a professionalisation of Chinese foreign policy, as those bureaucrats with particular expertise increased their input into the policy-making process. It also meant that the role of the leader diminished. Roy (1998: 66) writes:

> Deng Xiaoping intentionally took steps to decentralize the PRC's political system. Jiang Zemin, Deng's successor as top PRC leader, [has been] unable to personally dominate the policy process the way his predecessors did; indeed, it is unlikely that any individual will ever again command unquestioned control over the party, government and military simultaneously.

China has thus been in the process of moving away from a foreign policy dictated by the ruler (as was the case with Mao and the emperors before him), to a more pluralist system. However, Roy (1998: 65) does note that '[s]ince the PRC leadership considers foreign affairs an especially sensitive sphere of government, the foreign policy process has been particularly subject to secrecy and concentration at the top level of Party leadership'.

The opening of the Chinese economy has also led to a number of provincial and municipal governments becoming autonomous foreign policy actors. This is especially true of Shanghai, Guangdong and the Special Economic Zones. Thus in post-Mao China, central political authority has become decentralised with certain regions having a great deal of autonomy in their dealings with foreign governments. This decentralisation has led David Goodman (1997: 32) to assert that 'the nation-state may be a less appropriate comparative device for understanding China's development . . . than the notion of a continental system of great extent and diversity in which each province is regarded as a single, though not completely autarchic, social, political and economic system'.

The key bureaucracies in China's foreign policy apparatus are the MFA and the PLA. In the following section, the analysis will focus on how China has managed two competing foreign policy goals – regaining lost territory, such as Taiwan, while also ensuring its economic growth is maintained by enhancing regional stability via improved relations with neighbouring powers. Although a generalisation, it is the MFA that gives the latter priority, while the PLA prioritises the former. Consequently, these two bureaucracies often compete and contradict one another. This has been evident in the field of arms sales, a source of tension in recent US–Chinese relations. The MFA is keen to keep relations between Beijing and Washington cordial, especially at a time when China is seeking entry to the WTO. It is often, therefore, from the MFA that the US receives assurances that China will restrict the sale of missile technology, and the components and knowledge necessary to make weapons of mass destruction. However, although the MFA is acting in good faith, sales often still take place because it is the PLA that is responsible for Chinese arms transfers. An unclassified CIA (Central Intelligence Agency) report submitted to Congress in July 1997 concluded that: '[T]he Chinese [have] provided a tremendous variety of assistance to both Iran's and Pakistan's ballistic missile programs', and 'China [has] also [been] the primary source of nuclear-related equipment and technology to Pakistan and a key supplier to Iran' (quoted from Carpenter, 1998: 3–4). Such sales are an important source of revenue for the PLA, which views the US as the most likely threat to Chinese security and is thus less concerned with maintaining cordial relations. The Chinese President does have the power to ensure PLA arms sales are in compliance with the MFA criteria, but because the PLA uses arms sales to bolster its own funding, the President tends to side with the PLA. For example, when Deng was asked to settle a dispute between the MFA and PLA over the sale of missiles to Saudi Arabia, he asked the firm's representatives how much money they made. The answer, $2 billion, elicited from Deng the response, 'that's quite a lot', which thereby settled the matter (Roy, 1998: 76).

China's foreign policy apparatus, therefore, exhibits elements of both the unitary actor and bureaucratic models. The bureaucratic model is manifest in the competition between the MFA and PLA, but there also exists competition within the PLA. This is reflected in a generation gap between the older officers, who are more attached to the communist ideology, and the younger officers, who focus on technical competencies. Regionalism is another divisive factor. China's armies are regionally based, and the PLA commonly rotates provincial commanders to ensure that no one province gains too much influence. In recent times there has been concern that Shandong has become disproportionately powerful, and Jiang Zemin has been seeking to counteract this influence by promoting officers from his own Jiangsu province.

The role of the President, or at least the individual who heads FALSG (normally the Prime Minister), also indicates that the unitary actor model has its uses in understanding Chinese actions. Michael Swaine (1997: 108) has argued that the then Chinese Prime Minister, Li Peng, served as a 'foreign policy "bridge leader"' within the top leadership. In this capacity, he reportedly dominated foreign policy making, directing the formulation and implementation of critical policy initiatives and thereby limiting the influence of other Politburo Standing Committee members, including Jiang Zemin. While this may be true, Swaine notes that Li Peng probably consulted Jiang on many foreign policy issues, and certainly as President, Jiang was able to influence the tenor and direction of China's foreign policy.

The content of Chinese foreign policy: regional stability and regaining 'lost' territories

The pro-democracy protestors at Tiananmen Square brought home to the Chinese elite that communist ideology was no longer a source of CCP legitimacy. The 1990s thus witnessed the elite searching for alternative sources with which to bolster its legitimacy. The first source of legitimacy focuses on the CCP's role in providing the stability necessary for the continuing impressive economic growth of China, while the second emphasises the CCP's role in ending the century of shame and regaining the lost territory that was taken from China. These are not necessarily compatible goals and by examining three case studies – Diaoyu/Senkaku Islands, South China Sea and Taiwan – it will be possible to see which is having the greater influence over the direction of China's foreign policy. In essence, the more influential the need to create stability to enhance China's economic growth, the more China is seen as an emerging, responsible world power, which is learning the rules of the international game. The more the need to recapture lost territory influences China's foreign policy, the more China is seen as a dissatisfied, revisionist power, and the more prominent the talk of a 'China threat' becomes. Before examining the three case studies, though, it is necessary to appreciate just how impressive China's economic development has been.

China's economic growth since the 1970s has been achieved by engaging with the world economy. The lessons to be drawn from the experience of Albania and North Korea are that autarky and prosperity do not go hand in hand. The result of this engagement is that from being ranked thirty-second in world trade with a share of world trade at 0.8 per cent in 1978, by the mid-1990s China was eleventh with a share of 2.9 per cent of world trade. Between 1978 and 1982 foreign direct investment was about US$1 billion, by 1991 it had risen to US$4 billion and by 1993 it had increased ten-fold. For most of the 1990s, China received more FDI than any other country and was ranked second to the US in 1995. China's changing exports reflect the country's move towards development, with manufactured products representing 86 per cent of China's exports in 1995. According to the Ministry of Trade, nearly half the Chinese economy is 'related to the international market' (cited in Segal, 1997: 178). Consequently, China sought admission to GATT in 1986 (this issue was resolved in November 2001 with entry into GATT's successor, the WTO) and joined APEC in 1991.

China's engagement with the world economy, and perhaps more importantly the need for China to remain engaged in order to continue to prosper, has led to the prospect of China becoming constrained in its foreign policy as a consequence of its need for a peaceful external environment. Whether this is the case will now be examined with reference to, first, the Diaoyu/Senkaku Islands, then the island chains in the South China Sea, before concluding with Taiwan. In essence, the less influence the PLA has on the direction of Chinese foreign policy the more likely it is that China will act with restraint.

Diaoyu/Senkaku Islands

The Diaoyu Islands, known to the Japanese as Senkaku, comprise five uninhabited islets and three barren rocks which lie some 185 miles southeast of Okinawa and 125 miles northeast of Taiwan. Both Japan and China claim the island chain and in the 1990s two incidents occurred, in 1990 and 1996, which shed some light on the direction of Chinese foreign policy.

In the months following the Tiananmen Square events the CCP leadership sought to rescue its damaged legitimacy by appealing to Chinese patriotism and warning of internal and external threats to China. On 3 June 1990 Jiang Zemin warned of the dangers of 'peaceful evolution' – the danger that in opening China's market, and thereby benefiting from access to Western technology, China was also open to cultural and material influences from the capitalist world. These influences could undermine communist rule by spreading Western values, such as democracy and individual human rights. The Western response to the Tiananmen crackdown was to impose sanctions on China, but in July 1990 Japan announced its unilateral decision to resume official development loans to China. This placed Japan in a position to influence the flow of capital and development loans needed to bolster China's economic growth.

On 29 September 1990 it was reported in the Japanese press that Japan's Maritime Safety Agency was about to recognise a lighthouse built in 1978 on the main Diaoyu island as an official navigation mark. The Chinese responded on 18 October that such recognition would be an infringement of Chinese sovereignty. The situation deteriorated when Japan repelled an attempt by Taiwanese activists to reaffirm the Chinese claim by landing on the Diaoyu Islands. However, despite the rise in nationalistic furore on both sides, the CCP leadership adopted a conciliatory stance towards Japan. After the attempted landings by the Taiwanese activists the CCP issued a circular to local party committees stressing that tensions over 'these economically and strategically insignificant islands should not affect friendly relations between China and Japan'. Publicly the Chinese issued a mild condemnation of Japanese actions, for which Li Peng, the then Chinese Prime Minister, was heavily criticised by Hong Kong deputies for putting Japanese loans ahead of sovereignty issues. Even Beijing students, only a year after Tiananmen, distributed leaflets entitled, 'We Want the Diaoyu Islands, Not Yen' (Downs and Saunders, 1998–99: 131–2).

On 14 July 1996 the Japan Youth Federation erected a second makeshift lighthouse on the Diaoyu Islands and once again the conflicting claims created a crisis. The Chinese were this time more forthright in their condemnation, and Foreign Ministry spokesperson Shen Guofang stated, 'Japanese yen loans are helpful for promoting Sino-Japanese economic co-operation and trade, but as far as the issue of sovereignty is concerned, the Chinese government cannot make any compromise' (Downs and Saunders, 1998–99: 135). The situation deteriorated with the death of a pro-China activist, David Chan, who drowned trying to land on the Islands. However, as occurred six years earlier, it is evident that the CCP's desire to maintain stability for economic considerations was paramount in China's approach to resolving the crisis. As it had in 1990, the leadership banned anti-Japanese student demonstrations, and despite Shen's assertion that economic matters would not influence China's response, Erica Strecker Downs and Phillip Saunders (1998–99: 138) note that 'instructions issued by the central government in early October ordered provincial governments to place priority on domestic economic development'. The crisis eventually subsided by the end of October, but this time the Chinese leadership did come in for criticism from the PLA.

On 13–14 September the PLA had conducted military exercises on islands off Liaoning province, which it is thought were not just intended to send a message to Japan, but also to remind civilian officials that economic ties were not the only consideration. The government's approach to the territorial dispute also elicited a letter of protest from thirty-five army generals, who demanded stronger action. Although the political elite was able to favour the need for economic stability over the nationalist cause of regaining lost territory, it was noticeable that by the mid-1990s the PLA's influence over the direction of China's foreign policy was rising. This rising influence, and its subsequent fall, can also be witnessed in the next two case studies.

The South China Sea dispute

China claims sovereignty over much of the South China Sea, including the collection of reefs and islets known as the Spratly Islands that sit above reputably large oil and gas reserves. The Chinese claim is based on historic grounds, with the act of discovery said to have taken place during the Han Dynasty in the second century and with administrative duties functioning at the beginning of the Tang Dynasty in the eighth century. Beijing, throughout the 1990s, has sought to bolster its claim. In 1992 it adopted a Law on the Territorial Waters and their Contiguous Areas and at the 1995 ASEAN Annual Meeting in Brunei, Chinese Foreign Minister Qian Qichen agreed to defend China's sovereignty claims in accordance with the 1982 UN Convention on the Law of the Sea.

In addition to the Chinese claim, a number of ASEAN members also lay claim to parts of the South China Sea. Vietnam claims considerable areas of the South China Sea on historic grounds, while for the Philippines, geographical proximity is used to justify its smaller claim. The Malaysian claim is based on a number of reefs falling within its continental shelf, while the claim from Brunei is based on its Exclusive Economic Zone, which became active with the ratification of the 1982 International Law of the Sea on 16 November 1994. All participants, with the exception of Brunei, have sought to strengthen their cause by stationing troops on some of the reefs. In addition, Indonesia has also expressed concern that China has claimed part of its Natuna gas field (Austin, 1998; Sheng, 1995). China's actions throughout the late 1980s and 1990s have provided tangible evidence of its irredentist ambitions. In addition to seizing a number of reefs and building structures on them, including an airfield on Woody Island in the Paracels, the Chinese have also granted concessions for energy corporations to survey and drill for oil.

These actions have strengthened the China threat hypothesis, led to increased regional uncertainty about Chinese ambitions in Southeast Asia and ultimately have hindered China's ability to secure stable relations to support its economic growth. Michael Leifer (1997: 161) captures the dilemma of China's two policy goals – stable relations for economic growth and regaining of lost territory – when he writes:

> The Spratly Islands ha[ve] highlighted the problem of interdependence for China in its dealings with the states of Southeast Asia. It turns on how Beijing seeks to reconcile conflicting priorities of irredentist goals and good regional relations. In the case of the Spratly Islands, an untrammelled pursuit of irredentist ambition could run counter to the promotion of economic interests.

This duality in China's foreign policy can be clearly witnessed in the 1990s where China has engaged with the ASEAN members in a number of regional fora and entered into bilateral codes of conduct, only then to continue expanding the structures it had erected in the Spratlys. Thus while ASEAN had been successful in gaining a Chinese pledge not to resolve the South China Sea dispute through the use of force, and had also persuaded Beijing to discuss the dispute in the ARF, the 1990s ended with the discovery of Chinese construction work on the aptly named Mischief Reef.

The construction work at Mischief Reef, which was discovered in November 1998 and was finished in early 1999, reveals why China's dual policy objectives create the impression that while China talks of cooperation, its actions suggest that such cooperation is only achievable so long as China's territorial aspirations are not hindered. The Chinese claim that the construction work on Mischief Reef was carried out to repair the shelters they had established there in 1995 for their fishermen. A closer inspection, however, revealed that China was expanding the structure and appeared to be adapting the Reef for military use. The Philippines, which also claims the Reef, noted that the new concrete structures appeared to be garrisons with provisions for a helipad, gun embankments and berths for ships. The presence of Chinese warships around the Reef, meanwhile, violated the code of conduct Beijing had signed with Manila after an earlier Mischief Reef incident in 1995.

The establishment of a new military facility in the Spratly Islands clearly places doubts over the professed Chinese desire not to use force to resolve the dispute, while the presence of Chinese warships damages the credibility of China's willingness to adhere to confidence-building measures. Indeed, the Mischief Reef incident in late 1998 is one of many involving Chinese breaches of the code established with the Philippines. In January 1996 there was a minor skirmish involving Chinese and Philippine warships and between March and May of the same year the facilities on Mischief Reef were upgraded. In April 1997, tensions rose over the presence of Chinese warships near Mischief Reef, the establishment of structures on another reef, and the interception by the Philippine Navy of two Chinese vessels near Scarborough Shoal. It has also been reported that China destroyed foundations for what appeared to be a Philippine military structure on Scarborough Shoal in 1999 (*The Straits Times*, 2000).

The Philippines' response to the Chinese construction work on Mischief Reef reveals the sense of disquiet the ASEAN members feel about China's irredentist ambitions. It also reveals that not only does China's objective of regaining lost territory cause a worsening of regional relationships, it also encourages a more robust US military presence that is not conducive to China's great power aspirations. In October 1998, the Philippines agreed to the resumption of joint military exercises with the US for this first time since 1991. China's actions also led Philippine Foreign Minister, Domingo Siazon, to claim that the US would come to the aid of the Philippines if China attacked the country over the dispute in the South China Sea, and he warned of a proliferation of nuclear states in East Asia if the US wavered in its defence commitments. The Philippines also sought multilateral support via the United Nations, APEC and the Asia–Europe Meeting. The general disquiet over China's actions in the Spratly Islands also led Singapore and Australia to reaffirm the importance of a US presence in the region.

It would appear that, at least in the case of the Spratly Islands, Chinese foreign policy is more influenced by the potential gains to be achieved by asserting its claims in the South China Sea than by cultivating better relations with ASEAN members for economic considerations. The implication, as Ian James Storey (1999: 101) notes, is that the 'policy formulated by the Chinese leadership is influenced by senior generals within the PLA'. The influence of the PLA can also be seen in Rosemary Foot's (1998: 437) suggestion that the reason why the Inter-Sessional Support Group of the ARF was not very productive in March 1997 lay with the Chinese participants who felt it was necessary to be deliberately intransigent on home soil in the presence of PLA officials.

While the expansion of facilities on Mischief Reef does indicate a PLA influence over Chinese policy in the South China Sea, it would be misleading to suggest, however, that maintaining stability in the region was of less importance to Beijing. China has become an active participant in the ARF and the Indonesian-sponsored Workshops on the South China Sea. The Chinese leadership regularly reiterates its desire to settle the dispute peacefully and insist that China has no hegemonic ambitions. China has also engaged in dialogue with the ASEAN members in order to lessen fear of the 'China threat'. This dialogue includes negotiations over the establishment of an ASEAN–China code of conduct for the South China Sea. It is also worth noting that not only are the ASEAN claimants also establishing structures on the reefs and islets in the South China Sea, but they have been doing this for longer than the Chinese.

Therefore, while China's actions do indicate that Chinese foreign policy in the South China Sea is influenced by the PLA, it would be wrong to consider that China places defence of its claims in the Spratlys over good regional relations. However, while this may be true of the Spratlys and the Diaoyu/Senkaku Islands, Taiwan represents a different proposition since here China's sovereignty is almost universally recognised. Mel Gurtov and Byong-Moo Hwang (1998: 278) note that one of the reasons why China acted so provocatively towards Taiwan during the Taiwanese presidential elections in March 1996 was because 'the PLA wanted to send home the message to China's internationalists that *sacred national interests should never be sacrificed to economic interdependence*' (original emphasis).

Taiwan

Beijing regards Taiwan as a rebel province of China and one that will eventually reunite with the mainland. Indeed, with the return of Hong Kong in 1997 and Macau in 1999, reunification with Taiwan remains the final piece in ending the century of shame. The status of Taiwan as a province of China is known as the 'One China' policy, and thus Beijing treats the Taiwan problem as an internal matter. If Taipei should declare Taiwan to be a separate sovereign state, then this would be treated as an act of succession by Beijing, and the CCP have warned that a declaration of independence would be met by force.

Since 1979, China has followed Deng Xiaoping's policy of peaceful methods supported by military pressure in its dealings with Taiwan. With the need to reduce international tensions so that China's economy can develop, Beijing has pursued a non-confrontational approach towards Taipei known as 'peaceful inducement'. This policy has encouraged Taiwanese investment in China (now worth more than US$25 billion), has increased contacts between the island and the mainland and has helped lessen historical animosity. This is a policy also informed by a military logic as China lacks the wherewithal to subjugate Taiwan by force and is deterred further by the possibility of an American military response (O'Hanlon, 2000).

By the early 1990s, tension across the Taiwan Straits had dissipated and in 1995 Jiang Zemin called for equal bilateral consultations (implying that Taiwan was not being treated as a renegade Chinese province), including a summit, and spoke of Chinese not fighting Chinese. With greater economic and cultural exchange, Beijing reasoned that over time the status quo would sway in its favour. However, when Taiwan's President, Lee Teng-hui, visited the US in June 1995 and raised Taiwan's international profile, this was perceived in Beijing as the beginning of a process leading towards independence. Indeed, in 1999 Lee was referring to Chinese–Taiwanese relations as 'state-to-state'.

The granting of a visa by the US for Lee's 1995 visit undermined the credibility of Foreign Minister Qian Qichen, who had told the Politburo that US Secretary of State Warren Christopher had assured him a visa would not be granted. According to David Shambaugh (1996: 190), Qian and Jiang Zemin 'were both forced to make self-criticisms to the Central Military Commission'. Lee's visit was certainly not considered part of the peaceful inducement plan, and indeed it was thought that the time was right for military pressure. The 'carrot' approach favoured by the Foreign Ministry was replaced by the 'stick' approach advocated by the PLA.

The 'stick' approach was not intended to retake Taiwan by force but rather to avert a war with Taipei. The logic runs like this: (1) China would have to wage war against Taiwan if the latter declared independence, so (2) military threats would reduce the likelihood of a declaration of independence, and so (3) military threats would make a war less likely. The

Chinese embarked upon a series of military exercises near Taiwan which culminated in a highly provocative missile exercise during the March 1996 Taiwanese presidential election.

The use of military pressure in 1996 revealed the growth of influence the PLA had achieved in the direction of China's foreign policy. This influence was manifest with an increased military presence in both the Central Military Commission (CMC) and at the 14th National Party Congress. In 1992, three CMC members – Liu Huaqing, Zhang Zhen and Chi Haotian – wrote a protest letter to the CCP Central Commission regarding French and US arms sales to Taiwan. In 1993, a draft petition was signed by eight generals, demanding an apology from the United States when the US Navy stopped and boarded a Chinese freighter (the *Yinhe*) on suspicion of carrying ingredients for chemical weapons to Iran. In 1994, during the 8th National People's Congress, the PLA delegation was critical of the Foreign Ministry's policy towards the US and Japan, and Qian Qichen's resignation is also thought to have been sought.

Ellis Joffe (1997: 58) notes six factors that explain the rise in the PLA's influence. First, the lack of personal authority that Jiang Zemin held within the PLA compared to Mao and Deng, who both had revolutionary records of achievements and commanded long-standing loyalties from the military. Second, in addition to having the CMC as a vehicle of influence, the PLA since 1986 has also participated in the FALSG. The participation of Liu Huaqing and expected participation of Zhang Zhen in the Politburo Standing Committee provided the PLA with direct access to foreign policy decision making. Third, the military sees it as its responsibility to harness Chinese nationalism, and thus has sought to increase its influence over the direction of China's policy towards lost territories. Fourth, keeping Taiwan on the agenda and at a high level of tension has ensured that the PLA continues to receive a large military budget. Fifth, the change in military strategy away from territorial defence to forward projection provides the PLA with good reason to influence the direction of a foreign policy that could see the PLA deploying forces outside China. Finally, the extra-budgetary earnings of the PLA through arms sales ensures that the PLA has an interest in influencing the state of China's relations with other countries.

These factors notwithstanding, since Deng's death in February 1997, Jiang has consolidated his position in power, and in so doing the influence of the PLA has lessened. In 1998 Jiang ordered the PLA to withdraw from managing companies in non-defence-related industries, and he also revived the post of CMC Secretary-General and appointed a loyal supporter – Fu Quanyou. Jiang has also strengthened his position in foreign affairs by replacing Premier Li Peng with Zhu Rongji in March 1998. According to David Bachman (Downs and Saunders, 1998–99: 141), the restraint that China has shown towards Japan and the US over the Diaoyu Islands and Taiwan might reflect Jiang's growing control over the direction of China's foreign policy

This decline in PLA influence can be discerned in China's actions during, and in response to, the Taiwanese presidential election in March 2000. As had been the case in the 1996 election, Beijing sought to intimidate the electorate so that the pro-independence party – the Democratic Progressive Party (DPP) – led by Chen Shui-bian would not be victorious. In 1996 the intimidation had taken the form of military exercises; in 2000 it came in the form of a government white paper that stated that if Taiwan failed to engage in reunification talks, then China would resort to 'drastic measures' that included the use of force. Previously, China's threat to use force was tied to a Taiwanese declaration of independence, and while no deadline was set for reunification talks to begin, this was clearly an extension of the threat of war.

Beijing's intimidation failed as the Taiwanese electorate voted for Chen Shui-bian's DPP, bringing an end to fifty years of Kuomintang rule. The immediate response from Beijing was to lessen tension by saying that reunification could take twenty years, and although the DPP's Vice-President, Annette Lu, has infuriated Beijing with her pro-independence remarks, there is little sign that China intends to use military force to resolve the Taiwanese issue. This is particularly revealing with regard to the decline in the PLA's influence, because, in the aftermath of the 1999 NATO bombing of the Chinese embassy in Belgrade, Jiang and Zhu Rongji were reportedly under pressure from the military to be more assertive in international affairs. This is not to state that the use of force is not an option for Beijing; it clearly is, and if Taiwan shows signs of declaring independence, force is likely – Jiang will not want to be remembered as the leader who lost Taiwan. Rather, it is to state that at a time when mollifying the PLA has been evident, the CCP elite are adopting a conciliatory approach to managing Taiwanese relations with a pro-independence President.

Conclusion

At the beginning of a new century there are grounds for optimism regarding the prospects of stability in East Asia. The holding of the first North–South Korean summit since the end of the Korean War in June 2000 is perhaps the most tangible sign. The introduction to this chapter, though, highlighted the difficulties that have beset East Asia, and while these continue to exist, tension will be evident. It is the emerging Sino-Japanese relationship that will determine the region's stability.

One of the most encouraging signs for stability is that the PLA's influence over the direction of China's foreign policy appears to have declined since the mid-1990s. This, while not guaranteeing, nevertheless encourages the view that China will emerge as a responsible great power in the region. In addition, David Shambaugh (1996: 187) makes reference to China's tribute system to support the view that China can be seen as a benign power:

> Beijing . . . seeks to redress the Asian regional subsystem balance of power. History does not suggest that China seeks to conquer or absorb other countries in the region (except Taiwan and claimed territories in the East and South China Seas), but rather to place itself at the top of a new hierarchical pyramid of power in the region – a kind of new 'tribute system' whereby patronage and protection is dispensed to other countries in return for their recognition of China's superiority and sensitivities. International relations scholars recognize this as a classic benevolent hegemonic system.

Whether a benign China will emerge will, in part, be dependent upon the direction of Japanese foreign policy in the twenty-first century. While Japan's post-1945 reactive foreign policy suggests that Japan will respond to developments, rather than establish agendas for great power interactions, there are signs that Japan is seeking to reduce its reliance on the US. This can most clearly be seen with the launching of a five-year review of Japan's constitution, and most especially the prospects of changing Article 9. However, some caution is required because at the end of the 1980s there was much talk of Japan taking a line more independent of the US. These are therefore nascent and tentative steps by Japan, and whether they cause a worsening of Sino-Japanese relations will depend on whether they spark concerns of rising Japanese militarism in Beijing, and thus increase PLA influence over Chinese foreign policy.

Further reading

There has been a plethora of books written on the Asia-Pacific region during the last decade covering the key foreign policy issues of security and economic integration. Two useful volumes for placing current issues in their political context are McDougall (1997) and Yahuda (1996). The edited volumes of Ball (1996) and Yu (1997) highlight the key issues affecting the region, as does Alagappa (1998), which is one of the best books presently available. For books specifically on Japanese foreign policy the reader should consult Edström (1999), Fukushima (1999) and Hook et al. (2001). Chinese foreign policy is covered in great detail in Robinson and Shambaugh (eds) (1995) while Roy (1998) provides a very accessible read. An enormous number of articles has been published on the region and readers should consult the journals *International Security*, *Security Dialogue* and *Survival*. Region-specific journals include: *Asian Survey*, *Contemporary Southeast Asia*, *Pacific Affairs* and *Pacifica Review*.

References

Acharya, A. (1999) 'A Concert of Asia?', *Survival*, **41**(3), 84–101.

Ahn, C.S. (1998) 'Interministry Coordination in Japan's Foreign Policy Making', *Pacific Affairs*, **71**(1), 41–60.

Alagappa, M. (1998) *Asian Security Practice: Material and Ideational Influences*. Stanford, CA: Stanford University Press.

Allison, G.T. (1971) *Essence of Decision. Explaining the Cuban Missile Crisis*. Boston, MA: Little Brown.

Austin, G. (1998) *China's Ocean Frontier. International Law, Military Force and National Development*. St Leonards: Allen & Unwin.

Ball, D. (ed.) (1996) *The Transformation of Security in the Asia-Pacific Region*. London: Frank Cass.

Bessho, K. (1999) 'Identities and Security in East Asia', *Adelphi Paper*, **325**. London: International Institute for Strategic Studies.

Calder, K.E. (1997) 'The Institutions of Japanese Foreign Policy', in Grant, R.L. (ed.), *The Process of Japanese Foreign Policy: Focus on Asia*. London: The Royal Institute of International Affairs.

Carpenter, T.G. (1998) 'Managing a Great Power Relationship: the United States, China and East Asian Security', *The Journal of Strategic Studies*, **21**(1), 1–20.

Central Intelligence Agency (2000) *The World Factbook, 2000*. <http://www.odci.gov/cia/publications/factbook/>.

Chin, K.W. (1997) 'Japan as a Great Power in Asia', in Chan, H.C. (ed.), *The New Asia-Pacific Order*. Singapore: Institute of Southeast Asian Studies.

Dibb, P., Hale, D.D. and Prince, P. (1999) 'Asia's Insecurity', *Survival*, **41**(3), 5–20.

Downs, E.S. and Saunders, P.C. (1998–99) 'Legitimacy and the Limits of Nationalism', *International Security*, **23**(3), 114–46.

Edström, B. (1999) *Japan's Evolving Foreign Policy Doctrine: from Yoshida to Miyazawa*. Basingstoke: Macmillan.

Foot, R. (1998) 'China in the ASEAN Regional Forum: Organizational Processes and Domestic Modes of Thought', *Asian Survey*, 38(5), 425–40.

Fukushima, A. (1999) *Japanese Foreign Policy. The Emerging Logic of Multilateralism*. Basingstoke: Macmillan.

Funabashi, Y. (2000–1) 'Japan's Moment of Truth', *Survival*, 42(4), 73–84.

Gittings, J. (2000) 'Zhu Targets Corruption and Cults in China', *The Guardian* (6 March).

Goodman, D.S.G. (1997) 'How Open is Chinese Society?', in Goodman, D.S.G. and Segal, G. (eds), *China Rising: Nationalism and Interdependence*. London: Routledge, 27–52.

Gurtov, M. and Hwang, B.-M. (1998) *China's Security. The New Roles of the Military*. Boulder CO: Lynne Rienner.

Hook, G.D., Gilson, J., Hughes, C. and Dobson, H. (2001) *Japan's International Relations. Politics, Economics and Security*. London: Routledge.

Hughes, C.W. (1999) *Japan's Economic Power and Security: Japan and North Korea*. London: Routledge.

Joffe, E. (1997) 'How Much Does the PLA Make Foreign Policy?', in Goodman, D.S.G. and Segal, G. (eds), *China Rising: Nationalism and Interdependence*. London: Routledge, 53–70.

Korhonen, P. (1998) *Japan and Asia Pacific Integration: Pacific Romances 1968–1996*. London: Routledge.

Lawrence, S.V. (1999) 'Jiang's Two Faces', *Far Eastern Economic Review* (2 December), 16–17.

Leifer, M. (1996) 'The ASEAN Regional Forum', *Adelphi Paper*, 302, London: International Institute for Strategic Studies.

Leifer, M. (1997) 'China in Southeast Asia: Interdependence and Accommodation', in Goodman, D.S.G. and Segal, G. (eds), *China Rising: Nationalism and Interdependence*. London: Routledge, 156–71.

McBeth, J. (2000) 'Courting Danger', *Far Eastern Economic Review* (9 March), 18–19.

McDougall, D. (1997) *The International Politics of the New Asia Pacific*. Boulder, CO: Lynne Rienner.

O'Hanlon, M. (2000) 'Why China Cannot Conquer Taiwan', *International Security*, 25(2), 51–86.

Robinson, T.W. and Shambaugh, D. (eds) (1995) *Chinese Foreign Policy. Theory and Practice*. Oxford: Oxford University Press.

Roy, D. (1998) *China's Foreign Relations*. London: Macmillan.

Segal, G. (1997) 'Enlightening China', in Goodman, D.S.G. and Segal, G. (eds), *China Rising: Nationalism and Interdependence*. London: Routledge, 172–91.

Shambaugh, D. (1996) 'Containment or Engagement of China? Calculating Beijing's Responses', *International Security*, 21(2), 180–209.

Sheng, L. (1995) 'Beijing and the Spratlys', *Issues and Studies*, 31(7), 18–45.

Shibusawa, M. (1997) 'Japan's Historical Legacies: Implications for its Relations with Asia', in Grant, R.L. (ed.), *The Process of Japanese Foreign Policy: Focus on Asia*. London: The Royal Institute of International Affairs, 25–36.

Soeya, Y. (1998) 'Japan: Normative Constraints Versus Structural Imperatives', in Alagappa, M. (ed.), *Asian Security Practice: Material and Ideational Influences*. Stanford, CA: Stanford University Press, 198–233.

Storey, I.J. (1999) 'Creeping Assertiveness: China, the Philippines and the South China Sea Dispute', *Contemporary Southeast Asia*, **21**(1), 95–118.

Swaine, M.D. (1997) 'The PLA and Chinese National Security Policy: Leaderships, Structures, Processes', in Shambaugh, D. and Yang, R.H. (eds), *China's Military in Transition*. Oxford: Clarendon Press, 96–129.

The Straits Times (2000) 'Beijing Stops Manila from Building Structures on Disputed Shoal' (25 April).

United Nations Conference on Trade and Development (UNCTAD) (1993) *Trade and Development Report, 1993*. New York: United Nations.

World Bank (1993) *The East Asian Miracle: Economic Growth and Public Policy*. New York: Oxford University Press.

Yahuda, M. (1996) *The International Politics of the Asia-Pacific Region*. London: Routledge.

Yu, G.T. (ed.) (1997) *Asia's New World Order*. Basingstoke: Macmillan.

The world wide web

The Chinese Foreign Ministry can be accessed at: <http://www.fmprc.gov.cn/chn/index.html>. For the Chinese military, see <http://www.fmprc.gov.cn/chn/index.html>. The Japanese Foreign Ministry can be accessed at: <http://www.mofa.go.jp/>. The official site for ASEAN is <http:www.aseansec.org/>. The official site for APEC is <http://www.apecsec.org.sg/>. For keeping abreast of current events and for finding additional material from Asian web sites, see <http://www/asiaobserver.com/>.

Part Three
Conclusion

11 | The Challenge of Foreign Policy

Mark Webber

This chapter returns to some of the analyses of Part One using examples drawn from the case-study chapters of Part Two. It thus highlights certain issues relating to the book's central theme of transformation. In so doing it examines the nature and extent of change in the international system and relates this to the manner in which foreign policy has been shaped and altered. In addition, the chapter also touches upon some further analytical matters in the study of foreign policy – the importance of comparison and the continuing relevance of foreign policy analysis as an area of study.

Continuity and change in the foundations of foreign policy

We began our investigation of foreign policy in this volume by pointing out and describing the manner in which world politics has been transformed in recent decades and, in particular, following the demise of the Cold War from the late 1980s. These changes have meant that the context and the conduct of foreign policy have been fundamentally altered, something of which the case-study chapters have provided ample illustration. In this, the concluding chapter, we will revisit this central theme and take stock of just how sweeping and consequential this process of change has been.

In order to do this, it is perhaps useful to begin by reminding ourselves of some of the fundamental features of the process of transformation. In Chapter 2 it was suggested that the conduct of foreign policy has been changed by far-reaching alterations in three 'contexts' of the foreign policy arena: the international, the governmental and the domestic. This, in turn, has meant that the actors, issues and interests of foreign policy have also been profoundly affected. There has been a broadening of those who participate in influencing foreign policy making, a shift in the range and intensity of issues on the foreign policy agenda, and increasing ambiguities surrounding the notion of a national interest to guide foreign policy. The traditional view of foreign policy outlined in Chapter 1, with its emphasis on national security, the pursuit of clear national interests and foreign policies made and conducted by narrow elites within a system of states circumscribed by clear rules of engagement, has thus been thoroughly revised.

The case-study chapters have explored these themes and considered in some detail the manner in which the foreign policies of a number of states have been shaped by change. However, while it is clear that the foreign policies of these states have altered in fundamental ways (and this would be true of most other states too), it is important to bear in mind that the effects of the transformed world have been uneven. No state has been left untouched by the end of the Cold War and the accelerating processes of globalisation and international organisation (see Chapter 1), but the benefits and challenges which these processes have bestowed have differed markedly. One way to understand this differentiation is to consider typical foreign policy preoccupations in terms of regional settings much broader than those employed in the case studies. This type of conceptualisation is not unique to the post-Cold War period; attempts have long been made to categorise broad regions of the world and accord to them different characteristics. During the Cold War, for instance, the political divisions of the West, the communist countries and the Third World were familiar and more sophisticated formulations also existed which attempted to embrace global dynamics of an economic and social nature (Keohane and Nye, 1977). More recent formulations have, however, adopted new categories which reflect the scale and reach of global change. This was a notion we encountered in Chapter 3, for instance, when talking about the 'two worlds' or the core and periphery of international politics (Goldgeier and McFaul, 1992). Similarly, Singer and Wildavsky (1993) have posited a picture of 'zones of peace' and 'zones of turmoil'. In the former, foreign policy may be conceived as fixated less with preparation for and expectation of war and more with managing open and interdependent economies and societies, with confronting a multiplicity of transnational actors and with a strong international society. This description rings true certainly for foreign policies in much of Europe, North America and Japan. Conversely, 'zones of turmoil' are characterised by foreign policies fixated with traditional power politics, competitive local dynamics and the realistic threat of resort to force. This sums up well much of Africa, the Middle East and parts of the former Soviet Union.

Of course, a formulation on such a grandiose scale cannot be entirely accurate in its depiction of global dynamics, or fully capture the complexities of foreign policies which flow from them. There exist pockets of conflict within zones of peace (the former Yugoslavia) and areas of calm and cooperation within zones of turmoil (the states of the Association of South East Asian Nations in East Asia). The status of certain important states is also ambiguous – are China and Russia, for instance, part of a zone of peace or a zone of turmoil? Equally, the notion of two types of zone may convey some of the dynamics within the zones concerned, but equally important are the ways in which these zones (and states within them) relate to one another. To take two examples: Nigeria may occupy a zone of turmoil but some of its major foreign policy preoccupations concern its relations with Europe and the United States (US), and global financial institutions. The US, similarly, the key state within the Euro-Atlantic zone of peace, is nonetheless a global actor and its foreign policy is engaged continuously with zones of turmoil. Thus, as Buzan and Little (2000: 354) have suggested, 'the claim for two parallel modes of international relations seems plausible, even though there is significant overlap between them'.

Alongside the differential manner of change it is also worth noting another important qualification to the picture of transformation. In Chapter 1 it was suggested that change in world politics is often the product of long-term historical development, and to this one might add the point that the challenge of change thrown up by transformation is not unique to the period from the late twentieth century. If one is to take 1989 as a historical watershed, one should be aware that the years 1919 and 1945 arguably represented watersheds of similar importance (Roberts, 1991: 510). The evidence of the case studies also suggests that for many states particular circumstances are as important to their foreign policies as general patterns of global change. Some of these are coincident in time and, in some senses, linked with recent global transformation (as in the case of the end of apartheid in South Africa and the end of communism in Russia and Ukraine) but others are not (the American involvement in Vietnam, the 1979 revolution in Iran, the removal of the military from power in Brazil in the mid-1980s, etc.). Indeed, whether derived from local, regional or global conditions, coping with change is a perennial feature of foreign policy (Boyd and Hopple, 1987; Smith, 1981).

These important qualifications are worth mentioning. However, it has been argued throughout this text that something qualitatively different has attended the processes of change that have been apparent in the 1980s, 1990s and beyond. Foreign policy in many (arguably most) cases has not simply been about adaptation within narrow, perhaps predictable, limits, but adjustment in the face of change that has been sometimes sudden (the end of the Cold War), relentless (accelerating globalisation) and usually disorienting and uncomfortable. Indeed, the scale of change has been truly momentous; of such a profundity that, for some, it heralds 'one of the most decisive periods in human history – the first truly global age' (Booth, 1998: 353), or what Buzan and Little (2000: 357) have labelled 'a *sectoral transformation*: a shift from military-political to economic processes as the *dominant* (i.e. system defining) form of interaction' (original emphases). This does not yet mean a complete overturning of world politics but, for Buzan and Little, it does nonetheless raise the possibility of a revolutionary shift – from the modern to a 'post-modern' world order.

In this sense transformation is ongoing and unfinished, and a decade or so on from the end of the Cold War there continues to be much speculation as to the nature of the unfolding international order (Halliday, 2001). On the one hand, there are those who, without denying the overarching context of transformation, point to certain enduring features of the international system. It is, for instance, a system that is still characterised by the absence of world government and thus anarchy (albeit in a modified form in some regions owing to the development of international governance). It is a system also in which the sovereign state is still the principal focus and actor of international politics (even if sovereignty has been modified, state autonomy has been undermined and other actors have gained ground). It is, finally, a system which is underpinned by market capitalism. This economic order had been in the ascendant during the Cold War and has gained significant ground with the end of Soviet communism and the onset of market reforms in China from the 1980s onwards. Although some (Wallerstein, 1993) have imagined its passing, capitalism on a global scale will almost inevitably prevail (Buzan and Little, 2000: 364).

In light of these continuities, there is a temptation to argue that many traditional concerns of foreign policy will endure. Those writing in a realist vein, for instance, have argued that the uncertainties of international politics will not remove, and may indeed exacerbate, age-old concerns with the 'national interest', inter-state competition and expectation of war. The development of this trend, it is argued, will differ by region but, overall, the impact will be a world characterised by deepening competition and latent violence between states, including the great powers (Waltz, 1993). A somewhat more extreme version of this line of thought argues that the new issue agenda of international politics is equally alarming. Indeed, a whole school of thought has arisen, dubbed 'the new pessimism' (Maynes, 1995), that focuses upon issues of famine, AIDS, civil war, unchecked population growth, economic dislocation and inevitable great power competition to suggest that all states (even the seemingly better-off states in the West) can do little to curtail impending disaster. This line of thinking may be overstating the case. However, recent examples abound of how states (and their foreign policies) have appeared impotent or unprepared in the face of change, be this global movements of capital (the example given at the outset of Chapter 1), global alterations to the environment or the spate of civil wars that have blighted international politics in the 1990s and 2000s.

An alternative view, by contrast, highlights the more positive elements of transformation set in train by the end of the Cold War: the ongoing development of international organisation, greater prospects for regional cooperation and, perhaps most important of all, the end of the threat of global nuclear war (Freedman, 1998; Lake and Morgan, 1997b; Ruggie, 1992). What this means is that the end of the Cold War has altered foreign policy expectations. A predisposition towards militarisation, foreign policies of war preparation (or avoidance) and calculations based on the bloc politics of a world literally divided into two hostile camps has given way to a greater flexibility. This has not made the predicaments of foreign policy any less demanding – new challenges have proven to be as exacting as the old. However, what this line of thought argues is that the problem-solving potential of foreign policy has increased owing to the opening up of new avenues of dialogue, cooperation and interchange, in turn, buttressed by the stabilising effects of growing economic interdependence and a global 'wave' of democratisation (Ikenberry, 1996; Russett, 1993). As suggested above, there has, of course, been regional variation and the international politics of parts of the Middle East, Africa and the former Soviet Union still exhibit an agenda partly born of anxiety and fear. However, the general picture is an encouraging one such that for some the pessimists' picture of a post-Cold War world of irredeemable chaos can largely be dismissed as a 'myth' (Ikenberry, 1996).

One further matter for consideration concerns the configuration of power relations in world politics. At one level, our various case studies have highlighted this type of issue, in that a number of the regions of our concern tend to be dominated by a single power, be this Russia in the former Soviet Union (FSU), China in East Asia, the US in the Americas or South Africa in southern Africa. Within these settings, regional dominance is both a foreign policy objective of the state concerned and a preoccupation of the foreign policies of that state's neighbours. Only in the case of the Americas, however, does this dominance have a settled pattern. The positions of Russia, China and South Africa, by contrast, are more open to challenge either because they face potential combinations of regional rivals or because of the disruptive influence of recent domestic transitions.

At the broader international level, the situation appears more clear-cut, given the commonly-held view of American superiority. The fall of the Soviet Union has meant that, in material terms, the US enjoys an unassailable position in international politics. This is a position of no small historical importance. As William Wohlforth (1999: 7) has suggested, 'the United States is the first leading state in modern international history with decisive preponderance in *all* the underlying components of power: economic, military, technological, and geopolitical'. In this sense, Wohlforth continues, the international system is 'unambiguously unipolar'. There are those who would depart from this view, pointing for instance to Russia's possession of nuclear weapons as evidence of an existing rival pole of power (and hence of multipolarity) or of the rise of new powers such as Germany (or a unified Europe) and Japan (Layne, 1993). The evidence of the case studies in this volume, however, would seem to suggest that the US is likely to remain pre-eminent for the foreseeable future (see also Knutsen, 1999: 262). Russia may well possess nuclear weapons and a permanent seat on the UN Security Council, but it holds no other resource of global influence and many indicators suggest it is a power in decline. As for Germany and Japan, their foreign policies in the post-Cold War period have been marked by caution and hesitancy and have certainly not exhibited any conscious steps towards the acquisition of enhanced military capabilities (Germany, ironically, has been criticised by the US for *cutting* its armed forces and thus weakening NATO). These states, moreover, have remained allies, not rivals, of the US (see Chapters 7 and 10).

Talk of these regional and global power relationships needs to be placed in context. It is a preoccupation of traditional analysis of foreign policy to view international relations in terms of power (however defined). In Part One it was argued that this type of analysis, while not 'wrong' as such, offers an incomplete picture of the dynamics of change in world politics ·and a partial guide to the complexities of foreign policy making and implementation. The evidence of the case studies in Part Two, in turn, bears this out. This is not to deny that states still follow the prerogatives of military security, and are often fixated with ideas of status, competition and a national interest (however imperfectly defined). The traditional claim, however, that these prerogatives are fixed and dominant features of the foreign policies of all states is no longer valid (if it ever was). For many (arguably most) states, the issue agenda is now congested, fluid and dominated more by social, economic and political concerns than by military-security ones. It is abundantly clear that the foreign policies of the US, Brazil, Germany and Poland, for instance, while still involved with war and peace issues and matters of high national security, devote most of their energies to matters relating to engagement with international organisations and the management of external economic, social, environmental and other issues. This is arguably stating the obvious given the relatively stable regional environments of these states or the extent of their material resources. However, the statement carries some force also with regard to those states in much less favourable settings. China, South Africa, Nigeria, Ukraine and Israel, all of which reside in either war-prone regions or aside hostile neighbours, conduct foreign policies which are as much to do with the external management of their economies as they are the minimisation of external military threat.

Comparing foreign policies

That contemporary foreign policies have had to deal with a similar, bewildering range of problems and issues does not mean that the foreign policies of all states are the same. The type of generalisation made in the last section (that military issues have declined in importance) is precisely that – a generalisation. The reader should be aware that while generalisation is not impossible, considerable variation exists in foreign policies, be this in terms of the problem or issue confronted, the processes by which policy is made and implemented in response, and the manner in which one evaluates the performance (i.e. the success or failure) of the policy itself (Smith, 1989). Complexity of this sort means that 'grand theories' of foreign policy – 'trying to explain all aspects of foreign policy for all countries at all points in time' (Gerner, 1995: 30) – are difficult both to devise and to apply (see, for instance, the pitfalls of the 'rational actor' model in Chapter 3). One reaction to this type of problem may be to jettison theoretical efforts altogether and simply revert to a case-study approach, concentrating on trying to understand and explain individual foreign policies within single states. This approach is not without its merits, for knowledge of individual, perhaps unfamiliar, cases is always welcome. A fuller picture of foreign policy – even of individual cases – does, however, require comparative context (Smith, 1986: 25–6). What is unique or mundane, significant or inconsequential about a particular state's foreign policy can only be gleaned when set against the foreign policies of others. The declining global importance of Russian foreign policy, for instance, seems that much more obvious and dramatic when compared with the reach and influence of the US. Similarly, when comparing regional powers, common policy challenges and opportunities may be evident. However, in the case of South Africa and Nigeria – two of the regional powers considered in this volume – what is equally obvious are the differences. The fortunes of the former have been on the ascendant both regionally and globally, while the latter has suffered a diminution of status (see Chapter 8).

In fact, the benefits of comparison are many and Michael Hass (cited in Smith, 1989: 187–8) has outlined four of its uses. First, comparison permits a fuller *description* of particular foreign policies. A description of, say, Ukraine's aspirations towards European integration is that much more convincing when set aside similar and widely held aspirations among the majority of former communist states in Eastern Europe. Second, comparison allows one to forward explanations based on relationships of *causation*. Why Ukraine's policy of seeking European Union (EU) membership is likely to fail while that of Poland will probably succeed can be seen in terms of a range of factors that impinge upon both Poland and Ukraine and also upon the existing member states of the EU. A comparison of political, economic and social conditions along with geopolitical position and historical circumstance suggests that Poland is a much more attractive proposition to the EU and that Polish foreign policy has exploited this to the full. Third, and clearly linked, comparison facilitates *prediction*. It could reasonably be assumed that a communist restoration (or less likely, a military coup) in either Poland or Ukraine would result in a reversal of policies geared towards EU membership. It could also be assumed that in these circumstances the EU member states themselves would not be well inclined to either country. Fundamental alterations of domestic regime then create expectations of foreign policy change. Finally, comparison can be used to justify *prescription* or the assertion of a preferred state of affairs. Polish entry into the EU, if it was not simultaneous with that of Hungary and the Czech Republic (or, for that matter, Ukraine), could be used by these states as a means of justifying their own membership. In an analogous case, Polish entry into NATO in 1999 compounded a sense of grievance in Romania and the Baltic states at having been left out and thereby entrenched the objective of membership as a core foreign policy objective.

While comparison is thus useful, how the exercise of comparison itself should be conducted is not always straightforward. There are at least four steps to be taken in this regard (see Table 11.1). The first concerns the choice of the object of comparison. This may, at first sight, appear clear-cut. We are, after all, interested in comparing foreign policy. However, as the case studies in this book have illustrated, the foreign policy of a state is, in fact, an amalgam of foreign *policies*. Before we compare two or more states, we need to specify exactly which policy or policies are being compared. Is it issue-based, that is particular policies relating to, say, trade, arms control, peacekeeping and conflict resolution? Is it geographically-based, that is policies directed at a particular region? Or is the comparison directed towards an examination of over-arching objectives such as the promotion of security, economic welfare and status? The second step relates to the means by which comparison is undertaken. Are we, for instance, interested in comparing 'sets of variables' which serve as the source of foreign policy, be these the distinguishing characteristics of the decision maker, type of political regime (see Chapter 3), national identity (see Chapter 2), geographic location or economic development (adapted from Rosenau, 1980: 128–9)? Or are we interested, rather, in the urgency and immediacy of the foreign policy situation (crisis versus non-crisis decision making, as outlined in Chapter 3) and the types of instrument employed in the process of implementation (see Chapter 4)? The third step is to accommodate change. Given the core theme of this volume – that foreign policy is preoccupied with transformation – one plainly needs to assess the comparative impact of change. How do states respond to change? Is it by falling back on familiar habits of policy making, by engaging in method-ical policy reviews, or by sudden and makeshift adjustments? Do they, in other words, exhibit, styles that are 'habitual', 'deliberative' or 'convul-sive'? (Rosenau, 1972: 161–3). The fourth step, finally, concerns evalu-ation: the comparison of foreign policy performance. What criteria, in other words, can one utilise to judge the effectiveness of foreign policies in comparative terms? Intuitively this would seem to suggest the ability to satisfy a foreign policy goal. Such a standard, while simple, is insufficient. In foreign policy, goals are often unspecified, in contradiction, or unreal-istic and unobtainable. In this light, a somewhat more flexible set of cri-teria has been suggested by Smith (1989: 206). These criteria include the following: *clarity* of purpose, *consistency* in 'the matching of objectives, targets and techniques', *continuity* of perspective in the long term and, notwithstanding this, *adaptability*, an avoidance of rigidity in the face of change.

Table 11.1 Comparing foreign policies

<table>
<tr><th rowspan="2">Foreign policies to be compared</th><th colspan="3">Object of comparison</th><th colspan="3">Means of comparison</th><th rowspan="2">Response to change</th><th rowspan="2">Evaluation of policy</th></tr>
<tr><th>Issue</th><th>Geographic focus</th><th>Objective</th><th>Sets of variables</th><th>Urgency and immediacy</th><th>Instrument</th></tr>
<tr><td>trade</td><td>global</td><td>security</td><td>characteristics of the decision maker</td><td>crisis versus non-crisis</td><td>persuasive diplomacy</td><td>habitual</td><td>clarity</td></tr>
<tr><td>defence</td><td>regional</td><td>welfare</td><td>regime type</td><td></td><td>coercive diplomacy</td><td>deliberative</td><td>consistency</td></tr>
<tr><td>arms control</td><td>sub-regional</td><td>status</td><td>national identity</td><td></td><td>military intervention</td><td>convulsive</td><td>continuity</td></tr>
<tr><td>conflict resolution</td><td></td><td></td><td>geographic location</td><td></td><td></td><td></td><td>adaptability</td></tr>
<tr><td>peacekeeping</td><td></td><td></td><td>economic development</td><td></td><td></td><td></td><td></td></tr>
<tr><td>environment</td><td></td><td></td><td></td><td></td><td></td><td></td><td></td></tr>
<tr><td>migration</td><td></td><td></td><td></td><td></td><td></td><td></td><td></td></tr>
<tr><td>energy</td><td></td><td></td><td></td><td></td><td></td><td></td><td></td></tr>
</table>

Source: Adapted from Rosenau, 1972: 161–3; Rosenau, 1980: 128–9; Holsti, 1992: 82–114; Smith, 1989: 206.

Studying foreign policy

The transformation of world politics has presented states with new challenges in foreign policy. By the same token, the analysis of foreign policy has been tested also. As an academic field, foreign policy analysis (FPA) has, in fact, long been subject to periodic moments of doubt. Steve Smith (1986), writing in the mid-1980s, for instance, suggested that the field was beset by major problems, not the least of which was a misguided search for a general theory of foreign policy and an over-reliance on simplistic notions of national interest as a guide to foreign policy action. In a similar state-of-the-art overview written in the mid-1990s, Margot Light (1994: 100) noted how FPA had been buffeted by changes which seemingly undermined many of its analytical premises. These included the blurred distinction between foreign policy and domestic politics, the increasing constraints placed upon the state by the influence of other international actors, and the proliferation of new issues which rendered impossible a continued focus on 'high politics'. Changes such as these have led to the suggestion that in the face of transformation, FPA is increasingly irrelevant, for its object of analysis, the state, is so circumscribed. Much better, it is argued, to focus on the international system level if we want to explain state behaviour/foreign policy (White, 1999: 38).

Much of the analysis presented in this volume runs counter to a view of FPA as a marginal concern, however. Three issues can be used to illustrate this.

The first relates to the issue of structure – the contention just noted that the imperatives generated by the system determine the manner of action of the units (states) within it. This so-called 'agent-structure' issue is, in fact, a long-running one both within the broad discipline of International Relations (we noted in Chapters 1 and 3 that an emphasis on structure provides the analytical foundation of Neo-Realism) and within the Social Sciences more generally. In some respects, this position has something to commend it. The dictates of the international system do unquestionably lead states to behave in certain ways. However, we have already noted in Chapter 1 that the messages of the international system can be read in quite different ways. While a Neo-Realist would suggest that the international system's anarchic nature predisposes states towards foreign policies based on competition and self-preservation, a Pluralist perspective suggests exactly the opposite, that growing interdependence generates powerful imperatives towards cooperation. While drawing quite different conclusions, both Neo-Realist and Pluralist perspectives do nonetheless agree that the system exercises a determining influence on state behaviour.

More problematic for such structuralist perspectives are 'occasions when the unit [state] . . . does not behave in accordance with the dictates of the system' (White, 1999: 40). Neo-Realists have, for instance, suggested that systemic imperatives after the Cold War would lead Germany and Japan to acquire nuclear weapons. As noted above, however, the foreign policy of neither state has exhibited such a desire and to understand why requires consideration of the domestic and governmental 'contexts' of foreign policy as well as the international one (see Chapter 2).

A second issue concerns the relevance of the state in world politics. It has become almost a truism of International Relations that the state has suffered an irreversible demise of influence and that it has been 'crowded out' by the activities of other actors (Kegley and Wittkopf, 1999: 203–4). Indeed, this volume has been informed, in part, by this perspective. However, as was noted in Chapter 1, the state is still in important respects in rude health. The number of states has noticeably increased over the last two decades and the principles of statehood remain central to the ordering of international life. This is not to ignore the fact that both weak states and powerful non-state actors characterise the international system, nor is it to deny that states are often embattled in the face of external forces over which they have little control. However, many states have been capable of adaptation and accommodation, and this has been reflected in the conduct of their foreign policies. On the one hand, therefore, while it is clear that many weak states (in Africa and Latin America, for instance) have remained weak and some strong states (Russia) have weakened, it is clear also that some strong states (the US, Germany, Japan and China) have remained strong, and some weak states (Taiwan, South Korea and Singapore) have grown stronger (Pierre and Peters, 2000: 163–92).

Finally, we should consider the issue agenda. A proliferation of issues has undoubtedly occurred (see Chapter 2). However, far from undermining foreign policy as an object of analysis, these have, in fact, increased its importance, for as Light (1994: 101) has suggested, these issues 'represent the expanding range of concerns that are relevant to the subject'. The foreign policies of some states may indeed be overwhelmed by 'issue congestion' but the relevance of studying how the issue agenda is handled – what responses (or non-responses) it calls forth – is no less pertinent as a consequence.

Summary and conclusion

The analysis of foreign policy has not been untroubled by the fundamental alterations in its subject matter that have occurred since the late 1980s. This book, however, is informed by an assumption that foreign policy still matters and thus it remains important to analyse it seriously. FPA, despite the criticisms sometimes levelled against it, is not inherently backward-looking or intellectually nostalgic for a simpler age of traditional foreign policy concerns and the untrammelled supremacy of states as actors. While the analysis of this volume has been concerned with the foreign policies of states, our framework acknowledges that states increasingly coexist with other actors in the international system and that the agenda, instruments and possibilities of success in their foreign policies are ever-changing. It is the task of FPA to respond in a creative and flexible manner to these developments. This book, we hope, has made a worthwhile step in this direction.

Further reading

Much of the further reading listed under Chapter 1 is relevant here. In addition, a number of works provide thoughtful treatments of the nature of transformation, both globally and regionally. These are worth consulting for a sophisticated treatment of the long-term processes of change at work in the international system and for drawing out some of the implications of these processes for foreign policy. See in particular, Booth (ed.) (1998), Buzan and Little (2000), Lake and Morgan (eds) (1997a) and *Review of International Studies* (1999).

References

Booth, K. (ed.) (1998) *Statecraft and Security. The Cold War and Beyond.* Cambridge: Cambridge University Press.

Boyd, G. and Hopple, G.W. (eds) (1987) *Political Change and Foreign Policies.* London: Pinter.

Buzan, B. and Little, R. (2000) *International Systems in World History. Remaking the Study of International Relations.* Oxford: Oxford University Press.

Freedman, L. (1998) 'Military Power and Political Influence', *International Affairs*, 74(4), 763–80.

Gerner, D.J. (1995) 'The Evolution of the Study of Foreign Policy', in Neack, L., Hey, J.A.K. and Haney, P.J. (eds), *Foreign Policy Analysis. Continuity and Change in its Second Generation*. Englewood Cliffs, NJ: Prentice-Hall, 17–32.

Goldgeier, J.M. and McFaul, M. (1992) 'A Tale of Two Worlds: Core and Periphery in the Post-Cold War Era', *International Organisation*, 46(2), 467–91.

Halliday, F. (2001) *The World at 2000*. Basingstoke: Palgrave.

Holsti, K. (1992) *International Politics. A Framework for Analysis* (6th edition). London: Prentice Hall.

Ikenberry, G.J. (1996) 'The Myth of Post-Cold War Chaos', *Foreign Affairs*, 75(3) 79–91.

Kegley, Jr., C.W. and Wittkopf, E.R. (1999) *World Politics. Trend and Transformation* (7th edition). Basingstoke: Macmillan Press.

Keohane, R.O. and Nye, J.S. (1977) *Power and Interdependence. World Politics in Transition*. Boston, MA, and Toronto: Little Brown.

Knutsen, T.L. (1999) *The Rise and Fall of World Orders*. Manchester and New York: Manchester University Press.

Lake, D.A. and Morgan, P.M. (eds) (1997a) *Regional Orders. Building Security in a New World*. University Park, PA: Pennsylvania State University Press.

Lake, D.A. and Morgan, P.M. (1997b) 'The New Regionalism in Security Affairs', in Lake, D.A. and Morgan, P.M. (eds), *Regional Orders. Building Security in a New World*. University Park, PA: Pennsylvania State University Press, 20–44.

Layne, C. (1993) 'The Unipolar Illusion. Why New Great Powers Will Rise', *International Security*, 17(4), 5–51.

Light, M. (1994) 'Foreign Policy Analysis', in Groom, A.J.R. and Light, M. (eds), *Contemporary International Relations. A Guide to Theory*. London: Pinter, 92–108.

Maynes, C.W. (1995) 'The New Pessimism', *Foreign Policy*, 100, 33–49.

Pierre, J. and Peters, B.G. (2000) *Governance, Politics and the State*. Basingstoke: Macmillan Press.

Review of International Studies (1999) Special issue, 'The Interregnum: Controversies in World Politics 1989–1999', 25.

Roberts, A. (1991) 'A New Age in International Relations?', *International Affairs*, 67(3), 509–25.

Rosenau, J.N. (1972) 'The External Environment as a Variable in Foreign Policy Analysis', in Rosenau, J.N., Davis, V. and East, M.A. (eds), *The Analysis of International Politics*. New York: Free Press, 145–65.

Rosenau, J.N. (1980) *The Scientific Study of Foreign Policy* (revised edition). London: Pinter.

Ruggie, J.G. (1992) 'Multilateralism: the Anatomy of an Institution', *International Organisation*, 46(3), 561–98.

Russett, B.M. (1993) *Grasping the Democratic Peace*. Princeton, NJ: Princeton University Press.

Singer, M. and Wildavsky, A. (1993) *The Real World Order: Zones of Peace and Zones of Turmoil*. Chatham, NJ: Chatham House.

Smith, M. (1989) 'Comparing Foreign Policy Systems: Problems, Processes and Performance', in Clarke, M. and White, B. (eds), *Understanding Foreign Policy. The Foreign Policy Systems Approach*. Aldershot: Edward Elgar, 185–215.

Smith, S.M. (1981) *Foreign Policy Adaptation*. New York: Nichols Publishing.

Smith, S. (1986) 'Theories of Foreign Policy: an Historical Overview', *Review of International Studies*, **12**(1), 13–29.

Wallerstein, I. (1993) 'The World-System after the Cold War', *Journal of Peace Research*, **30**(1), 1–6.

Waltz, K. (1993) 'The Emerging Structure of International Politics', *International Security*, **18**(2), 44–79.

White, B. (1999) 'The European Challenge to Foreign Policy Analysis', *European Journal of International Relations*, **5**(1), 7–66.

Wohlforth, W. (1999) 'The Stability of a Unipolar World', *International Security*, **24**(1), 5–41.

Glossary

Actors used in two senses in this volume. Actors refer, first, to identifiable participants in international affairs be these states (and their national governments) or various 'non-state' actors such as international organisations (whose members are states), non-governmental organisations, multinational corporations, transnational political protest movements and so on. The range of actors in this sense has broadened considerably in the period since at least the 1970s. Second, actors (or 'agents') refer to those individuals and groups involved in the making and implementation of foreign policy (see Chapters 2, 3 and 4).

Cold War the inter-bloc rivalry between the Soviet-led communist camp and the Western camp. This had economic, ideological and, most dangerously, military aspects. The Cold War's most obvious manifestation was in the shape of a divided Europe and the military stand-off there between the Warsaw Pact and NATO. The Cold War also had powerful global implications. It involved military interventions on the part of the Soviet Union and the US throughout the so-called 'Third World' (notably in places like Afghanistan and Vietnam), the competitive search by these two states for Third World allies and the consequent orientation of local foreign policies in terms of stances that were either pro-Soviet, pro-Western or non-aligned. The Cold War was effectively ended by the *rapprochement* which occurred between the Soviet Union and the West after 1985, resulting in the unification of Germany, agreements on nuclear and conventional force reductions, and joint diplomatic efforts in seats of regional conflict in the Third World. The collapse of communism in Eastern Europe in 1989–90 and, shortly after, the collapse of the Soviet Union brought the Cold War to an end.

Dependency   a condition in which certain regions and states are disadvantaged by asymmetries of power. Such asymmetries result in economic underdevelopment and political and economic subordination to richer and more powerful states and international organisations. A dependency perspective suggests that in foreign policy the dependent state has few realistic policy choices and few resources to ensure effective foreign policy implementation. This approach was influential in analysing Latin America in the 1970s and 1980s. It has a continuing relevance in this regard, an obvious application in the case of African states and some relevance when considering the foreign policies of a number of weak, former communist states.

Foreign policy   the goals sought, values set, decisions made and actions taken by states, and national governments acting on their behalf, in the context of the external relations of national societies. It constitutes an attempt to design, manage and control the foreign relations of national societies. This definition focuses on foreign policy as an activity of states but emphatically places this within an international context in which states co-exist with other important actors and are subject to a complex range of domestic and external influences. It is not, therefore, a 'state-centric' view of foreign policy as held by Traditional perspectives (see below).

Foreign policy analysis   the academic study of foreign policy and part of the broader academic discipline of International Relations. Usually concerned with an examination of the factors (both domestic and external) which influence the making and implementation of foreign policy, the instruments deployed in the conduct of policy and cross-national comparisons.

Foreign policy arena   the terrain upon which foreign policy is conceived and executed. The arena can be understood in terms of three interrelated foreign policy *contexts* – the international, the governmental and the domestic – which shape the conduct of foreign policy. These contexts are, in turn, characterised in terms of foreign policy *actors*, *issues* and *interests* (see Chapter 2).

Globalisation   the increasing global spread of primarily economic forces (trade, currency and investment flows, for instance) accompanied by the rise of interconnected social and political phenomena (global communication networks, movements of population, transnational protest movements, etc.).

Globalist an approach to the analysis of foreign policy based on the logic of globalisation. It assumes that foreign policy occurs in a very indeterminate world of shifting power structures and a multiplicity of external influences. In the face of these forces, the foreign policies of all but the most powerful states are seen as being of little effect.

Identity in the study of foreign policy applied to the inhabitants of a state ('national identity') and assumed to reflect a sense of similarity born from a national history, common experience and exposure to the same myths and symbols of nationhood. National identity consequently generates a sense of the state's place in the world, its national interests and its aspirations, and thus points to the appropriateness of certain courses of foreign policy action.

Implementation the mechanisms through which, and the instruments with which, decisions are translated into action and outcomes (see Chapter 4).

Interests traditionally viewed as the self-evident goals of foreign policy and usually expressed in terms of a monolithic 'national interest'. The interests of a state are, however, often ambiguous, difficult to define and open to differences of interpretation. Foreign policy is concerned with the complex task of defining, reconciling and pursuing interests internationally and, in so doing, asserting and sometimes reconciling these interests with those of other states.

Issues the matters of substance towards which foreign policy is directed. Taken together, issues constitute the agenda of foreign policy. Global transformation has altered and in many ways broadened this agenda.

Marginalisation the condition by which states and regions, and the peoples who populate them, lack participation in the main currents of international development. In this sense, sub-Saharan Africa, for example, is often deemed to be marginal given its lowly contribution to the global economy and the lack of influence its states possess in global economic regulation and political affairs (see Chapter 8).

Neo-Realism emphasises the conditioning influence of the anarchic structure of the international system upon its 'units' (i.e. states). From this analytical position foreign policy is inferred to be an activity concerned ultimately with security, the pursuit of advantage in relations with other states and the enhancement of state capabilities. Forms of cooperation between states are not ruled out but they are seen as fragile, being based on expediency and short-term gain.

Pluralism the pluralist perspective on foreign policy is informed by a view of world politics characterised by a proliferation of issues and actors. Consequently, foreign policy is not seen as preoccupied by military and security concerns. These still matter, but so too do economic, social, environmental and other concerns. These sorts of issue, moreover, involve varied and often intense forms of cooperation between states.

Policy making the processes by which actions are conceived and formulated by actors (be these individuals or groups). These typically culminate in a policy decision (see Chapter 3).

Political images of foreign policy making approaches which share an assumption that policy making is the outcome of political activity broadly defined (involving elements of power, influence and interests). This typically involves bargaining processes among those groups and individuals which make up or influence government.

Psychological images of foreign policy making based on the central assumption that what matters in the framing of policy are the perceptions and beliefs held by policy makers, which are, in turn, subject to bias and distortion. This approach helps to explain the motivation of policy makers and the manner in which they adjust (or fail to adjust) policy in response to altered circumstances.

Rationality a supposedly inherent quality in policy making and implementation. Judgements as to whether a policy is rational turn on several more or less exacting definitions of this quality (see the 'rational actor' images outlined in Chapter 3). Among the most clear-cut is so-called 'procedural rationality' where a policy is premised on a clear notion of the problem to be addressed, the selection of an appropriate goal or objective, and the use of the most efficient instruments to achieve that goal.

Realism a long-influential approach to the study of International Relations. It places an emphasis on power relations between states and a consequent need in foreign policy to pursue objectives which safeguard security and sovereignty. This approach attributes state behaviour as much to qualities which inhere within the state (the quality of leadership or the quest of leaders for power and glory) as to the effects of anarchy (see Neo-Realism).

Traditional view of foreign policy this regards foreign policy in terms of a 'state-centric' view of the world. States are the main actors in world politics and states, guided by a narrow elite, pursue a closed and hierarchical set of foreign policy objectives in which security is paramount owing to the existence of an anarchic international system characterised by distrust and competition. This is a view commonly associated with Realist and Neo-Realist perspectives on foreign policy.

Transformation far-reaching processes of change which have characterised world politics (and the global economy). These processes have long origins, but were increasingly being felt from the 1970s onwards, owing to alterations in the global economy, the rise of transnational actors and a widening of issues of foreign policy relevance. A more important watershed occurred at the end of the 1980s/early 1990s with the end of the Cold War (see above), the dismantling of communist political systems in Eastern Europe and the dissolution of the Soviet Union.

Index

Notes
1. **Emboldened** page numbers indicate chapters and glossary definitions; *italicised* page numbers indicate statistical tables
2. The following abbreviations are used: FP – foreign policy; SSA – sub-Saharan Africa; US – United States